HISTORY of the 565TH ANTIAIRCRAFT BATTALION

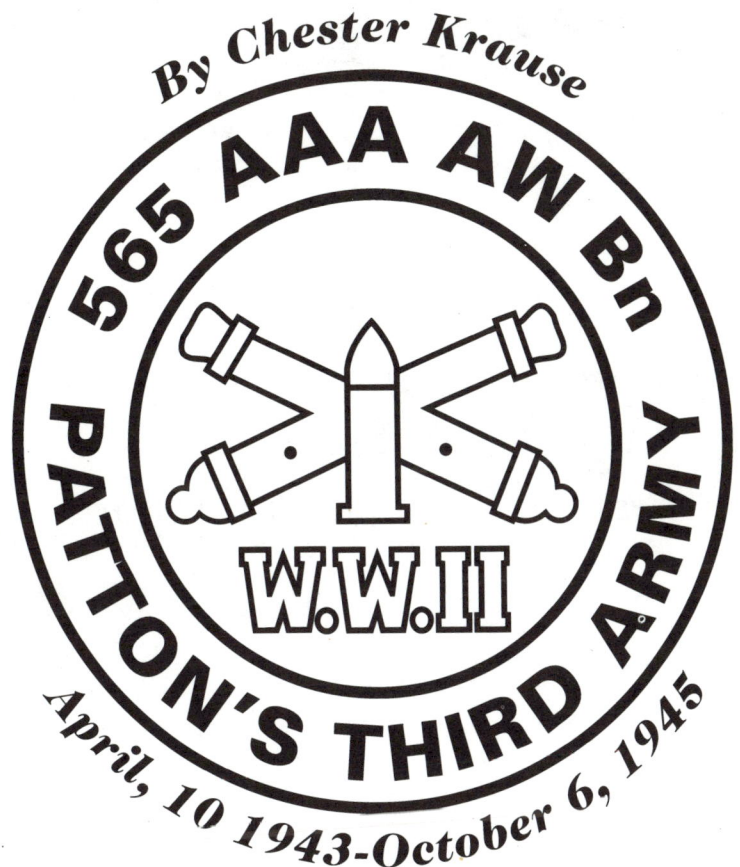

By Chester Krause

565 AAA AW Bn
PATTON'S THIRD ARMY
April, 10 1943 – October 6, 1945
W.W.II

**European Theatre of Operations
October 1944 – February 1946**

12th Corps

8th Corps

20th Corps

Battle of the Ardennes • Battle of Rhineland • Battle of Central Europe
• Chanor Base • Camp Top Hat • Belgium, 1945/46

© 1993 Chester L. Krause

All rights reserved. No portion of this book
may be reproduced without permission.

Published by:

krause publications

700 E. State Street • Iola, WI 54990-0001
Telephone: 715/445-2214

ISBN: 0-87341-224-9

Printed in the United States of America

Dedicated to those who died in the service of the 565th AAA AW Bn.

Clifford Drake
June 28, 1943
D Battery

Preston C. Ragsdale
November 1943
Battery C

Ernst C. Tilton
April 29, 1945
Battery C

Frank Orlandella
June 26, 1945
Battery A

About the Author

Chester L. Krause (Chet) was born and reared in and near Iola in central Wisconsin. He went to a one-room school and graduated from Iola High School in 1941. During high school and immediately thereafter, he took automotive courses in the evenings at local garages and machine shops.

Chet's farming background lent itself to his association with mechanics after entering military service on Feb. 11, 1943. He attended basic training in Camp Wallace, Texas for six weeks. He was then sent to auto mechanics school at Camp Davis, North Carolina before joining the 565th AAA as a headquarters auto mechanic in June 1943. His tenure with the unit was continuous until he transferred to the 563 AAA in mid-September 1945, about three weeks before the 565th AAA was desolved.

After his military service, Chet served the Iola area as a freelance carpenter until 1957. In 1952 he began to publish Numismatic News, a newspaper serving coin collectors. Since that time he has continued as a full-time publisher in many varied fields.

In addition to Chet's interest in the various activities of the 565th AAA, he's also interested in all forms of antiaircraft equipment, including guns, trucks and trailers, and he owns several of these items.

Contents

About the Author 4
Foreword 6
Frontispiece 7
Preface 8
Planning & Operations Summaries 12
Chapter 1
(April 1943 to mid-October 1943) 26
Chapter 2
(October to mid-January 1944) 29
Chapter 3
Departure from Camp Stewart
(Mid-January to September 1944) 31
Chapter 4
(October 1944 to Dec. 16, 1944) 36
Chapter 5
(Dec. 16-31, 1944) 41
Chapter 6
(Jan. 1-31, 1945) 48
Chapter 7
(Feb. 1-28, 1945) 54
Chapter 8
(March 1-31, 1945) 58
Chapter 9
(April 1-30, 1945) 64

Chapter 10
(May 1-8, 1945) 72
Chapter 11
(May 9-July 10, 1945) 74
Chapter 12
(July 10 to Oct. 1, 1945) 78
Order of Battle 87
Monthly Operations Reports 97
Weekly AAA Intelligence Reports 121
Lessons Learned & Conclusions 151
Special Orders #1 155
Fighting Assignments of the 3rd Army 161
Commendations 162
Unit History 163
Medical Reports 165
History of the 565th AAA A/W BN 167
Ten Days in April, Twelve Days in May 168
Since I Left the United States 171
One Year Furlough 173
Combat Locations 174
Battery Maps 178
Basic Military Map Symbols 180
Conclusion 183
Bibliography 184

Foreword

Writing a history of an army unit 50 years after the fact leaves a lot to be desired, but in the case of the 565th AAA (AW) Bn, we did have about 2,000 pages of handwritten records that were available from the archives at Washington, D.C. Additionally, the battalion has had reunions for nearly 20 years, bringing out much of the oral history.

I've visited nearly 40 former battalion members at their homes and I've had many one-on-one conversations, including one with our former commanding officer, Col. Kenneth Yarnell (Ret) in June 1992. Letters containing tidbits of information have also flowed to me.

Thus, what follows is a condensation of all this information. I regret that few original photos are available. In that absence those within these covers have been gathered from hither and yon to typify what we saw and experienced while in the ETO.

The maps contained herein are perhaps as virgin to you as they were to me. They are of three types: first, the ones I have compiled of each battery's trek across Germany; second, reprints from the after-action reports of the Third Army; and third, those taken from official government books that show the overall situation of the war from the book, "The Last Offensive."

Enjoy.

Chet Krause

Patton's statue as it appears today at Ettlebruck, north of Luxembourg City.

Preface

I suppose the need for antiaircraft began when Orville and Wilbur Wright first took to the air. However, it was several years later before it really surfaced. In fact, Brig. Gen. Billy Mitchell suggested that the need for antiaircraft would never exist because the airplanes would become so superior that armies would never again need ground fire to control enemy aircraft. How incorrect he was! However, the U.S. Army did develop a three-inch antiaircraft gun that was standardized in 1927. It was a good weapon for the planes of that period because they flew at relatively low speeds, low levels and were fairly easy targets.

However, as the Italo-Ethiopian War and the Spanish Civil War progressed, it soon became evident in the 1930s that the old three-inch gun was really not an effective gun for the U.S. armed forces. However, as the elevations of targets increased, the complexities of trying to hit a mere speck in the sky were extraordinary. This then became a three-dimensional attempt, as opposed to conventional artillery which shoots from a fixed position at a fixed target with fixed ammunition.

Thus, the philosophy of antiaircraft defense was a steady barrage of fire in the general direction of the airplane, and that rapidly cycling guns were probably best for hitting an aircraft. However, rapidly cycling guns required an extravagant amount of ammunition, and it was probably more scare than accurate or productive. While this type of defense and ammunition prevented close end attacks, it was no match for high flying bombers with sophisticated sights. Soon it became evident that the U.S. forces really needed guns that had a high muzzle velocity and an armor piercing capability so that once it did hit or explode near the target, the shrapnel created would penetrate the armor of the aircraft. There were some elements of both fire power and defense within the army that could be adapted to antiaircraft; the most basic was a machine gun. Once an airplane got above two to three thousand feet, a 30- caliber machine gun was very ineffective because at that distance the bullets had about spent their energy. Even if they hit a plane, the force couldn't knock it down.

The 50-caliber machine gun was much better. However, its mount was heavy and cumbersome, and it couldn't be moved into another position very quickly.

It soon became evident that the military needed a more sophisticated tracking device. With the larger caliber, we needed some kind of fuse that would explode when it came within proximity of the target, but not necessarily a point detonating projectile (which must hit something to explode).

Some of these objectives were obtained. In 1940, it took 2,500 artillery shots to hit an airplane, and by 1944 that number was reduced to 300. Several things happened to the 50-caliber machine guns. In its initial state it had a water-cooled barrel. That led to a lot of problems if armies were fighting in a desert or in cold weather. The water-cooled barrel was heavier, and this increased the crew necessary to operate it. Someone had to operate a water pump to make it function. These problems were corrected to some degree by the air-cooled barrel which increased the diameter's cooling surface, allowing the barrel to cool faster. The air-cooled barrel also increased the length from 36 inches to 45 inches, providing even more of a cooling surface and allowing for a faster firing rate. Remember, the number of shots armies put into the air was considered the greatest defensive weapon for that time.

Fortunately, for the U.S. Army, the 50-caliber machine gun had changes that were fairly complete by 1940; the only things that had to be corrected after that were the mounts. From an antiaircraft standpoint, the 50-caliber gun evolved from a 550 pound tripod, which originally sat on the ground, to a revolving turret mounted on most any kind of truck. The turret had its own power plant, and it could be traversed 360 degrees and elevated 90 degrees. It had just two M-14 guns on it. Later, it was equipped with four guns; the 565th remembers this gun as the M-51. The M-51 was mounted on a two-ton tandem trailer and pulled by a 2-1/2-ton GMC truck. The same type of quad mount, an M-45, was mounted in two other ways while we were in the service. One was on a little two-wheeled, air-transportable, M-20 trailer. (The M-45 and M-20 trailer was called an M-55.) The M-45 was also mounted on an M-3 halftrack, called an M-16, and was an integral part of a self-propelled antiaircraft battalion.

In the late 1930s, it became very evident that the Army needed guns bigger than a 50-caliber. American military engineers began working and decided they would design a 37mm on a four-wheel mount. They were developing this about the same time that Great Britain was working with a Swedish patented gun, a 40mm Bofors. While 37mm guns were effective, it is arguable whether or not the carriages that America built were superior to those that the British were building. The U.S. version could be put up and let down hydraulically, but it weighed about 500 more than the British version.

Inasmuch as we were using much of the same type of weaponry as the British, it was decided that U.S. forces would use the 40mm. Therefore there would be a common gun between the British and U.S. forces for interchangeable parts and ammunition. The 565th remembers this gun very well because it was our basic weapon. It was on a four-wheeled carriage, and by the time we got a hold of the gun, it had directors that controlled oil gears, controlling both azimuth and elevation. (This was the sophistication that was developed by the British.) The 565th, of course, learned that

Half-track quad mount. This is an M-16A1, the armor of an M-16 folded down.

in cold weather and combat, these oil gears weren't effective enough. This fact has been noted in many of the daily journals and after action reports, especially those of the 3rd Army, of which we were a part.

A 40mm antiaircraft gun.

It took awhile before America got into production of 40mm; it wasn't until 1940 that America received any naval models, and it was after that before the U.S. Army got any of models. Then we had some problems because all of the measurements were in millimeters. At that time in our machine shops we were not prepared to produce metric system measurements, and it took us a long time to get all the blueprints translated in order to produce interchangeable parts.

It wasn't until the summer of 1943 that the U.S. military completely obsoleted the 37mm gun. Today they are tremendously scarce. (I've been looking for one for my collection ever since I began collecting, and I have yet to locate such a piece of equipment.) The 40mm was not without its complications, not only mechanically, but also ballistically. Sometimes it needed to use tracer ammunition, and sometimes it needed armor piercing ammunition. The 40mm needed a common cartridge that could be shot both in the United States and in Great Britain. U.S. military forces had not used this caliber before, and therefore we had little experience in developing the ballistics for such a caliber.

During the fighting in North Africa, it was learned that firepower with a minimum amount of vehicles was the greatest asset the army could get. Out of this need came a twin 40mm that was mounted on a light tank chassis designated as an M-19 (Duster). But it wasn't until late 1944 that any of these were released for actual use. Some of these were seen in Camp Stewart, Georgia, before we left there in October 1944, but I do not recall seeing them myself. However, I was told that these twin 40mm were effective once they did hit combat. There were M-55 Quad 50s used for air transportable purposes in both gliders and C-47s (civilian DC-3s). There was also an air-transportable 40mm produced, known as an M-5; it was mounted on two little wheels, very similar to the M-55 50-caliber, and could be transported via gliders and C-47s. Both of these guns became popular as conventional weapons in the Korean War era. I do remember seeing both the M-55 and the M-5 at Camp Stewart while I was there in 1944.

Bombers and their fighter escorts were well beyond the range of both the 37mm and the 40mm guns. Thus, a gun with greater range needed to be developed. While the Army did have some 75mm, which are the equivalent of a three-inch that was adapted for antiaircraft, they were never used en masse. Work began in the late 1930s on a 90mm 3.6-calibur gun. The reasoning behind this cartridge size was its 40-pound weight. This is about the weight one man could handle on a sustained basis.

A 90mm M-1 known as the two-wheeled 90.

The 90mm 3.6-caliber gun was ready for use in 1940. It was a hand-loading gun: The fuse had to be set and rammed into the chamber by hand. This weapon was called an M-1. The M-1 could probably shoot anywhere from 15 to 17 rounds per minute, which was considered slow. In due course, a 90mm M-2 was developed; this weapon was a four-wheeled 90mm. It was much heavier than the M-1, a two-wheeled 90mm, and had to be pulled by big tractors. It shot 27 shots per minute and had semi-automatic loading and automatic fuse cutting. The 90mm M-2 was more of a high performance gun than the old M-1 we saw around Camp Stewart, Georgia. We saw some of these newer M-2s at the camp before we went overseas.

A 90mm M-2, also known as the four-wheeled 90.

The most important thing that happened in the ETO (European Theater of Operation) was the use of the proximity fuse, a fuse in a 90mm that would explode when it got close to an object. The buzz bombs, or the V-1s, that the Germans were using in the winter of 1944 and 1945 as they came over the British coast were duck soup to the 90mm. Sometimes the 90mm was up to 60 percent or 70 percent effective on the V-1s. Thus, the need for antiaircraft diminished greatly during this period, and the need for more sophisticated, higher-shooting guns became unnecessary. In fact, 90mm outfits carried the proximity fused ammunition with them at Normandy, France, but could not use them for fear an unexploded round might fall into German hands. The 90mm were initially pulled by 6x6 six-ton Whites or Corbetts, but these proved to be too small. Thus, as 90mm units went overseas, an M-4 tractor became the standard prime mover.

A 120mm M1 and antiaircraft mount M1 in traveling position.

A larger 120mm gun was also designed. In fact, very few were made, and none got overseas. They were basically used in the coastal areas of the United States and Alaska. I expect if the war had continued, these huge guns would have played a far greater role in winning the war. The 120mm gun was finished despite the fact it wasn't needed anymore. It had a muzzle velocity of 130 feet, faster than the 90mm. It had a 50-pound projectile, and it had an altitude of 56,000 feet, about 10 miles. Thus, it was a tremendous weapon. The 120mm guns were used during the Korean conflict. Some of its negative aspects were that it weighed 30 tons, was 123-1/2 inches wide, and would occupy an entire road (while most equipment was under 100 inches wide). There were only 450 of these guns manufactured, with four of these sent to Ireland. (To the best of my knowledge, the only 120mm guns are at the Air Defense Museum in Fort Bliss, Texas and Raritan Arsenal in New Jersey.)

After reading so much literature on the weapons used in World War II, I think I should comment that the weapons developed for antiaircraft during World War II were, indeed, a very ingenious gathering of weaponry. It took a real mechanical genius to put these various guns together and use them. They didn't always work: the cold weather stopped the oil gears of the 40mm, and the Zeiss sights didn't always function properly. However, the 40mm shot very well with open sights, and AAA shot hundreds of airplanes out of the sky. The 90mm guns became tremendous weapons once radar was attached. Their use made searchlights obsolete and eliminated both the German and Japanese Air Force.

The use of antiaircraft as strictly an antiaircraft weapon soon gave way to a general ground force weapon. That is, the 50-caliber quad mounts were such an antipersonnel gun that they remained current in the Army through the Vietnam War. The 40mm could be used against light armor. In fact, while the 565th was in Luxembourg City during the Battle of the Bulge, all our guns were assigned to a defensive position on the road from Echternach, Luxembourg leading into Luxembourg City as a defensive position. Granted, they were probably only good for one or two shots at a German 88, but if a German tiger tank came down the road, we could cause some serious damage.

This introduction wouldn't be complete if I didn't explain the organization of antiaircraft as it emerged from the coast artillery.

The coast artillery was organized as regiments. The first battalion would be a gun battalion; the second battalion would be either automatic weapons or self- propelled; the third battalion would be searchlights. As World War II progressed, the need for searchlights diminished, thus decreasing the need for searchlight battalions. Also, the Army needed flexibility of movement for their battalions. As antiaircraft emerged from coast artillery on March 9, 1942, the battalions all became independent, and the CA brigade headquarters became antiaircraft artillery (AAA) group headquarters. This independence allowed the battalions to move from one group to another. This was especially true in combat. The 565th was a prime example of this. We served in several different groups, and our batteries were not assigned to the same group at all times. It gave the AAA much more flexibility. Normally, an automatic weapons or a self-propelled battalion was attached to a division. Then the next unit in the ground forces was a corps. This usually contained three divisions with probably one or two antiaircraft battalions at their disposal. These were usually 90mm gun batteries. The 565th was attached to the 3rd Army, and there were eight battalions, generally attached to 3rd Army headquarters, operating under three groups. A divisional antiaircraft unit was located where the fighting was going on. A corps was probably protecting supply dumps, and in our particular case, the 565th was protecting 3rd Army headquarters, a neighboring gun battalion, a steel mill and similar defense. But nonetheless, it's important to note that the old rigid triangle of a gun battalion, automatic weapons battalion and a searchlight battalion broke down. Our battalion went from a position of being rigid, as in coast artillery, to one of being highly mobile. We were organized as the 565th CA AA Battalion on April 10, 1943. It was June 1943 when we were redesignated as the 565th AAA Battalion (AW), with the CA designation dropped from our title.

With regards to searchlights, the first successful radar the Army developed was an SCQ268. Later the SCR584 was tied directly to a 90mm, eliminating the need of a searchlight. This was only successfully tested just before the troops left for Europe and landed on the beaches. Because of this new combination as a weapon, searchlights, per se, became obsolete. However, they continued being used a great deal in Europe, principally to light battle fields or to illuminate an area if engineers were crossing a river. On a cloudy night searchlights could project their lights at the bottom of clouds, and the reflection would light the whole river basin. This gave the engineers the potential to be in operation 24 hours a day.

Searchlights could also illuminate a pontoon bridge once it was in place in order to guard it against flooding

Searchlight with 60-inch diameter, 800,000,000 candle power, and a range of 30 miles.

objects. In our instance, the 70th Division field artillery was assigned to shoot objects that were floating in the Rhine River toward the bridge. There were a couple of searchlights that were panning the river for any objects. Our particular mission was antiaircraft defensive, and an engineering unit built and maintained the bridge. This shows how several units of the Army would combine to install and maintain a facility. This was a particularly unique crossing at the Rhine River because the water was so swift; a bridge had never before been in place there, and even today there isn't a bridge. But nonetheless, searchlights played an important role in Europe.

Two-hundred foot double triple Bailey Bridge under construction at Paris.

Planning & Operations Summaries

Reprinted from the 3rd Army After Action Reports

CHAPTER I
PLANNING IN UNITED KINGDOM

Although the Advance Detachment, Headquarters Third U. S. Army, actually arrived in England on 28 January 1944, the report of the Command Group begins as of 26 January 1944, when, by secret order, LIEUTENANT GENERAL G. S. PATTON, JR. assumed command.

The planning phase for the participation of Third U. S. Army in the operation "OVERLORD" which was to involve the seizing and securing of a base in France, prepared for further operations on the Continent occupied the entire time of the Command Group during its stay in England. This planning period can properly be divided into four phases. First, there was a reorganization and adjustment of the Command Group and the Staff to comply with the Army Commander's requirements as to personnel and policies. Secondly, there was the intensive study of the proposed operation, tactically and logistically. There was also the reception, acquisition, training and briefing of Third U. S. Army troops with regard to the operation, and finally, there was a coordination of the operational plans and supply matters with the various higher headquarters concerned, and adjustments between the headquarters of Army level.

Prior to the arrival of the main echelon of the Third U. S. Army Headquarters on 22-23 March from the United States, several officers who had served with the Army Commander in Africa and Sicily arrived in England. These officers included BRIGADIER GENERAL HOBART R. GAY, Deputy Chief of Staff (formerly Chief of Staff of the Seventh U. S. Army); COLONEL PAUL D. HARKINS, Deputy Chief of Staff, Tactical; COLONEL OSCAR W. KOCH, Assistant Chief of Staff, G-2; COLONEL HALLEY G. MADDOX, Assistant Chief of Staff, G-3; COLONEL WALTER J. MULLER, Assistant Chief of Staff, G-4; COLONEL ELTON F. HAMMOND, Signal Officer; COLONEL ROBERT E. CUMMINGS, Adjutant General (formerly Deputy Chief of Staff, Administrative, of the Seventh U. S. Army), and LIEUTENANT COLONEL KENNETH E. VAN BUSKIRK, Special Services Officer.

These officers, combined with the personnel of the Advance Detachment of Headquarters Third U. S. Army, from the United States, and established Headquarters at PEOVER HALL, Cheshire, England by 1 March 1944. MAJOR GENERAL HUGH J. GAFFEY, formerly Commanding General of the 2d Armored Division, was appointed Chief of Staff, and reported for duty 20 March 1944.

With the arrival of the main body of Headquarters on 22-23 March, the Army Commander assembled the officers and men, informed them of his policies, the standard of performance he expected of them, and what the Third U.S. Army would be expected to accomplish in its forthcoming mission.

Daily Staff conferences were held in the War Room, commencing on 27 March. At these conferences, Section Chiefs were briefed on security instructions, operational plans, G-2 estimates, and Staff policy in connection with operation "OVERLORD." Sections and new sub-sections were assigned or established and Headquarters personnel shifted in order to have adequate personnel in the proper places for the mission. Thus, the G-5 Section (Civil Affairs) and the G-6 Section (initially combined Public Relations and Psychological Warfare Sections) were added and staffed; a Tank Destroyer Section was added to the Army Staff, and air sub-sections were added to G-2 and G-3, as well as additional sub-sections to G-4 and AG; all of these to meet the problems incident to the particular operation. (For details see Staff Section Reports).

Rigid security measures were adopted and a new classification "TOP SECRET", pertaining to the handling of highly secret documents was directed by Supreme Headquarters, and the machinery for compliance was set up. This necessitated a Top Secret Control Room under the Adjutant General within the Command section headquarters.

During this period every effort was made to familiarize the Army Staff with the personnel and problems of the Army troops, corps, and divisions assigned to the Third U.S. Army so that every possible assistance could be rendered them in preparing for the operation.

In early March, and continuously thereafter, plans for the operation "OVERLORD" prepared by Supreme Headquarters Allied Expeditionary Force, First U. S. Army Group, First U. S. Army, and the Communications Zone, were completed and studied in the light of Third U. S. Army's mission. The Command Group, assisted by the sections concerned, made detailed studies of these plans together with the Third U. S. Army directives received from higher headquarters, and prepared insofar as possible, both tactically and logistically for its participation in Operation "OVERLORD." Terrain, ports, enemy-battle order, logistics and plans of other participating armies were studied within the scope of the directives issued to Third U. S. Army.

Inasmuch as it is necessary to brief corps and Army units and higher headquarters, presentations were organized for this purpose in which the G-1, G-2, G-3, G-4, Signal, and the Engineer Sections participated. Realizing the possible changes in plans that might occur, alternate plans and additional studies in connection therewith were made under the supervision of the Command Group to meet foreseeable eventualities. The details of this planning will be found in the reports of the various sections.

During this period, troops assigned and attached to the Third U.S. Army were trained, administered and briefed on the part they were to play in operation "OVERLORD." Plans were made and carried out for the training and utilization of additional troops due to arrive at later dates in the United Kingdom. The Army Commander and the appropriate staff officers spent considerable time visiting the corps and divisions assigned or attached to Third U. S. Army, prescribing training programs, witnessing combat exercises and testing-firing of weapons. Emphasis was particularly placed on the use of tanks in support of infantry, the use of tank destroyer battalions and the use of armor to reduce strong points and other types of defenses. The Army Commander wrote and published three "letters of Instruction," dealing generally with troops in combat, which stated the general principles under which he expected Third U. S. Army troops to operate. (see Annexes No. 1, 2, and 3.) He personally visited all principal units of the Third U. S. Army and talked to the assembled officers and non-commissioned officers of each unit. A letter of instruction with regard to the employment of tanks with infantry was also written, and a further letter of instructions on the employment of Tank Destroyers was prepared by BRIGADIER GENERAL HERBERT L. EARNEST, Commanding General of the 1st Tank Destroyer Brigade, at the request of the Army Commander and published to units of the Third U. S. Army. (See Annexes No. 4 and 5.) An administrative school was conducted under the direction of the Adjutant General for all Third U. S. Army troops, and uniform procedure in handling administrative matters was set up and disseminated by lectures to the personnel from Third U. S. Army units.

It developed during the planning phase that a tremendous amount of coordination and adjustments with higher headquarters required the presence of Third U.S. Army personnel in LONDON almost constantly. In view of such conditions, a Third U. S. Army Headquarters was established in LONDON and functioned as a liaison between all headquarters established there.

Close liaison was initially established with the Western Base Section, and later with the Southern Base Section, in connection with the equipping, marshalling, and movement of Third U. S. Army troops to the Continent. This enabled Third U. S. Army to keep in close touch with the development of operational plans and supply problems which were ever prevalent in connection with the operation.

With movement to the Continent imminent, on 29 June Third U.S. Army Headquarters moved to BREAMORE, England.

After "D"-Day, 6 June, efforts of the Third U. S. Army command were directed largely to completion of training, equipping and the proper phasing of certain units to meet the ever-changing tactical emergencies.

On 23 June an advance detachment accompanied the VIII Corps to the Continent, where liaison with the First U.S. Army was established and a site for Headquarters selected. On 6 July advance elements of Headquarters Third U.S. Army set foot on the Continent and established Headquarters at NEHOU (T19), on the COTENTIN Peninsula.

CHAPTER 2
PRE-OPERATIONAL ON CONTINENT

Headquarters Third U.S. Army, except for a small rear detachment left in the United Kingdom, closed in the bivouac area on 7 July. The succeeding days were spent in preparing for the entry of the Third U.S. Army into active field operations.

The XIX Tactical Air Command, having been designated to support Third U.S. Army upon entry into active operations, established headquarters adjacent to the Army Headquarters. Detailed arrangement's for close air-ground cooperation were begun.

The XII Corps, commanded by MAJOR GENERAL GILBERT R. COOK, assigned to the Third U.S. Army and at this time remaining in the United Kingdom, was designated in charge of the movement and equipping of all Third U.S. Army units remaining in England. For this task GENERAL COOK was named Deputy Army Commander. The detachment of the Third U.S. Army remaining in the United Kingdom was attached to the XII Corps and worked under their supervision.

Constant and intensive study was carried on by all Staff Sections on the tactical situation, terrain estimates, and the many alternate plans envisaged for the employment of the Third U. S. Army. Daily briefings were held for all Section Chiefs during this entire period and many matters under discussion were thus brought to the attention of the entire staff.

During this period the tactical situation dictated that several divisions and supporting troops ultimately to be assigned to Third U.S. Army were called upon for use at the front. The Army Commander and members of the staff visited each of these units to observe and familiarize themselves with their characteristics and their problems.

Constant readjustment of supply plans were necessary due to the tactical situation and the plans for the future. Liaison was established with the 21 Army Group, British, First U. S. Army, and later with the Twelfth U. S. Army Group when its headquarters became operational on the Continent.

On 22 July the Third U.S. Army received its first operational directive. Tentative boundaries were assigned, units were designated, and an indication was given that the Third U.S. Army would soon assume an active role on the Continent. Based on this directive and conferences between the Army Commander and the Commanding General, Twelfth U.S. Army Group, corps and division commanders were briefed on the roles they were to play and were directed to initiate plans for the forthcoming operations.

In order to provide some actual experience, arrangements were made with the First U.S. Army to supplement the First U.S. Army service units operating behind the corps and divisions with service units that would eventually be assigned Third U.S. Army. Third U.S. Army dumps were established and wherever possible Third U.S. Army units took over the actual operation of service installations.

On Friday, 28 July, the Commanding General, Twelfth U. S. Army Group verbally directed that the Army Commander personally supervise the operational control of all troops then in the VIII Corps area, acting as Deputy Army Group Commander. The assumption of this role by the Army Commander fitted generally into the plans for the coming operation, as initially it was planned that the Third U.S. Army would assume command of the VIII Corps and XV Corps at 1200 hours, 1 August 1944. At this time the breakthrough of the American forces in the vicinity of COUTANCES (T25) had progressed sufficiently to justify the exploitation of their success. Plans of the Third U. S. Army were based on this exploitation.

On 31 July the Forward Echelon of the Third U. S. Army moved to a new Command Post location generally north of MUNEVILLE le BINGARD (T26) preparatory to becoming operational.

At 1200 on 1 August Third U. S. Army officially became operational although it had actually been controlling the operations of VIII and XV Corps since 28 July.

CHAPTER 3
AUGUST OPERATIONS

Following a conference on 1 August with the Commanding General, Twelfth U. S. Army Group, at which the Army Commander and the Commanding Generals of the XV and XX Corps were present, new boundaries were established and certain arrangements made with regard to the mission of Third U. S. Army.

The 90th Division had already been started for an area south of the SEE RIVER, and the Forward Echelon, Headquarters Third U.S. Army, moved to a new position north and northeast of BEAUCHAMPS (T23) from which the Command Group could better direct operations. Arrangements were immediately made for the future use of the XV and XX Corps in active operations.

Two problems confronted the command; one was to hold open the corridor through AVRANCHES (T21) between the SEE and the SELUNE RIVERS against constant enemy counterattacks; and the second was the exploitation of the breakthrough already accomplished.

On 3 August the decision had been reached and detailed orders were issued which provided for an adequate force to contain any enemy counterattacks against the corridor and free the remainder of Third U.S. Army for a movement to exploit the situation in BRITTANY and to the south and east.

By 4 August the exploitation of the breakthrough into BRITTANY had been sufficient to justify a concentration of movement to the east, and the Commanding General of the XV Corps was directed to seize river crossings at MAYENNE (Y87) and LAVAL (Y64) the next day. The mission was accomplished.

As a result of the enemy threat against AVRANCHES (T21), the XX Corps was directed to the northeast and rear of the German Army confronting the beachhead, and was given DREUX (R33) as its objective. The frequent changes of Corps objectives during the move east were caused by the fluid state of enemy resistance and in reality was a compromise between a desire to destroy the enemy partially trapped in the MORTAIN (T51) pocket and the advantages to be gained from proceeding east as rapidly as supply lines would permit before newly organized resistance could slow the pace.

On 13 August, the XII Corps became operational and proceeded east on the right of the XX Corps. Portions of the XV Corps turned north on ARGENTAN (U21) and the remainder, consisting of the 5th Armored Division and the 79th Infantry Division moved east to MANTES GASSICOURT (R66) where the 79th Division established a bridgehead across the SEINE River. The VIII Corps had been given the mission of reducing the strong points in the BRITTANY Peninsula during this advance.

On 25 August the XV Corps was transferred to the First U. S. Army and the advance of the Third U. S. Army continued south and east of PARIS (S04) with two Corps of one Armored and one Infantry division each. CHALONS (T54), TROYES (Y27) and NOGENT (X89) were the objectives. From there the XX Corps moved to the MARNE River, captured CHATEAU THIERRY (S86), and continued on to take REIMS (T37). The XII Corps at the same time took VITRY (T61) and CHALONS-SUR-MARNE (T54). Orders of higher headquarters directed that the Army Commander keep an armored division on his right flank against any enemy threat from south of the LOIRE River and arrangements were made to draw on the forces in the BRITTANY Peninsula for such mission. By the end of the month XII Corps had secured a bridgehead across the MEUSE River at COMMERCY (U42), and the XX Corps, using the 7th Armored Division as a spearhead had seized and secured a bridgehead across the river at VERDUN (U26).

As the month drew to a close there was an indication that the advance would necessarily have to slow its pace in order to permit supply echelons to make readjustments that would enable them to keep up with the rapid advance. There was at this time one more river before the Siegfried Line and GERMANY proper, the MOSELLE, and it was believed that a delay in the advance at this time would result in an enemy build-up in the path of the Third U. S. Army. During these operations to the east, the VIII Corps was actively engaged in the occupation of the BRITTANY Peninsula, and by the end of the month most of the Peninsula was occupied, with the exception of the major ports of BREST (V99), LORIENT (G72) and ST. NAZAIRE (N56) which were being contained and were to be reduced in the future one at a time. At this time the Third U. S. Army was responsible for operations on eastern and western fronts which were 600 miles apart and responsible for a flank of over 1,000 miles which it covered with less than two divisions. However, it should be stated that though there was actually no army reserve as such, the XIX Tactical Air Command was always considered a potential threat to any concerted enemy effort that could develop and if such a condition arose plans were always envisaged that the fighter bombers could break it up, delay or destroy it, while ground forces were being directed to points of contact. That no such threat ever developed was probably the result of the constant pounding from the air done on enemy concentrations each time they were discovered.

During this period of operation, the Command Group was in daily contact with the corps and divisions - L-5 and Cub planes and 1/4-ton trucks were at times the only means of communication. Frequent conferences were also held with the Commanding General, Twelfth U. S. Army Group, with regard to all aspects of the operation, tactical as well as the logistical. Special briefings for the Command Group were instituted during the operational period, at which time details which were not provided in the General Staff conferences held every morning were furnished, consisting mostly of G-2 reports and evaluations and G-3 situation briefings. Special subjects such as river crossings, reduction of strong points and other operational matters were also studied. The entire operation during the month of August had to be coordinated with the plans and activities of the Second British Army, the First Canadian Army and the First U. S. Army, and this likewise occupied considerable time and study.

On the whole, Third U.S. Army had, during the latter phase of this action, advanced with four divisions through the very heart of FRANCE with uncovered flanks, but the risks calculated and accepted by the Army Commander in such an advance proved well taken when the rapid collapse of the German forces in FRANCE are considered.

During the rapid advance of the Third U.S. Army in its movement west through the BRITTANY Peninsula and east to the MOSELLE in the months of August and September, there developed a very close relationship between the infantry-tank and tank-air combinations. Although the advance of the ground troops constantly left the air forces working in the fields far to the rear, the support throughout the whole campaign was magnificent. When tank and tank destroyer columns moved they carried infantry on their backs. When they hit obstacles, the infantry would dismount and in many places assist in clearing the way - and move on again. The air would talk to the leading tank columns, telling what was in front and in many cases answering questions of enemy on their flanks. It was a great treat to match these combinations develop.

CHAPTER 4
SEPTEMBER OPERATIONS

The outstanding characteristic of this period was the abrupt change in the pace of the advance of the Third U.S. Army. This was followed, after a period of enemy build-up and change in weather conditions, by a type of warfare considerably different from that employed after the breakthrough at AVRANCHES on 1st August.

Whatever the cause, it was apparent by the 1st of September that the mobility of the Army had become seriously impaired by an acute shortage of gasoline for Third U. S. Army units. From that point on, other shortages developed to such an extent that the time and energy of the Command Group was substantially diverted to the logistics of the situation. The shortages were such that no operational plans could be considered without a prior survey of the present and potential future reserve stocks of gasoline and ammunition, and both strategic and tactical plans were necessarily modified to meet the limitations imposed by available supplies.

The efforts of the Command Group to remedy the shortage of supplies through higher headquarters revealed theater shortages in supplies and available transportation facilities, which in turn necessitated an allocation as between army groups and as between the armies of their respective group commands. By 2 September the allocation to Third U. S. Army had been made. On a tonnage basis, it was too small to permit anything other than limited offensive operations against the enemy.

Efforts were made to obtain again control of the XV Corps and certain divisions which had been diverted for special tasks during the movement across FRANCE to the east. On 2 September the Army Commander received assurances that the 79th Infantry Division, the French 2nd Armored Division and the 6th Armored Division would eventually be released to Third U.S. Army. Additional effort was made to obtain release of the 83d Division which was promised as soon as a replacement division could be moved into position in the BRITTANY Peninsula. Plans were made to assemble the XV Corps, when it returned, on the south flank of the Army in the vicinity of SENS, and the Army, operating on a three corps front, was to move forward with ultimate objectives in GERMANY. Based entirely upon supplies available, a limited offensive was commenced to secure bridgeheads across the MOSELLE River and secure a line of departure which, when gasoline and ammunition was sufficient, would be used to jump off on a large scale offensive operation. On 8 September the XX Corps attached to secure a bridgehead across the MOSELLE in the vicinity of and north of PONT-A-MOUSSON. On the 11th of September the XII Corps attacked across the MOSELLE River south of NANCY to secure a bridgehead and capture the City of NANCY. NANCY was captured on the 15th of September. XV Corps attacked on 11th of September to the east and generally south of XII Corps, leaving a minimum essential force to guard the south flank of the Army.

On the 18th of September the ammunition allowance to Third U. S. Army was so drastically reduced that even the limited offensive operations under way had to be curtailed. The limited offensive thus conducted revealed that the Germans had been able to build up a substantial defense in front of the Third U. S. Army and progress to the east, across the MOSELLE, was both difficult and slow.

On the 23d of September the 7th Armored Division was relieved from assignment to the Third U. S. Army and attached to 21st Army Group; and by the 25th of September decision had been reached by higher headquarters that the XV Corps, with the 79th Infantry and French 2nd Armored Divisions, would be assigned to the Sixth Army Group.

After careful study, the Army Commander met with his Corps Commanders at Army Headquarters and outlined future limited operations in detail, stressing particularly the methods by which they were to be conducted. These instructions were subsequently confirmed in writing in "Letter of Instructions Number 4," which is attached hereto as Annex No. 6.

At the close of the period counterattacks against XII Corps became so harrassing that the Army Commander ordered an offensive to eliminate this threat.

CHAPTER 5
OCTOBER OPERATIONS

Generally the static tactical situation which obtained in September persisted throughout October, with the difference that there was a planned offensive to be organized and a definite date for its execution fixed.

The attention of the Command Group was directed principally to the solution of three major problems in preparation for this new offensive.

First was the accumulation of sufficient supplies to sustain the offensive which was to carry to the RHINE. To this end the entire supply situation was re-examined and studied with a view to conserving ammunition and weapons during the static period. Likewise, steps were taken to obtain every possible benefit from the material at hand and accumulate the required surplus stocks. Wherever possible definite arrangements were made for future deliveries. Thus, captured enemy weapons and ammunition were used extensively as was other captured equipment. Tactical operations, including use of transportation and artillery fires, were limited to the bare situation requirements and every effort was made to obtain adequate additional wet and cold weather clothing and overshoes for the combat soldiers. The armored and other vehicles received the necessary maintenance to bring them to a high operational condition. Careful utilization of all available facilities resulted in the accumulation of substantial surpluses in ammunition and gasoline and, with well established supply sources, agencies and routes, assured support of a major offensive.

The second essential step in preparation was the assembly and regrouping of troops. Every effort was made to obtain all of the combat units assigned to the Third U. S. Army. Certain of these units had reached the Continent but had not yet moved up to Army area. Steps were taken to expedite their movement, particularly that of the 95th and 26th Infantry Divisions and the 10th Armored Division. Because of Theater shortage in transportation, movement of these units to Third U. S. Amy area was both involved and difficult. The solution of this problem received considerable attention by the Command Group. Even the organic transportation of most of the units in rear areas as well as personnel to man them had been cannibalized by the requirements of the supply situation.

Although it had been necessary to bring scattered organic transportation and personnel in from all over FRANCE where they had been engaged in work incidental to the operation of the Communications Zone, the last week in October found the units up to T/O and T/E strength and in position in the Third U. S. Army area.

The third item of major importance was the planning for the proposed large-scale offensive. Plans were being developed during the entire period but had become largely crystalized by the middle of October. In conformity with these plans certain limited offensives were executed to secure the most favorable line of departure on the large scale coordinated offensive. These limited offensives also served to keep the enemy from becoming too aggressive, and as specialized experience for the combat units. The principal limited offensives in the XII Corps area included one executed by the 35th Infantry Division and 6th Armored Division on 1 October and another by the same units together with the 80th Division on 8 October. Both attacks were quickly successful and the results excellent. The enemy was surprised and a substantial number of prisoners taken. A successful attack by the 26th Infantry Division on 25 October also had the purpose of baptizing the 26th Division into battle.

In the XX Corps sector, the METZ (U85) forts presented a problem in a type of fixed fortifications with which the Army had had little experience. A partially successful attack in battalion strength by the 5th Infantry Division against Fort DRIANT (U75), one of the strongest of the forts guarding XETZ (U85), was continued during the early part of the month and the experience gained thereby was instrumental in determining the tactical plan for future operations against METZ (U85) and provided a basis for training in assaults on fixed fortifications. Battalions were rotated during this operation with that purpose in mind. The other attack in the XX Corps zone was that of the 90th Infantry Division on MAIZIERES LE METZ (U86). This was executed by the 357th Infantry Regiment, and was in anticipation of the future large-scale offensive.

Meantime, the plan for the new offensive as approved by the Army Commander on 18 October was submitted to the Army Group Commander the following day. This plan involved a large-scale attack for the reduction of METZ (U85) by encirclement by XX Corps and its subsequent advance with XII Corps on the right to the SAAR River, the establishment of bridgeheads across the SAAR and a breach of the Siegfried fortifications. The details of this were coordinated with Sixth Army Group Air Corps, and XV Corps of the Seventh Army prior to approval by the Twelfth Army Group.

During the latter part of the period the Command Group concentrated upon the preparation of the Army for the execution of this plan, although the approval had been delayed pending an attempt by Twelfth Army Group to coordinate the proposed attack with an attack along the entire front by all Armies then in contact. On 22 October the Army Group Commander gave his approval and fixed a time (to be determined by weather) after 5 November 1944 for the commencement of the attack by Third U. S. Army.

The Army Commander visited the new units, including III Corps and 95th Infantry Division, in Third U. S. Army and spoke to a selected group of officers and noncommissioned officers.

Finally, the Chiefs of Sections of the General and Special Staff, Headquarters Third U. S. Army were assembled on 31 October and discussed the final details with the Army Commander. D-Day was announced as between the 5th and 8th of November, but not later than 8 November.

Distinguished visitors to Third U. S. Army during the period included General George C. Marshall, Chief of Staff of the Army (7-10 October); General Dwight D. Eisenhower, Supreme Commander, Allied Expeditionary Force (17 October); Lieutenant General Omar N. Bradley, Commanding General, Twelfth Army Group (7, 11, 22 October); Lieutenant General Thomas T. Handy, Deputy Chief of Staff of the Army (7-10 October); Lieutenant General Jacob L. Devers, Commanding General, Sixth Army Group (17 October); Lieutenant General John C. H. Lee, Commanding General, Communications Zone, European Theater of Operations (25 October); and Lieutenant General Carl A. Spaatz, Commanding General, United States Strategic Air Forces (21 October).

CHAPTER 6
NOVEMBER OPERATIONS

During this period, the Third U. S. Army launched its second large-scale offensive. The early part of the period was spent in intensive final preparations which included the accumulation and placing of vital supplies, additional studies of terrain, fortifications and supply routes, and changes in the details of the plans already formulated to give effect to the new conditions caused by the elements and the changing tactical situation. Also included was the personal briefing by the Army Commander of participating personnel on the purpose and objectives of the imminent offensive.

Last minute changes in plans were made necessary first, by the Postponement of the proposed coordinated attack along the entire Western Front and, secondly, by the flood conditions existing on the MOSELLE and SEILLE Rivers and in the entire valley, which materially affected the proposed tactical operations.

On 2 November, the Army Commander was informed by the Army Group Commander that the proposed coordinated attack had been postponed, but at the same time he was given the authority to attack with the Third U. S. Army as scheduled if he deemed it advisable. The Army Commander directed that the attack would be launched not earlier than 5 November and not later than 8 November, the actual time to depend on the weather conditions for the planned aerial bombardment.

Priority targets for the medium and heavy bombers were established by Third U. S. Army and approved. The Army Commander talked to officers and men of each of the divisions participating in the attack during the 3rd, 4th and 6th of November. The attack was coordinated with the Seventh Army and its XV Corps, which was protecting the right flank of the advance.

As the target date approached, the weather continued unsettled, and the steady, persistent rainfall caused the worst flood conditions in 35 years in the areas selected for the attack, with even worse conditions in prospect. The aerial bombardment scheduled to precede the attack and fixed for 5 November could not be flown because of weather, nor could such missions be flown to cover the selected targets on 6 or 7 November. But, the urgent necessity for attack against the increasingly strong German positions continued.

Therefore, without benefit of the aerial bombardment, in rain and with unprecedented flood conditions prevailing, the attack by the XII Corps jumped off on 8 November. In spite of the handicaps of terrain, mud, and water, the attack proceeded steadily, and by 10 November most of the armored elements of the 4th and 6th Armored Divisions were across the SEILLE River. German prisoners later stated that the offensive had achieved tactical surprise in that the enemy considered it impossible for Third U. S. Army to launch an attack under such unfavorable weather and terrain conditions.

On 9 November, the XX Corps attacked with the 90th Division on the north near THIONVILLE (U88), and the 5th Division on the south flank attacked in the direction of CHEMINOT (U83). The first objective was the encirclement of METZ (U85). The attack by the 90th Division across the flooded MOSELLE River at THIONVILLE (U88) was brilliantly executed and the envelopment of METZ (U85) proceeded rapidly, with the 95th Division making an attack from the north and west against the German bridgehead on the west bank of the MOSELLE. By 17 November, elements of both the 5th Division (from the south and east) and the 95th Division (from the north and west) had entered the city limits of METZ (U85), and the 90th Division was within four miles of BOULAY (Q16), its objective east of METZ (U85). By 19 November, the encirclement of METZ (U85) was completed by contact between the elements of the 5th and 90th Divisions approximately six miles east of the city. The mopping up of METZ (U85) continued during the 20th and 21st of November, at the end of which time only four forts, VERDUN (U85), DRIANT (U75), JEAN D'ARC (U75), and ST. PRIVAT (U85) were holding out. METZ (U85) was officially declared captured on 19 November, releasing additional troops for the advance to the east. The task of reducing the remaining forts was given to the 5th Infantry Division.

In the meantime, commencing on the 18th of November, the pressure of the Third U. S. Army was such that the Germans were forced into a limited but general withdrawal along the entire Third U. S. Army front. German transport, confined to the roads because of the weather, was heavily and successfully attacked by our air forces. XII Corps, which had been advancing steadily, pressed the withdrawing Germans, and on 23 November the 4th Armored Division on the Corps right flank crossed the SAAR Canal and established a bridgehead at MITTERSHEIM (Q42).

In the central sector of the XII Corps and in the north of the XX Corps sector, the advance to the SAAR River continued, with elements reaching a point to the east of ST. AVOLD (Q25) and about four miles from SAARGUEMINES (Q55) by 27 November. In the XX Corps sector, the 10th Armored Division and the 90th and 95th Infantry Divisions were nearing the SAAR River in the direction of SAARLAUTERN (Q28) and DILLINGEN (Q29), and plans were being prepared for an attack by the Army across the SAAR River and through the Siegfried Line, to jump off early in December.

Of particular interest during the period was the capture of METZ (U85), by storm for the first time in its history as a fortified city. Moreover, during the advance toward the SAAR, the Third U. S. Army had passed through the Maginot Line in many sectors including the hinge at ST. AVOLD (Q25).

Operationally, one of the most successful of the experimental missions was the use of "DUKWS" by the 90th Division in connection with its river crossing in the vicinity of THIONVILLE (U88). Likewise, the tremendous importance in the Army advance, because of the flood conditions was the successful and difficult bridging of the MOSELLE and SEILLE Rivers by the Engineers and their constant road maintenance necessary to give effect to the Army advance.

During this period, final arrangements were completed for the use of considerable French troops within the Army boundary for numerous security purposes in rear of the Third U. S. Army.

Distinguished visitors for the period included General Dwight D. Eisenhower, Supreme Commander, Allied Expeditionary Force (15, 24 November); Lieutenant, General Omar N. Bradley, Commanding General, Twelfth Army Group (2, 13, 24, 26 November); Lieutenant General Walter B. Smith, Chief of Staff, SHAEF (28 November); Lieutenant General Lucian K. Truscott, Commanding General, Fifth Army (28 November); Lieutenant General Carl A. Spaatz, Commanding General, United States Strategic Air Forces, and Lieutenant General James H. Doolittle, Commanding General, Eighth Air Force (9 November); General Giraud, French Army (23 November); Bishop Hobson, Secretary of the Board of Army and Navy Chaplains (4 November); Mr. Averill Harriman, U. S. Ambassador to Russia (27 November); Mr. Herbert H. Lehman, Director of the United Nations Relief and Rehabilitation Administration (30 November); and six industrialists from the United States, accompanied by Brigadier General Browning (28 November).

CHAPTER 7
DECEMBER OPERATIONS

The period of the report covered by this chapter opened with offensive preparations designed ultimately to breach the Siegfried Line in the vicinity of the ZWEIBRUCKEN (Q77) area, and ended in a coordinated attack by the VIII and III Corps (neither of which was operational under Third U. S. Army on 1 December) to reduce and, if possible, pinch off the enemy-held ARDENNES salient and reestablish contact with the First U. S. Army. The interim involved a tactical situation to the north changing at kaleidoscopic speed, an indefinite deferment of Third U. S. Army's plans for a breach of the Siegfried Line south of the MOSELLE River, toward which the offensive commencing 8 November had been directed, a change in front by three Corps of the Third U. S. Army which was executed with an indescribable urgency, the reassignment of the VIII Corps and certain of its supporting troops to the Third U. S. Army, and the launching of a new offensive in a new direction in a new area.

The events of this period were somewhat unusual in Third U. S. Army. The suddenly obscure tactical situation which arose, commencing 16 December, in the sector of the VIII Corps to the immediate north of the Third U. S. Army boundary required a most difficult and complex tactical and logistical readjustment on the part of the entire Third U. S. Army. Generally, the sequence of events which follow are without attempt to pin-point all of the tactical moves or achievements of the combat units.

As of 1 December, the SAAR offensive was still in progress with XX Corps on the north and XII Corps on the south advancing mostly by frontal attack against the German pocket on the west of the SAAR River which denied the Army a line of departure for direct assault against the Siegfried Line. The four remaining forts in the METZ (U85) area were being contained by the 5th Division. Part of the Maginot Line had been secured in our advance toward the SAAR, and on the extreme southern flank, XII Corps had established a bridgehead over the SAAR and was advancing north against the outer German defenses of the Siegfried Line in that area. The Army was continuing to advance along its entire front from MERZIG (Q29) south through SAARGUEMINES (Q52) to reach the SAAR and prepare for an assault against the Siegfried Line across the river. By 10 December, the XX Corps had forced a bridgehead across the SAAR at DILLIGEN (Q82) to the north of SAARLAUTERN (Q72) and at SAARLAUTERN (Q72). XII Corps had bridgeheads in the vicinity of SAARGUEMINES (Q52) and SETTINGEN (Q55) on the south. Aggressive offensive tactics continued, expanding the established bridgeheads across the SAAR and cleaning up the German bridgehead west of the SAAR, preparatory to the attack on the Siegfried line.

Meantime, plans for the all-out attack against the Siegfried Line were completed. The Army Commander and the Commanding Generals of the United States Strategic Air Force, Eighth Air Force, Ninth Air Force, and XIX Tactical Air Command, had coordinated a plan to breach the Line with an air blitz of unprecedented enormity in the vicinity of ZWEIBRUCKEN (Q77) - KAISERSLAUTERN (R09), such air attacks to continue for a period of three successive days, each attack to be followed by a ground assault, which seemed to assure the accomplishment of the desired results. Additional preparations including (1) the acquisition on 10 December of needed infantry replacements from ten per cent of Army and Corps troops, totalling more than 4,000 men (trained through III Corps Training Center established at METZ (U85), (2) the enlarging of the bridgeheads across the SAAR, (3) the accumulation of supplies and the establishment of new forward supply Points, (4) preparation of ST. AVOLD (Q25) as the new Third U. S. Army Advance Command Post, and (5) the regrouping and movement of all divisions concerned to the designated assembly areas, occupied the attention of the Command Group.

While the eyes of the Army were primarily directed to the proposed "main" effort, III Corps had been made operational on 15 December, the 87th Division had arrived and relieved the 26th Division in the XII Corps sector (11-12 December), which, in turn, had assembled in the METZ (U85) area under the III Corps, and the final METZ fort, JEAN D'ARC (U75) had surrendered to the 26th Division on 13 December.

The date of the assault on the Siegfried Line had been fixed by the Army Commander to commence on 19 December, and support of all arms involved had been coordinated for that date. Although the Army stood, by 15 December, 12,000 men short of T/O strength, principally in combat infantry, there was a confidence in both Army and Corps Headquarters that this effort would accomplish the breach of the Siegfried Line and reach the RHINE River rapidly.

Came 16 December. The XX Corps was in the process of shifting troops preparatory to assaulting the Siegfried Line. Likewise, the XII Corps was regrouping and moving units into the line for the assault. The date for the coordinated air-ground offensive was postponed to 21 December in order to secure the best possible line of departure. The III Corps, with the 6th Armored Division, 26th Infantry Division, and attached troops, was assigned a sector of the Army front and moved into position to prepare to pass through a portion of XII Corps and exploit the initial successes expected to be gained in the first, assault. Advance Headquarters Third U. S. Army was alerted for movement to ST. AVOLD (Q25) 19 December.

Reports had reached Army Headquarters in NANCY (U81) of a German offensive in the VIII Corps sector in the ARDENNES on the north flank of XX Corps. On 18 December, the Army Commander was summoned to LUXEMBOURG (P81) with certain members of the staff by the Army Group Commander. There, the known details of the German breakthrough in the ARDENNES were explained, and the Army commander was asked when the Third U. S. Army could intervene, to which he replied that he could do so with three divisions very shortly. Difficulty in changing the front involved the necessity of disengaging certain divisions already committed. However, the 4th Armored and 80th Infantry Divisions were halted immediately, and one combat command of the 4th armored Division moved at midnight that night on LONGWY (P50), to be followed by the remainder of the division at dawn. The 80th Division was started to move to LUXEMBOURG (P81) at dawn, 19 December.

At the direction of the Army Group Commander, the Commanding General, III Corps, and the forward echelon of his headquarters were ordered to report to the Chief of Staff, Twelfth Army Group at LUXEMBOURG (P81) on the morning of 19 December. The Corps Commanders, Commanding General, XIX Tactical Air Command, and the General Staff, Third U. S. Army, were assembled at Army Headquarters 0800, 19 December, the urgency of the situation was explained, and preparations immediately commenced for operations against the southern flank of the German penetration in the ARDENNES to the north. The Army Commander then proceeded to VERDUN (U26) where a conference was held by the Supreme Commander, the Army Group Commanders, and certain assembled staffs.

On the assumption that the VIII Corps would be assigned to Third U. S. Army, a plan for the employment of the III and VIII Corps was drawn up, envisaging three possible lines of attack: NEUFCHATEAU (P33)-ST. HUBERT (P36); ARLON (P52) - BASTOGNE (P55); and LUXEMBOURG (P81)-DIEKIRCH (P84) - ST. VITH (P88). The conference with the Supreme Commander at VERDUN (U26) resulted in a directive to the Sixth Army Group to take over the southern front as far north as the southern boundary of the XX Corps; the 6th Armored Division to remain in the SAARBRUCKEN (Q47) area until relieved by elements of the Seventh Army; the 42nd (which had been allocated to Third U. S. Army but never had actually come under its operational control) and 87th Infantry Divisions of the Third U. S. Army to pass to the Seventh Army.

Third U. S. Army would consist of the VIII Corps in the vicinity of NEUFCHATEAU (P33), with 101st Airborne Division and elements of the 28th Division, 9th and l0th Armored Divisions, and elements of the 106th Infantry Division, plus Corps troops; III Corps in the vicinity of ARLON (P52), with the 26th Infantry, 80th Infantry, and 4th Armored Divisions; XII Corps, to be assembled in the vicinity of LUXEMBOURG (P81), consisting of the 35th, 4th and 5th Infantry Divisions, elements of the 9th and 10th Armored Divisions, and 2nd Cavalry Group, Reinforced; XX Corps in the vicinity of THIONVILLE (U88), with the 90th and 95th Infantry Divisions and 6th Armored Division, when relieved by the Seventh Army; XX Corps also had 3rd Cavalry Group. At the conference, with the Supreme Commander at VERDUN (U26), the Army Commander stated that he could attack north with the III Corps on 23 December.

The Army Commander then directed that the 26th Division be moved 20 December to the vicinity of ARLON (P52), advance detachment to move at once; XII Corps to disengage and Corps headquarters with artillery to move to the vicinity of LUXEMBOURG (P81), 21 December, leaving a working headquarters at the old location until such time as it could be relieved by the XV Corps of the Seventh Army; 35th Division to be withdrawn from the line and assembled at METZ (U85), Tac Echelon, Third U. S. Army headquarters to move to LUXEMBOURG (P81) 20 December; the Forward Echelon, headquarters III Corps to move to ARLON (P52) at once.

On 20 December, after a visit to Twelfth Army Group Headquarters at LUXEMBOURG (P81), the III Corps, VIII Corps, 4th Armored Division, 4th and 26th Infantry Divisions, the 9th and 10th Armored Divisions, and Advance Detachment of the 80th Division, the Army Commander directed that the VIII Corps hold BASTOGNE (P55) with the 101st Airborne Division and attachments, and prepare demolitions and road blocks in other critical areas. The III Corps was directed to attack for the purpose of relieving BASTOGNE (P55) at 0600 on 22 December. The Commanding General, 10th Armored Division, was placed in temporary command of the troops in the vicinity of LUXEMBOURG (P81) pending the arrival of the Commanding General of the XII Corps, and was directed to coordinate with one combat command of the 9th Armored Division in that vicinity. Commanding General, 9th Armored Division, with his headquarters, was sent to the VIII Corps to take over the two combat commands, one of the 9th and one of the 10th Armored Division, in the vicinity of BASTOGNE (P55). Arrangements were made for the immediate movement to the new front of all self-propelled tank destroyer battalions and separate tank battalions, necessary ammunition, engineers, and hospitals. The 5th Division was disengaged at SAARLAUTERN (Q72) and moved on LUXEMBOURG (P81) that day, two RCTs arriving by midnight with one company of the 818th Tank Destroyer Battalion. The highly complicated road and supply movements, under the necessity of moving large bodies of men, supplies, and equipment over a limited road-net, in a short space of time, with limited communications and without the issuance of a written order, were successfully and expeditiously accomplished.

On 22 December, the III Corps attacked. The defenders of BASTOGNE (P55), denying its use to the enemy, were still holding out, despite the fact that they were then entirely surrounded and cut off. In the XII Corps sector, north of LUXEMBOURG (P81), the 10th Infantry Regiment of the 5th Infantry Division attacked northeast on ECHTERNACH (L03), driving the enemy toward the SAUER River. On 23 December, excellent flying weather gave seven fighter-bomber groups, eleven medium-bomber groups, one division of the Eighth Air Force, and elements of the RAF an opportunity to operate in support of the Third U. S. Army. XX Corps launched a diversionary attack in the direction of SAARBURG (L11). The 35th Division closed in METZ (U85).

The following day, the XII Corps had cleared the SAUER River from DIEKIRCH (P84) to ECHTERNACH (L03), and the 6th Cavalry Group, reinforced with one company of Engineers and one company of tank destroyers, had moved to join the III Corps which was continuing its attack to the northeast towards BASTOGNE (P55). On Christmas Day, the 6th Armored Division in the XX Corps sector was ordered to the XII Corps, and the elements of the 10th Armored Division in the XII Corps ordered to METZ (U85). The 35th Division was ordered from METZ (U85) to ARLON (P52), to close on 26 December, prepared to attack between the 26th Infantry and 4th Armored Divisions on the morning of 27 December. The 80th Division was attached to XII Corps, affective 1800 hours, 26 December. On Christmas Day, the Army Commander visited every front-line division.

On 23 December and again on the 26th, it was necessary to drop supplies, consisting principally of rations and ammunition, to the 101st Airborne Division and other units in the BASTOGNE (P55) defense zone. This alone was a vital and difficult mission both to coordinate and execute, with C-47s of the Troop Carrier Command flying from ENGLAND and FRANCE, and with a limited drop area surrounded by enemy units capable of throwing up a tremendous amount of flak. Its great success is a tribute to the skill and courage of the pilots and enabled the defenders of BASTOGNE (P55) to carry on most effectively.

Also, because of the over-running and capture of almost the entire medical personnel among the BASTOGNE (P55) defense units, a surgeon was successfully flown in by cub plane on 25 December, and a surgical team flown in by glider on 26 December. Later, on 26 December, Combat Command "R", 4th Armored Division, by a very determined and daring attack, entered BASTOGNE (P55) at 1645 with one battalion of armored infantry and one battalion of tanks. That night this Task Force escorted 40 truckloads of supplies into beleagured BASTOGNE (P55). The corridor thus opened was held and expanded during the remaining days of the period. The total time from the moment when the 4th Armored Division left the SAARBRUCKEN (Q47) sector till the relief of BASTOGNE (P55) was seven days; the distance covered was 120 miles; the distance gained by combat during the four days was 16 miles. Directly participating effectively in the BASTOGNE (P55) relief were the 4th Armored Division, the 318th Infantry (less the 3rd Battalion) of the 80th Division, and Combat Command "A" of the 9th Armored Division.

The 87th Division, 17th Airborne Division, and 11th Armored Division, then SHAEF reserve, were requested by the Third U. S. Army. The 11th Armored Division and 87th Division were released to Third U. S. Army, assigned to VIII Corps, and moved to assembly areas near NEUFCHATEAU (P33) on 29 December with orders to attack to the northeast west of BASTOGNE (P55) on HOUFFALIZE, (P57) at 0800, 30 December. The 6th Armored Division closed north of ARLON (P52), preparatory to attack on the axis BASTOGNE (P55) — ST. VITH (P88) on 31 December.

30 December was the critical day for the operation and it involved a concerted effort on the part of the Germans, using at least five divisions, to again isolate BASTOGNE (P55). On this day, with the 11th Armored Division on the right and the 87th Division on the left, VIII Corps attacked at 0800 and encountered the flank of a German counterattack of one Panzer and one Infantry Division headed southeast to cut off BASTOGNE (P55). The attack turned the Germans back. The German repulse on this day was greatly aided by the action of the XIX Tactical Air Command, which was able to fly most of the day despite very bad weather. On 31 December, in snow and sleet, III Corps launched its attack to the northeast of BASTOGNE (P55), with the 6th Armored Division on the left and the 35th Division on the right. So, at the close of December, the III, VIII, and XII Corps were attacking to seal off the German penetration, and the XX Corps engaged in an aggressive defense in the SAAR - MOSELLE triangle and along the SAAR River to the south.

On 28 December, the remainder of the Forward Echelon, Headquarters Third U. S. Army moved to LUXEMBOURG (P81) to join the Tactical Headquarters established there on 20 December.

The really critical phase of the German penetration appeared to be almost terminated. The BASTOGNE (P55) defenses had stood firm against the best the Germans could muster. Additional combat troops were being assembled both in the Third U. S. Army area to the south and west of the bulge and on the north by First U. S. Army for a drive to erase it once and for all. The Germans had already paid dearly in men, material, and morale for their big gamble and it appeared that their expenditures in this direction would be made greater before they could extricate themselves.

Distinguished visitors during the period were: Lieutenant General Jacob L. Devers, Commanding General, Sixth Army Group (5 December); seventeen members of the House Military Affairs Committee, United States House of Representatives (6 December); Lieutenant General Carl A. Spaatz, Commanding General, United States Strategic Air Forces, and Lieutenant General James H. Doolittle, Commanding General, Eighth Air Force (6, 31 December); Major General Hoyt S. Vandenberg, Commanding General, Ninth Air Force (6 December); Major General Thomas B. Larkin, Communications Zone, Sixth Army Group (16 December); Major General Stayer, Chief Surgeon, NATOUSA (16 December); and Brigadier General Frank A. Allen, Public Relations Officer, SHAEF (21 December).

CHAPTER 8
JANUARY OPERATIONS

This period opened most appropriately, when at 0001, 1 January, all guns of the Third U. S. Army fired New Year's greetings on the enemy for twenty minutes. Between this and the close of the period, the final phase of the Battle of the Ardennes Salient had been fought and won, Third U. S. Army had made contact with the First U. S. Army in the vicinity of HOUFFALIZE (P57), the dangerous salient southeast of BASTOGNE (P55) had been sealed off and liquidated, and the Germans forced to retire within the Siegfried defenses east of the OUR River. The period was characterized entirely by attack with only such pauses as were necessary for shifting units and changing directions in order to strike the enemy from a new direction. That the Germans were thoroughly beaten in this operation was conclusively established by mounting masses of evidence, not only in the ground lost, material captured and destroyed, condition of prisoners, the dead, but in captured documents, evidences of hasty flight and other miscellaneous intelligence material gathered from various sources.

In harmony with the current theme, the period closed with an attack by the VIII Corps in the northern sector of the Third U. S. Army front, west of PRUM (L07), but this time with a different objective; i.e., to cross the OUR River and force the Siegfried Line.

The period likewise produced a build-up of the Third U. S. Army to its greatest strength, with a total of seventeen divisions, including eleven infantry, two airborne and four armored, one hundred and three battalions of field artillery and six engineer general service regiments, combat battalions and antiaircraft and other supporting troops. Also, within the period came the transfer of a substantial number of combat troops to other areas, either in support of prospective new offensives or as security against a possible new enemy offensive in some other sector. At the close of the period, as far as combat strength was concerned, the Third U. S. Army was not the equal of the Army assembled on the 16th of December prepared to attack the Siegfried fortifications in the SAARBRUCKEN (Q47) area. However, its combat efficiency was unimpaired as indicated by its accomplishments.

As mentioned in the preceding chapter, the really critical phase of the ARDENNES operation appeared to be almost over by the first of the year, but the Germans were not willing to concede that they had been stopped.

Enemy air was especially active on the 1st of January. The anti-aircraft of the Army claimed 45 planes shot down. Likewise, numerous delaying actions and constant counterattacks directed principally against the base and tip of the BASTOGNE (P55) salient, coming from both east and west, reached a climax on the 4th of January when 17 counterattacks by elements of eight enemy divisions were launched against the Third U. S. Army divisions in the line, from the 87th on the left of the Army to the right of the 26th Division, generally in the direction ESCHDORF (P64).

On the 2nd of January, the Army Commander conferred with the Commanding Generals of the III, VIII, XII, and XX Corps and coordinated the plans for attack against the Siegfried Line. Generally, XX Corps was given an aggressive defensive mission and directed to construct secondary defense lines in its area. XII Corps was to launch an attack north from the vicinity of DIEKIRCH (P84), spearheaded by the 5th Infantry Division, while the VIII Corps, reinforced by 17th Airborne Division, was to attack on the morning of 4 January to the northeast to effect a junction with the VII Corps of the First U. S. Army in the vicinity of HOUFFALIZE (P57). The XII Corps attack was indefinitely postponed by higher headquarters which favored an attack north of a point further from the shoulders of the Ardennes Salient. The remainder of the attack was held up until 9 January and progress was thereafter slow due to the terrific cold and snow conditions under which the troops fought, making rapid progress next to impossible.

The principal immediate task of the III Corps was to force the enemy to reduce his pressure against the eastern and southeastern forces of the BASTOGNE (P55) salient and for this purpose the 90th Division, having been relieved in place in the XX Corps zone by the 94th Division, was moved to the III Corps area preparatory to attacking northwest through the 26th Division, while the 6th Armored Division in conjunction with the 35th Division, launched attacks to the southeast to join with the 90th Division. By 10 January, there were indications that the Germans were trying to pull out of this salient before the trap could be sprung, and the XIX Tactical Air Command successfully attacked retreating enemy columns in the vicinity of DONCOLS (P65).

The attack launched by the VIII Corps on the 9th of January included, in addition to the 87th Infantry Division supported by the 11th Armored Division on the Corps left flank, the 101st Airborne Division, supported by the 4th Armored Division, to the northwest of NOVILLE (P56). Considerable progress was made on that day, but on 10 January, higher headquarters directed the withdrawal of the 4th Armored Division from the BASTOGNE (P55) area to an area southeast of LUXEMBOURG (P81) prepared to meet a possible German attack in the MOSELLE area southeast of LUXEMBOURG (P81). The positions occupied by the 4th Armored Division were now outposted by the 6th Armored Division. The attack of the III Corps to cut off the pocket to the southeast of the BASTOGNE (P55) salient was ordered continued.

To counteract possible enemy offensive operations in other sectors of Third and Seventh U.S. Army areas, armored divisions were moved into strategic places to be held in SHAEF Reserve. Thus, the 4th Armored Division was in position southeast of LUXEMBOURG (P81), the 9th Armored Division moved to the vicinity of THIONVILLE (U88), and later, the 8th Armored Division arrived at PONT-A-MOUSSON (U73).

On 11 January, elements of the VIII Corps occupied ST. HUBERT (P36) and contacted the British XXX Corps northwest of the city. On 13 January, the all-out attack of the VIII Corps was pressed with the heaviest resistance being encountered in front of the 101st Airborne and 11th Armored Divisions striking north towards HOUFFALIZE (P57).

By this time the Germans were completely on the defensive in the entire bulge area. These attacks were generally successful and it appeared that shortly contact would be made with the First U.S. Army in the vicinity of HOUFFALIZE (P57).

Based upon the situation, XII Corps was ordered to prepare to attack north of the DIEKIRCH (P84) - ST. VITH (PBS) road on 18 January, and the 4th Armored Division was released to the XII Corps for this purpose. The Army Group Commander visited this headquarters to discuss a new plan of attack involving one strong corps from First U. S. Army and two corps or more from the Third U. S. Army to attack south and north respectively on the ST. VITH (P88) - DIEKIRCH (P84) axis. By 16 January, Third U. S. Army had made contact with the VII Corps of the First U. S. Army in the vicinity of HOUFFALIZE (P57) and the first phase of the Battle of the Ardennes Salient, had been completed. From there on it became a bulge. On the same day, the 90th Division, advancing to the north and west along the HEINERSCHEID (P86) - BASTOGNE (P55) road and to the north from below NIEDERWAMPACH (P65), succeeded in cutting off the former German penetration at the base of the BASTOGNE (P55) salient and turned to take up new positions in preparation for further advances to the east.

From 16 January on, orders from higher headquarters transferred combat units from Third U. S. Army control, which caused a modification in its plans of attack. First, the 10th Armored Division was ordered moved from the XX Corps sector to CHATEAU SALINS (Q12). On 18 January, the 101st Airborne Division, together with supporting tank destroyer and antiaircraft battalions, was ordered moved to Sixth Army Group, move to start on 19 January. On 22 January, the 35th Division, less one combat team, was ordered turned over to the Seventh Army to be moved to the vicinity of SAVERNE (Q71).

On 18 January, the attack of the XII Corps jumped off at 0300. By nightfall elements of the 4th and 5th Infantry Divisions had two combat teams across the SAUER River and had made satisfactory advances, with the 80th Division capturing the village of NOCHER (P75), and high ground in the vicinity.

On 21 January, the III and VIII Corps resumed their advances and registered gains of eight to ten kilometers causing the withdrawal of the enemy in their immediate front.

It was during this period that substantial damage was done to the enemy, both by the XIX Tactical Air Command and Army artillery in the attempts to withdraw east across the OUR River. On 22 January, the XIX Tactical Air Command had one of its best days, knocking out approximately 1,500 motor transports destroyed with an additional 500 damaged. As the German withdrawal to behind the Siegfried Line continued, the III, VIII, and XII Corps were forced into a slow pursuit principally because of the bad road and weather conditions. On 25 January, elements of all three corps were against the so-called Skyline Drive, which is the high ridge road paralleling the OUR River to the west and running directly in front of the Siegfried Line. In the XX Corps sector, after a few limited objective attacks in the MERZIG (Q29) - TRIER (L22) - REMICH (P90) triangle by the 94th Division and relief of the 95th Division in the SAARLAUTERN (Q72) bridgehead by the 26th Division, the sector remained relatively static.

The III, XII and VIII Corps drew up against the OUR River line until on 29 January, when the VIII Corps attack jumped off with the 87th Division on the left, the 4th Division in the center, and the 90th Division on the right, against the heavily fortified German positions in the northern sector of the Army front. This virtually marked the start of a new campaign for Third U. S. Army. The Battle of the Ardennes had been completed and the enemy forced from all the ground he had gained in the breakthrough.

As the period closed with the VIII Corps on the attack in the northern sector of the Army zone, alternate plans were being prepared for an attack either by the XII Corps or the XII and XX Corps jointly across the OUR River in the vicinity of ECHTERNACH (L03), the role of the III Corps holding the middle sector on the right flank of the VIII Corps., was relegated to a holding attack and demonstration to cover the main effort.

Thus, at the close of the month, just 45 days after the commencement of the German offensive, the enemy had been forced back within the Siegfried fortifications on the Third U. S. Army front, and all but a small portion of the territory over-run regained by Third U. S. Army. Contrary to the expectations of the German High Comand, the counterattack had not succeeded in long dislocating the offensive preparations being made in other sectors for the advance to the RHINE, and was considered in some quarters to be the last desperate gamble prior to the crack-up of the once proud conqueror.

"The German winter offensive which met initially with a rapid series of successes was stemmed, thrown back, and again the American armies were linked together. It had cost the Germans over 100,000 troops and countless thousands of vehicles and tons of other equipment — very expensive—and must certainly have a tremendous effect on the morale of the German Army as a whole. It cost the Allies 50,000 men — killed, wounded, and missing — and somewhere in the neighborhood of five to ten thousand tons of equipment, plus a delay in their plans for taking the offensive and retaking the initiative, but the German strength was at an end. On all fronts we were advancing."

Distinguished visitors for the period were: General Omar N. Bradley, Commanding General, Twelfth Army Group (1, 6, 10, 12, 15, 22 Jan); Major General Levin C. Allen, Chief of Staff, Twelfth Army Group (12 Jan); and Mr. Leon Henderson (18 Jan).

CHAPTER 9
FEBRUARY OPERATIONS

After the readjustments which the impending relegation of Third U. S. Army to the mission of maintaining an aggressive defense in its sector had been made, the period was marked by some relaxation from the previous driving efforts required in the reduction of the ARDENNES bulge and the accompanying preparations for an immediate assault on the Siegfried Line. The principal concern of the

Third U. S. Army now was to prevent the Germans, if possible, from strengthening their fortified Siegfried Line positions on the Third U. S. Army front and preventing him from shifting his troops to other sectors, while complying with orders from higher headquarters.

Early in the period, it was learned that the main effort to reach the RHINE would be made in the north by the troops under the command of Field Marshal Montgomery, protected on the right by the American First Army. In the south, in the Sixth Army Group sector, plans were under way in preparation for an offensive there.

Third U. S. Army was facing the EIFEL, a rugged country, with poor road nets and many rivers, where everyone realized the mounting of a large-scale offensive would be difficult to mount and maintain. Immediately in front of the defenses in that sector facing the Third U. S. Army front, lay the flood-swollen OUR River. Then came the fixed fortifications of the Siegfried Line in depth, anchored in the north by a road net centering in the town of PRUM (LO7) and to the south by the BITBURG (L15) controlled road net. Facing the XX Corps was the difficult and well defended SAAR - MOSELLE triangle, with the ancient city of TRIER (L22) as its focal point. Over all were the steep broken hills and ravines, poor roads, and the cold, wet, muddy February weather. Aggressive defense was in order, but its application in the situation gave a new tactical meaning to the term.

Throughout the month, Third U. S. Army steadily lost combat strength through the planned transfer of combat units. On 2 February, two field artillery groups and six battalions of field artillery were ordered transferred to the Ninth Army. On the same date, the 95th Infantry Division was likewise transferred to Ninth Army. On 5 February, 17th Airborne Division was alerted for removal from Third U. S. Army area, and the 10th Armored Group was nominated, upon orders from higher headquarters, for transfer to the Ninth Army. On 11 February, III Corps Headquarters was transferred to the First Army in preparation for the plans already mentioned. Three engineer combat battalions were also relieved from Third U. S. Army and assigned to First U. S. Army, 15 February.

On 19 February, against these losses, Third U. S. Army obtained the right to use the 10th Armored Division for limited operations in the XX Corps sector, in exchange for the 90th Infantry Division which was put in SHAEF Reserve in Third U. S. Army area, and on 26 February was assigned the newly-arrived 89th Infantry Division. Although these various shifts and changes were designed to assist in other higher priority operations, they greatly complicated the problems inherently present in the maintenance of the aggressive defense.

The entire attention of the Command Group was concentrated on the accomplishment of its assigned mission consistent with the constant adjustments and improvisations that were necessary because of these changes.

On 1 February, the Commanding General, XII Corps, presented the Army Commander with a plan of attack against the Siegfried Line in the vicinity of ECHTERNACH (LO3) using the troops then assigned to XII Corps. The Army Commander approved the plan and directed it be put into effect 5 February, but directive was suspended at the request of the Twelfth Army Group commander, pending a decision as to where the main effort would be made. At this time, the VIII Corps was closing up against the Siegfried Line, attacking in its sector east of ST. VITH (P88) with the 87th, 4th and 90th Infantry Divisions from left to right.

On 2 February, the Army Commander attended a meeting with the Commanding Generals of First and Ninth U. S. Armies, and Commanding General, Twelfth Army Group, at which time directive from higher headquarters as to future operations was outlined and adjustments made between armies to give effect to such plan. Pursuant to this directive, the transfers described above were made.

On 3 February, the Commanding Generals of the III, VIII, XII and XX Corps met with the Army Commander to discuss future operations, in the light of the directive received from higher headquarters. As a result of the conference, XII Corps was directed to attack the night of 6 - 7 February in accordance with the plan previously approved, and the VIII Corps was directed to continue its attack with the troops now assigned to it. The immediate objective of the XII Corps was BITBURG (L15) and of the VIII Corps, PRUM (LO7), the explicit Army objective being the seizing and holding the general line: NEUENSTEIN (P85) - PRUM (LO7) - PRONSFELD (LO7) - and the high ground generally north and east of GROSSKAMPENSBERG (P97). This, in effect, changed the direction of the VIII Corps from the northeast to the southeast against PRUM (LO7). The attack of the VIII Corps was approved at a conference between the Supreme Commander, Twelfth Army Group Commander, and the Army Commander at BASTOGNE (P55), 5 February. Its partial purpose was to protect the flank of the First U. S. Army in its proposed attack to the RHINE in support of 21st Army Group, and prevent the withdrawal of enemy forces to the north for use against 21st Army Group and First U. S. Army.

By 5 February, the 4th Division had made substantial gains in the VIII Corps sector and breached the main line of resistance of the Siegfried Line in the vicinity of RUTH (P94) and SCHEID (LO6), reaching a point approximately 4 kilometers from PRUM (LO7). The supply situation because of the poor roadnet and wet, cold weather in the VIII Corps zone was so bad during this entire operation that running rights on the roads in the III Corps sector were granted to VIII Corps to supply their divisions (8 February) and repeated partial supplies of VIII Corps troops were made by air drop throughout the entire period.

On 7 February, XII Corps, having completed its readjusting in preparation for the attack, jumped off at approximately 0100 hours, 5th Infantry Division attacking immediately north of ECHTERNACH (LO3) and the 80th Division north of the 5th Division. The 417th Infantry Regiment of the 76th Division on the right flank of 5th Division, attacked across the SAUER River. At the same time, in the III Corps sector, demonstrations by the 6th Armored Division and 507th Parachute Regiment of the 17th Airborne Division were successful in crossing the OUR River. Flood conditions and the strong defensive fortifications across the OUR River made the crossing on all fronts decidedly difficult.

Although the advance was slow and bitterly contested, by the 12th of February the VIII Corps had captured PRUM (LO7), and the 4th Infantry Division had extended a bridgehead across to the east bank of the PRUM River. VIANDEN (P85), west of the OUR River, had been cleared by the 6th Cavalry, and in the XII Corps, the bridgeheads of the 5th and 80th Divisions were joined and consolidated on a 10-mile front approximately 2 miles in depth.

With the transfer of the III Corps to First U. S. Army on 11 February, boundary adjustments and reassignments of units had to be made between the VIII and XII Corps which took over control of the III Corps area. While the VIII and XII Corps were maintaining aggressive defense in the EIFEL sector, plans were developed for an attack by the XX Corps to clear the MOSELLE - SAAR triangle, which included MERZIG (Q29) and TRIER (L22). The 10th Armored Division was released for three days by higher headquarters for the specific task of clearing out the MOSELLE - SAAR triangle. This attack was fixed for 20 February, with the 94th Infantry and 10th Armored Divisions making the main effort. On 20 February, the 94th Division advanced more than 3 miles to the east and took the high ground overlooking the SAAR River and the city of SAARBURG (L11). 10th Armored Division broke through the positions gained by the 94th Division and reached points within three miles of the junction of the SAAR and MOSELLE Rivers. The 2d Cavalry Group of the XII Corps, which had crossed the MOSELLE River on the night of 19 - 20 February, captured the town of WINCHERINGEN (LO1) and made contact with the 10th Armored Division.

On 21 February, the Commanding General, Twelfth Army Group, visited headquarters and outlined the future plans for the Third U. S. Army. As a result, the Army was to continue its active defense, but if breakthrough should be made, troops were to be pushed rapidly to the RHINE River in the exploitation of such a breakthrough.

By 24 February, the VIII Corps and XII Corps for the most part, were against the PRUM River, with a bridgehead established across the PRUM River by the 5th Division in two places. In XX Corps Sector, the 10th Armored Division crossed the SAAR River south of SAARBURG (L11) and the 94th Division which had previously crossed at SERRIG (L10) expanded its bridgehead.

On 25 February, the Army Group Commander conferred with the Army Commander, Commanding General, XIX Tactical Air Command, and the Commanding Generals of the VIII, XII and XX Corps concerning future operations. The Army Group Commander authorized an attack by the VIII Corps east of the KYLL River and to secure bridgeheads there if resistance was not too heavy; XII Corps to attack, less the 80th Division in Corps reserve, and seize crossings over the KYLL River; the 89th Division to be committed on the south flank of the Corps; XX Corps to continue its attack to enlarge the bridgehead and seize TRIER (L22), supported by a combat team from the 26th Division, then in SAARLAUTERN (Q72), after its relief by the 65th Division which was to move into the SAARLAUTERN (Q72) bridgehead.

Pursuant to the orders, at the close of the period, in the XII Corps sector, the 76th Division was advancing to cross the PRUM River, cut the BITBURG (L15) - TRIER (L22) road, and attack TRIER (L22) from the north, and had reached GILZEM (L14) and IRRELL (L03) on the BITBURG (L15) - TRIER (L22) road. The 5th infantry Division had entered BITBURG (L15) and the 4th Armored Division had reached the KYLL River and was preparing for a crossing. In the VIII Corps, 6th Armored Division and 6th Cavalry Group had crossed the PRUM River and had established a bridgehead some 1 - 3 miles deep, while the 4th Infantry Division had crossed in three places preparatory to further advance. To the south, in the TRIER (L22) area, the 10th Armored Division had moved northward to the outskirts of PELLINGEN (L22), captured ZERR (L21) and two bridgeheads north and south of SAARBURG (L11) had been joined.

During this month, the way had been prepared for decisive action in the near future. There is not much doubt but that the German high command had not anticipated an aggressive defense of this nature in the EIFEL area and was not equipped to meet the threat of a complete breakthrough in this sector. As the captured G-3 of the 277th German Volksgrenadier Division said: "The locations of the U. S. First and Ninth Armies were well known, but one was not sure where the U. S. Third Army was. It was believed that it was to be committed through the bridgehead of the U. S. First Army across the ROER or in the worst case they expected an armored thrust through the AHR Valley. But nobody believed that this long-feared thrust would come where it actually did. It was a complete surprise; which threw the German Armies off balance."

Distinguished visitors for the period were: General Omar N. Bradley, Commanding General, Twelfth Army Group (25 Feb); Lieutenant General John C. H. Lee, Commanding General, Communications Zone, European Theater of Operations (28 Feb): Lietenant General Ben Lear, Deputy Theater Commander, European Theater of Operations (14 Feb); 14 Major General Charles H. Bonesteel, Chief, General Inspectorate Section, European Theater of Operations (28 Feb); Major General Gladeon M. Barnes, Office of the Chief of Ordnance, War Department (28 Feb); Major General Levin C. Allen, Chief of Staff, Twelfth Army Group (25 Feb); Major General Walter A. Wood, War Department General Staff (16 Feb); Major General Thomas B. Larkin, Deputy Chief of Staff, European Theater of Operations (14 Feb); Major General Paul R. Hawley, Chief Surgeon, European Theater of Operations (14 Feb); Major General Geoffrey Keyes, Commanding General, II Corps (9 - 12 Feb); Brigadier General Morgan, Assistant to Surgeon General, War Department (27 Feb); Dr. Isador Lubin, Personal Adviser to the President of the United States (18 Feb); and Mr. Sawyer, United States Ambassador to Belgium and Luxembourg. (10 Feb).

CHAPTER 10
MARCH OPERATIONS

This was the critical and decisive period. It was critical for the Germans in their attempts to maintain a cohesive front against the reassembled Allied offensive in the west and decisive for Third U.S. Army in that it had reached a point where by continued skillful use of bold, aggressive tactics and by taking carefully calculated risks, it could once and for all time destroy the power of the Wehrmacht to carry on the struggle. It was in this period that the accumulated effect of past actions since Third Army's operational birth on 1 August 1944 paid the dividends towards which it had constantly directed its efforts from the very beginning. The way had been prepared in those bleak days of January and March. It remained to travel the road.

In a tactical sense the actions of the period were divided into three distinct phases. First, while conducting an aggressive or action defense, there was the breakthrough to the RHINE which contributed immeasurably to the total destruction of the 19th German Army to the north. Secondly, there was the outflanking movement across the MOSELLE to the south which enveloped and destroyed the two best of the remaining cohesive German Armies (1st and 7th) on the Western Front. And lastly, there was the crossing of the RHINE to complete the mopping up of the last remnants of the Wehrmacht and the occupation of the territory from which the power to continue further in organized combat would have to come. In the official reports by campaigns, the three phases described here were the last part of "The Eifel to the Rhine and the Capture of Trier," all of "The Capture of Coblenz and the Palatinate Campaign," and the first, and most critical phase of the "Forcing the Rhine - Frankfurt on Main - and Across the Mulde Campaign."

As noted, the first phase had been set up previously and the decisive action came early in the period. The Siegfried Line on Third U. S. Army front had been destroyed, the important road centers had been captured, and the necessary bridgeheads were being established all for a breakthrough to the RHINE River.

As the period opened, XX Corps troops entered TRIER (L22) and the 76th Infantry Division established contact with the 10th Armored Division north of TRIER (L22). In the XII Corps sector, the 5th Infantry Division had prepared to seize a bridgehead across the KYLL River, and in the VIII Corps sector, the 6th Armored Division had advanced to the NIMS River, and the 87th and 4th Infantry Divisions were making slow but steady progress to the east. The RHINE did not seem too distant.

As TRIER (L22) fell, the 10th Armored Division crossed the KYLL and MOSELLE Rivers towards WITTLICH (L35), supported by a combat team of the 76th Infantry Division. The SAAR-MOSELLE triangle was no more.

Then, dramatically, and with great tactical surprise to the enemy, the 4th Armored Division attacked through the 5th Infantry Division bridgehead across the KYLL in the XII Corps sector and made a clean breakthrough to the east. By 7 March, the 4th Armored Division had reached the RHINE River. All available transport and other means were used to advance the infantry close behind to mop up by-passed pockets of resistance.

Pressure was maintained in other Corps sectors to keep the enemy from shifting to meet this breakthrough. In the VIII Corps sector, while initially the attack progressed more slowly, the 11th Armored Division was able to pass through the 4th Infantry Division on 8 March and the next day capture the key city of MAYEN (L69), also establishing contact with the 4th Armored Division east of that city. This with the capture of WITTLICH (L35) by the 10th Armored Division in the XX Corps sector completely finished the cohesive German resistance along the Third U. S. Army front north of the MOSELLE. By 12 March most of the pockets of resistance on the west bank of the RHINE (with the exception of COBLENZ (L89)) had been cleared of enemy resistance and a regrouping was in order so that the Third U. S. Army could soon proceed on the second phase: crossing the MOSELLE to the south. Thus concluded the first of the three decisive phases after approximately 35 days of aggressive defense and five days of offense in the EIFEL.

During the first phase, the 6th Armored Division had been ordered into SHAEF Reserve (4 March) and later moved to Sixth Army Group. Likewise, on 10 March the 4th Infantry Division was ordered to Sixth Army Group - both in preparation for the frontal assault on the Siegfried Line protecting the SAAR Basin. Following the first phase, three operations were deemed essential: (1) occupy COBLENZ (L89) in the RHINE-MOSELLE triangle, (2) attack south across the MOSELLE along the RHINE to assist the Seventh U. S. Army in its frontal attack on the SAAR Basin Siegfried defenses, and (3) attack on the direct flank of the Siegfried Line out of a bridgehead between TRIER (L22) and SAARBURG (L11) south of the MOSELLE. XII and XX Corps were selected to make the main effort. The VIII Corps was to make the secondary effort attacking COBLENZ (L89) and ultimately maintaining a defensive position along the west bank of the RHINE to the south as it was uncovered by the XII Corps.

On 11 March a conference of Corps Commanders was held to coordinate the Third U. S. Army plans with the proposed Seventh U. S. Army offensive. Pursuant to the decisions reached in this conference and in accordance with directives received from higher headquarters, the XX Corps launched an attack through the TRIER (L22) - SAARBURG (L11) bridgehead south of the MOSELLE with the 94th Infantry Division flanked by the 3rd Cavalry Group on the left, 80th Infantry Division in the center, and the 26th Infantry Division on the right flank, while the 65th Infantry Division made demonstrations in the SAARLAUTERN (Q72) bridgehead.

Meantime, alternate plans had been under consideration by the Command Group. First considered was a plan to seize a bridge or force a crossing of the RHINE River in the COBLENZ (L89) area. Secondly, there was the possibility - as the west bank of the RHINE was uncovered to the south - of seizing a bridgehead in the MAINZ (M35) - WORMS (M41) area. These were examined and carefully considered but final decision had to be postponed until the tactical situation developed further.

On 14 March the XII Corps attacked south across the MOSELLE from the vicinity of TREIS (L67) and succeeded in establishing substantial bridgeheads against moderate resistance. On 15 March the 4th Armored Division attacked through the bridgehead thus established, towards SIMMERN (L85) where they seized a bridge intact before midnight and reached the vicinity of BAD KREUZNACH (M03) the next day. The envelopment of the enemy SAAR Basin defenses was well under way. On the night of 15-16 March, the VIII Corps crossed the MOSELLE with its objective the city of COBLENZ (L89). The bridgehead was established and the attack against COBLENZ (L89) proceeded against moderate resistance, culminating in the complete capture of the city and surrounding area by 19 March. Meantime, Third U.S. Army troops in the XII and XX Corps sectors were rapidly approaching the inter Army Group boundary line, and by authority of higher headquarters, arrangements were made with Seventh U. S. Army whereby Third U. S. Army units could continue into the rear areas within the Sixth Army Group zone for the purpose of completing the envelopment.

On 16 March the Supreme Commander visited the headquarters and after examining the tactical situation and personally visiting the XX Corps sector, authorized the use of another armored division in that area and such other troops as were necessary to complete the execution of the proposed plan of Third U. S. Army. To this end, Twelfth Army Group made the 28th Infantry Division available from First U. S. Army to protect the west bank of the RHINE in the VIII Corps sector, replacing the 11th Armored Division. The 12th Armored Division was ordered to move from Seventh U. S. Army to XX Corps to attack through the 26th Infantry Division on the right of the 10th Armored Division, and the use of the 10th Armored Division for an advance on KAISERSLAUTERN (R09) was authorized. The 11th Armored Division was assigned to XII Corps to give depth to the advance of the 4th Armored Division. It was to attack across the MOSELLE through the 89th Infantry Division with the objective WORMS (M41). The objective of the attack of the 4th Armored Division was changed to MAINZ (M35) with instructions to seize a bridge across the RHINE, if possible.

Compared with the confusion in rear of the German defenses in the XII Corps sector, the attacks of the 94th, 80th and 26th Infantry Divisions encountered stiff opposition, although the 26th Division on 16 March captured the stubbornly defended MERZIG (Q29).

By 18 March, the 4th Armored Division had a bridgehead across the NAHE River; the 90th Infantry Division was clearing the city of BINGEN (M15); BAD KREUZNACH (M03) had been captured; the 11th Armored Division was along the NAHE River from MARTINSHEIM (N71) to KIRNSULZBACH (L72) with infantry across; the 12th Armored Division was attacking east through the 94th Infantry Division and had two columns west of WEISELBACH (R41) and BAUMHOLDER (L71); the 10th Armored Division had reached WOLFERSWEILER (L50), REITSCHEID (L50), and the outskirts of SAN BAUDORF (L50); the 26th Infantry Division was in the rear of the Siegfried Line opposite SAARLAUTERN (Q72). The complete success of the envelopment was assured.

It remained for the 90th Infantry Division to capture MAINZ (M35), the 4th Armored Division to capture WORMS (M41), the 11th Armored Division to close on the RHINE River south of WORMS (M41), the 12th Armored Division to seal off LUDWIGSHAFEN (R49), and the 10th Armored Division to overrun KAISERSLAUTERN (R09), all by 22 March, and certain elements of the XI Corps to spend several days thereafter completing the encirclement.

On 21 March the Third U. S. Army rejected an offer of airborne troops to assist in establishing a bridgehead across the RHINE on the grounds that the 14 days required for their preparation was too long.

Plans were immediately laid for the third phase of the operation which was to exploit the advantages gained by the destruction of the German forces defending the SAAR Basin; i.e., the immediate crossing of the RHINE before enemy defensive positions could be established. Already there were signs that the enemy was attempting to collect combat units and organize such defensive positions. The VIII Corps was directed to prepare for an assault crossing of the RHINE River in the vicinity of BOPPARD (L88) with another crossing further south if feasible, and the XII Corps was directed to prepare to cross the RHINE in the vicinity of OPPENHEIM (M43) - NACKENHEIM (M44). While this was being accomplished, the 10th Armored Division of the XX Corps was directed on LANDAU (R26) and the 12th Armored Division headed south toward SPEYER (R48).

Representatives of the Third U. S. Army were briefed by Twelfth Army Group on 22 March with respect to the over all plans for the conquest of Germany east of the RHINE. They were informed that again the main effort would be made in the north by the 21st Army Group under the command of Field Marshal Montgomery with troops consisting of 24 and possibly 35 divisions, that the nine American divisions in the REMAGEN (F61) bridgehead in the First U. S. Army sector would be permitted to continue to exploit the bridgehead, and that only nine additional divisions - a portion of which would be allocated to the Seventh U. S. Army - would be permitted to cross the RHINE because of the supply situation. The Army Commander, Third U. S. Army, was authorized to force a crossing of the RHINE in the OPPENHEIM (M43) area, but it was suggested that not more than six divisions on the outside could be used to exploit such crossing.

On the same day (22 March) under the direction of the XII Corps, the 5th Infantry Division commenced its assault crossing of the RHINE, the first in history, at 2200 hours, and by 0800 hours, 23 March, had six infantry battalions across with supporting tank destroyers. Resistance was light. The Germans had not had enough time and enough material to provide an adequate defense. This was the beginning of the third phase, the final decisive phase of the action in this period which commenced with the crossing of the KYLL in the EIFEL, gathered momentum with the crossing of the MOSELLE to the south near the RHINE, and ended with the establishing of a secure bridgehead across the RHINE. Within a day after the assault began, the entire 5th Infantry Division was across the RHINE, plus one combat team of the 90th Division, and the bridgehead was approximately four miles deep and nine miles wide. The XX Corps continued regrouping to point its troops toward the east across the RHINE. During the next few days and for the remainder of the period, the XII Corps bridgehead across the RHINE and that established by the VIII Corps in its attack on the night of 24 March were exploited. The 4th and 6th Armored Divisions in that order passed across on 24 March, and by night, 4th Armored Division had reached DARMSTADT (M64). On 25 March, the 4th Armored Division had seized three bridges across the MAIN River, one just south of HANAU (M87); and the 5th Infantry Division had moved into the MAIN River zone preparatory to move north toward FRANKFURT (M67); the 6th Armored Division was within eight kilometers of FRANKFURT (M67); and VIII Corps was busy expanding its bridgehead with the 87th and 89th Infantry Divisions to take the high ground overlooking the proposed American bridge sites at MAINZ (M35). The operation was so successful that by the end of the period ten divisions were authorized by higher headquarters and had crossed the RHINE into the bridgehead. The crossings had been progressively expanded until now they included points from south of KASSEL (C20) to the FULDA River and to HERSFELD (H35), ROSDORF (C52), and DARMSTADT (M64).

On 28 March the Third U. S. Army was given a new directive for the advance to the east eventually with XX Corps on the north, XII Corps on the south, and VIII Corps in the center. Regrouping was in order as OHRDRUF (J15) was captured on 1 April and the period closed.

Thus ended another decisive month in Third U. S. Army history. It had assisted in the destruction of two German Armies, had broken the backbone of German resistance in its sector, and was engaged in destroying the capability of the Germans to continue further to resist in the west by deep penetrations into its industrial, communications and defensive areas in the heart of Germany.

Distinguished visitors for the period were: General of the Army Dwight D. Eisenhower, Supreme Commander, Allied Expeditionary Force (16 - 17 Mar); General Koeltz, Deputy Chief of Staff, French Army (11 Mar); Lieutenant General Walter B. Smith, Chief of Staff, SHAEF (16 Mar); Lieutenant General Ben Lear, Deputy Theater Commander, European Theater of Operations (16 Mar); Major General James G. Christiansen, Chief of Staff, Army Ground Forces (20 Mar); Lieutenant General Alexander M. Patch, Commanding General, Seventh U. S. Army (23 Mar); Major General Arthur Wilson, Continental Advance Section, Communications Zone (9 Mar); Major General Robert Littlejohn, Chief Quartermaster, European Theater of Operations (11 Mar); Major General Richard Crane, Office of the Chief of Ordnance, War Department (23 Mar); Mr. Henry Taylor, representative of Scripps-Howard Newspaper Syndicate (13 Mar); Mr. Patterson, United States Ambassador to Yugoslavia (7 Mar); and Mr. Harvey Gibson and wife, American Red Cross (9 Mar).

CHAPTER 11
APRIL OPERATIONS

This was the final phase of the European War. For Third U. S. Army the period surveyed in this chapter was chiefly one of occupation and mopping up operations. After the RHINE had been crossed (22 March) the Command had every reason to expect that the resistance encountered would be spotty and ineffective - and it was. There was fighting, in rear areas as well as forward. There were mine fields, and extensive demolitions. But nowhere could the enemy concentrate enough strength to hold up more than temporarily the advance at the point of resistance. In fact on 23 March the Commanding General, Twelfth Army Group had stated that in his opinion German resistance in the West had been definitely broken and any Army could cross the RHINE at any place and time of its own choosing.

As applied to the German resistance east of the RHINE, this forecast likewise proved extremely accurate. First and Ninth U.S. Armies speedily enveloped the RUHR and thereby isolated a large number of German troops. That disintegration of the German Army had been accomplished was evident from the size of the German units surrendering and the comparatively small American casualties. On the Third U. S. Army front the number of prisoners increased and U. S. casualties decreased daily.

At times fierce enemy resistance was met in restricted areas, but with these isolated exceptions, road blocks and defense of towns and cities was the limit of his capabilities and a practically uniform method of dealing with these defenses was developed. If the city refused to surrender, artillery was laid on and then the infantry moved in.

The Army's advance to the east was restricted until the RUHR pocket could be liquidated and thus free an additional Army to make the penetration to cut Germany in half. Third U. S. Army was restrained from further advance to the east at HERSFELD (H35), OHRDRUF (J15), JENA (J66), and the MULDE River. Although the Command knew that these restrictions were in part the result of arrangements with the advancing Russians, it was difficult to overcome the habit of moving when possible to prevent potential defensive position from being established and maintained.

Meantime stories of the defense of the National Redoubt accumulated. Forces were concentrated against this contingency, including those of the Third U. S. Army.

A summary of the operations follows: With Third U. S. Army headquarters at OBERSTEIN (L72) on the NAHE River 1 April, the Army was informed by Twelfth Army Group that its advance would be halted on a north-south line through the point of furthest advance as of 1700, 1 April. The advancing armor (4th and 11th Armored Divisions) in the XII Corps sector had reached positions east of EISENACH (H76) - MEININGEN (H82) line, in the vicinity of those cities, with the infantry well up behind, while in the XX Corps zone, troops which had advanced northeast on KASSEL (C20), had infantry in the city (80th Infantry Division), with armor (6th Armored Division) turned east below KASSEL (C20) to a point near SPANGENBERG (H38).

As the period opened, disorganized or cut off enemy groups were still in considerable force well behind our advanced elements and the VIII Corps was mopping up in its zone as well as the 71st, Infantry Division of XII Corps in the Corps rear areas. To aid in clearing out these pockets, in the wooded areas and mountains northeast of WIESBADEN (M36) toward BAD NAUHEIM (M54), the Army Commander received permission from Twelfth Army Group to use a small task force from the 13th Armored Division.

At 1700, 1 April, Twelfth Army Group fixed the restraining line for Third U. S. Army advance to a north-south line of MEININGEN (H82) OBERHOF-(J13) - LANGENSALZA (J08) - MULHAUSEN (H89) inclusive.

On 2 April new Corps boundaries were fixed to give the VIII Corps a zone in the Army center for an anticipated further advance east, with XX Corps on the left and XII Corps on the right.

At this stage, Third U. S. Army encountered the first elements of what was to prove a most complicated and difficult problem even after the last shot had been fired; namely, the overrunning of great numbers of displaced persons and the recapture of countless prisoners of war from all Allied nations. Conferences were held with representatives of Twelfth Army Group, Air, and Communications Zone to work out speedy evacuation arrangements for those to be moved west and holding in place and feeding those to be moved east. Military operations required that they be kept off the highways and fed, clothed and housed until they could be moved. Much of the energies of the Army and all the personnel, equipment and facilities that could be spared from operations were used to administer and control these people, and the weight of this effort had to be constantly considered against the necessities of the tactical and logistical situation.

On 3 April the Forward Echelon, Headquarters Third U. S. Army, moved across the RHINE to the northern outskirts of FRANKFURT-AM-MAIN (M67). It was indicated that Third U. S. Army would be ordered to change the direction of its attack from east to southeast between DRESDEN (F29) and MUNICH (Y85) and on 4 April the Commanding General, Seventh U. S. Army, conferred with Twelfth Army Group Commander and Third U. S. Army Commander on possible new Army and Army Group boundaries. The next day Army was notified that its north boundary had been fixed as KASSEL (C20) - SOMMERDA (J39), which adjustment left most of the XX Corps units in First U. S. Army zone. KASSEL (C20), just captured by 80th Division, went to First U. S. Army.

Corps Commanders met with the Army Commander on 5 April to complete the details of objectives, boundaries and troops prior to a further advance east. Third U. S. Army had at this time again reached its restraining line, but hoped to be permitted to attack east again shortly. XX Corps, consisting of 80th and 76th Infantry Divisions and 6th and 13th Armored Divisions, was to advance to the ELBE River and capture DRESDEN (F29). VIII Corps, with 65th, 87th and 89th Infantry Divisions and 4th Armored Division in reserve, was to be prepared to advance east in zone after consolidating along the general line GOTHA (J06) - OHRDRUF (J15). XII Corps, with the 26th, 71st, 90th Infantry Divisions and 11th Armored Division was to consolidate along the line OBERHOF (J13) — MEININGEN (H82), prepared to advance southeast in zone. The Corps regrouped for these missions.

On 7 April, 13th Armored and 5th Infantry Divisions were assigned to First U. S. Army to assist in meeting a possible threat by the Germans to break out of the RUHR pocket. The 4th Armored Division was assigned to XX Corps to replace the 13th Armored Division and a limited offensive for all three Corps was set for 10 April, with a full scale offensive to follow on 11 April. The main effort was to be made by XX Corps to attack east and seize a bridgehead across the ELBE River. XII Corps on the Army right flank was to seize the high ground northeast of BAYREUTH (075). As the offensive got under way 11 April, the Army was directed by Group not to advance to the east beyond a line generally on the west bank of the MULDE River as far south as GLAUCHAU (K35) - ZWICKAU (K34) - PLAUEN (K12) - HOF (099) - BAYREUTH (075), except for the establishment of limited bridgeheads over that river. By 17 April all troops had reached the halt line and the 4th Armored Division, having seized some bridges over the MULDE River intact, had established a bridgehead reaching to the outskirts of CHEMNITZ (K66). Plans had been made to move the Forward Echelon, Headquarters Third U.S. Army, to WEIMAR (J57) on 16 April, but this was suspended 15 April pending a decision on a change of front.

On 16 April, Third U. S. Army received a new directive. Under this plan, First U. S. Army was to take over the VIII Corps and the MULDE River line, Third U. S. Army to receive the III Corps which was completing mopping up in its area in the RUHR pocket, and attack southeast with three Corps on Group order on the axis REGENSBURG (U15) - LINZ (V88) to contact the Soviet forces advancing west and northwest from VIENNA (X49). Seventh U. S. Army was to continue its offensive on our right flank with the mission of reducing the Redoubt and sealing the Swiss-German border. With VIII Corps, Third U. S. Army would lose the 6th Armored Division and 76th, 87th and 89th Infantry Divisions and temporarily the 4th Armored Division. In addition to III Corps, Army would gain the 13th, 16th and 20th Armored Divisions, and 86th and 99th Infantry Divisions. Third U. S. Army also was to have the XVIII Airborne Corps with 5th and 8th Infantry Divisions and 4th Armored Division to assemble near FULDA (H31) and held in reserve to be committed on Army Group order.

This required a change of front with a fairly complete regrouping of troops. The scheme of maneuver permitted the XII Corps on the left flank with 26th, 90th, 97th Infantry Divisions and 11th Armored Division to pivot south, the XX Corps to move south to the center across VIII and XII Corps rear and assemble the 65th, 71st, 80th Infantry Divisions and 13th Armored Division for advance along the REGENSBURG (U15) - LINZ (V88) axis, and the III Corps on the right with the 86th and 99th Infantry and 20th Armored Divisions. Several of the new divisions were not available immediately, and the regrouping was complicated by the available roadnet, but the target date was set for 21 April and the divisions and corps started movement for their new zones. A conference of the Corps Commanders with the Army Commander concerning the new mission was held 17 April. On 18 April, the XVIII Airborne Corps and 8th Infantry Division, assigned Third U. S. Army 17 April, were relieved from such assignment. Date of Third U. S. Army attack was postponed to 22 April and Army was informed there would be no limiting line.

On 22 April Third U. S. Army launched its attack. On the III Corps front only a partial advance by elements of the 86th and 99th Divisions could be made because of the movement of the 45th and 3rd Infantry Divisions and 14th Armored Division of Seventh U. S. Army across its front. Elements of XX Corps were on the DANUBE by midnight of the 23rd, and the XII Corps advance, spearheaded by the 11th Armored Division, had reached CHAM (U58), while the 97th and 90th Divisions blocked the passes into Czechoslovakia on its left flank. The 20th Armored Division was exchanged with Seventh U. S. Army for the 14th Armored Division to facilitate troop movements, and the latter attached to III Corps. On 24 April elements of III Corps reached the DANUBE and the 11th Armored Division had reached REGEN (U95) in the XII Corps sector.

By 26 April elements of XII Corps were in Austria and the XX and III Corps had established bridgeheads across the DANUBE. REGENSBURG (U15) fell to 65th Infantry Division of the XX Corps on 27 April and by the following day elements of the 13th Armored Division had advanced across the ISAR River at PLATTLING (U73), while the III Corps advanced to a point 15 kilometers north of the ISAR.

As the period closed, the 4th Armored Division came back to Third U. S. Army; V Corps of First U. S. Army took over the 1st and 97th Division areas north of XII Corps; the XII Corps had elements attacking towards LINZ (V88) in Austria, and was moving on PASSAU (Q21) at a point six kilometers from the INN and DANUBE Rivers; the XX Corps had elements advancing east along the DANUBE.

During the last ten days of the period, divisions were relieved, assigned, attached and placed in SHAEF Reserve so rapidly that reference is made to the Operations Report for the details. Assignments were made, boundaries changed, and divisions withdrawn on the basis of expediency. The penetrations into remaining enemy-held territory were so extensive by this time that it was obvious that only one principal pocket remained to be dealt with, in Czechoslovakia. The final end was not far away.

Distinguished visitors during the period were: Major General Cecil R. Moore, Chief Engineer, European Theater of Operations (1 Apr); Lieutenant General Leonard T. Gerow, Commanding General, Fifteenth Army (4 Apr); Lieutenant General Alexander M. Patch, Commanding General, Seventh U. S. Army (4 Apr); General of the Army Henry H. Arnold, Commanding General, United States Army Air Forces (5 Apr); Mr. Elmer Davis, head of Office of War Information (6 Apr); Assistant Secretary of War, Mr. John J. McCloy (8 Apr); Major General Ray W. Barker, G-1, SHAEF (8 Apr); Mr. Bernard Baruch, Special Representative of the President of the United States (10 Apr); General of the Army Dwight D. Eisenhower, Supreme Commander, Allied Expeditionary Force, and General Omar N. Bradley Commanding General, Twelfth Army Group (12 Apr).

CHAPTER 12
MAY OPERATIONS

This is the concluding chapter of the "After Action Report" from the Command point of view. Tactically, finis was written on the enemy in the previous chapter. The problems which confronted the Command in the brief period covered by this report were political and administrative. Germany had been defeated and neither its armies nor its people were capable of continuing the war. There remained to complete occupation and administration of Germany, the removal of recaptured Allied prisoners of war and displaced persons to their proper destinations, the surrender and demobilization of German Army personnel, and the removal of surplus United States troops from the Theater. The ECLIPSE Plan came into practical operation. More and more over-run territory was being taken over by Third U. S. Army and organized under the ECLIPSE Plan, and the last organized centers of resistance, most of them on the Third U. S. Army front, were liquidated.

As the period opened, Seventh U. S. Army requested a change in boundaries to permit an advance, through a zone occupied and over-run by III Corps, in order to take SALZBURG (Z92) in an attack from the east along the Autobahn. This meant the sealing off of III Corps from further combat operations and the withdrawal of its troops to a point north of the INN River. Third U. S. Army interposed no objection to this proposal, and III Corps was removed from further participation in active combat. The new boundary established by arrangement between the Army Groups was - North of FREISING (Y98), no change - below FREISING (Y98) - MULDORF (Z57) - INN River to Junction of INN and SALZACH Rivers, thence southeast to STRASSWALCHEN (V14) - thence east and northeast., south of the SALZBURG (Z92) - LINZ (V88) road generally along the foothills to the junction of the DANUBE and ENNS Rivers. A railroad running north from the ENNS River and DANUBE junction was to be the United States - Russian international boundary.

3d May the XX Corps crossed the INN River and advanced on LINZ (V88) from the south and west. In XII Corps sector, the 11th Armored Division was within six miles of LINZ (V88) from the northwest by midnight.

Forward Echelon, Headquarters Third U. S. Army, moved from ERLANGEN (031) to REGENSBURG (U15). On 4 May, V Corps, consisting of the 1st, 2d, 97th Infantry and 9th Armored Divisions, was assigned to Third U. S. Army. By Twelfth Army Group order, two Corps of Third U. S. Army were to attack northeast into CZECHOSLOVAKIA. The main axis of attack was to be REGENSBURG (U15) - CHAM (U58) - PILSEN (LO4) - BUDEJOVICE, (R88). While the Corps involved were changing direction, XX Corps troops advanced to within four kilometers of LINZ (V88) and 11th Armored Division was negotiating the surrender of the City.

The new V and XII Corps attack jumped off 5 May. By 6 May PILSEN (LO4) had been captured by V Corps and most of the troops of both Corps had closed on the restraining line. Russian signals could be seen from the line of advance at night.

On 7th of May, word was received of the surrender of all German forces to the Americans, Russians, and British. Forward movement of all troops was stopped. Only movements to close up in designated areas were authorized.

On 8 May the final German capitulation was announced. Only the carrying out of the details of the surrender terms remained.

It is noteworthy that during April and May, Third U. S. Army overran some of the worst horror camps in Germany, captured the gold and currency reserve of the German Reich (6 April) in a salt mine near MERKERS (H65) and gold and art treasures of the Austrian Government (7 May). It also participated in the reduction of the last German resistance.

That the end was close was known on 2 May when all the German Armies in ITALY surrendered to the Fifteenth Army Group. On 3 May the German Armies in HOLLAND, DENMARK, and east and west of LUBECK (S98) in northern GERMANY surrendered to Field Marshal Montgomery. On 4 May, 11th Panzer Division surrendered to XII Corps. 5th of May, Army Group "G", consisting of 1st and 19th German Armies surrendered to Sixth Army Group.

Distinguished visitors for the period were Lieutenant General John C. H. Lee, Commanding General, Communications Zone, European Theater of Operations (1 May); Lieutenant General Ortiz, Major General Beltran and Brigadier General Rodriguez of the Mexican Army (4 May); Under Secretary of War Robert S. Patterson (6-7 May); General Omar N. Bradley and Major General Levin C. Allen, Commanding General and Chief of Staff, respectively, Twelfth Army Group (8 May).

In conclusion, the final General Order (Number 98) published under combat conditions, is most appropriate and self-explanatory.

HEADQUARTERS
THIRD UNITED STATES ARMY
APO 403

9 May 1945.

GENERAL ORDERS

NUMBER   98

SOLDIERS OF THE THIRD ARMY, PAST AND PRESENT

During the 281 days of incessant and victorious combat, your penetrations have advanced farther in less time than any other army in history. You have fought your way across 24 major rivers and innumerable lesser streams. You have liberated or conquered more than 82,000 square miles of territory, including 1500 cities and towns, and some 12,000 inhabited places. Prior to the termination of active hostilities, you had captured in battle 956,000 enemy soldiers and killed or wounded at least 500,000 others. France, Belgium, Luxembourg, Germany, Austria, and Czechoslovakia bear witness to your exploits.

All men and women of the six corps and thirty-nine divisions that have at different times been members of this Army have done their duty. Each deserves credit. The enduring valor of the combat troops has been paralleled and made possible by the often unpublicized activities of the supply, administrative, and medical services of this Army and of the Communications Zone troops supporting it. Nor should we forget our comrades of the other armies and of the Air Force, particularly of the XIX Tactical Air Command, by whose side or under whose wings we have had the honor to fight.

In proudly contemplating our achievements, let us never forget our heroic dead whose graves mark the course of our victorious advances, nor our wounded whose sacrifices aided so much to our success.

I should be both ungrateful and wanting in candor if I failed to acknowledge the debt we owe to our Chiefs of Staff, Generals Gaffey and Gay, and to the officers and men of the General and Special Staff Sections of Army Headquarters. Without their loyalty, intelligence, and unremitting labors, success would have been impossible.

The termination of fighting in Europe does not remove the opportunities for other outstanding and equally difficult achievements in the days which are to come. In some ways the immediate future will demand of you more fortitude than has the past because, without the inspiration of combat, you must maintain - by your dress, deportment, and efficiency - not only the prestige of the Third Army but also the honor of the United States. I have complete confidence that you will not fail.

During the course of this war I have received promotions and decorations far above and beyond my individual merit. You won them; I as your representative wear them. The one honor which is mine and mine alone is that of having commanded such an incomparable group of Americans, the record of whose fortitude, audacity, and valor will endure as long as history lasts.

/s&t/ G. S. PATTON, JR.,
General.

Chapter 1
(April 1943 to mid-October 1943)

While the exact date the 565th Antiaircraft Battalion became organized was April 10, 1943, its early beginnings were dated Jan. 16, 1943 in Camp Davis, North Carolina. The 565th was scheduled to be, and eventually was, activated in Camp Stewart, Georgia. Its early identity was the 123rd AW (Automatic Weaponry) Battalion (Provisional). The following officers were designated as part of that original battalion: Maj. Frank A. Courtenay of New Orleans, commanding officer; Maj. John T. Efford of Stanford, Connecticut, executive officer of New Orleans; Capt. Charles R. Griffin of Dayhead, New Jersey; Capt. James T. Collier of Atlanta, Georgia; Capt. Marion D. Chapman of Monroe, Louisiana; 1st Lts. Robert Nesbit, Jr. and James E. Bowron of Birmingham, Alabama, Franklin H. Hazzard, Alexander S. Pierce; 2nd Lts. Rodger A. Hughes, John M. Clark, William S. Evarts and Harvey C. Goodman. Maj. Efford was relieved on Jan. 25, 1943, and he was subsequently replaced by Maj. Anthony R. Bayer.

The organization was moved from Camp Davis, North Carolina to Camp Stewart, Georgia on Feb. 12, 1943. Several of the officers went to various schools, and some of them went on leave before the activation. Finally, on Feb. 25, 1943 the 123rd was redesignated as the 565th CA (Coast Artillery) Battalion AAA (Antiaircraft Artillery). It was attached to the 490th CA Battalion AAA for rations and quarters until March 5, 1943 and then to the 493rd CA Battalion AAA.

April 10, 1943 was the day of activation. A large group of officers and enlisted men, known as the cadre, arrived to staff the battalion well in advance of the troops. Many of the names that are listed here stayed on with the battalion until it was dissolved in 1945. However, many of them only stayed a short while. The table of organization as of April 10, 1943 was as follows: Maj. Frank Courtenay, commanding officer; Capt. Anthony R. Bayer, executive officer; 1st Lt. Alexander S. Pierce, adjutant (S1); Lt. Jack Studley, intelligence officer (S2); Lt. Franklin H. Hazzard, plans and training officer (S3); 2nd Lt. Roger H. Hughes (S4), supply officer.

Of the names mentioned earlier, Capt. Collier became the battery commander of Battery "A," 1st Lt. Bob Nesbit became the commander of Battery "D," and James Bowron became the commander of Battery "C." At this writing, the commander of Battery "B" was unknown, and in the course of the history of headquarters battery, there were several officers who would have been battery commander. It almost seems that the battery commander of headquarters battery was utilized in many capacities, and if the battery needed an officer somewhere, they would easily transfer him there. He often went to the "B" Battery as commanding officer. It is interesting to note the battery commanders of "C" and "D" were with us from basic training on through the war, while "B" Battery had several commanders. Capt. Collier was replaced by Capt. Harry Gray in the fall of 1943 before leaving for Tennessee maneuvers.

To put the organization of the 565th into perspective, backtrack to 1942. In December, the U.S. 3rd Army (headquartered in Texas) was transferred from Tennessee, where it had been a Headquarters Unit for the training of troops and maneuvering, to England. Also, Maj. Gen. George Patton, who was to become the U.S. 3rd Army's commanding officer, had been relieved of his previous command because he slapped a soldier in Sicily. The fact is, when just a handful of the 3rd Army personnel landed in England, the general appeared before them and said, "I'm your new commander." He was immediately assigned the 2nd Armored Division which was the first of the divisions that was to appear with him in the 3rd Army.

Just a little history; the U.S. 3rd Army did not figure heavily into the invasion of beaches, but rather it was part of the 1st Army Group. But there were divisions in those invasions that were to become part of that 3rd Army; as the divisions broke off, they became the 3rd Army and what was left of the 1st Army Group became the 1st Army. Together they were the U.S. 12th Army Group under Lt. Gen. Omar Bradley.

In the Mediterranean, the U.S. 8th Army Forward Units entered Tunisia, and then in February the Germans made a counter attack there. The Germans had their famous breakthrough at the Kasserne Pass in Tunisia against the American II Corps and the Allied's 1st Army. Later on, the U.S. 8th Army takes Medenine, and on the 25th the American forces retook the Kasserne Pass, both in Tunisia. In late February, the Germans attacked the Grant's Gap in Tunisia. Also, up in Norway, commandos destroyed the heavily watered installation at Norsk Hydro, depriving the Germans of raw materials for A-bomb research. In the United Kingdom in February, 252 civilians were killed, and 347 were injured. In early March the African Corp attacked. Medenine, Tunisia was repulsed with heavy losses that forced Germany's Gen. Rommel to leave Africa. The U.S. 8th Army continued with several battle successes. In the United Kingdom, casualties for March were 993, and 439 were injured.

On March 10, 1943 the 565th received news that their activation would not take place before April 20th, and they would be designated as "white troops." At that point, our officers were working out with the 493rd on their training. In 1943 there were black troops, as well as white troops, and they were not integrated. Integration did not take place until after World War II.

On March 12th all the cadres went through an obstacle course, including the commanding officer. He reported that everyone was in fair physical condition, but that he had a little bit of trouble. In quoting his officers, they desired to have more study on guns and wanted to start troop school. They were very anxious to get through with training.

On March 15th, nine new second lieutenants were assigned. They are as follows:

Richard F. Spencer, William Stall, William Sternberg, Charles H. Stockman, James M. Stokes, Jack H. Studley, Frederick J. Szeles, Charles K. Thiebauth, Carl A. Tomlin.

On March 22nd, the 565th received word that activation would be on April 10th. I guess that was probably considered a rumor at that particular time, because other dates had been projected as possible activation dates for the battalion. On March 23rd, the battalion commander noted in his diary that he was resting quietly at noon, and then all of a sudden he heard that ninety cadre men would arrive at 1:00 p.m. and move into the H-1 area at Camp Stewart. He did receive eighty-seven enlisted men at 2:30 p.m. and also received five new second lieutenants: Melvin J. Berg, Morris H.

Berkowitz, Robert B. Carr, Clarence L. Slagle and William E. Smiley. Second lieutenant Charles E. Coleman was assigned but did not report. The 565th was supposed to start a mutual mess with the 564th, but rations hadn't arrived. Some men ate at the cadre pool as usual.

Apparently the battalion commander reviewed the enlisted men that arrived as cadre and didn't think too highly of some of them. On March 24th he made some adjustments in the enlisted men's cadre and hoped that there would be replacements available for some unfit men. Rations did arrive for the mess which would start the next day.

On March 28th another group of second lieutenants arrived, and they were: C.F. Gilgun, J.A. Stajduhar, W.S. Eldredge, R.T. Farnsworth, M.S. Eaton, S.H. Froistad, F.R. Fahringer, N.R.Wiley. The usual cadre training continued, as often noted in the commander's diary.

(In an overall note, both in the early part of the 565th and later on, many second lieutenants were assigned to us. I suppose many second lieutenants were assigned to battalions other than ours. It has always been my feeling that as second lieutenants or officers came out of officers training at Camp Davis, North Carolina and arrived in our camp, they were then assigned to some unit just so they would have a home. This arrangement allowed them to have a place to hang their hat and pick up some training until being reassigned to a regular unit. Once in a while there was an officer who arrived late in the picture and became a regular officer in the 565th; however, most of the ones that went overseas with us were early cadre and stayed on.)

After the arrival of the cadre on April 10th, the battalion commander's diary (the only source of direct information that we have at this particular point in our 565th history), indicates that except for an occasional officer going on or coming back from leave, nothing significant happened. However, the cadre would take some small hikes or do some physical exercises. Nothing of importance was happening during the next month until the actual recruits started arriving.

As the 565th waited, the war in North Africa continued as the British American 8th Army continued its attack from the west against Germany, and the Americans continued their pressure from the east, meeting at Tunisia. Also, there was a new protection plan formulated for American ocean vessels enroute to Europe: American ships would travel in convoys protected by submarines.

On Saturday, May 1st, the cadre had their usual cleanup duties, and there were some strong rumors that 125 recruits would arrive the next day. So, they drew rations and secured trucks through group to transport the recruits to the area. As it turned out, the recruits did not arrive, and the information stated they would not arrive until Tuesday. The battalion had the rations on hand, so along with the first of the rookies, they remained fairly inactive. On Monday, May 3rd, the battalion (the cadre of both enlisted men and officers) made a road march covering approximately six miles. This, of course, would have been the cadre of both enlisted men and officers. The battalion commanders diary noted that on May 4th, when the first 125 recruits arrived at 9:00 a.m., he called them castoffs from the paratroops. Then there were another 125 recruits that arrived at 9:00 p.m., making a total of 250 new recruits that day. Also, there were actually some antiaircraft airborne being trained in Camp Stewart, Georgia. However, there is no notation whether these recruits came from those particular units or whether they came from some infantry paratroop units.

The next day, recruits were out training and cleaning the area. Capt. Bayer was promoted to major on May 3rd. The area the recruits moved into was brand new and had not been completed until the 565th moved in. We were its first troops. Thus, there was a lot of cleanup to do behind the carpenters and those who cleared the forest. This work kept the new recruits busy.

On May 6th another 125 recruits arrived, making 375 total recruits. As the recruit drill continued on May 7th, the area cleanup also continued along with all the medical examinations and inoculations. Then on Saturday, May 8th, 221 new men from Fort Ogelthorpe, Georgia and 85 new men from Camp Upton, New York arrived, making 681 total recruits as of midnight that day.

On Monday morning, May 10th, 200 recruits from Camp Grant, Illinois arrived at approximately 5:00 a.m. making a total of 881 new men. The new men were all comparatively young and eager to learn. The commanding officer indicated that a lot of work was getting done and that some preliminary training had already been started during the previous week.

On Thursday, May 13th, notes indicate that the 565th was transferred from the 29th to the 27th Group and from the 55th Brigade to the 1st Divisional Training Brigade. Those were all commands within Camp Stewart and, except for the commanding officer, it probably made little difference to those of us in the 565th.

As training continued, on Friday, May 21st, the first 565th Battalion parade took place. I can imagine that it was like a bunch of sheep in a field. Certainly in those few days, there wasn't enough time for people to understand how to march in formation. On May 25th the battalion took a two-mile hike that took thirty-five minutes, which probably wasn't a bad speed for that time. On May 27th the 565th received a new designation: the 565 AAA AW Battalion (Mobile).

Prior to this, when we were designated as coast artillery, the makeup of the coast artillery often was as follows: The brigade was the highest command and was commanded by a general; There were three groups under a brigade, each commanded by a colonel; Under each group there were three battalions, each commanded by a lieutenant colonel. Each one of these groups would have a battalion of automatic weapons, 40-mm and 50-mm machine guns, such as the 565th. Each would have a battalion of searchlights and a battalion of 90-mm guns.

Several things were happening at this time which made that particular table of organization very obsolete. First of all, with the use of radar it was unnecessary to have searchlights, making them obsolete. Searchlights certainly weren't an integral part of fighting a war, especially an antiaircraft war. Also, by breaking up battalions from group, it was possible for them to be much more flexible. If an objective was more to an advantage, a battalion could either stay in place or move and be attached to a different brigade without having to stay within that rigid structure. Also, the army was undergoing a complete change in its overall structures to become more mobile, and thus antiaircraft was moved out of coast artillery, which was a very natural move.

Antiaircraft was a very special group of men. In the readings that I have done on this, the need for antiaircraft became critical in the late 30's and the early 40's with the Battle of Britain and the Blitz of German and Japanese aircraft. Allied forces could just not depend on anything if we weren't able to knock airplanes out of the sky. And, with the antiquated coast artillery pieces that we were trying to use for that purpose, it became an impossible job. Therefore, the sophistications of weaponry were such that it took a more technical group of men. There were nearly 1 million men in antiaircraft at one time. In choosing these men, the military leaned toward men with above average mechanical aptitude, as well as anyone who had ever had any artillery training.

Looking at our own 565th, we had 123 vehicles. Then added to that we had numerous power plants and guns, totalling nearly 225 mechanical devices; thus, there was need for mechanical ability. Also, we had sixty-four guns to man, and there were thirty-two gun crews consisting of fifteen men each. It took a special breed of person to do this, making antiaircraft personnel a cut above the normal person who entered the military service. (To that degree, the 565th was privileged to have served one another and to have served in antiaircraft.)

Going along with the war, on May 12th Gen. von Armon surrendered the bulk of the Axis forces in North Africa, and the second Washington Conference started. The conference was with Churchill, Gen. Eisenhower and their chiefs of staff.

The month of June continued with a full schedule of training and a few people moving in and out to specialized schools. It was very hot, and toward the end of the month there were a few days with rain and more rain. The commanding officer, Maj. Courtenay, called June 24th the "Day of Infamy. [with] No furloughs until completion of the 18th week [of training]." Officers and men did not appreciate this. I expect that with the very hot weather, this certainly came as very bad news to them.

On June 28th, Pvt. Drake of "D" Battery was accidentally shot and killed on the "C" range. This was a tremendously tough scene for a new battalion such as ours to have witnessed. One of the cadre men, Sgt. Dreeland, was discharged to accept a position as a warrant officer at the end of the month. So here we see both the cadre men being promoted, as well as tragedy. June 30th, just two days later, was payday and was very busy, with headquarters and "C" Battery leaving for a two day bivouac.

The rain that had started in late June continued through the first week of July, and after that it became extremely hot again. The commanding officer mentioned the heat practically every day. Evidently, we were beginning to develop a need for some courts martial in our new unit. The commanding officer himself received the rank of lieutenant colonel on July 12th. We had probably been firing our 40mm during the day; it's noted in the end of the month we were beginning to do some night firing and making final preparations for bivouac.

Back to the war, the Allies dropped airborne forces in Sicily as a prelude to invasion, and Operation Husky, the allied invasion of Sicily, got underway. Also, the U.S. hunter/killer groups were in action against submarines in the Atlantic, and twelve U-Boats were sunk in July. Thus, we were beginning to take charge of the waters that separated the Americas from Europe. The Canadians captured Caltagirone in Sicily, and the U.S. 7th Army, under Maj. Gen. George S. Patton, captured Palermo, a port city in Sicily. The meeting of the Fascist Grand Council decided all military power would revert to the Italian crown. The Royal Air Force raided Hamburg, Germany, killing 20,000. Mussolini resigned and was arrested.

Marshall Badoglio formed a new government. Hamburg, Germany was bombed by the United States Army Air Force by day and by the RAF at night. The Fascist party in Italy was dissolved, and the RAF incendiary raid on Hamburg generated a fire storm. The United Kingdom lost 167 people during July, with another 210 injured.

During the month of August there was very hot weather in Camp Stewart, Georgia. Occasionally it would rain, giving us some relief from the heat. On Monday, Aug. 2nd, the outfit pulled out for bivouac at 11:00 a.m. We stayed out all week, getting back Friday evening.

This had been our first long time out in the field, and once we returned to camp everyone was hurrying trying to get things in shape after being gone for so long. It is interesting to note that on Aug. 7th, Col. Courtenay was upset about something. I don't quite know what it was, but according to the next entry on Sunday, Aug. 8th, we were to work all Saturday evenings from this point forward. So apparently Courtenay was really "ticked off," and we were all confined to camp for a while.

Apparently, we were getting ready for another bivouac in the middle of the August. On Sunday morning, Aug. 15th, we loaded the trucks and took off just before midnight. We went to the area of Glennville, and thirty men transferred to the AAA, also at Camp Stewart. On Tuesday, the commanding officer told us how nice it was to go swimming in Glisson's Pond; he said it felt swell. I don't know if everyone was able to go swimming or if only the colonel went. We came back by way of Glennville and Ludowici, and got back to camp mid-afternoon on Friday, Aug. 20th.

In the world at war, RAF continued their raid on Hamburg, Germany. Total losses in August exceeded 40,000, with another 37,000 seriously injured.

The Red army captured Oreland in Belgorod, Ukraine, on the eastern front. The British and U.S. forces entered Randazzo, north of Etna, Italy. Also in Italy, Rome was declared an `open city,' and Marshall Badoglio sent a peace mission to Spain. Italy was getting ready to surrender to the Allies. U.S. forces reached Messina, Sicily, and all German resistance in Sicily had ceased. The Russians had captured Kharkov, Ukraine. The Quadrant Conference in Quebec, Canada between Churchill and Roosevelt ended on the eighth day.

The month of September could be characterized by two major events. First, we were coming to the end of our eighteen-week training. We were firing small arms such as M1s and carbines. During that time there was intermittent rain which made firing very difficult on ranges. However, the extreme heat of the summer had passed, and with the prospect of furloughs, the 565th was in a much better mood. Finally, later in the month we started receiving furloughs. On Saturday, Sept. 25th, our AARTC (Antiaircraft Recruit Training Center) at Camp Stewart, Georgia, granted the furloughs.

In the World War, Marshall Badoglio signed the Italian Armistice. In the United Kingdom during September there were five civilian casualties and eleven injuries.

While everybody was off on furlough, Capt. Marion D. Chapman became the battalion commander. He stayed back with a handful of other people while the rest of us were off on furlough. Apparently, they got their chance to leave later on. Col. Courtenay returned on Oct. 14th.

October was an interesting month. Most of the enlisted men and officers were on furlough during the first half of October. When we returned on Oct. 12th, the 565th received an announcement that the battalion was going into permanent bivouac, better known as "tent city." We would also go into a field problem, and on the 28th, we would go to Tennessee on maneuvers. After enjoying our furloughs at home, we were busy with problems like becoming the newest troops in camp, living in tent city, going on a bivouac and eventually moving to Tennessee. In retrospect, this was probably be the worst part of the service that we had endured in our entire three years with the 565th.

Chapter 2
(October to mid-January 1944)

The war continued. In Italy, the 5th U.S. Army captured Naples and the Allies reached Foggia; the 5th Army also took Benevento and the British commandoes landed at Termoli. The Australians captured Finschafen at the end of the Huon Peninsula in New Guinea. The U.S. Navy opened bombardment on Wake Island in the central Pacific. The 5th U.S. Army in Italy reached the Volturno river, north of Naples. Italy declared war on Germany which, of course, was a turn-about, after having been their ally early in the war. Civilian casualties in the United Kingdom continued; 118 were killed, and 282 were injured.

The month of November started out on a very confusing note. First, many of the personnel, both officers and enlisted men of the 565th, were sent to Tennessee maneuvers as umpires for other units. As a result, the 565th was sent replacements for those that were on temporary leave. Many of the officers that normally would have served our units were not in place. Except for our commanding officer, Col. Courtenay, and Maj. Bayer, who commanded the battalion, the enlisted men sort of had shotgun ranks. I don't recall a substitute enlisted man being put in place in our section. However, I do find notes that Capt. Carter E. Martin was assigned to the "B" Battery as its commanding officer (I believe he was the supply officer). The advanced party left on Sunday morning, Nov. 7th, and was led to Tennessee by Maj. Bayer.

The rest of the 565th did not depart until Saturday, Nov. 13th at 6:00 a.m. It was a cold and clear morning. I guess it was the first time we had actually loaded everything we owned onto the 123 vehicles that the battalion had under its command. Of course, we found it very crowded. We made our first overnight stop at Madison, Georgia; the second stop was at Fort Oglethorpe in Atlanta. We arrived there about 5:00 p.m. and camped at the Chickamauga battlefield grounds. The weather was clear and dry.

Upon leaving Chickamauga, we went by Lookout Mountain. While passing through the Cumberland Mountains we saw a rare sight worth remembering. There, going up Mt. Eagle, was a Japanese submarine being transported on a very large truck. Our whole group had to make room for it to pass. We arrived in Murfreesboro, Tennessee on Monday, Nov. 15th, at about 5:00 p.m. and made camp in an old onion field. It started raining and continued throughout the night, which was a very welcome or unwelcome scenario, depending on who you were. However, it was kind of a harbinger of what Tennessee maneuvers were going to offer the 565th. Apparently, we had been spoiled by the sands of Georgia and weren't used to picking a camp site in Tennessee.

On the following day, Nov. 16th, we moved to a hill about a mile away where conditions were much better. There was reveille every morning. One of the hardest things we had to do was wear those uncomfortable steel helmets. Previously, we would only wear them when we had to and could get away without wearing them most of the time, but now we always had umpires looking at us. In fact, they would stand reveille with us on occasions when they weren't goofing off. This was our first exposure to "the real thing." At this time the battalion was attached to the 50th Brigade of the 35th Division.

While the 565th was in maneuvers, a problem would begin on a weekend and end on a weekend (it would start on a Sunday night or a Monday morning and run through Friday afternoon or Saturday morning). Thus, we were always scheduled to move on those days and sometimes once or twice in between.

On our second week in Tennessee, things got underway about 6:00 a.m. on Monday, and we proceeded to a location about sixteen miles away. In Tennessee we never made long moves; sometimes it was only a matter of a mile or two. But when we were in Camp Stewart, Georgia, we could make quite long moves. At about 4:00 p.m. on Tuesday we moved three miles down the road. The next day the problem was over; then, we moved about twelve miles from Lebanon to a rest area. It was cold "as all get out." It was almost Thanksgiving, so on Friday, Nov. 26th we had a Thanksgiving dinner. A large portion of the battalion was on pass because many of our enlisted men came from the Tennessee and Georgia areas.

During our third week there, on Sunday, Nov. 28th, we got march orders at 2:00 p.m. to move fifty feet by 4:00 p.m. That was actually a real problem! However, it was merely meant to get people back in off furlough; and if I recall correctly, a lot of men were late.

On Tuesday, we moved again, about six miles into a new position. Then the 565th traveled about twenty miles in blackout and occupied a new position at 11:00 p.m. (Please note that I'm not using Army time in this historical document because most of us are civilians now and have forgotten military time.) This week of manuevers ended on Thursday, Dec. 2nd. About noon there was a light rain falling, and we moved to a rest camp near Carthage, about twenty-five miles north of Lebanon. The weather was much warmer. We set up bivouac in a pine grove; it was really quite pleasant. On Sunday the line batteries left, moving out for the next week's problems; the headquarters battery and their personnel remained behind. The commanding officer's diary notes that the present area was very wet, muddy and dreary, with more rain expected that night. The total number of men without leave was quite high, nearly forty percent. The field problem was over on Thursday, Dec. 9th. Unfortunately, it continued to rain and was very miserable. On Dec. 10th we moved about forty miles in the miserable, wet rain and bivouacked about fifteen miles from Murfreesboro, Tennessee in a large field. At this point, twelve- and twenty-four-hour passes were available; of course there was a lot of paperwork involved with granting passes, and it was a very difficult job for those who worked in personnel. The wet and cold weather really hampered their efforts. In looking back, it almost seems that they were giving passes to people who were actually AWOL.

The battalion moved out at 6:00 p.m. for the problem that began on Sunday, Dec. 12th; however, headquarters stayed in a rear echelon and moved only about one-half mile. This was quite a common occurrence. I served in the headquarters battery, and usually we would stay removed from the batteries themselves. This was also a very sad week for our colonel who was relieved of his command. Maj. Bayer assumed command on Dec. 16th. On the next day, Friday, Dec. 17th, we moved into Camp Forest, Tennessee to reorganize. Apparently, our equipment was in very bad shape. Many people were sick with colds; we had never been issued rubber footgear, and a lot of people were still AWOL.

However, the days at Camp Forest, Tennessee were not wasted. There were various classes that could be held indoors, while those of us that were involved with equipment, worked outside. I remember there was a particular problem with the undersides of vehicles, tires, and particularly, propeller shafts, gear boxes and universal joints. When there is extremely cold weather, a lot of these problems occur. While we were able to make some of those repairs, little did we know how bad everything was until we got back to Camp Stewart, Georgia in early January. While I didn't witness it firsthand, I can imagine that the guns also suffered problems similar to those our vehicles had.

The day after Christmas we moved to Carthage, Tennessee and remained overnight for another field problem. Again, it was wet and rainy, and respiratory problems were on the increase. Even though we had some rest while at Camp Forest, Tennessee, it certainly wasn't a cure-all for everything. On New Year's Day we were making preparations to move to Westmoreland, Tennessee, which was about forty miles away. The weather was warm and clear, but by the following day it got wet and cool again. The position was a sea of mud. On Monday, Jan. 2, 1944 the battalion prepared to move in the afternoon, but the trucks were still being winched out of the mud and moved to a new position about five miles on the other side of Westmoreland. By Wednesday, the weather was still wet and cold, and the battalion wore mosquito nets, which were part of our training. A soldier in "D" battery was killed in a truck accident. On Saturday, Jan. 8th, it snowed; we had some very cold weather.

On Sunday, Jan. 9th, the 565th moved to a point near Lebanon, Tennessee, getting there in mid-afternoon. The weather was still tremendously cold. However, the new position was quite good; it was a natural shelter away from the wind. The weather continued to be cold, and it was taking its toll on both men and equipment. On Wednesday, we again made another move near Murfreesboro, Tennessee to a miserable location that was very muddy and wet. On Thursday, Jan. 13th, staff Sgt. Ragsdale, a soldier in "C" Battery, was killed in a truck accident at Cripple Creek, and several other men were injured. On Friday, Jan. 14th, 1944, we learned that we were going to return to Camp Stewart, Georgia on Monday. What a relief for all of us in the battalion! On Saturday it snowed, as if to give us a final signal that the Tennessee maneuvers were not a good experience for the 565th.

Getting up-to-date on the war in general, the 8th Army had crossed the Moro River in Italy, and the second Cairo Conference with Roosevelt and Churchill ended. Gen. Rommel was appointed as commander-in-chief for the fortress of Europe, and the U.S. 5th Army took San Pietro, Italy. On Dec. 25th, the 1st and the 7th U.S. Marine Division units landed in New Britain. On December 26th, the U.S. Marines landed at Cape Gloucester, New Britain. In the Battle of North Cape, the German battlecruiser Scharnhorst was sunk by the British fleet. It was headed by Admiral Fraser on the battleship Her Majesty The Duke of York. On Dec. 29th, U.S. Marines captured Cape Gloucester airfield. In the United Kingdom only ten people were killed and forty-one injured during the month.

Chapter 3

Departure From Camp Stewart (Mid-January to September 1944)

In early January, Gen. Rommel assumed command of the German Army Group B, which was defending northern France, Belgium and the Netherlands. Gen. Mark Clark commanded the U.S. 5th and the 7th armies in Italy. At the same time, the U.S. 5th Army assaulted the Gustav Line east of Cassino, Italy, and Sir Oliver Leese commanded the 8th Army in the Adriatic coast. The 5th Army captured Cervaro. The Russians took Sarny, with the Germans counterattacking near Kiev, both in the Ukraine. Eisenhower was appointed Supreme Commander of the Allied Expeditionary Forces. The British X Corps crossed the Garigliano River south of Cassino, Italy. On January 24th, the U.S. 5th Army occupied Anzio and Nettuno, Italy. By January 30th, the U.S. 5th Army successfully broke into the Gustav Line.

To summarize the trip into Tennessee which began in early November and ended in mid-January, we went up there as recruits who had entered the service in the early part of 1943, and six months later we departed for this road trip that took us some three days. We arrived in Tennessee in November, which was the beginning of the real winter season. Even though we had been on maneuvers and bivouacs in Camp Stewart, Georgia, nothing compared to living out in the open twenty-four hours, for days on end, especially when we were putting up with cold winds, moisture and all the bad vagrancies of Mother Nature.

From that experience, we also came back into a camp where they weren't used to having soldiers like us around. That is, Camp Stewart was a recruit training center: the trucks, equipment and uniforms were always immaculate. We probably came back a little like would-be doughboys; our uniforms had not been pressed in many months, and our trucks and guns were in terrible condition. By the standards of Camp Stewart, all of the vehicles needed repainting or refurbishing. I recall at one time, even in our little headquarters battery that had just fifteen or sixteen vehicles, half of them were on what we called "dead line"--they couldn't be taken out on the highway. We came back without the commanding officer we went with and were soon to lose our executive officer, Maj. Bayer. These two top officers needed to be replaced. Those of us already in the 565th were no longer recruits, and since recruits had first dibs on barracks, the rest of us often lived in tent cities. Because of the absenteeism that took place during the maneuvers, there seemed to be an endless list of courts martial for people who had gone AWOL (absent without leave). We went into a rigorous retraining, both in shooting our guns, as well as staying in bivouac. We spent much of our time from then, until we left in early October, in tent cities. We would never again enjoy the tranquil setting of Camp Stewart as we first knew it.

I'm not sure which was worse, living in tent cities or on bivouac. But, bivouac was more favorable because at least we didn't have to put up with dusty streets and living quarters in such close proximity with one another.

When maneuvers were over we were again faced with a three-day road trip back to Camp Stewart, Georgia. This merely meant retracing our steps, with an overnight stay at Ft. Oglethorpe in Chattanooga, Tennessee, the first night and in Madison, Georgia on the second night. Of course, camping there was a rather minimal experience compared to what was happening in the bivouac or maneuver area proper. We arrived back in Camp Stewart, Georgia about 5:00 p.m. on Wednesday evening and entered some barracks. On Thursday, we immediately began to clean our equipment because it looked like it had just been pulled through a mud hole. Not only was it dirty, but it was very scratched and dented.

Oil was leaking out of bearings and seals, and the AARTC (Antiaircraft Recruit Training Center) started on our case immediately. So, we began working on this, not limiting ourselves to any eight-hour days. From an administrative standpoint, all the required court martials that needed processing took a lot of time and paperwork. Some of those who had gone AWOL were still missing. They had to be found and brought back to Camp Stewart.

When the 565th returned back to Camp Stewart, Georgia, on Wednesday, Jan. 19th, Maj. Bayer was transferred, leaving us without an executive officer.

On Jan. 6th, 1944, Lt. Col. Carl Santilli assumed command of the 565th. The 565th was still on maneuvers in Tennessee at this time.

During the next several days, several things happened with respect to officers. Jumping ahead, on Monday, Jan. 31st, we received two officers who would stay with us for the duration. They were Maj. Charles D. Fry, who was to become our S3 (operations officer) and Maj. Calvin M. Pentecost, who was to become our executive officer. Records indicate that several officers were again being shuttled in and out of our battalion. (This continued to happen while we were at Camp Stewart). I expect that this was also happening to many of the veteran battalions, because as officers were graduating from Officers Candidate School at Camp Davis, North Carolina, they would come down to Camp Stewart, Georgia, and join an existing battalion while waiting for their permanent assignment. The battalion commander's diary notes that AARTC was inspecting us daily, putting pressure on us to shape up. On Monday, Feb. 7th, Capt. Stouier assumed command of Battery "B," and as mentioned earlier, this battery had several commanders.

Even though I found no written record of these events, a couple of things happened after we returned to Camp Stewart, Georgia. First, the 565th started its training with a 50-caliber machine gun on a tripod. This was a single, air-cooled gun. That was what we had during Tennessee maneuvers, but when we returned to Camp Stewart, we were issued M51's. An M51 included an M7 trailer with an M45 quad-mounted 50 caliber machine gun mounted on it; it was pulled by a 2 1/2-ton GMC truck. This was a very effective weapon, one that was not only used by us, but by half track units where this same quad 50 was mounted on the back of an M3; this was designated as an M16. These same M51's were part of 90mm units as part of their perimeter defense. Second, we had four forward observers posts (two in each battery), each manned by two men. After maneuvers, a third observer came in so that there were now three observers in each outpost. Every battery was assigned two observation crews. The crews were all issued a jeep, a 1/4-ton trailer and an SCR593 radio. In all, we had eight obser-

A nighttime array of M51 fire at the beaches.

vation teams consisting of 3 men each. It's interesting to note that the enlisted men from the letter battery stayed assigned to them and were never transferred to headquarters battery until well into the war, after we got to Europe where the new third person was already assigned.

The commanding officer's diary notes that we began firing on "C" range in mid-February.

After coming back from Tennessee maneuvers we were all rather disenchanted. We didn't know whether the officers had failed us, if we had failed them, or whether we failed each other. Or perhaps, the events of the war were such that they just didn't need anymore antiaircraft in Europe until after the invasion. In retrospect, the latter probably was the case. The 565th had a gut feeling that we might be dissolved because of the problems, but, apparently we got both our guns and our act back together. Now AARTC was going to make sure the 565th stayed together instead of seperating us. Being in Tennessee on maneuvers and then bivouac made us a very experienced field unit, but it wasn't until Wednesday, Feb. 9th, when we were alerted that we were going on our first field problem in Camp Stewart since returning from Tennessee maneuvers that we were reassured we were going to be retained as a unit.

In June 1992, I had occasion to visit Col. Kenneth Yarnall (Ret), our commanding officer from Aug. 24, 1944 to July 10, 1945, which covered our trip overseas as well as combat duty.

I recall his assignment to the 565th AAA. He told of how he was on the firing range with a different unit in a different East Coast camp. He received an urgent call to report to Camp Stewart. He was aware that there were two unpopular units there, the 563rd and the 565th, and he was hoping that his assignment wasn't one of them.

This was not the case. When he arrived at Camp Stewart, the commanding general gave him the command of our unit. He was able to speak to Lt. Col. Santilli about an hour before his departure. I gathered that his opinion of him was the same as the 800 officers and men that comprised our unit.

Here's what faced this class of '39 West Pointer: a battalion with a bad reputation among the top brass of AAA command (that's not to say we deserved it). Yarnall had no time to train his unit as we were already in the pre-departure phase of deployment to the ETO. We sailed Oct. 6th. Our equipment was unloaded in France, the men in England. It took three weeks to get the equipment to us. No time to train! We departed for France, lay at anchor for a week, unloaded on Dec. 16th. The day the Battle of the Bulge began, there was no time for a refresher course. On Dec. 21st, we were at battle stations in Luxembourg City.

In reflection, Yarnall feels that the commanding general at Camp Stewart was a proud man who was going to have two of his units broken up and transferred as replacements to other cadres and units. As a senior AAA general, his feelings prevailed.

Recorded on Feb. 7th in the archives, General Order 3 describes the general guard duty that was performed in and around the battalion. Apparently we had had a prior general order during our earlier stay there, but it took several days to get a new one prepared as we set up in a new area.

Turning to world events, in early February, Operation Overlord, the plan for the invasion of northwestern Europe or France, was approved in Whitehall, Ohio. Germans were involved in some heavy counterattacks in Anzio, Italy. The U.S. Task Force opened assault on Truk, Micronesia. The airfields there were wrecked by U.S. naval fire, with 400 tons of shipping and 270 aircrafts destroyed. The German Air Force, the Luftwaffe, began it's "Little Blitz" on London, and U.S.

troops began landing on Eniwetok atoll in the South Pacific. The civilian casualty toll in the United Kingdom was becoming very high. In February, there were 961 killed and 1712 injured. By mid-January there was heavy attack produced at Cassino, Italy, which was preceeded by some heavy aerial bombardments. Remember, a lot of the war in Italy had been held up because of bad weather and fog. Heavy raids were also being conducted over Hamburg, Germany, where three thousand tons of bombs were dropped. The Royal Air Force raided Nuremberg, Germany, and ninety-five aircraft were lost. In March in the United Kingdom there were 279 civilians killed and 633 injured. The first weekend in March the 565th went on bivouac at a place near Cherry Hill School. By mid-week, there were heavy rains, and the ground became very swampy. On Friday, March 9th, we moved into what was called administrative bivouac near Metter, Georgia. I rather expected that was a tent city, although I wasn't familiar with what this term meant at the time.

The wet weather continued, and by March 11th we moved a third time into a new area. When we put a shovel into the ground, we struck water. This wasn't too unusual in the Camp Stewart area in Georgia. There's an old adage that Georgia is the only place in the world where you could stand in mud up to your bottom and get sand blown in your eye.

By March 15th we moved to a place called Reidsville. The sand was easy to dig, which wasn't the case when we were up in Tennessee. In Tennessee, the only way we had of disposing of garbage was into slit trenches. We also had to dig slit trenches for our toilets, as well as slit trenches and foxholes for our own protection. Often after we would leave a bivouac area, the wild hogs of Tennessee would come in and root up our garbage and string it all over the place. Then we would get reprimanded for not covering our garbage properly, so we had to go back and dig yet a deeper hole to get rid of it. We certainly didn't have that problem in Georgia.

We left for bivouac in early March. Finally March 17th we moved back to camp, arriving there mid-day. It was very hot, and the heat continued for days. At this time the line batteries were practicing on the firing ranges. On March 22nd, several officers arrived and left, with some officers going to the infantry in Fort Benning, Georgia. (All of antiaircraft, as indicated earlier, was once part of the coast artillery. In 1943, about the time the 565th was being organized, it had it's own designation as AAA. It had nearly 1 million men at times because we needed a lot of men that were used to being around artillery and mechanical devices. Some of the recorded histories note that some antiaircraft units were parked in Europe during WWII, especially the semi-mobile ones. Their equipment, personnel, jeeps, 3/4-ton trucks and 2 1/2-ton trucks were used as infantry replacements, which were very scarce. I expect by March of 1944, the overall Army command could see that the necessity of training more antiaircraft officers was probably an exercise in futility. What the Army really needed were those trained as infantry troops.) So this note in our battalion commander's diary was probably a harbinger of just that particular item in military strategy. On March 28th rain was still falling after a week. The following day the sunshine broke out and it was a beautiful day.

There is little information recorded in battalion commander Santilli's diary for the month of April except for the words "busy" or "a quiet day." Officers, as well as enlisted men, just continued to come and go in the battalion.

In regards to the battles around the world, the Russians had entered Romania, and the British forces in Kohimia, India were surrounded. The Red army had liberated Odessa. In the Ukraine, the Red army had also captured Simferopol and Feodosia and liberated Yalta and Tarnopol, cutting the Axis front in half. During the war when American forces were over there in '44 and '45, the Germans were being squeezed. These, of course, were just some of the early indications of how the Russians were beginning the push from the east. Casualties in the United Kingdom continued to be high, with 146 people killed and 226 injured during April.

In May there were few notations that actually took place, although notes indicate that Capt. Holt took over as CO of headquarters battery after Capt. Stouier had been relieved. The notes do indicate, however, that by May 20th, we were in a bivouac area in the field near Reidsville, Georgia. The weather was quite hot. Later, on May 24th, we moved to Metter, Georgia and some of our men were sent to the infantry. While I have no way of proving this, I expect that some of the men who didn't have the proper training for antiaircraft were being shuffled between the various branches of the Army because of the great need for men in the infantry.

On the world front, on May 11th the U.S. 5th and the U.S. 8th Armies prepared to join the onslaught on the Gustav Line in Italy. The last of the German forces had evacuated the Crimea. Kesselring ordered controlled withdrawal of the Germans from the Gustav and Adolph Hitler Lines. The U.S. 5th and 8th Armies finally penetrated the Gustav Line. Apparently these actions were taking place in Italy. The Canadian troops were breaking through the Adolph Hitler Line in Italy, under strong air support from the United States, in an operation called Buffalo. British troops launched an all-out breakthrough at Anzio, Italy. The Anzio troops linked with the U.S. 5th Army at Terracina, Italy. At last there were no civilian casualties in England.

Once again, in the month of June, the diary used two words: "quiet" and "busy." Apparently, either things were booming, or the days were very slow. (Note: June 6th was D-Day in Europe, the day the allies landed on the beaches in France.) As far as our diary is concerned, it was also a very busy day for us. On June 15th, the battalion was to go on a problem with a searchlight battalion.

While that was probably an interesting exercise, let me share something that I have learned in the intervening years. Searchlights were a very obsolete bit of equipment for shooting down airplanes. The radar that had been hooked to the 90mm guns no longer required searchlights to find a plane. In fact, all 90mm guns sent to Europe had radar, as opposed to height finders and directors, which were left in Great Britain. The statistics that have been quoted as to the number of British casualties each month declines precipitously. The cause was twofold: first, radar and second, proximity fuses. These were used on at V1 rockets on the coastal areas only. So any dud would fall into the English Channel. The U.S. Army took no chances on the Germans getting hold of one. This is why the casualty rate became so low. So really there was not a lot of use for searchlights at this point in the army, or particularly in the field of combat except for one reason: they were used for illumination. Searchlights were particularly helpful in Europe on a cloudy night when the engineers wanted to build a bridge across the river. They would shine searchlights against the bottom of clouds and the beams would illuminate the area. The enemy that wished to shoot at these troops would then be revealed to our forces. U.S. artillery or armor could easily spot the enemy and eliminate them. These searchlights also had a very important part to play in the war that was to come.

Notes state that the 565th was getting ready to go on furlough again at the end of June. We were busy preparing all the paperwork, and the first furloughs left Camp Stewart, Georgia, on Friday, June 30th. Of course, with the thought that we would eventually end up in Europe and be part of the fight in the European Theater of Operation (ETO), we were very interested in what was happening there.

A lot was going on in England in preparation for the Allied invasion of Europe on June 6th, 1944, D-Day. There was bad weather in the English Channel, and as landings were made on both Utah and Omaha beaches there were many casualties. The operations on the beaches did not go as well as expected. It wasn't until June 10th, four days after the invasion, that the American and British forces actually linked up their beachheads. Gen. Montgomery was the overall commander on the beaches at that time.

On June 13th, the first of the V1 flying bombs landed in England. They continued to fall there day and night. In the Pacific, the U.S. Fleet destroyed fourteen Japanese warships, including three aircraft carriers, during the Battle of the Philippine Sea. In Europe, the U.S. 3rd Army drove toward Cherbourg, France and liberated Cherbourg on June 29th. One thousand bombers attacked Berlin, Germany. The U.S. troops mopped up the Cotentin Peninsula of France. Again there were a lot of civilian casualties in the United Kingdom; 1,935 were dead and 5,906 injured mainly as a result of the V1 bomb. Most of the 565th had left on furlough at the end of June.

There was little work being done for the first couple of weeks in July. By mid-July the entire battalion was taking training in mine fields. How well we remember that! We would get down on our hands and knees with bayonets and stick them in the ground at about six inch intervals rather than have any kind of mechanical device or mine sweepers locate the mines. During the months of June and July several promotions were made. This, no doubt, was an adjustment of people who had been reduced in rank while on maneuvers. Also, they were just filling the table of organization from transfers and gun sections who had never received all the rank that was required to begin with.

Some of the special orders we have in our files, note that several of the officers and enlisted men who missed going on furlough at the end of June, began going in the July instead. This was all an indication that we were getting ready for overseas duty. At the end of July, work was completed on all permanent records. I'm not exactly sure what that means, but I expect there were a lot of temporary records or special orders that hadn't been posted on the individual records.

Let's look at the changes in the world. (From this point forward, basically only European changes will be noted because that is where the 565th was headed.) The British 2nd Army launched the offensive around Caen, France, drawing German forces into battle in preparation for Operation Cobra, six days later. Remember, when looking south toward the north coast of France, the British landed to the left and the Americans to the right. The British commander, Gen. Montgomery, was in overall charge of the landings. However, Gen. Bradley was in charge of the 1st Army Group which later became the 1st Army under General Hodges. Also, a couple divisions split off and became the 3rd Army under Gen. Patton. On Aug. 1st, Gen. Bradley assumed command of the 12th Army Group (1st and 3rd Armies). Gen. Patton was to the right of the 1st Army, and his 3rd Army went toward Cherbourg, France. The Canadian army was to the extreme left of the British army's command.

While the records for the month of August are a bit sketchy, it appears that the 565th went into the field in early August; however, we also had to pull guard duty at Camp Stewart. Bear in mind, it didn't take the entire battalion to pull guard duty on the post; however, it took a lot of them, and it was a bit of a hassle to commute between the field and the post to do the duty.

Apparently, Col. Santilli left on furlough because he came back on Aug. 5th to assume command. He also may have been on some kind of leave because, looking ahead now, we were to leave Camp Stewart on Oct. 6th. The records note that the battalion supply office got new clothes which were issued to all the enlisted men; this was an indication that we were going overseas. In all probability, as enlisted men, we probably knew that or highly suspected that. On Aug. 9th we received movement orders. All the beneficiary stencils were cut, which was a long job because they state the benefits the men and officers can receive.

On Aug. 12th, we assisted the 198th Gun Battalion on post guard. Apparently, they were understrengthed; the 565th helped them because we were just more or less "lazing around" Camp Stewart, waiting for our departure. On Aug. 16th, the roster of advanced parties were forwarded to higher headquarters. The AARTC wanted the battalion to leave camp. (They wanted us to get out of barracks and go out into a tent city.)

In the war in Europe, it is interesting to note some of the table of organization changes that took place on Aug. 1st. When the American forces split the 1st Army Group into the 1st Army and the 3rd Army, Gen. Omar Bradley took over the group command as the 12th Army Group, and Gen. Hodge assumed command of the 1st Army. The British and the Canadian armies under Gen. Montgomery were called the 21st Army Group.

On the Italian front, the U.S. 8th Army did reach Florence. In France, the 3rd Army took Rennes and also reached the outskirts of Brest, but it was months before the area was taken. It was highly fortified and eventually, all the U.S. 8th Army ever did was sit on the outskirts of town and keep the people in Brest occupied. We were never able to use Brest as a port. Over on the extreme left flank of the front, the Canadian forces were driving south toward Falaise, France. By Aug. 9th, Gen. Eisenhower set up his headquarters in France, and the U.S. 3rd Army turned toward Falaise or to the east and approached St. Malo and mopped up in Le Mans. By Aug. 11th, the 3rd Army was in high gear headed east towards Paris, taking Angers; Falaise Gap was closed to less than twenty miles. On Aug. 13th the Germans begin to withdraw through the Falaise Gap. On Aug. 15th, Operation Anvil began as the Allieds invaded the southern coast of France and were coming up the Rhone River Valley. The Canadians finally took the Falaises on Aug. 16th. Field Marshal von Kluge, commander of the German Army Group D, committed suicide on Aug. 19th. The two German armies then surrendered in the Falaise-Argentan pocket.

Gen. Patton and his forces reached the Seine river on each side of Paris, France, but did not enter the city. The 3rd Army formed a bridgehead across the Seine at Mantes-Gassingcourt. The Falaise Gap closed, and the French troops liberated the port city of Toulon, France.

On Aug. 25th, under France's Gen. LeClerc, the French 2nd Armored Division liberated Paris, France, with the aid of U.S. troops. U.S. troops continued to assault Brest, France, but never did take it. The British 2nd Army crossed the Seine river at Verdun, France. On Aug. 28th, the port city of Marseilles was liberated in southern France. French troops liberated Soissons, France, on Aug. 29th. By the 31st, the British 2nd Army reached Armiens in northern France and captured the Somme bridges intact. The U.S. 8th Army attacked the Gothic Line in Italy. Gen. Montgomery was promoted to Field Marshall, commanding the 21st Army Group (Canadian 1st and British 2nd Armies). Civilian casualties in the United Kingdom were down somewhat, with 1,103 killed and 2,921 injured for the month of August.

Over a period of the next several days, within the battalion there was a lot of work being done to get ready for our overseas movement. While it isn't recorded anywhere, I recall that in the motorpool we were very busy making boxes, lining them, and finally hauling them to the railroad station. The 565th turned in all of our trucks, but those did not go overseas; however, our guns did go overseas. Once we would get to England we would draw new trucks.

In our preparation for overseas movement, several people from AARTC in Camp Stewart, Georgia, inspected us. They had come in from higher headquarters. The office closed each day after 4:00 p.m., so we could engage in sports. We were just killing time because we really had nothing to do, and after some time, had no equipment to do anything with; therefore, we were at our wits' end to entertain ourselves. I also recall one meal we had during that time - seven kinds of beans. Apparently, we were in the process of cleaning up all the various kinds of rations that were in our kitchens.

On Aug. 23rd, Col. Santilli announced he had been relieved of his duties and that on the 24th, Lt. Col. Kenneth L. Yarnell would be arriving to take over as the battalion's commanding officer. This was a surprise to most of us. Col. Yarnall had graduated from the U.S. Military Academy in West Point in 1939, and apparently, he was well trained in operations of an antiaircraft battalion. The 565th knew very little of him, and because we were going overseas soon, we never had an opportunity to see him operate in the field or get acquainted with him. Be mindful, enlisted men and officers didn't do a lot of fraternizing.

On Aug. 26th the advanced party left for Europe. This group included: Lt. Olsen, our S1; Capt. Martin, our S4 or supply officer; T/Sgt. Lesko, his chief enlisted man; Mr. Dreeland, personnel; and Lt. Spencer. (They actually went to France, but the rest of the 565th ended up in England, far away from our supplies.)

In Europe, the Red Ball Express was well under way. After we arrived in Europe, we used to see trucks that had a red ball painted on their bumper. We thought the Red Ball Express was taking place during December and January during the war. However, the Red Ball Express actually began on Aug. 22nd, and it was made up of many transportation companies. The front had moved so rapidly to the east that the Allies had literally outrun their source of supply. The distance from the harbor beaches to the front was now 560 miles. In order to get supplies there, trucking companies hauled supplies to the front with 2 1/2-ton 6x6's to four-ton cargo 6x6's. They were known as the Red Ball Express and had soup kitchens, rest areas, and relief and tire patching stations along the way. The same type of operation, only not quite so formalized, continued on throughout the war. It wasn't until April that the front didn't need truck-in supplies.

During the month of September, our commanding officer's diary is rather sketchy and rather incomplete. However, it does indicate that the unit was involved in activities to stay busy. On Labor Day, Sept. 4th, the temperature was 102 degrees farenheit, which didn't allow a great deal of activity in the first place. Notes did indicate that we worked in the evening, as opposed to during the day. It was very hot again the following day, and we were working on files. It does indicate that we were going to have a parade on Sept. 9th, and also that Staff Sgt. Talarico, one of our original cadre men, was discharged. I don't know whether the parade was called for him, but it does indicate that the parade was postponed and held the following day, Sept. 11th.

We had another battalion parade on Sept. 14th, and apparently, this was to keep everyone busy. The second week in September indicates there were a lot of meetings with officers, especially meetings between the CO and people at higher headquarters. On Sept. 15th, the CO became the father of a baby girl. On Sept. 18th, notes indicated that this unit was to be in a staging area by Oct. 1st, 1944. Again, on Sept. 28th, we had a parade with the 140th Group, which indicates it was more than one battalion, probably three. Also on that day our beds were taken away from us and on Sept. 30th, we left Camp Stewart, Georgia by train at 9:00 a.m. We traveled all day.

Meanwhile, the Red Ball Express in Europe continued to operate with the distance it traveled stretching further and further. In some cases it went nearly one thousand miles. On Sept. 25th, the U.S. 3rd Army assumed a defensive role, and this is kind of the tip of the iceberg. In the eyes of the Americans, Gen. Montgomery was always interfering with the war and liked to shove his weight around. Gen. Eisenhower was Supreme Commander of the Army, yet politically he had to get along with the British. Gen. Montgomery actually had the same rank as Eisenhower, and because he had a direct voice to Churchill, Montgomery always seemed to be stirring the waters. He had convinced the high command that they should run the offensive in northern Europe as opposed to southern; therefore, the U.S. 3rd Army, which was on the southern flank of the 12th Army Group at that time, was ordered to stay in place. To keep them there, the U.S. 3rd Army wasn't given gasoline. By this time the defensive line was now the Canadian Army in the north, then the 2nd British Army under the 21st Army Group, headed by Gen. Bernard Montgomery. The next ones in line were the U.S. 1st, 3rd and 9th Armies making up the 12th Army Group under Lt. Gen. Omar Bradley. The U.S. 7th Army and the First French Free Army were to the south of that, making up the 6th Army Group headed by Gen. Devers, who had arrived from the south of France via the Rhine River Valley. This was to be the makeup of the table of organization for the rest of the war, although there were some movements of corps and armies. The XV Corps, which had been part of the U.S. 3rd Army, was transferred to the U.S. 7th Army to its right.

The Allied invasion of Europe took place in early June. In July, August and September their front had made great milage advances. They actually reached the Moselle River and the Siegfried Line, making some penetrations there. However, the line of supply became so long that it became almost impossible for the Allies to advance any further until these supply lines could be shortened.

As we look ahead to the Battle of the Ardennes, because of our own lack of supplies we gave the German forces seventy-five days to set up an offense.

In the meantime, the American forces were struggling to rebuild bridges all the way from LaHavre, France on into eastern France, into Luxembourg and Belgium. We also needed to restore the harbors at Antwerp so we could receive supplies there, thus making the line of supply much shorter.

The British dropped paratroops across the Rhine river at Arnhem in the Netherlands. The bridges were cut off there, and the British suffered a defeat and had difficulty getting their soldiers back. The British 2nd Army did make some progress getting closer to the Rhine River in the north. The British 2nd Army also widened the Nijmegen saliant. The last survivors of the Battle of Arnhem were withdrawn.

In Italy, the U.S. 8th Army crossed the Rubicon river in Italy. Canadian forces finally finished taking Calais in northern France. In the United Kingdom, the civilian death count was 90, with 360 injured.

Chapter 4
(October 1944 to Dec. 16, 1944)

As the 565th traveled north by the train on Oct. 1st, we passed through Washington D.C. about 6:00 a.m. We finally reached Camp Kilmer, New Jersey, about noon. We went into a Barracks Number 3, which is kind of insignificant, except for the fact that we were used to being in tent city. The weather was cool, which was a great change from what we had been experiencing in Georgia. Some of the boxes that were required for headquarters work were opened, and we changed and updated some of the battalion's records.

Meanwhile, over in Europe, the Allies also had supply problems. Their blanket situation was beginning to improve, and a critical shortage of winter clothing, raincoats and overshoes was beginning to be rectified. The Germans, who quickly retreated across France, were concentrating on the northern front, opposite the British 2nd Army.

In the meantime, at Camp Kilmer, New Jersey, we all stood reveille and generally just messed around, while those that were preparing records stayed busy. The next day, on Oct. 3rd, we had a physical inspection. Again, I expect it was a matter of keeping busy.

In Europe, the 9th Army took a new position north of the 1st Army and south of the British 2nd Army position. Thus, as the U.S. armies lined up, the 9th Army was to the north, the 1st Army was in the middle, and the 3rd Army was to the south. These made up the U.S. 12th Army Group under Gen. Bradley. South of that was the U.S. 7th Army and the 1st Free French Army under the 6th Army Group, commanded by Gen. Devers.

In the meantime, on Oct. 4th, we had an abandon ship drill in our preparation for sailing on the 6th. Arrangements were made for a partial payment so we would have some money when traveling overseas. Since it was Sunday, Chaplain Bird conducted services. On Oct. 5th, the records indicate that two men from Battery "C" were AWOL. Another man was in the hospital; and, 157 men who had initially made allotments, had changed them, creating a lot of paperwork for the people in headquarters. On the 5th, we began our trek to the ship, which would take us overseas. To get to the ship we took a ferry that went through Newark and Jersey City, New Jersey to Staten Island, New York, where we boarded our ship at midnight on Pier 17. While the band played, the battalion ate donuts and drank coffee. At 11:45 a.m. on Oct. 6th, we set sail on the U.S. army transport Cristobal of the Panama Line. The Panama Line was a fruiter, which was a high speed freight boat that hauled bananas from the Caribbean to the east coast. It had been refitted to haul troops to Europe. (The USAT Crostobal wasn't retired from service until just a few years ago.)

In the meantime, the 90th Division was supposed to guard Brest, France, and the entire southern flank of the rest of the U.S. 3rd Army as it swept across northern France, to eventually concentrate near Nancy. It took about ten days for the forces to move into position. Up on the northern front, the Canadians assaulted the Breskens, Netherlands pocket in the low countries. The U.S. 3rd Army occupied Echternack and Grevensmacher, Luxembourg. This was done by the 20th Corps which was the northern most corps of the U.S. 3rd Army. (An army is usually made up of three corps, and each corps has three divisions.)

Aboard ship on Oct. 7th, a voice announced that six short blasts and one long blast meant to abandon ship. On Sunday, Oct. 8th, church services were conducted on the gun deck, and we set our watches one hour ahead. The post exchange (PX) was open. On the 9th, we had boat drills to test our abilities for timeliness. Our second try with a time of 3 1/2 minutes was accepted as being good enough. We began having special service programs for entertainment. On Oct. 10th the weather was quite rough as we proceeded across the North Atlantic. At this point of the journey, we were part of a very large convoy.

On the war front, the Canadians broke through into a pocket towards the Scheldte river on the northern front. At SHAEF Headquarters in Europe (Supreme Headquarters Allied Expiditionary Forces), a meeting was called by Gen. Eisenhower at Verdun, France, relative to the U.S. Army's role in upcoming operations. It was attended by Gen. Bradley's U.S. 12th Army group, Gen. Patton's U.S. 3rd Army, Gen. Hodges' 1st Army and Gen. Simpson's 9th Army. Bradley was the general in charge. Patton, Hodges and Simpson, were each commanding officers of an army.

Aboard ship the weather continued to be rough for the next several days, sometimes to the point where we weren't allowed on deck. And, there were people that were seasick. Some were seasick for the entire journey, but fortunately, I was only sick for three days.

The U.S. 12th Army Group, under Gen. Bradley, had many more troops than the 21st Army Group had under Gen. Montgomery. Sooner or later Montgomery was going to ask for one of the U.S. armies; after all, U.S. forces had four armies, and he only had two. Gen. Eisenhower felt that transferring either the U.S. 1st or 3rd Armies, who were used to working together, would be in error. At that particular time, from north to south, we had the U.S. 1st, the U.S. 9th, the U.S. 3rd under Bradley's 12th Army Group, and the U.S. 7th in Devers' 6th Army Group. Thus, Eisenhower issued orders to transfer the U.S. 9th to the 21st Group under Gen. Montgomery, and inserted it in the line between the British 2nd Army and the U.S. 1st Army.

Later, comments reflected that the transfer was probably a good change because the U.S. 9th had not become so ingrained in the command of Gens. Bradley and Eisenhower. There were a few minor changes; Some of the army corps were shifted as a result of the transfer. As the U.S. 9th Army shifted to the north, the U.S. 1st Army assumed the command of the XIX Corps, and the VIII Corps remained under the 1st Army's command. Some of the corps that were under the U.S. 1st Army were reassigned to the U.S. 9th Army.

By this time, the waters of the North Atlantic had become extremely rough, so the 565th didn't have any boat drills on some of the days. Also, we weren't able to get on the top deck. Besides that, on Oct. 12th orders came down to quit gambling. We had first aid drills and many activities to keep us busy. On Oct. 14th, we were issued K rations for debarkation, in case we weren't able to have a meal somewhere along the way. On the 16th, we sighted Land's End, which is the extreme southwest tip of England. When this happened, we left the convoy and headed for the harbor on our own. We had been on the water for eleven days. We were supposed to disembark on Oct. 17th, but it was post-

Arranging a camouflage net over a truck.

poned. So, the anchor was dropped in the harbor at Plymouth, England.

Finally on Oct. 18th we did disembark in the early evening, leaving for Leek, England, by train just before midnight. We arrived there the next morning and were taken by trucks to an old British army camp, Blackslaw-Moore. While at the time none of this seemed to be too unusual to most of us, in retrospect, I imagine we were something like a bunch of lost sheep. We were supposed to have unloaded in La Harve, France, where all of our equipment was, and we found ourselves in the midlands of England with no equipment. It took several days to get all the gear to England.

From October until early December, life for the 565th at Blackslaw-Moore was very similar to the closing days in August and September in Camp Stewart, Georgia, where we had little, if anything, to do. As a matter of fact, the first days that we were in Blackslaw-Moore, we had nothing to do because we had no foot lockers and no equipment, all of which had been sent to La Harve, France. Subsequently, this equipment had to be shipped back across the channel and transported by rail up to Leek, England. We also had to draw new trucks in Liverpool, England and drive them to our new camp.

Generally things were just in a period of flux. The weather was cold, damp and snowy. We were living in Nisson huts and heated with charcoal burners. While we had charcoal to burn, it often came from a pile that had been there for a long time and was heavily covered with snow. We had to become experts in firing wet charcoal in order to stay warm.

In the meantime, in Europe, SHAEF had called a meeting at Verdun, relative to the U.S. 3rd Army's role in the Group. Gens. Bradley, Patton, Hodges and Simpson attended. Taking the Saar region and crossing the Saar River was outlined as the objective of the U.S. 3rd Army. This movement was tentatively scheduled for Oct. 23rd. The 1st Army and the 9th Army would be at the Ruhr River, further to the north.

There were a few respites from the boredom that took place such as the groups of drivers and work crews that were sent out to unload boats or process materials that were coming in from the United States to other areas of England. But all in all, it was a rather boring and unproductive time for us knowing that there was a war going on just a few hundred miles from us.

Finally, in early December, we got word that we were ready and would be transferred across the channel. We soon started preparing vehicles and rosters for men for our move to South Hampton, England. Finally, on Dec. 7th, at 5:30 a.m., we departed. We arrived at South Hampton at 10:00 p.m. As in Blackslaw-Moore, South Hampton was very muddy.

On Dec. 8th, we went to the docks, and our trucks and equipment were loaded onto the ships. We boarded about 6:00 p.m. The ship I was on was the USS Charles M. Hall; headquarters and headquarters battery were also on this ship. It took several ships for the entire battalion to cross the channel. We pulled out in the South Hampton Harbor, anchored overnight, and on Dec. 10th, we crossed the channel to La Harve, France; however, we did not unload until Dec. 14th.

Antiaircraft crew watches for enemy planes.

We unloaded at the very end of a dock that was built by the engineers. Once off the ship, we were sent to the area where the lettered battery trucks were being unloaded and put into landing crafts by booms from ships anchored in the harbor. As these landing crafts would come up to this unloading area, the trucks would start driving off the landing craft; however, the trucks needed aid getting up on shore, and we would hook our winches to these trucks to get them onto dry land. Once on land the trucks headed for the Red Horse assembly area, near Rowen, France, about twenty-five to thirty miles down the road.

In the meantime, the Germans were building up a considerable amount of hardware just east of both the 1st and the 3rd Armies. This, of course, was a concern to Gen. Patton, but to him, his information fell on deaf ears. It was a surprise to everyone when the Germans broke out on Dec. 16th; however, it wasn't an unexpected move for the Germans. They certainly had the men and equipment to launch such a move.

For a clearer understanding of our abilities, the U.S. 3rd Army was considered to have the best intelligence in the ETO. It was standard that divisions in the 3rd Army would capture a handful of prisoners each day. The 3rd Army tried to find out what units the prisoners were from, what kind of equipment they had and any other information. Thus, through this information they were able to know what units they were facing and what kind of equipment those units would be using.

As a winter offensive was being planned by the Allies, the Germans attacked the Ardennes region of Luxembourg and Belgium on Dec. 16th. Thus, the Germans upstaged the Allies when it came to launching aggressive action. Perhaps their intelligence picked up our intent, and they beat us to the punch.

There were some unique things going on in the ETO. The Allies lost many infantrymen and set up an infantry training center near Metz, France, where new soldiers from other branches of service could be trained. There was a constant shifting of divisions from one corps to another and, in some cases, from one army to another.

The Red Horse assembly area near Rowen, France was a muddy field much like what we saw in Tennessee; however, here at Red Horse you could get around on gravel roads, whereas in Tennessee it became a quagmire. We were at Red Horse on Dec. 16th when the Germans came across the front and began what was to become known as the Battle of the Bulge. At this time, the U.S. 1st Army headquarters was in Spa, and that is where we had been assigned. The U.S. 3rd Army headquarters was south at Nancy, France. When the 565th arrived there five days later, we didn't realize we'd be attached to the 3rd Army. As a matter of fact, our advance parties, including Col. Yarnell and his battery commanders, went to Spa, Belguim and found the 1st Army headquarters almost abandoned. They were packing to go westward deeper into Belgium. In the meantime, our executive officer, Maj. Pentecost, received orders to proceed to Luxembourg City and set up defense of Lucky Forward (3rd Army G2 and G3) which was moving to Luxembourg City from Nancy, France. The commanding officer and his advance party intercepted us on our way to our destination.

One of the greatest gambles of history—a nation threatened and surrounded by an angry conqueror which aided, in a thousand ways, nations fighting for their lives

THE TRUE STORY OF SWEDISH NEUTRALITY

Condensed from The Minneapolis Tribune
Ralph Wallace

ONE of the greatest gambles of history was played out in Scandinavia during World War II. Until now, only a few high American and English statesmen knew that Sweden—so often accused of pro-German leanings—actually aided the Allies with vital military supplies and information from the outbreak of war.

Only two men, both high Swedish officials, knew that information gathered by Sweden's far-flung intelligence network funneled directly to the Allied legations. That information told what occurred day by day in Hitler's headquarters. It furnished details of the V-1 bomb months ahead of the initial attacks on London. It even included accurate

RALPH WALLACE, well-known American writer and publicist, recently spent several weeks in northern Europe. This first comprehensive story of Sweden's amazing part in the war is based on his lengthy interviews with high Swedish, British and American officials, as well as leaders of the Scandinavian undergrounds, and on extensive investigation in Washington, London, Stockholm and Copenhagen.

microfilm maps of the Calais coastal batteries bombarding England.

Completely encircled, Sweden was forced to make a pretense of neutrality. Yet even in the first war years, clandestine shipments of ball bearings and other priceless equipment were reaching the United States and Great Britain. The Bofors 40 mm. anti-aircraft gun, one of the war's outstanding weapons, was smuggled to the United States in 1940 and produced here by the thousands. Generals and colonels—no lower officers were trusted—sweated in blacked-out armories to pack cases of machine guns and hand grenades for the Danish and Norwegian undergrounds.

"With all that went on during war years," Per Albin Hansson, prime minister of Sweden, told me a few weeks ago in Stockholm, "it is a miracle that Sweden survived at all."

After weeks of intensive investigation in Sweden, I am convinced that all but a small minority of business and governmental leaders always privately worked and hoped for German defeat. German sympathizers

Copyright 1946, The Minneapolis Star-Journal and Tribune, Minneapolis 15, Minn.
(The Minneapolis Tribune, August 18 and 19, '46)

A reprint from Reader's Digest mentions how the first 40mm was smuggled out of Sweden.

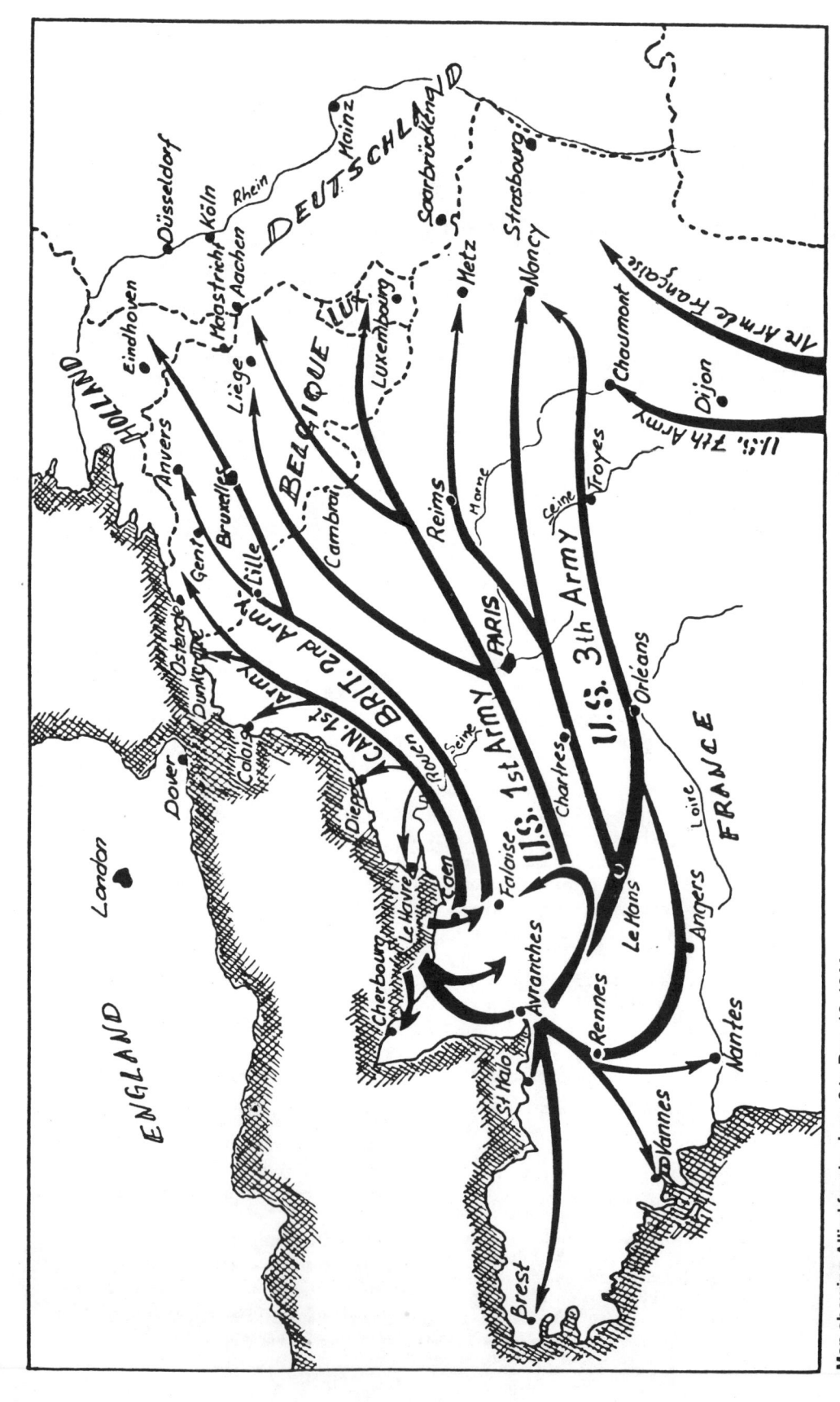

Map showing Allied fronts, June 6 to Dec. 16, 1944.

Chapter 5
(Dec. 16-31, 1944)

On Dec. 16th, the day the Battle of the Bulge began, the U.S. 3rd Army was poised for an attack to the south of the Luxembourg/French border, but the weather wasn't good, and the attack was delayed.

That's when things got out of hand up north, and the Bulge began at Echternach, Luxembourg, a city twenty miles northeast of Luxembourg City. This was where the German Panzer divisions broke through. The extent of the break was not known for several days. This was the area that the U.S. 9th Army had been defending for a long time. The German side had the Eifel, a series of very steep hills, deep valleys and fast-flowing rivers; the Luxembourg/Belgium side had the hilly Ardennes. Thus, the topography of this area would not make a likely battleground, and the 9th Army somewhat abandoned this place. Perhaps forces could fight up the valleys, but even then they were in very close proximity of enemies shooting down at them from both sides. Because the 9th Army wasn't occupying the area, it was several hours before the entire U.S. forces knew that a full scale German offensive was underway here.

A day after the Bulge, Gen. Patton learned of what was going on, and he immediately assigned the XX Corps to defend his entire line to the east. He moved all the other corps north to the shore up the southern flank of the Bulge (salient). On Dec. 18th, Gen. Patton traveled to Luxembourg City. The 12th Army group headquarters was already there at the Alfa Hotel, across the street from the railroad station. Gen. Bradley asked Gen. Patton to do a ninety degree turn to the north and Patton sent one armored and two infantry divisions into the area within twenty-four hours. The 4th Armored and the 80th Infantry had to withdraw west across the Saar and the Moselle Rivers, moving about 125 miles. The 26th Infantry had four thousand untrained men; Patton wasn't too happy about committing them to such a battle, but he had little choice. The Bulge hit in the 1st Army area, but left the VIII Corps of the 1st Army intact to the south. As the Bulge expanded to the west, the VIII Corps literally strung out along the southern border of the Bulge, awaiting reinforcements from the U.S. 3rd Army. And as it turned out, the 3rd Army was to gather the VIII Corps on the west end of the Bulge. The III Corps was to hit into the center of it, and the XII Corps was to be on the north and east. The XX Corps of the 3rd Army was to stay in position and hold the position that it had prior to the Bulge's formation on the 3rd Army's southern flank, southeast of Luxembourg City.

In the meantime, at the headquarters of SHAEF in Verdun, France, Gen. Eisenhower called Gens. Bradley, Devers and Britain's Tetters in for a conference. (Actually, Gen. Montgomery should have been there, too, but the rift between him and the U.S. forces had grown very wide.)

On the 20th of December, the 565th left the Red Horse assembly area near Rowen for Luxembourg City, passing through Reims and Soissons, France. We arrived at Neidercorn, Luxembourg (about six miles southeast of Luxembourg City) about 9:00 p.m. In the meantime, Lucky Forward had moved into Luxembourg on Dec. 19th. The 12th Army Group was headquartered in the Alfa Hotel near the railroad station, just up and over the railroad bridge from the 565th AAA Battalion Headquarters, until it was moved to Namur, Belgium.

On Dec. 21st, the 565th then pulled into positions in and around Luxembourg. "A" Battery defended Luxembourg City to the west, with "D" Battery to the east. "B" Battery moved to the airstrip east of the city. "C" Battery moved northeast about six or seven miles to the towers of Radio Luxembourg. Somewhere along the line we became assigned to the U.S. 3rd Army, 38th Brigade, 207 AAA Group, but initially operated under the 207 AAA Group that had been cut off from the rest of the 1st Army. The other troops attached to the 1st Army, which was cut off because of the salient, were also assigned to the 3rd Army. The 38th Brigade remained in Nancy, France; the 207 AAA Group was located in Luxembourg City, Luxembourg. In all probability, 16 AAA Group was also part of the 1st Army that was left behind.

As we sat in Luxembourg City, I'm sure few of us realized what infantry division or combination of troops was really protecting our flanks. The 3rd Army was at the southern flank of the salient. The army stretched from the far west end, well west of Bastogne, Belgium, east to Echternach, Luxembourg, then south along the Moselle river. But in our immediate area, the 565th was protected by the XII Corps, which consisted of the 4th and 5th Infantry Divisions, the 10th Armored Division, minus Combat Command "B", plus the Combat Command "A" of the 9th Armored Division and the 2nd Cavalry Group. (An armored division was made up of Combat Command "A", "B" & Reserve Command.) We also had the 35th Division, which was in a reserve mode at Metz, France, immediately south of us. The 4th and 5th Infantry Divisions were immediately north and to our east, and we were depending on them to keep the Germans from coming into Luxembourg City.

From an aerial standpoint Dec. 22nd proved to be a great day when sorties from the 19th TAC (Tactical Air Command) flew 558 missions and claimed 412 vehicles, 34 tanks, 26 guns and 56 railroad cars. This was of great help to the U.S. forces because it thwarted a lot of German plans.

At this point, the 565th's communications center was recording all the messages that were coming and going from the batteries and from the battalion headquarters to the batteries. The center was ladened with radios and telephones that were out of order. We were getting messages such as when planes were going over, if we shot at them, why they didn't shoot, what direction the enemy came from and which way the enemy went.

Since the 565th was attached to the 16th AAA Group, we were part of the 38th Brigade. The 38th Brigade was actually the command unit of the 3rd Army, and it would have anywhere from three to four antiaircraft groups under it at any given time. There were as many as eight antiaircraft battalions attached to the 3rd Army headquarters at one time, which meant that they were receiving orders directly through at least three AAA Groups.

The 565th's initial assignment was probably with the 16th AAA Group that was operating in the Luxembourg City area and assigned to the 1st Army, whose headquarters was at Spa, Belgium. The 38th Brigade was the 3rd Army Highest AAA Command and located at Nancy, France.

Lt. Col. Yarnall recalls that he and the five battery commanders left the Red Horse assembly area well ahead of the battalion proper to report to the 1st Army headquarters at Spa.

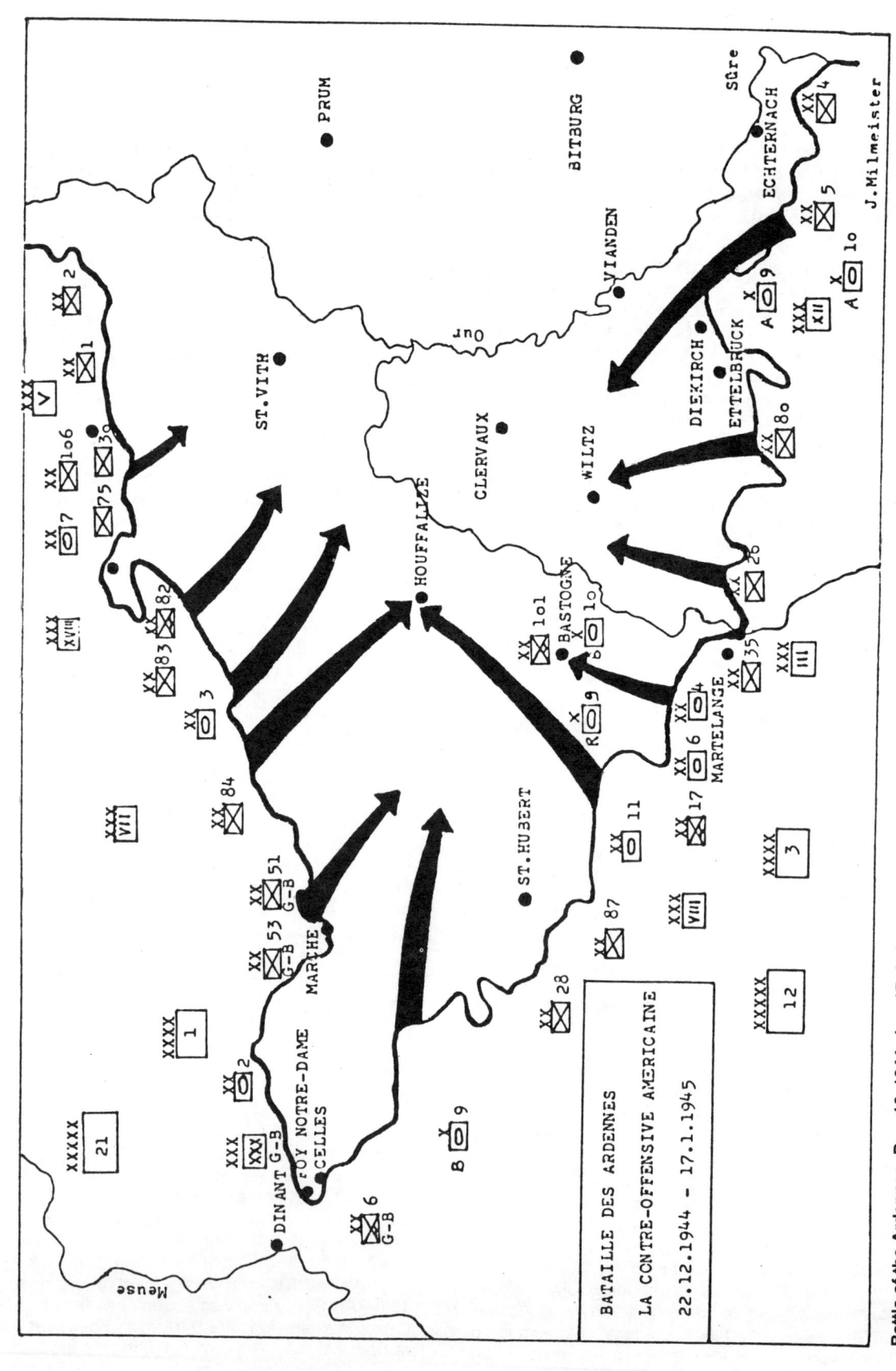

Battle of the Ardennes: Dec. 16, 1944; Jan. 17, 1945.

An M-15, two 50-caliber machine guns and a 37mm rifle, the second half of a self-propelled AAA unit. This employed a turret arrangement on the reverse of a half-track.

An M-16 half-track used by self-propelled AAA units. The M-16 allowed for rapid deployment from one area to another.

A 90mm gun ready to fire in the snow-covered Ardennes.

Upon arrival there, they were informed that the headquarters had left the building and that they should find their way to the 16 AAA Group (still part of the 1st Army) at Luxembourg City. Aware of the German offensive, they took a long circuitous route west before turning south. Eventually they arrived at Arlon, France and met the battalion as it arrived from Rowen.

At this time the city of Bastogne, Belguim was completely surrounded by the Germans, and the U.S. forces were fighting gallantly to relieve that. At one time there was somewhere between seven hundred to thirteen hundred wounded in need of treatment in the Bastogne area. Moreover, the Germans had really fortified the ground around the city and had launched an all out effort to gain control of it. After all, it was the key road in the center of that part of Belgium and northern France.

On Dec. 24th we fired our first shots, expending 174 rounds of 40mm at 90mm bursts. We used 82 rounds of 50-caliber, had seen targets, and yet we claimed no results. At this particular time nine Weissights were inoperative and in the process of being repaired. These sights must have been rather ineffective because such notations were very common throughout the unit reports until the end of the war. It must be that they just did not work properly, at least not in cold weather.

By Dec. 25th, our records indicate the position of all the gun batteries and their coordinates, as well as all the outposts around the city of Luxembourg.

The 3rd Army reported at this time that there were nine Panzer divisions and fourteen infantry divisions effective in the Bulge. It was assumed that Hitler had the ability to launch another powerful attack at the Echternach or Trier areas generally north and east of Luxembourg City. It was assumed that the enemy had eleven divisions, or about eighty thousand troops opposing the U.S. 3rd Army, north of the Moselle River. This was somewhat less than their opposition against the 1st Army: sixty-three thousand troops made up of eight divisions.

Strafing and bombing by the enemy continued to increase in the 3rd Army area. Of the 143 planes making ninety-four raids to this date, AAA shot down 17 and claimed 6. On Dec. 25th our unit report indicates we fired 190 rounds of 40mm at 90mm bursts and 50-rounds of 50 caliber at seen targets with no results. By this time there were fourteen Weissights in for repair. On the north flank of the 1st Army, the 1st Armored Division stopped the Germans about four miles short of the Moselle River. Overall, antiaircraft fire claimed 11 planes and 11 probables, out of fifty raids and 103 planes. The 35th Division, which had been in reserve at Metz, France, left for the 7th Army. The XIX TAC flew 600 missions, claiming 756 vehicles and 74 armored vehicles and tanks.

After the 565th apparently took a look at the situation, we found that the guns would be more effective at a different location. On Dec. 26th we moved some of our guns to new positions. We fired 155 rounds of 40mm high explosives and 450 rounds of 50-caliber ball ammunition and tracers. We had fifteen Weissights inoperable and being repaired. Six ordinance men were attached to our battalion to repair this equipment.

One P-47 with U.S. markings strafed an ambulance near one of our gun positions and dropped a bomb near another at about 10:00 a.m. Later that evening, an M-51 in Section 15 of Battery "B" was strafed. Also, two JU-88's flashed their white wing lights twice, indicating the proper code for identification before strafing, and attacked the B Battery air strip at 8:00 p.m. Another P-47 strafed the road in the vicinity of "C" Battery and was definitely recognized by two officers of "C" Battery who state they could see no markings other than "U.S.A.A.F." on the plane.

Still on Dec. 25th, the 4th Armored Division made contact at Bastogne, and at this point, it was concluded that the only spot that the enemy might make a successful counterattack was at the Saar region in Germany. South of Luxembourg City, the front held north of Saar River, Germany and the Sure River, Luxembourg. Enemy aircraft made 148 raids that day, consisting of 234 planes attacking communications supply routes, installations and highway traffic. AAA shot down 26 planes and claimed 21.

On a historical note, the Sauer and the Our rivers merged north of Echternach, Luxembourg, and thereafter it was the Sauer River which emptied into the Moselle River, twenty-five miles further south.

Dec. 27th was a bad day for the Germans because they found themselves low on supplies in the Ardennes forest. First, the 565th had a good day and shot 337 rounds of 40mm and 1,230 rounds of 50-caliber. Both "A" and "D" Batteries observed one 40mm hit on an enemy plane. Both "B" and "D" Batteries engaged a plane. Throughout the battalion we also saw a lot of planes dropping flares. While we made no claims that day, we had a field day shooting at enemy aircraft.

Overall, 3rd AAA claimed three planes and eight probables. There were seventy-four planes and thirty-five raids. The skies were clear, and 652 patients were evacuated from Bastogne, Belgium.

On the 28th more gun positions were changed. We did fire 74 rounds of 40mm and 454 rounds of 50-caliber. We claimed one probable. Later, I believe the probable was confirmed and changed to a Category I. Also, a JU-88, engaged by "B" Battery, was later seen at minimum altitude by an infantry person north of "B" Battery. He reported that apparently it was in serious trouble and in distress.

With regards to claiming a plane, we could shoot and claim a hit, knock down or disable an E/A. Yet, in order to actually claim that plane, someone had to investigate it and see that the plane was actually down. If a battery hit a plane, and it flew back into Germany, then there was no way of finding it. Or if the plane was shot at and flew out of sight, there were certainly more important things to do than investigate the hit in order to officially claim the plane. Many times anti-aircraft sections were never able to claim planes they shot down. In our entire operation in the European theater of operation (ETO), we were only given credit for destroying one plane, with one probable. This is a prime example of the underestimated amount of damage that we really did. A chart here shows what probably happened.

In the following days we found things were happening. Very often spent bullets landed in and around our gun sections, as well as by headquarters. Also, flares were being dropped at night. Anyway, it was something new that we had not seen before.

Beginning on Dec. 30th there were several reports of mortars and bombs dropping in and near our gun positions; this hadn't happened before, indicating that civilians or infiltrators were in the area actually giving positions of our anti-aircraft guns to someone who would then broadcast that to the Germans across the Moselle River. The mortars and bombs were getting too close for this to be an accident. On Dec. 31st we didn't see much aircraft flying but we were being subjected to incoming mortar shells, indicating again that there were spies in the area reporting our positions.

On Dec. 31st there was a verbal instruction from S1, the executive of the 16th Group, that a B-25 carrying important persons would land at A97 of the airstrip. (This is now Luxembourg International Airport). Couriers should disseminate this information without delay to all gun sections, with instructions not to fire on this plane. This B-25 was assigned to Gen. Eisenhower as he moved his headquarters from England to the continent. The reports of December 31st are replete with explosions taking place all over our battalion area in the form of mortars, flares and most any kind of explosive. We were given orders that some kind of a mechanical stop should be placed over windows so that spent bullets from dog fights and other kinds of fighting would not come into buildings. Once a bullet was inside a concrete room it would fly around, easily injuring anyone there.

The unit report of Dec. 31st indicated that 40mm expended 240 rounds, and 6,520 rounds of 50-calibur were used. The report also explains at great length the height of the enemy aircraft they sighted, what direction they were going and what happened.

Incidentally, no claims were made that day. With the amount of planes in the air and the amount of ammunition expended, certainly those planes didn't go home completely unscathed. Also on the 31st, a P-47 chasing an ME-109 over Luxembourg City was erroneously shot down. The P-47 was not supposed to be in our area. Luxembourg City was designated as an IAZ (Inner Artillery Zone). This meant that no aircraft within a five-mile radius or ten thousand foot elevation should be in the area. Anything therein was fair game.

KILLED & DISABLED AIRCRAFT

DATE	TIME	BTRY	PLANE	CAT I	CAT II	CAT III
Dec. 21	1200	Became Operational				
Dec. 27	2233	A				x
	2234	B				x
Dec. 28		B	JU88			x
Dec. 30	1847	A				x
Dec. 30	1932	D	JU88			x
Dec. 30	2150	A	JU88			x
Dec. 31	1226	A	Reported E/A falling as a result of a dogfight.			
April 13		D	ME109	x		
April 23	2300	B	JU88			x
April 25	2230	B	JU88			x

Signalman uses a tree to set up telephone communications to an M-51.

During daylight hours the area over the city was supposed to be defended by antiaircraft; evidently the P-47 had picked up the ME-109 in Germany and, not realizing where he was, chased him over our area. That is not to say the 565th would shoot down a friendly plane that came into our area; however, when the gun section came up on the plane we didn't realize there were two planes in the area and just shot down the first one that came into the sights.

Col. Yarnall and Major Fry were asked to discuss this with Gen. Bradley. The colonel, in describing it, indicated it was a friendly discussion, not the repremanding type, rather, what could be done to prevent further occurrences.

Pescatore, Luxembourg (1988). Site of 3rd Army headquarters, 1944-1945.

Chapter 6
(Jan. 1 - 31, 1945)

On New Year's Day, seven enemy aircraft were seen over the area where sixty-eight rounds of 40mm ammunition were fired. To our northwest at Bastogne, Belgium, the enemy was still committed to taking that city.

The U.S. 7th Army to our south was committed to take in over more of the southern exposure of the 3rd Army that had been vacated as the 3rd Army moved north, particularly that of the XX Corps. The enemy was quite inactive, although they did send 308 aircraft over the 3rd Army area that day and produced an air raid at Metz, France, destroying 20 of our P-47s. Sixteen of these enemy aircraft were shot down by antiaircraft guns. The total losses that day were 63 planes. There was no change in the area immediately north and east of Luxembourg which was held by the XII Corps. The supply situation was changed for the better except for our lack of rubber footgear.

On the northern front in the 1st Army Group area where the British and the 1st Canadian armies were concerned, the frontier was quite inactive. Some British Mosquitoes flew into the 3rd Army area, and the adjacent antiaircraft batteries fired at them (although "C" Battery, which was at Junglinster, had not fired on the aircraft.) Apparently this was of great concern to the group because a message was received that someone from "C" Battery should personally go to all the batteries requesting that they not fire upon these aircrafts. It was also requested that we did not fire upon friendly aircraft. We should make every effort to record the numbers of the friendly planes and report them back to group headquarters.

That afternoon some P-38s fired at "C" Battery installations at Junglinster. More red flares were reported during the evening hours. Also, there appeared to be some mortar fire in the "D" Battery area. Some of the officers from 3rd Army headquarters joined those from the "D" Battery of the 565th to investigate a wooded area, and the area in question was brought under surveillance by armored cars to await the daylight.

On Jan. 2nd, Willie Copeland, a cook from headquarters battery, was wounded by spent 50-caliber machine gun bullets from a dog fight taking place over the city. He was evacuated to the 104th Evacuation Hospital in the city. Other bullets from the same burst broke windows in rooms; some windows broke in the rooms where we (I) slept.

During the time from Dec. 22nd to Dec. 30th we had engaged forty-six enemy aircraft and had fired 1,467 rounds of 40mm ammunition and 9,444 rounds of 50-caliber ammunition. Nine of those raids were made at night whereby the 40mm were firing at 90mm bursts, and seven raids were at seen targets during daylight. During that time we had one Category 3 claim by "B" Battery. It was also noted that Bastogne, Belgium, received relief. The XII Corps which had its headquarters in Luxembourg City had the 4th, 5th and 90th Infantry under its command was protecting the area immediately north and east of Luxembourg City. They were the units we looked to for support.

Intent upon retaking Bastogne, Belgium, units of the 6th Panzer division from the German 1st Army front that had been on the northern front of the Bulge arrived in the Bastogne area. There was no change in the units that occupied our area but there was little air activity because of bad flying weather.

On Jan. 4th, Lt. Dale E. Nelson of "D" Battery was brought in about 4:00 p.m. with shrapnel splinters in his leg. He went on to the hospital. Mortar shells were again reported in the evening, and these continued for the next several days. There were reports that several people found remnants of the mortars that they heard explode overhead. The 3rd Army requested these be sent to them for evaluation. The XII Corps was ordered to clear the area south and west of the Moselle and Sauer Rivers and attack north of Diekirch, Luxembourg, toward St. Vith, Belgium, to monitor movements of the German troops.

On Jan. 5th, the 565th's journal notes that there were many bombers flying overhead. We could literally look anywhere in the sky and see these bombers accompanied by fighter planes as they were dropping bits of tin foil to confuse German radar. The U.S. planes were headed for the southern part of Germany.

Shellings from the night before continued, and reports were brought into battalion headquarters regarding the exact locations of all the explosions that took place near our gun sections. These explosions continued to be a mystery both to ourselves and to the 3rd Army. The officers from the 3rd Army visited our headquarters to find the exact coordinates of all the bursts and continued to look at the fragments of all the shells that could be found. Resistance in the Bastogne, Belgium, area was somewhat less than it had been previously.

The 90th Infantry Division that had been on the southern flank to our east near the Sauer River was moved to the III Corps near Bastogne. The 94th was assigned to take its place in the Luxembourg, area.

The weather continued to be bad. There were few, if any, flights going on by the XIX TAC, and it was estimated that about a third of the cold weather gear had arrived. While that may seem like a small amount, anything was a lot better than what we had prior to that time.

Lt. Dale Nelson of "D" Battery was awarded the purple heart because he was wounded a few days earlier. (He originally entered the service through the state of Wisconsin. After the war, our 565th reunion organization has never been able to locate Lt. Nelson.)

On Jan. 6th we were notified that there was going to be some friendly aircraft overhead that night; we should hold our fire unless advised otherwise. Fighting was on a much slower scale throughout the 3rd Army area, and we felt the enemy was about to pull back to a new defense line from Houffalize to St. Vith, Belgium. Perhaps the biggest piece of news on Jan. 7th was that we got seven sacks of mail! This was the first mail we received since leaving England. We made a lot of effort to determine the exact locations of all those mortar shells or whatever was dropping on us each evening; we were requested to get coordinates in six digits, as well as the exact time the shell landed.

The 15th Army was assigned to the 12th Army Group. Little is said about the 15th Army because it was unlike anything that was in battle. The 15th Army was to command the 12th Army Group reserve forces, receive new units for England, prepare them for combat, and reorganize and re-equip the units that were returning from battle from the 12th Army Group (the 1st and 3rd Armies).

On Jan. 9th we received large amounts of mail. Some of it came from as far away as Camp Stewart, Georgia; we left there Oct. 6, 1945. Certificates from the medics were received on Lt. Nelson. The weather was cold and cloudy. On a clerical note, the battalion headquarters typewriter broke down. This must have been a complete calamity! The journal indicates that it cost 430 francs to get it fixed. (I believe at that time a franc was worth about two cents.)

The 565th also received word that Pvt. George E. Ford was to be returned to the zone of the interior (the United States) because he was accepted for entrance to the U.S. Naval Academy.

Explosives were found by "D" Battery; this was placed in the bridge by German engineers. A guard was placed on the bridge in the "D" Battery area after blocks of TNT were found tied to its pillars. The explosives remained there until a group came to investigate the incident and remove them.

On Jan. 9th there were several meetings relative to our batteries being assigned to anti-tank positions. There was a threat that Luxembourg City would be attacked from any one of four directions; therefore, each of our gun positions was assigned a roadblock or a road position, whereby we could fire from a anti-tank position, as opposed to an antiaircraft position. Particularly, we were to cover the roads to Merche Sandweiler-Oetrange and Junglinster. The 16 AAA Group notified us that there would be friendly aircraft over the area that evening, and we should hold fire; an enemy thrust from Luxembourg to Metz, France, was being given high consideration by the Germans. SHAEF advised the 3rd Army to be prepared to send four armored divisions from Bastogne, Belgium, to an area southeast of Luxembourg. AAA was to be used as anti-tank units under the direction of the 16th AAA Group in the 38th AAA Brigade to coordinate with 3rd Army AAA efforts. A lot of winter clothing was received at LaHarve, France, but there was limited transportation to get it to Luxembourg. Personnel from S1 went to Lucky to see if they could arrange to have Pvt. Willy Ford, the wounded cook from headquarters battery, moved to a replacement depot near Luxembourg City so that upon his recovery he could be transferred back into the 565th. They must have accomplished something in their mission because he did return in due course.

On Jan. 10th, a man from "C" Battery was seriously burned as he worked alone while repairing a twenty-man cooker outside a tent. He was taken to the hospital.

Overall, small advances were made in most every major area of the battle front. The weather was good, and the 19th TAC sent off 325 sorties that day.

When we got up in the morning Jan. 11th, we found that sleet fell during the night, putting a coating of ice on all the trees and roads. Things were rather static because transportation couldn't move; however, it was very picturesque. Sgt. Haroldson of "D" Battery was awarded the Purple Heart because he had frostbitten feet. 1st Sgt. Misch was sent to the hospital in bad condition, but the CO was to write a letter requesting that Misch be returned to the unit when he was able to do so. Shelling began at 8:15 p.m. and battery headquarters wasn't able to tell whether it was an invasion, if it was 90mm fire or something else. Nonetheless, we could see flashes and hear the reports of high velocity guns.

We did not have 90mm guns in the city of Luxembourg per se; instead, they were down at Differdange, Luxembourg, to the southwest. Also, all the anti-tank, as well as some anti-paratroop defense, had been set up in the area mentioned earlier. The anti-paratroop defense was something new, and it was set up along a line from Mamers, France, to Berchem, Belgium. At 4:00 p.m. we received word that there would be friendly aircraft over the area west of the city in the evening, and we were to withhold fire unless told to do otherwise. That evening, reports of explosions in the area were plentiful; every battery reported one or more of them.

From a German standpoint, the Ardennes offensive was turning into a defensive one. It was expected that the Germans would open a new front, probably in from the Saar River area. This was in the XX Corps area to our southeast. The 4th Armored moved from Bastogne, Belgium, to an assembly area south and east of Luxembourg in the XII Corps area, while advances continued in the III and the VIII Corps areas, which were west of Bastogne. It was bad flying weather.

The 8th and 9th Armored Divisions were assigned to the 3rd Army for administration and supply. These were armored divisions, previously assigned to the 1st Army which was on the north flank of the Bulge.

Starting about 9 p.m. on Jan. 12th, mortar shells were very plentiful again. They were seen by almost all the gun sections and were coming in very frequent intervals. There was also a very large explosion that had an unknown source. An M-51 in Section 5 of "A" Battery received severe damage from an explosion at about 9 p.m. and was badly broken. This M-51 was replaced with a M-16 half-track, which was also a quad 50-caliber gun.

Explosions that evening continued; it almost seemed that there wasn't a gun section that didn't receive or report one every evening. While we were receiving all these incoming explosions, an unidentified projectile fell in Luxembourg near a mobile laundry and the 104th Evacuation Hospital. Seven people were injured, and their equipment was very damaged. Overall, in the Ardennes it was now considered that the enemy only had means of defensive action in their salient. The weather was still lousy, just as it had been ever since Dec. 16th.

On Jan. 13th, shelling started some time before midnight and continued until 8:00 a.m. For the most part these explosions were in the "A" and "D" Battery areas; this was Luxembourg City. There were some reports from "B" Battery, which was immediately east of the city at an airstrip (today Luxembourg City International Airport). Few explosions, if any, took place in the "C" Battery area, which was about six miles northeast at Junglinster, Luxembourg. Aerial explosions occurred and everything hit the ground. Our journal noted that the weather was getting better; however, it was still very cold. The wind chill factor really made it a difficult climate.

There were 551 sorties flown by the XIX TAC. Also on this day something new happened. We were alerted that since P-51's would be flying in our area for a couple of hours. There was hostile aircraft being tracked north of the city, and the Air Force intended to intercept them rather than let them come over to the city and let antiaircraft work on them. Tonight there would be a lot of Allied aircraft over the area. These were bombers from the 8th Air Force coming from England headed into Germany. Batteries "A" and "D" continued to report that shells were dropped into their area and that projectiles were heard going through the air.

On Jan. 14th, we had good weather again, and TAC flew 633 sorties. The drive to reduce the salient continued. The 87th Infantry Division joined the 3rd Army.

Our coal supply was low, and the 35th Division, which had been on the west end of the Bulge, was sent into the reserves near Metz, France. The 35th Division had been with the 3rd all across France, but, when it again became active, was reassigned to both the 7th and 9th Armies.

On Jan. 15th Lt. Nelson was sent back to the hospital with an infection in his leg. The 565th journal notes don't reveal this, but apparently he had returned to the battalion after receiving some aid in area hospitals. Also on the 15th, we hadn't received our password from 3rd Army; it was missing. After conducting searches, Pvt. Billings from the message center brought it in. He had left it in the map compartment of one of the vehicles.

A very common scene at war's end was truckloads of GIs traveling across the Rhine. Six-by-sixes were a synonym for a 2-1/2-ton GMC 6x6.

All fuel in the ETO was gasoline; it was all handled in five-gallon cans that could be loaded by hand in the back of trucks for bulk transport. Individual cans could be strapped to all vehicles.

While there wasn't a lot of explosion activity on the 15th, "A" Battery saw a two-motor single tail airplane approach from the east, circle the city and continue to the east, flying at a very high elevation. Pvt. Engle thought he saw a bomb falling straight down, just prior to an explosion. Engle reported hearing a plane about this time, but he was unable to see it. Several sections of "A" Battery reported hearing an object approach the city from the northeast, making a whirling noise. Cpl. Cantrell of Section 3 reported hearing the same noise and observed a trail of flames at approximately fifteen hundred feet.

The U.S. 1st and 3rd armies linked up at Houffalize, Belguim, which then completely stopped the Germans from possibly moving in a Westward direction. The 4th Armored was assigned to the XX Corps, the Corps that now operated immediately east of Luxembourg City. The 87th remained in the Corps area. The weather was fine, and the XIX TAC flew 472 sorties. A captured German trigger mechanism for small rifles and machine guns was adapted for use on small ordnance for the U.S. Army; this allowed operators of these weapons to be able to wear mittens. Also, all the telephone cables had been replaced from Esch to Luxembourg City.

On Jan. 16th the 565th could see that things were lightening up a little bit. Orders came down that the machine gunner on a M-51 no longer had to be in the turret itself; instead, he could be in the revetment. This, of course, provided a great deal of comfort for him because the turret was a terrifically cold spot to occupy on a continual basis. Again, there were many reports in the "A" and "D" Batteries regarding explosions in and around their areas. Both P-47s and P-51s dropped explosives, and even though no one was hurt, the fragments did considerable damage to telephone poles and left craters in the ground. As a result of this attack the wire communications were out in "D" Battery.

Also on the 16th, the 1st Army reverted to the 12th Army Group, going from Gen. Montgomery's command to Gen. Bradley's. Advances were made in the III and the VIII Corps areas, and the XII Corps was in a stable front all around us. The XIX TAC flew 504 sorties.

It was noted that during this cold weather and frozen ground, steel tracks on tanks made traveling very difficult, so steel lugs were welded to every fifth lug. In the case of the rubber tracks, a steel block was equipped on every fifth lug.

It is indicated that five men returned from the 17 Reinforcement Depot. Some had been in the hospital in England and were being returned to their units. No shelling took place on this date which was a great relief after many days. The weather was warm and cloudy and snow began falling in early evening. Jan. 18th was recognized as the end of the Bastogne campaign.

While the enemy was retreating, the U.S. forces believed they could attack at any time on a limited offense if so desired. There was an estimated 54,500 enemy troops against the 3rd Army. This was the equivalent of 6 1/2 divisions, 170 tanks or assault guns, and this was a decrease of about 20,000 troops and 150 tanks from seven days earlier.

The Germans were unwilling or incapable of reinforcing their infantry in the Ardennes; this was a major factor leading to their defeat. A major adjustment in the order of battle relative to the 15th Army was that the 35th remained in reserve, and other divisions were going into rest areas as well. The XII Corps, northeast of Luxembourg, advanced across the Sauer River and made good progress against moderate resistance. This had been a quiet front. No pre-artillery had been fired, but a four hour barrage kicked off H-hour. There was a small amount of return fire this date, and it became much heavier the next day. There was very poor visibility during this limited offensive. Generally, the 3rd Army continued its advanced north and east with daily attacks. The weather was partly cloudy and a bit warmer.

At night we saw several explosions in the "B" Battery area around the airport, as well as the "D" and "A" Battery areas. The 12th and 6th Army Groups set up new boundaries by Jan. 20th. These were the boundaries between the 3rd and the 7th Armies. The XII Corps continued its attack at the juncture of the Sauer and the Moselle Rivers and the 5th Infantry Division captured Diekirch, Luxembourg. The weather was overcast and prevented much flying; therefore, there was little activity. There was strong pressure in all segments of the 3rd Army area. Seven hundred tons of winter clothing arrived in Longwy, France, on this date, which was a great relief to much of the 3rd Army.

Warm weather arrived on Jan. 19th, which was a welcome relief, although it came with light rain that later turned to snow. There was no shelling the night before, and this too was a great relief. This was the beginning of what was to be a long stay in Luxembourg City without any shells or any enemy aircraft overhead. In Junglinster, Luxembourg, three P-47s with American markings flew over at about three-thousand to five-thousand feet. Section 4 of "C" Battery observed one of the planes drop one bomb which appeared to land in Eschweiler, Germany. It was later reported that the town was Beidweiler.

And as a result of this bomb, four people were trapped in a house, and a barn was set on fire. We were supposed to pattern-paint winter camouflage on any canvas that could not be concealed. Fifteen explosions occurred during the afternoon in or near the 565th defended area. Officers from Verdun, France, investigated these explosions, and in their opinion, they were all the same type that had occurred during the past several weeks. Many explosions were preceded by the sound of a minor explosion. At least two projectiles hit the treetops first, but they didn't explode until they fell to the ground. Very small craters were formed, and no unusual fragments were found.

From Gen. Bradley's headquarters, XII Corps commanders were ordered to continue to attack certain segments to eliminate the Bulge. Generally, all troops realigned before again pursuing an aggressive role. The 35th Division was assigned to the XX Corps. The weather was fairly decent, and 150 sorties were flown. The 3rd Army now consisted of three hundred-fifty thousand men. They were about thirty-four thousand men under strength; these were mostly riflemen. The Bulge had all but been eliminated. The 101st Airborne, which was so instrumental in holding Bastogne, Belgium, was released and assigned to the 6th Army Group to the south under the direction of Gen. Devers.

Sunday, Jan. 21st, was cold and clear. On this particular day the observation posts that were operated by the 565th were going to be moved from about a five mile radius to a seven mile radius.

Although there weren't many, the journal still indicates that we were having some incoming explosions. The Germans' order of battle placed only two divisions in the Bulge area. They had no Panzer divisions in reserve, but they did have troops in the Trier, Germany, area or at least in the triangle region south of Trier. It was concluded that the enemy had no Panzer reserves in the west. The only Panzer divisions left were on the Russian front, and they did not have many replacements for the infantry. The boundaries for the U.S. 1st, 3rd and 7th Armies all changed on this date. The weather was bad, and there was little flying.

On Jan. 22nd the 35th Division attached to the 7th Army. In the meantime, the 1st and 3rd Armies moved toward St. Vith, Belgium, the last German stronghold. It was beautiful weather; 627 sorties were flown, and 1,177 German vehicles were destroyed.

The 3rd Army, having swung around the west flank of the Bulge, started pursuing in a northeasterly direction.

Six-foot antenna mounted atop an SCR 584 radar was used to direct the fire of a 90mm AA gun.

The after-action reports of the 3rd Army on Jan. 22nd state, "The pace of the enemy's withdrawal from the Ardennes was intensified. Rapid pursuit by the III and the VIII Corps forces and the relentless pressure of the XII Corps' attack, combined with the effort of the all-out Russian drive on the Eastern front which in eight days had carried it to within 150 miles of Berlin, served to bring this about. He raced to cross the Our River, with the result that hundreds of his vehicles concentrated in the vicinity of the few available crossings, notably at Eisenbach and Gemund, were persistently attacked throughout the day by all available aircraft of the XIX TAC, as well as all available artillery of the 3rd Army. The enemy suffered a severe blow, losing an estimated 1,800 vehicles destroyed or damaged and untold numbers of personnel.

Little is noted on Jan. 23rd except that there would be friendly bombers over the skies at night, and that all of our observation posts had completed occupying new positions. This resulted in changing the diameter of the IAZ to nineteen miles. The 3rd Army pushed up from the south and around the west end into the Bulge area, and then the 1st Army gathered its forces, combining in an effort to eliminate the Bulge. This necessitated a lot of realignment as far as divisions and Army Corps were concerned. As a result, the U.S. 8th, 7th and 4th Divisions came from the XII Corps and went to the VIII Corps. The 76th Division from the VIII Corps went to the XII Corps, and the 95th Division from the XX Corps went to the VIII Corps. The 17th Airborne went from the VIII Corps to the III Corps, and the 26th went from the III Corps to the XX Corps. The 90th went from the III Corps to the VIII

Corps. Of course, as previously mentioned, both the 35th Division, as well as the 101st Division, was moved to the 7th Army to our south. Much of the artillery that had been attached to Army headquarters was shifted to Corps headquarters, particularly the III, XII and VIII Corps. The divisions that had been close to us were the 4th, 5th and 90th.

The Roermond Triangle north of Aachen was eliminated on Jan. 25th. The greatest seaborne evacuation in history was also beginning; up to 2 million Germans were taken from Courtland, Pomerania and Prussia across the Baltic, away from the advancing Russians.

The troop alignment of the XII Corps immediately east of Luxembourg City from south to north was now the 2nd Cavalry Group, the 4th Armored, the 76th, the 5th, the 80th Infantry Divisions; the 76th relieved the 87th which moved to the VIII Corps. This front was extremely quiet.

Jan. 26th proved to be a bonanza for mail; we received many delayed Christmas packages. Out in the field there were reports that bombers would be over the area tonight. There was a very large explosion a mile northeast of "C" Battery CP. Capt. Bowron of "C" Battery CO reported that a V-1 went over at about 6:00 p.m. the night before. "A" Battery reported a large ball of fire the size of the sun going southeast to northwest. It hit on the other side of the ridge, approximately three miles from Section 2. It was a very big explosion. The impact and explosion of this bomb was observed by Batteries "A," "B" and "D," but it occurred outside of our areas so nothing was damaged. These were reported to the 16th AAA Group.

On Jan. 27th the weather remained extremely cold. We were notified that friendly bombers would be over the area at night.

On the Army battle front it appeared that the enemy was using the Sigfried Line as its western defense front. One or two Panzer divisions were moving to the east.

The 4th Division was relieved by the 5th, and the 80th was to assume their positions on the front. The 3rd Army had been receiving twenty-eight thousand replacements during the previous two weeks. The bad weather continued.

It was cold on Jan. 28th, but the sun broke out which allowed the XIX TAC to do its duty. On the 28th, the last vestige of the Ardennes salient was reduced. The Germans had one hundred-twenty thousand dead, wounded or POWs. U.S. losses were eighty-six hundred dead, forty-seven thousand wounded and one thousand missing. The Siegfried Line was the next objective for Allies in Europe.

It was still cold on 29th. That night we were going to have friendly aircraft over the area; these were B-24s and B-17s headed for Germany.

Quoting from the 3rd Army After Action Reports, it is interesting to note that on Jan. 29th it said, "In accordance with the instructions from the SHAEF, arrangements were made to establish a new boundary in the Army area, which was to be known as the Army Group Rear Air Boundary. Aircraft Defense of the installations forward of this line was to be the responsibility of the Army. Anti Aircraft defense of installations to the rear were to be to be the responsibility of the 19th Air Defense Command."

The location of this boundary was to be determined by mutual agreement between the Army Group Commander and the Air Force Commander. The initial boundary agreed upon excluded the area of Army responsibility. The ordinance installation and the airfield Etain as well as the airfield east of Conflans, an airfield southwest of Metz. Anti Aircraft units of the 9th Air Defense Command, which had been defending these fields, had been attached to the 3rd Army for Operational Command and were relieved when the 9th Air Defense Command took over responsibility for defense of the airfields. The 3rd US Army was to continue to exercise operational control over all Anti Aircraft units inside the Army area." It's also interesting to note, that the 12th Army Group had requested that they obtain dog teams to assist in the evacuation of patients through the deep snows of the Ardennes and the Eiffel that were being encountered at the time by the 3rd Army Divisions. As a result of the experiments made in the XIIth Corps, plans were made to provide litters with snow runners. Bad weather continued into the 30th of January and was complicated by a freezing rain.

January 31, payday. We've had a couple of them since we arrived in Europe, but they were always a day that we looked forward to.

Chapter 7
(Feb 1-28, 1945)

The weather was warm on Feb. 1st, to everyone's joy. We received a bit more mail and eight replacements, which were assigned to various batteries.

In the southern front, the U.S. 7th Army had reached the outer limits of the Siegfried Line. As the new month rolled in, the 95th Infantry and the 8th Armored Division were transferred to the 9th Army, which was covering a front between the American 1st Army and the British 2nd Army. A plan to attack the Siegfried on the 3rd Army front was to take place at Echternach, which was twenty-five miles northeast of Luxembourg City. This attack would use the XII Corps, which had been there as our protectorates for quite some time. The plan was to launch that attack on Feb. 5th, but the 12th Army Group vetoed that. Their tanks were a bit light in the front ends, and they wanted to take some time to get more armor on their Sherman tanks. They took eighteen inches of armor off the front of disabled Sherman tanks and attached it to the fronts of those that were still operable. This put a lot of armor on the front, which was quite effective. The 12th Army Group also contracted with European companies still in business to make some permanent armor as opposed to these makeshift affairs.

Because we were in the dead of winter, coal was also in short supply. Both the Army and the civilians were in great need of it.

The weather had hampered the Germans as well as the U.S. Forces. Although the enemy was incapable of launching an attack, they were in a position to be a great spoiler because of the deep snows, melting snows and the muddy side hills. To describe it mildly, traveling was terrible. The weather continued to be warm and melting snows raised many rivers in the area, making it almost impossible to bridge them for an attack.

The 12th Army Group did direct the 3rd Army to attack parallel with the 1st Army northeasterly from Echternach, Luxembourg to Bitberg, Germany, continuing the attack toward the Rhine River. This attack was decided to take place on Feb. 6th and 7th. That evening, the combined U.S. and British forces launched 1,000 B-17 bomber attacks, with 900 fighters on Germany. At this time, we were reporting to the 207th Group as opposed to the 16th Brigade.

The enemy order of battle included the shifting of infantry troops north with less pressure immediately ahead of the U.S. 3rd Army and more pressure in front of the 1st and 9th Armies. Also, the XII Corps were using searchlights in a ground role to help build bridges over the Moselle River. The searchlights worked wonderfully in cloudy weather because the lights would shine against the bottoms of the clouds, illuminating the entire area for thousands of yards around.

On the highest level, the Yalta Conference opened and the U.S. troops captured the first of the Roer Dams.

The 565th received a letter of commendation from the 115th AAA Gun Battalion for men who had instructed them on the M-51s. Understand that in a 90mm battalion, each battery had four M-51s for local protection; they had four 90mm guns for high altitude E/A.

The weather remained rainy and foggy, which led to further thawing of the deep snows in both the Ardennes and the Eiffel. It is also noted that over ninety men from a searchlight battalion were attached to the 565th for administration and rations.

At this point in the war the Cavalry converted from M-59 to M-24 light tanks, which were much faster and more maneuverable. The guns changed from 37mm to 75mm.

Authority was given to reestablish local mail and telephone service between Luxembourg City and Esch and all the southern part of Luxembourg. The 95th Division was transferred to the 9th Army, and the British and the Canadian forces of the 21st Army Group kicked off the Rhine River offensive.

Early February continued to be warm and foggy, which led to more melting snow, rising rivers and muddy highways. The Eiffel, the hilly country immediately north and east of Luxembourg, became almost impossible to travel in; and, while the 565th was not specifically there, the infantry and armored divisions were there battling with the Germans. At this time it was felt that the enemy could still launch some delaying tactics, but because of the terrain and the weather, it would be impossible for either the Germans or U.S. forces to launch a major offensive. The XII Corps, however, did use artillery across the Sauer River. The 5th, 76th and the 80th Infantries crossed the river, and the 11th Infantry used searchlights in their efforts to secure a bridgehead on the opposite side. The weather was good enough so that 240 sorties flew that day.

The 5th Infantry had gone to the 9th Army and the 3rd Army rear eschelon, which had been in Esch, France, was moved to Luxembourg City.

To the north, the German engineers had wrecked more dams on the Rhine River, this time at the Schwammanuel Dam. Also, a gun in "D" Battery and another one in "C" Battery were being repaired. And in the last thirty days, there had been no enemy air raids that were engaged by guns of the 565th. Our cumulative report showed we had fired 1,460 rounds of 40mm ammunition and 9,444 rounds of 50-caliber ammunition since we entered combat on Jan. 21st.

Strategically, it was indicated the Monte was to become active up north along with the 9th Army, which was now under his command; but the 12th Army Group continued to extend its bridgeheads beyond the Sauer and the Our rivers using searchlights when necessary and when the opportunity arose. This was what they called the role of an aggressive defense.

Railroad cars were in short supply. The railroad bridges between La Harve, France, and the battle front had been repaired, and a major portion of our supplies were coming by means of railroad. However, a lot of the cars and the locomotives had been destroyed along with the railroad bridges in the fight across northern France. By this time, the melting snow had made the river crossings in the Eiffel extremely hazardous and none were being attempted. The Canadian army did jump off on the northern sector, and the 12th Army Group headquarters moved from Verdun, France, which was about fifty miles west of Metz, to a more tactical position at Namur, Belgium. The move was about seventy-five miles.

On Feb. 9th, the 226th Searchlight Battalion, Battery "B," was attached to the 565th for operations and rations.

A 3rd Army reconnaissance indicated there was a new German Panzer Division identified on the battle front in the area of Trier, Germany, and there were fifteen to twenty rail cars moved into the area as well. This led to the speculation that the Germans may have more reserves than had been anticipated. A search began to determine what was happening there. The bridgeheads in the VII Corps area, which was the 1st Army immediately to the north of the 3rd Army, had joined the XII Corps area immediately east of Luxembourg City.

On Feb. 10th, a truck from "A" Battery overturned, severely injuring one person. "A" Battery also reported that due west of Section 17, a big flare of lights, such as a fire, occurred; it lasted 35 or 40 seconds. The light started, slowed and then died down. There were no sounds, but a few minutes before a 90mm fired. During firing, a noise of bombing or heavy artillery was heard.

The III Corps was reassigned to the 1st Army; recall that they were the Corps that had originally been assigned to the 1st Army's southern flank before the Battle of the Bulge. The VIIIth Corps assumed III Corps area. This movement all happened during the time of bad roads and high water.

Two M-51s, one in "C" Battery and one in "D" Battery, were inoperative because they needed repair. Also, cumulative totals since we arrived in Luxembourg showed that we had been engaged in forty-seven raids and we had expended 1,469 rounds of 40mm and 9,444 rounds of 50-caliber.

For the first time in several days, the weather was clear. On Feb. 12th, the 17th Airborne was transferred to the 1st Army, which was immediately north of the 3rd Army.

The Yalta Conference ended.

At 9 p.m. we got a phone call from "B" Battery reporting that Sims, a man from Section 42, was walking to the quarters from the 40mm gun when some unknown person grabbed him from behind. Sims turned to hit the man, but he slashed Sims with a knife, cutting his shirt but not injuring him. The man ran off and Sims fired at him from a distance of thirty yards but missed. It was not determined if the attacker was a civilian or an enemy soldier because of the extreme darkness.

On Feb. 13th the civilian government was now in full cooperation with the military government. The military must have been relieved to have civilians taking over their former positions. Also, we ceased operational control of our remaining searchlights. The 565th was short twenty-four men and two officers.

On Feb. 14th, Lt. Farnsworth, of "C" Battery, reported that he saw a P-47 crash about three miles northwest of Gun Section 6 and 7. The plane was headed southwest. Also, a message from "C" Battery said that a B-17 was sighted flying northwest at a distance of two miles. Five men were seen bailing out of the plane as it was falling. "A" Battery indicated that they noticed three flares about one mile north of Section 12. They appeared to come from the ground and were red and yellow. Also, Section 14 of "A" Battery saw two white flares southeast of their section about two minutes apart. The section heard and saw no planes. Both flares traveled the same course, but their range was indefinite.

Meanwhile, the bridgeheads over the Our and the Sauer rivers were expanded and the narrow gauge railroad east of Luxembourg started hauling supplies to the 5th Division.

The 565th had one M-51 and one 2-1/2 ton truck that were inoperable. The Battalion was short three officers and twenty-seven enlisted men. The narrow gauge railroad was being loaded at Dommeldange and then unloaded at Junglinster, where "C" Battery was located, and then a little farther up the line at Consdorf.

On Feb. 15th, several officers changed their duties. Lt. Olson, who had been the S1 or personnel officer, was detailed as the battery commander of Headquarters Battery. Capt. Holt was relieved as headquarters CO and assigned as CO of "B" Battery. Lt. Newman, from "D" Battery, was assigned to headquarters as S1 or personnel officer.

We were inspected by Col. Gettys, the commanding officer of the 38th Brigade. There was shelling the night before in the vicinity of "D" Battery, which was in the eastern part of the city of Luxembourg. Both "D" and "B" Batteries were reporting explosions in their area during midday. ("B" Battery was a bit farther east at the airport.) This was a recurrence of something that hadn't happened for several days, but these explosions were very much like the ones in late January. Lt. Carr reported by phone that a P-47 crashed about four miles southeast of Section 32; this was the "C" Battery area near Junglinster.

Again, a 2 1/2-ton truck was reported as inoperative. The front axle of the rear bogie assembly went out. We removed it and chained up the end of the springs to the frame. It was not able to haul loads, but it could travel on its own, using the front-wheel drive. We moved it from one location to the next and finally found a front bogie and installed it ourselves.

By this time, the front had moved well away from Luxembourg City. We remained in Luxembourg because 3rd Army headquarters was there. We were receiving inspections from our higher commands on a very regular basis, probably just to make sure we weren't sleeping on the job. While we certainly weren't in a communication zone, we were a long way from the front. The war had reached beyond the Sauer, the Our and the Muse rivers; while we were still within range of the guns in Trier, Germany, which was twenty-two miles away, we weren't seeing quite the action that we once saw. The guns that had molested us for weeks had been silenced. We hadn't even seen an enemy plane in several days.

Our stay at Luxembourg had gotten to the point where we could actually get a pass to go into the city, and we often did so.

Electricity was restored, and there was some gas every once in awhile in the apartment building where we were billeted, allowin us to take warm showers.

On Feb. 20th, the journal notes that it had been raining for a couple of days. This certainly didn't help with the amount of moisture that was running into rivers in the Eiffel.

We received ten reinforcements who were assigned to the lettered batteries, with one going to headquarters battery. Apparently they weren't from the antiaircraft, because they needed training.

Even though this isn't noted in a lot of history books, a new bulge had developed between Prum and Echternach ^_ referred to as the Vianden Bulge. Both the VIII and the XII Corps devoted a lot of time to eliminating this bulge. This was happening immediately across the river, about twenty-five miles from Luxembourg City.

Feb. 21st could be known as a great day. First, Gen. Bradley visited Gen. Patton at his headquarters, and they agreed that Gen. Montgomery wasn't doing too much in the north and that the 1st and the 9th Armies were kind of sitting on their backsides, and that the war was really being fought by the 3rd Army, and Bradley gave Patton a green light to do so.

The Moselle Sauer Triangle was a bit of land that laid south and east of Trier, Germany, and it was bounded on the south by the Sauer River, on the west and north by the Moselle River, and on the east by the Siegfried Line. It was hard territory to capture, but nonetheless, as the city of Trier fell, it was a great step toward the beginning of the Rhineland offensive. There was a lot of activity in the Vianden

Bulge, and the XX Corps gained control of everything west of the Sauer River.

For the last several nights, heavy bombers flew over the area, and we were told to hold our fire. We did have a few explosions the night before but not to the degree that had been happening days earlier.

On the battlefront itself, the bad terrain still existed east of Prum/Bitberg area, and hard fighting lay ahead in the Vianden Bulge. The 10th Armored cleared what remained of the Moselle Sauer Triangle.

At this point, the 565th was missing several pieces of equipment: four directors for an M5A1 40mm; eight oil gears that drive the gun, receiving messages from the M5 director; and four cable systems that were used to connect the guns and the directors. Most of the veterans of the 565th will tell you that they didn't depend an awful lot on the M5 directors while in Europe; instead, they used their iron sights and tracer ammunition in most cases.

The 3rd Army after-action reports note that tire patches were in very short supply. This is no surprise after going through the Battle of the Bulge, the very difficult roads, along with the off-road travel that trucks and guns did. Only two explosions took place during the night of Feb. 23rd.

An enlisted man from "C" Battery found a booby trap on a railroad near the end of a tunnel. It was made out of a couple of U.S. hand grenades and wires and would have caused a minor explosion. On Feb. 25th, a recommendation was made to award several men in the battalion the good conduct medal.

Also, work had begun on the paperwork for men who wanted to transfer to the Infantry. Infantry replacements were the hardest to come by: They were first to suffer great casualties and had the least training. (I recall talking to a fellow from the 70th Infantry Division after the war. They had trained three groups of soldiers in the United States before departing for the ETO. Each time the division had been stripped of its infantry men, and they were sent to the various theaters as replacements.

Several from the 565th did volunteer to go to the Infantry.)

From the enemy standpoint, the Panzer Divisions moved to the northern front and the 3rd Army captured a high German command post and many prisoners. The Vianden Bulge was eliminated. Also on Feb. 25th, 434 sorties flew and the weather was improving greatly.

On Feb. 26th, the battalion command post moved from a location near the railroad station, to an area in the east-central part of Luxembourg City. Section 5 of "D" Battery reported that eight American paratroopers or crew members bailed out of a bomber in the vicinity. Lt. Clark arrived at the battalion CP reporting that 1st Lt. Norval R. Porrit landed near a cemetary. Pvt. Ward of "D" Battery obtained an ambulance for him, and took him to the 104th Evacuation Hospital. New information was received, informing us that he was a member of a B-17 crew, and that the rest of his crew was probably scattered over an area of thirty miles behind the plane. His unit was the 94th Bomber Group, 410th Squadron

Bob Currie, Battery "C," on his 40mm.

based in the United Kingdom. Also on Feb. 26th, the 12th Army Group had placed the 90th Infantry in reserves.

During February, the U.S. Army continued its attack on the Siegfried Line during this period. They captured Bitberg and nineteen other small towns and closed in on Trier, Germany, one of the oldest cities in western Europe. A general lack of civilian medical personnel and facilities in occupied sections of Germany threatened to place an excessive burden on the military medical units. To eliminate this possibility, military government public health officers reestablished and improvised hospitals, relocated civilian doctors and salvaged the medical supplies.

On Feb. 27, 1,200 bombers from England flew over the 3rd Army territory, and U.S. artillery maintained a continuous barrage on German antiaircraft battalions' positions.

As February came to a close, it meant payday for all of us, which was great. As I recall, we received that pay in Luxembourg francs. Bitberg fell, which was great. There was only one badly damaged Panzer Division left in the German army.

Ables, Herndon, Jones, Revetti, Capt. McCoy, M/Sgt. Grant, Allen, Childress, Daughtery. Battalion headquarters in background.

Chapter 8
(March 1-31, 1945)

In March 1945, the American troops advanced over the Muse River but didn't quite reach the Rhine River. The 10th Armored entered Trier from the south. On March 1, 485 sorties flew, and a bit farther north, the 9th Army captured Monchen-Gladbach, Germany. The 565th, of course, remained back in Luxembourg City in defense of 3rd Army headquarters. To a large degree, this area was beginning to get like a communication zone. We even got passes to allow us to go to Paris.

There was an occasional report of a German airplane in the area, but few were ever seen. The bombs that had plagued us in January and February were no longer dropping in our area because they had been flying from Trier and Trier had fallen to the 10th Armored. On the German side, Gen. Modell was replaced by Von Runstad, and the 3rd Army started its drive toward the Rhine River with the 4th Armored and the 5th Infantry Divisions.

At an Army level, the 90th Infantry was transferred from SHAEF, and the 6th Armored was transferred to SHAEF in reserve.

It was beautiful weather on March 3rd, and 545 sorties flew.

Plans were being made to supply the II Corps for the kickoff to the Rhine River. At an Army level, military government was beginning to be set up at a civilian status, but this was hard to do because it was difficult to know who were Nazi sympathizers and who were not.

Capt. Russell left on March 5th with a detail of eight trucks and an assistant driver to haul reinforcement troops to the front. Cash deposits from 565th members were taken to finance (we really didn't have any place to spend it).

Enemy strength in front of the 3rd Army was now estimated at 45,000 and the equivalent of fifty tanks, which made up about 5 1/2 divisions. A third of the western front confronted the 3rd Army.

SHAEF headquarters instructed the 21st Army Group (Gen. Montgomery) to penetrate and cross the Rhine River. The 12th Army Group had advanced to the Rhine, taking all of the German area north of the Moselle where it joins the Rhine. The 6th Army Group was to stay in a defensive position to the south of the 3rd Army. At this point, the 3rd Army had taken about 200,000 prisoners.

On March 6th, the 3rd Army was told to proceed to Koblenz, Germany. The weather was bad in all of Europe and little activity took place that day. The group that had been sent to Paris returned on March 7th. Maj. Pentecost and Cpt. Moss ventured into Germany to visit the 26th AAA Group to get information and their first look at German territory. (I rather expect that many of the enlisted men had already made such a trip because good Moselle wine was readily available back in Luxembourg, and this wasn't something that you requisitioned from the supply depots.) It was noted that there were 25,000 Germans north of the Moselle, yet west of the Rhine.

While the 3rd Army was well positioned to capture these, Hitler issued an order that they had to fight to the last man. Thus, many German lives were sacrificed.

The weather continued to be unsettled as the 4th Armored rolled on toward the Rhine River.

In the meantime, the engineers had rebuilt many of the railroad bridges from LaHarve, France, and we were beginning to receive railroad supplies as far as Ettelbruck and Diekirsh, Luxembourg. They were delivered there by communication zone people and in just a few days the railroad was opened on to Prum, Bitberg and Trier. Bad weather continued. Due to the absence of the German Luftwaffe coming over our territory, we were flying tracking missions occasionally, just so our gunners could get practice. On the Army front a large pocket had developed between the 1st and the 3rd Armies called the Eiffel Pocket. This area occupied a lot of troops for the next several days, mainly the XII Corps on the south. In the meantime, the 3rd army began our southeasterly drive west of the Rhine.

On March 10th there were reports of a prowler in or near "D" Battery. A guard fired some forty-five rounds at the intruder but missed, so we never knew what that was all about.

More of the mysterious explosions were coming during the evening near Section 5 of "A" Battery; this area had a gun placed immediately outside the 3rd Army headquarters. Accounts in Patton's book indicate that the battery commander of headquarters battery 3rd Army was killed in that explosion.

Weather began to get better and on March 10th 347 sorties flew. Also, the railroad was extended to Thiensville, France just south of the 565th. On March 11th, the west bank of the Rhine had been contained, and a bridgehead at Reamagan had been made.

Despite a low ceiling, 205 sorties flew that day. Also, two 80mm mortars struck within Luxembourg City that day, killing two enlisted men and causing much damage. The airfield at Trier had begun operations; it was basically a TAC field, but it was used to some degree to fly in supplies.

Eighteen shells were heard exploding within the areas defended by "A" and "D" Batteries and near "B" Battery, east of "D" Battery, at the airport. There was no damage to any of the material or people of this battalion.

On March 12th the altitude of Internal Artillery Zone (IAZ) Area 16 was changed to 10,000 feet until midnight. This IAZ was an area with a seven-mile radius in and around Luxembourg City. The antiaircraft guns were supposed to be on defensive in that particular block of air, and any aircraft that did fly into it was considered a target for antiaircraft guns. Occasionally elevations of IAZs would change, and therefore the enemy, unaware of this, would fly into the zone thinking it was safe. However, if the IAZ changed, the enemy planes would become targets. I'm not sure whether or not the IAZ was changed this time to confuse the enemy.

At the 3rd Army level, isolated pockets north of the Moselle River and west of the Rhine River were continuing to be mopped up. The Eiffel campaign had concluded, and the city of Trier had been taken. The troops were beginning to capture the city of Koblenz, Germany, and the Palatinate Campaign was poised to begin. (The Palatinate is the geographic area west of the Rhine, south of the Moselle and east of the Hunsrvek and Haarot mountains.)

On March 13th, elements of the XII Corps crossed the Moselle River and joined units of the 7th Army to envelope the enemy in the Sauer/Moselle/Rhine area. Under orders from SHAEF, the 12th Army Group was given an order to cross the Moselle River, head southeasterly in behind the German lines to meet the 7th Army coming up from the south. The 7th Army had a bit of trouble getting through the

Engineers put the final touches on the rubber pontoon bridge at Boppard.

Siegfried Line earlier, and therefore, their end of the battle front somewhat lagged behind compared to the 12th Army Group in the center of the allied line. Anyway, instead of heading due east like the 3rd Army had been, it took a southeasterly direction and headed through literally unoccupied territory on the entire west bank of the Rhine River. Thus, a triangle of encircled Germans developed with the Saar to the west, the Moselle to the north and the Rhine to the east.

March 15th had great weather conditions, and XIX TAC flew 625 sorties. The XIIth Corps did a half right and the XXth Corps stayed put, thus placing the XXth Corps north, rather than south, of the usual XIIth Corps. Then the 3rd Army continued its attack southeast into what was to become 7th Army territory. At some point, the 565th, at least Hq "B" & "C" Batteries, were to be attached to the XXth Corps. This is why we were attached to the XXth rather than XIIth, which had always been in the front immediately to our east up to this particular point in the war.

On March 17th, one officer and eighteen trucks were sent on a detail to the Quartermaster Depot #91. There would be a lot of allied bombers over the area this evening, and again, the IAZ Area 16 would be 10,000 feet.

In Germany on the 3rd Army front, the 4th Armored had captured Bad Kreuznach and fighting continued inside Koblenz. The railroad had now been extended to Trier, which is on the east side of the Moselle River and immediately east of Luxembourg City.

On March 18th, Pvt. Clarence Sanders was wounded by a .45-caliber bullet, which had been accidentally discharged from a submachine gun. He was taken to the evacuation hospital by the battalion surgeon. Also, there would be friendly bombers over the area this evening. Again, the IAZ rules for Area 16 were 10,000 feet until midnight. On March 18th, the 87th Infantry Division finished capturing Koblenz, Bad Kreuznach was cleared, and we were threatening Frankfort, which was across the river between the Mainz and Worms. The Germans now had to fear not only the Reamgan Bridgehead, but one downstream at the Ruhr in the 21st Army Sector. There was also possibly a threat of yet a third crossing in the 3rd Army Sector. The VIII Corps was to take over the west bank of the Rhine, south to Bingen, and relieve the XIIth Corps for duty to the South.

The XXth Corps now contained the 4th and 90th Infantry Divisions, the 2nd and 4th Armored Division plus the 2nd Cavalry Group. There were 714 sorties flown on March 18th.

Due to the great toll the war had taken on the Army's wheels, tire changing and tire repair teams were set up around the main highways. The Saar Triangle had been completely cleared that is the area south of Trier bounded by the Moselle River on the west, the Siegfried line on the east and the Saar River on the south.

There wasn't too much of importance happening within the battalion itself; after all, we were back in Luxembourg City and one hundred miles from the front. It wasn't going to be long before we started moving to catch up to the rest of the 3rd Army.

On March 19th, 605 sorties were flown, and the resistance was beginning to crumble. The 3rd Army had captured 950 square miles of the Rhine Gorge from Koblenz to Bingen, Germany. Supplies were beginning to be a problem because they were one hundred miles from the Trier railhead, and tank transporters and trailers were used to get supplies to the front.

By March 20th all the Corps had reached the Rhine River. On that particular day, 655 sorties flew. 3rd Army anti-aircraft shot down 25 planes and claimed eleven more since the Battle of the Bulge. The VIIIth Corps was now at Bingen and the XIIth Corps was at Ludwigshafen.

The first of the German's 262 jets appeared in the skies that day. Only 18,500 troops were out in front of the 3rd Army now; this was the equivalent of fifteen tanks or about 2 1/2 Divisions.

On March 21st, our "C" Battery moved to an area near Trier to guard a bridge, leaving the towers of Radio Luxembourg to others. It was now the mission of the 3rd Army to seize and secure the crossings over the Rhine River between Koblenz and Gimbsheim and continue the attack to the northeast. In the meantime, the triangle that had been formed from the 3rd Army's southeasterly drive, linking up with the 7th Army coming up from the southwest, was all but mopped up.

On March 22nd, "C" Battery was attached to the 456th AAA Automatic Battalion. Some officers and men departed for Paris on leave. Also, cards were received at battalion headquarters whereby the soldier's number of service points could be denoted. This, of course, was anticipating that the war would be over soon, and this started to set up a priority of who would be discharged first.

Battery "C" became non-operational, and the 481st Automatic Weapons Battalion assumed its position. Also, there were a lot of divisional transfers within Corps on the entire front. Troops started across the Rhine at Oppenheim at 10:30 p.m.; this move was kept secret for a while.

Overall, the capturing and handling of prisoners was beginning to become a problem. The men on the front line weren't equipped to handle all the prisoners that were being overrun and those that were surrendering to us.

Perhaps the best account of the first crossing of the Rhine River appears in the book called "Patton" by H. Essame. Essame states:

"That night at 2200 hours, the 23rd Regiment of the 5th Division, in assault boats and on rafts, without artillery preparation, air bombardment or dropping of airborne troops, slipped so quietly into the water that they surprised not only the enemy but the rest of 3rd Army as well. Before dawn on March 23, the division had six Battalions on the far side with the loss of only eight killed and 20 wounded.

"That morning sunlight flooded the room in the Chateau de Namur where Bradley was having breakfast. Suddenly, he was called to the telephone. Raising the instrument he heard the familiar high-pitched voice: 'Brad, don't tell anyone but I'm across.... I sneaked a division over last night. There are so few Krauts about they don't know it yet. So don't make any announcement: we'll keep it secret until we see how it goes.'

"In the evening he telephoned again: 'Brad, for God's sake, tell the world we're across. We knocked down 33 Krauts when they came after our pontoon bridge. I want the world to know 3rd Army made it before Monty starts across.'

"Next morning Patton himself proceeded to Oppenheim, passed through the town to the barge harbor and then led the way across the low bridge spanning the Rhine. Half-way across he stopped. 'Time for a short halt', he said, and standing on the edge of the bridge, relieved his bladder into the Rhine. 'I have been looking forward to this for a long time', he said, buttoning his breeches. He then walked on to the far bank: here he deliberately stubbed his toe and fell to the ground as Scipio Africanus and William the Conqueror had done in similar circumstances, saying that they saw in their hands the soil of Africa or England. He now saw in his own hands the soil of Germany. For all eternity, he would be in company with his peers. George Patton never under-rated himself. He left that to others: some of them his own countrymen, but not of the 3rd Army."

On March 23rd, there were 775 sorties flown; they encountered 154 Luftwaffe planes: eighteen were downed

Convoys roll across the bridge at Boppard.

and fifteen were probables. Corps indicated that a couple additional planes were probables as well. During the period of March 18th to March 24th, antiaircraft encountered 138 enemy aircraft; they downed twenty-eight of them and claimed six other ones. They occupied land five miles south of Koblenz on the east side of the Rhine. The 3rd Army was still in what was known as the 7th Army Zone to the south. The 7th Army was supposed to have come northeast to occupy it, but they were still being slowed down trying to get through the Siegfried Line to the south. Staff Sgt. Erwin and Sgt. Palmisano from Batteries "A" and "B" left by plane at noon for a trip to the Riviera. In the meantime, people took other trips back to Paris, too. Several of the outposts moved and reported to their new locations. Again, the IAZ rules in Area 16 were set at 10,000 feet. The elevation of the IAZ varied over the days so the enemy wasn't always sure that it was going to be at midnight. "C" Battery became operational at the railroad bridge in Germany, just near Echternach, Luxembourg, on March 23rd.

On March 24th, the German Air Force continued to concentrate its efforts against the Oppenheim crossings in the XII Corps. Antiaircraft scored heavily when they shot down twenty-six of the 138 attacking airplanes; six other planes were probably destroyed. On the following day, the heaviest attacks yet made on the bridgehead took place when 230 aircraft struck at the bridges, troops and installations. Antiaircraft destroyed 29 of the raiding planes and claimed 23 probables. Attacks were unceasing and around the clock. They were made from altitudes from twenty feet to 15,000 feet in each of the bombing attacks. Only three planes appeared over the remainder of the XXth Corps Zone. One plane was destroyed and one was probably destroyed. These losses to the German Air Force, combined with the losses at fighter fields which had been overrun by the advancing 3rd Army armored infantry, reduced the threat to the bridgehead which we now firmly established. The IAZ, with a radius of 15,000 yards and a ceiling of 15,000 feet established for the Oppenheim Crossing, aided considerably in its defense.

Enemy aircraft efforts at Boppard at St. Goer were confined to less than thirty planes. Of these, four were shot down and three were probably destroyed during the first five days of the operation.

The 3rd Army Forward Command Post was moved from Luxembourg to Idar-Oberstein, Germany.

It is not surprising with the Lucky Army Forward Headquarters Units moving forward that the 565th would soon follow; however, we were not chosen to protect Lucky Forward, but were assigned to a new mission. We had seen action and were experienced troops in the eyes of many of the AAA units in Europe, so we could assume a more responsible battle role.

Several enlisted men left for the Riviera on March 26th and OCS's applications for Staff Sgt. Harlen, Cpl. Seftel, Pvts. Casey and Monahan were returned from the Army because of visual defects.

1st Sgt. Kuykendall's application was returned because it was incomplete. We received word on the 27th that "C" Battery would again move at its own time to a spot near Apach. This was on the east side of the Moselle southeast of Luxembourg City. We also received word from 207th Group that "A," "B" and "D" were to operate under unrestricted rules for firing for twenty-four hours. This, in effect, said to shoot at anything that comes into the area because neither friendly aircraft nor enemy aircraft are supposed to be there.

On March 28th, we received word that we would be moving and that equipment should be prepared to leave. Some of it was to be loaded and others ready to load on very short notice. On March 28th, our executive officer proceeded to 3rd Army headquarters expecting the 38th Brigade (3rd Army's AAA Command) to be assigned to protect the Lucky Forward at Idar-Oberstein, Germany, but this didn't materialize. There was some thought given to at least following the three batteries that remained in Luxembourg City to assume defensive position somewhere forward of Luxembourg. Later we did learn that we would be relieved of our mission in Luxembourg City and we were to await further orders.

In the entire front other interesting things were happening. There were pockets of Germans left throughout the area. The 70th Division was to stay west of the Rhine for the purpose of mopping up these pockets. They were also supposed to generally keep the country in a stable orderliness until civilian governments could be set up. The 38th Brigade was to assume all of the AAA defense of crossings at the Rhine River. We were also warned not to travel as lone vehicles, but rather to travel in small convoys because of the small enemy pockets and individual German soldiers that might attack us.

The Red army had reached the Austrian border and the 2nd British Army started to drive toward the Elbe River. On March 29th, the 565th, including headquarters and all four batteries, began its move at noon for Simmern, Germany which was a territory, as well as a city, immediately west of the Rhine River. A rear echelon party stayed on to clean up the quarters and the gun sites we had vacated. Another antiaircraft battalion, the 795th, moved in to replace us.

March 29th was bad flying weather and little was done regarding enemy aircraft, what little was left of it. Receiving supplies was again becoming a problem because the railheads were still in France and Luxembourg. A railhead was opened at Mainz, Germany, on April 3rd, and 2 1/2 ton trucks were used to move gasoline forward from that point on. That evening, the battalion arrived at Hausbay, which is a settlement south and west of Boppard, Germany. HQs Batteries "B" and "D" CP's all stopped at the same location that evening. We'll recall that "C" Battery was already in Germany protecting bridges, so their point of beginning that day was different from those who had left from Luxembourg. "A" Battery moved across the Rhine at Boppard, and "C" Battery located northwest of Boppard in support of field artillery battalion. It is true that the headquarters of "B" and "D" and headquarters of headquarters Battery all went to Hausbay. The 1st platoon of "B" Battery went on to protect the 578th Field Artillery Battalion, and the 2nd platoon went to protect an air strip near Lunsbur. In the case of "C" Battery, the 1st platoon protected the 277th Field Artillery Battalion, and the 2nd platoon protected of the 63rd field artillery battalion. In the case of "D" Battery, the 1st platoon gave "AAA" protection to 174th Field Artillery Battalion and the 2nd platoon gave protection to the 578th Field Artillery Battalion. This was on the east side of the Rhine and they crossed at St. Goer.

Having just left Luxembourg City, it's interesting to note that our total consumption of ammunition while we were there was 2,057 rounds of 40mm and 9,444 rounds of .50-caliber.

On March 31st we moved from Hausbay to Boppard and set up our battalion headquarters in a hotel that overlooked the Rhine River. Batteries also moved to Boppard to protect the pontoon bridge. Field artillery had the obligation of shooting and destroying any objects in the river. Antiaircraft had the responsibility of shooting anything that was coming in by air. At night, a searchlight battalion illuminated the river.

When we reached the Rhine we were now under the command of 113th AA Group as opposed to the 207th that we had left back in Luxembourg City.

It is also interesting to note that the 113th AA Group was only concerned with antiaircraft that was east of the Rhine, and anything west of the Rhine would revert to the control of the 7th AAA Group Battalion. We had free access to cross the Rhine by infiltration at Boppard anytime we wanted to without having to get prior permission.

On March 31st, we received a whole new set of objectives. Battalion CP was moved to Boppard. In the case of "A" Battery, the 1st platoon was in defensive of the bridge there. "B" Battery's 1st platoon was assigned to the 578th Field Artillery Battalion and the 2nd platoon was to protect an airstrip. "C" Battery 1st platoon was to protect the 277th Field Artillery Battalion, and the 2nd platoon was assigned to the 663rd Field Artillery Battalion. In the case of "D" Battery, the 1st platoon was in protection of the 174th Field Artillery Battalion and the 2nd platoon was in protection of the 578th Field Artillery Battalion. Remember that field artillery are at least 105mm guns, therefore, they are quite vulnerable to aircraft attacks. The smaller field pieces are usually part of the infantry.

The battalion commander's diary notes that while we were stopped in Simneru, we were attached to the 113rd Group, but as of 6 p.m. on March 31st, the battalion passed control to the 7th AA Group, commanded by Col. Dutton. When we moved to Lorch, battalion HQ, "B" and "C" were on the east side of the Rhine River, "A" and "D" Batteries were on the west side of the Rhine. In our initial move, "D" Battery went across the bridge at St. Goer then came back across the bridge at Boppard moving south to Lorch where we were protecting the floating Bailey Bridge Crossing. Our troops were mixed on both sides of the river for a period of time. Also, this area had been taken so fast that there were small pockets of German soldiers still in the area. The night the headquarters battery had moved in Hausbay we were alerted around midnight that there were German soldiers coming into town seeking food. We, of course, knew little about infantry fighting and how to contain such an attack. A platoon from the 70th Infantry came into town, and we served as a supplement to whatever they did to repeal the attack.

The 3rd Army had determined that they needed four bridge crossings at the Rhine below Oppenheim. There were bridges at Boppard, Lorch and Bingen and assault boats at St. Goer. There had been a pontoon bridge at St. Goer, but it had very unstable anchors so the floating bailey was built at Lorch to replace it. Because there were still crossings made by boats at St. Goer, a defense was needed there. The 128th gun battalion set up at Boppard; the 120th gun battalion set up at St. Goer; the 565th AW was at Lorch; and the 815th AW set up at Bingen. Searchlights were attached and, in the case of the 565th, two lights were from "B" Battery of the 226th searchlight battalion. We all operated under the 7th AAA Group, which operated under the 38th Brigade. Thus, while our original missions were in and around Boppard because the bridge at St. Goer was not anchored well and was merely a pontoon bridge, a floating Bailey bridge at Lorch would be built. We were then assigned to that particular site. The outposts were then coordinated by the 38th Brigade and all the outposts from all four battalions were coordinated under one central command. This move necessitated bringing some of our units in that had been attached to field artillery battalions and guarding small air strips. The 70th Division occupied the west side of the Rhine to clean up small pockets of resistance that still existed there. AAA needs in the area would be coordinated by the 7 AAA Group. We were instructed to establish communications with an infantry battalion of the 70th Division and exchange information with them.

Typical scene at war's end.

Chapter 9
(April 1-30, 1945)

The air above the bridges from Boppard to Lorch was known as IAZ 38. There would be a 1,200-yard radius on either side of the river, with the standard 10,000-foot ceiling. However, that was often cancelled, and the batteries were given a "blank check" permission to fire on any enemy plane they saw at any elevation.

On April 3rd, Lucky Forward moved to Frankfurt, a move of some eighty-five miles from Oberstein. Fighting began in Eisenach far to our northeast. (Some of our battalion moved there on April 10th or so.) The Corps now lined up in the 3rd Army with the XX Corps to the north, the VIII Corps in the center and the XII Corps to the south.

On April 4th, the 4th Armored captured Gotha and Ordruff, and the 89th Infantry Division from the 1st Army began mopping up the area. The 3rd Army's XXth Corps now bumped up against the 89th of the 1st Army at the southern boundary of the 1st Army and the northern boundary of the 3rd Army. The weather was great and the 3rd Army flew 455 sorties.

On April 5th, we arrived at Lorch, which was on the east side of the river. Gradually, "A" and "D" Batteries moved in on the west bank, and "B" and "C" on the east bank. The general defense of a bridge was that antiaircraft would take care of airplanes flying overhead, searchlights would watch for floating objects in the water and field artillery would fire and destroy these objects, whatever they happened to be, so nothing could destroy the bridge. In case of an air raid, the lights were to be doused. While "A" and "B" Batteries were in IAZ 38, "C" and "D" Batteries were in IAZ 39, south of Lorch. Eisenach was captured. There were 269 sorties flown that day, and the armored advances were now somewhat limited to the infantry's ability to mop up behind them. The 3rd Army rear echelon moved to Frankfort, 135 miles from its former headquarters in Trier.

Also, Capt. Franklin, our battalion dentist, requested relief from active duty. His request was sent to the 7th AAA Group. (Capt. Franklin was well into his thirties, making him the oldest man in our battalion; he was having a difficult time keeping up with the rigors of the harsh winter and the outdoor living.

It was also noted that all units of the 565th and two from 128th gun battalion were in the IAZ 43 that was centered at Lorch for 12,000 yards. We also received word that the commanding officer from the 128th Gun Battalion was responsible for operating the four battalions that were guarding the bridges over the Rhine for the 3rd Army; our own Col. Yarnell was to be the defense coordinator.

On April 9th, we received a message from a group asking for a detail of eighteen trucks to haul gasoline and volunteers to be in a unit for a military police detachment. Capt. Grey and Lt. Springer volunteered from "A" Battery, and their names were submitted to Group for consideration. It was also indicated that the eighteen trucks that were requested reported to an airport to haul gasoline. The round trip took about twelve hours. They also asked for an additional five trucks for a different detail, if we could find them. Apparently we did get their trucks.

The 9th was Easter Sunday, and it was beautiful weather. It seemed a lot of people had colds as a result of the spring weather that had come upon us with warm then cool days. Sleeping in rather cool, damp quarters didn't help our health, either.

We received word that we should send two batteries of our choice at once to an airfield near Schwalbach, replacing the 456th AAA by infiltration. That means that they would move at their own speed whenever they were ready. "A" and "D" Batteries were notified to move to this location which was near 3rd Army Headquarters at Frankfurt. The advanced party came to the battalion for further information. The 7th AAA Group was notified that "A" and "D" Batteries would be going. It is also noted that the resistance of the 3rd Army now was estimated at 21,000 of low grade troops that had the equivalent of 110 tanks and guns. The communication zone took over railheads, and all supplies west of the Rhine River. Also, new Pershing tanks were released to the 3rd Army and given to the 40th and 11th armored divisions.

On April 9th, we again sent a convoy of eighteen trucks to Group to haul gasoline; they returned. The weather was cold and the battalion received orders from the 3rd Army ordering Sgt. Kuykendall to the Infantry OCS to depart on April 10th. Also, there was a large amount of money waiting to be sent home because the men really didn't have any place to spend it since they arrived in Germany.

We received word that the two searchlights that were with us at Lorch were to be sent upstream to Bingem on that crossing. Also noted on April 9th: A gasoline pipeline had been completed across the Rhine to Mainz, and 549 sorties were flown.

On April 10th we received word that we would get march orders later in the day; they came at 5:00 p.m. We were to head for the vicinity of Eisenach and would be attached to the 112th AAA Group and the XXth Corps. This was the first time we had not been attached to the 3rd Army. We started very late in the day; the roads were very dusty, the trip very arduous. The drive took all night.

Part of the trip was over a German super highway. The weather was cool at night but warm during the day. "A" and "D" Batteries stayed behind at Schwabach and attached to the VIII Corps. The 120th AA Gun Battalion, which had been with us on the Rhine, also received marching orders. There is nothing to indicate whether they came with us or went someplace else. Nonetheless, they were relieved at the pontoon bridge at Boppard and Lorch.

In the area where we were headed, the 4th armored swept to Erfurt and 535 sorties were flown by TAC that day. In other areas of the front, the 9th Army had reached Hanover and the Canadians crossed the River Ijssel.

Churchill announced to the British that the Commonwealth casualties of the war to date were: armed forces, 1,126,820; the Merchant Navy, 34,161; and civilians, 144,542.

We received orders to move out at 4:00 p.m., and at 5:30 we were underway for Eisenach. We were to report to the 112th Group, which was in command of antiaircraft operations for the XXth Corps. Headquarters "B" and "C" left in this convoy. "A" and "D" had already moved to Schwalbach, near Frankfurth. I'm not sure just how many miles this convoy covered, but it took a good bit of time to get there as we did not arrive until the following morning. We moved into the Grossen/Behringer area because it contained airstrips to which gasoline and ammunition were being by flown by

A 40mm (not 565th) set up in front of the Frankfurt Opera House.

C47s and gliders. They were being strafed by enemy aircraft. Therefore, they needed AAA protection quickly.

In a normal convoy, the headquarters motorpool was always the last to move out. The column was headed by the commanding officer; the battalion motorpool consisted of a jeep and the battalion motor officer, a parts truck and the battalion wrecker, which were always the last vehicles in the convoy. It was generally my job to ride on the wrecker. There was usually a crew of three or four with the wrecker and parts trucks: a driver, an assistant driver and a couple of mechanics. If a truck broke down, the battery maintenance units would try to take care of it. If they couldn't or if the repair was going to take a lot of time, they would move on and catch up with their battery, leaving the truck until the battalion maintenance section arrived.

On this particular occasion, as we got closer to our destination, we had seven or eight trucks in the convoy led by Capt. McCoy and M/Sgt. Grant, four or five "B" & "C" battery trucks, the parts truck and the wrecker.

A bit east of Eisenach, on our way to Brossen-Behrengher, we were stopped at an intersection by a German or a civilian, apparently dressed in GI clothes, who told us we had gotten into an area that had been cleared and that we could put the lights on the lights of our lead vehicle. Never having had an instruction like this before and not being used to this, we foolishly complied. A little ways down the road we were strafed. Fortunately for us, the lights on the lead vehicle had just rounded a corner and the rest of the convoy was at a right angle to the jeep with its lights on. The strafing took place between the jeep and first truck.

I was riding in one of the last vehicles, and I recall that along with the noise, it looked as if somebody was striking an arc welder as those shells were being delivered from the strafing plane. As we stopped and got out of the trucks, we could hear the plane departing and immediately manned some of our ring mounts (.50 caliber machine guns) that were with us, but the plane never came back to give us a second treatment. The plane, of course, would have met a hail of .50-caliber bullets, as we probably had an M-51 along with several ring mounts traveling with us on the various trucks.

Our new headquarters was only a short ways ahead, but we missed it and went farther down the road. We halted in a small village to see if all the trucks were still with us. (I

Antiaircraft weapon protects Danube crossing.

had moved forward to a different vehicle after we were strafed.) The wrecker was missing so we stayed there while Capt. McCoy went back to see what happened. He found the wrecker had run off the road and rolled down a hill. In the process, it had injured M/Sgt. Grant who was riding in the passenger side of the cab, and also T/4 Ravetti, a mechanic, who was riding in the back of the wrecker. After identifying the town we were in, we determined that we were well beyond where we were supposed to be.

We immediately turned around and went in the direction from whence we came. When we arrived at the wrecker, Cpl. Herndon and I were dropped off to guard it. This was 4 to 5 o'clock in the morning, and we really couldn't see much. As daylight arrived, we began cleaning up the mess that was on the side hill. It included everything from tires to boxes of small tools as well as larger ones. The people who left us promised to return for us once they found their way back to where we were supposed to be and attended to the men who had been injured when the wrecker ran off the road.

We had been up about 24 hours at that time, and I'm sure we probably had some food with us in the form of C or D rations. In a short while a plane started circling overhead, and we identified it as an ME 109. We didn't have any way of defending ourselves. Fortunately, we found a cattle pass nearby; a cattle pass is a concrete culvert, probably six feet high and six feet wide. We crawled into it. The plane assessed the situation and took off for greener pastures. The crews from headquarters came back, and we rolled the wrecker up on its wheels, reloaded the tools and returned to headquarters still sleepless. We never got to bed until that evening. I recall it was the first time I'd ever gone 1 1/2 days without any sleep. It was a new experience for me.

It is noted in the CO's diary that the present location of the CP was very near the battle front. Immediately to our north was the 1st Army. I doubt there was any infantry or field artillery or any other kind of troops in the area except us,, who were guarding airfields. "C" Battery was at Langensalza to our north and "B" Battery was at Weingenlupmitz to our south. We were not in contact with anyone from the 1st Army. We literally were guarding our perimeters as well as the air.

Headquarters battery had just arrived in Grossen-Behringen when 112th Group requested fifteen 2 1/2-ton trucks to haul infantry. This was a natural request from us. After all, we had just arrived and we were probably the only ones in the area that had transportation of any kind.

The 4th and 6th armored and the 80th infantry were ahead of us a little bit, and they had gained about forty miles that day. They captured Weimar and Erfurt.

There was no doubt the Germans were beaten, but they continued their delay tactics. When they got into a city such as Gera, Weimar, Gotha or Erfurt, they would have snipers and mines all over the place. It was a delaying action, not one of aggression. Our infantry had to proceed with a lot of caution, and the city had to literally be taken street by street and door to door. Enemy aircraft also wanted to strafe the fields where our C47s and gliders were landing. There were 540 sorties flown that day by the XIX TAC.

Farther south, 3rd Army headquarters moved to Hersfeld, about eighty-five miles from Frankfurt. That would have been the forward position of the Army. G2 and G3 were called Lucky Forward, "lucky" meaning the 3rd Army.

April 12th was nice and warm. Headquarters battery and Batterys "B" and "C" were now attached to the XXth Corps. HQ battery was located at Behringer, "C" Battery at Lancansalza, and "B" Battery at Weingenlup, near Ohrdurf, the infamous concentration camp -- all north of Frankfurt.

"A" Battery had been reassigned orders attaching them to the 38th Brigade, then assigned to the 113th Group and attached to the 635th AAA AW battalion for operation control. Their mission was to provide a defense of the 578th Field Artillery in the case of the 1st platoon and the 2nd platoon to the 63rd Field Artillery.

Their CP was at Rehestadt. Later that day, the battery was relieved and reassigned to an airfield at Rohrensee. The 2nd platoon was assigned to an AA protection of C1 III supply dump.

The assignment to the 113rd Group also included "D" Battery. They, in turn, were assigned to the VIIIth Corps. In other words, they were assigned to the AAA Group attached to the VIII Corps.

The last bridge, which the 565th protected, was built across the Rhine at Lorch. It was a heavy-duty bridge built of steel pontoons with double Bailey Bridge railings.

The bridge at Lorch carried heavy loads of traffic. Note the slight depression in the area on which the convoy is traveling. On lighter bridges, vehicles were spaced much farther apart.

In the meantime, the enemy was quite stubborn in the Erfurt area. The 4th Armored did gain twenty miles and bypassed Gera. Erfurt was finally cleared and some of the troops of the 4th Armored enter Gera by the end of the day. The Communication Zone Supply notified the 3rd Army that it was about to open a supply dump at Eisenach, right at our back door. Perhaps the most notable thing that happened on April 12th was the death of President Roosevelt and Vice President Harry S. Truman taking office.

On April 13th, we moved our battalion supply along with "C" Battery to the vicinity of Weimar, although the Germans still occupied a good bit of the city. We were set up about three miles south of Weimar near an airstrip, again protecting the incoming supplies. This was some fifty miles east of Grossen-Behrengen. Without regard to specific assignment, the CO's diary says that our missions before moving were the AAA defense of airstrips at Lancansalza, Wenigenlupnitz, Berka, Vacha and Rohrensee. The most important thing that happened this day, on the 13th, was that Pvt. James Vann in "B" Battery shot down a plane with a .50-caliber ring mount, the only kill credited to the 565th.

"D" Battery was assigned to the 635th AAA Battalion for operational control and its missions were supply routes and bridges at Berka, Vacha and Tunnroda. "A" Battery was assigned to positions at Rehestadt and Rohrensee. Batteries "B" and "C" were located near the battalion headquarters near Weimar.

"A" Battery was at Bethy and "D" Battery was located about twenty miles from "A" Battery. Both "A" Battery and "D" Battery still remained under operation control of other AAA battalions. "D" Battery was actually located at Tunnroda, just south of Bad Berka. When "C" Battery moved to the airfield near Weimar, they then sent its trucks back to move "B" Battery. Remember we sent "B" Battery 2-1/2-ton trucks to move the infantry. Apparently, they hadn't returned and it was necessary for us to use trucks from "C" Battery to move "B" Battery to the Weimar airport.

In the meantime, the 4th Armored had driven within four miles of Chemnitz. Gera was captured by the 80th Division and nearly 300 sorties were flown that day.

The 3rd Army troops were within fifteen miles of Lepzig and stopped about five miles north of Chemnitz. Plans were made to advance the communication zone deliveries from Eisenach to points at Erfurt and Weimar, which were another 50 miles closer to the front. This was a total of 195 miles from Mainz.

In the meantime, our immediate command, the 112th Group, which had been in Gera, had moved to Meerane. The 281st Ordinance, which was our contact for maintenance, was now in Gera.

On the greater front, immediately to our east, was an estimated 15,000 enemy that had the equivalent of 65 tanks and guns. The 474th Infantry Regiment was moved to Weimer to clear it of all enemy personnel. The 6th Armored drove to points directly north of Chemnitz, and the 4th Armored maintained positions west and northwest of Chemnitz.

Territorial rights were being negotiated with the Russians getting Berlin and some of the area now occupied by the 3rd Army around Chemnitz.

There were 365 Sorties of the XIX TAC on this date, and the German airfields were getting scarce. Thus, the XIX TAC had driven many of the German planes from their home fields. The SHAEF kept the 3rd Army from moving forward. The 120th Evacuation Hospital, serving us in our area, was moved to Ettersburg to provide medical services to the Buchenwald inmates.

Late in the afternoon on April 15th, a group of us in the battalion motorpool got into one of our 2-1/2-ton trucks and journeyed to Buchenwald, the infamous concentration camp, northwest of Weimar. I don't know whether we were the first ones from the battalion there, but we were among the early arrivals because it is noted that in the following days several people went there.

When we arrived, we were met at the gate by a 17-year-old who could speak English. He then became our host for our visit to the camp. He immediately took us to the camp hospital whose chief surgeon, who was Belgian or Dutch, took over as our escort along with the young man. He showed us the hospital first, which contained a Supreme Court Justice from Belgium as a patient. He also had a fellow who evidently was a native of a European country but had played second base for the Philadelphia Phillies. They were all elite patients. He had asked us if we had any K Rations with us (K Rations is a chocolate bar). He said he didn't want the inmates to eat chocolate because it was too rich for their systems at the moment. We returned to the truck and got what we had and gave it to him. Thereafter, we followed him throughout the camp, the first stop being a house of ill repute.

Apparently, they had several "women of the street" there, and for the few pennies that the inmates made, they could have sexual contact with these women. There were guards outside the doors so they wouldn't be harassed.

We moved from there to what was known as the Upper Barracks, or the non-Jewish people, and were able to speak English to some of those inmates. While they were rather thin and gaunt, they were certainly not in the dehydrated condition in which we found Jews in the lower camp.

The lower camp contained the building of which you see so many pictures, where the bodies of men are nothing but skin and bones and where men are dying in regularity. I recall that these were long, narrow buildings. On one end of it was a room about eight feet square; it contained those who had died in the last 24 hours. When we were there, bodies hadn't been removed to the crematory because the camp wasn't functioning in a normal manner. There were even bodies that had not been removed from their bunks.

There were six shelves about six feet wide by about six feet high on either side of the aisle as you walked down this barracks. Each man had about one square foot of space to sleep on; they were packed in there like sardines. When someone died, he was merely pushed aside or you slept alongside him.

Historically, there had been a couple of death marches out of the camp just prior to the American's arrival, so therefore, the population wasn't as great as it had been. I recall when coming into camp that we saw many a body lying on the shoulder of the road, some of them sitting against a tree and still propped there in death.

We moved on to the crematory where we found a hay rack load of bodies on a wagon and a huge SS Trooper who had committed suicide the day the Americans liberated the place. We then went down into the cellar of the crematory where bodies were processed.

As each inmate went down a stairway and turned right, entering an open room, a guard with a large wooden maul hit each man in the forehead, crushing his skull and killing him. The dead men would then be taken to the crematory next door.

Bodies were stacked three to a furnace in the process of cremation. As I recall, there were two stories of furnaces: one in the basement and another one on the the ground floor. In back we saw the pile of bones and ashes that were the remains of the bodies.

We returned to the battalion motorpool and told others of our escapade. In the course of the next couple of days, almost everybody had seen Buchenwald. A day or two earlier, we had seen parts of the camp at Ohrdruf, which was something similar to this, but not to such a great extent, or perhaps we didn't see the worst of Ohrdruf.

Bodies stacked at the Buchenwald concentration camp at Weimar, Germany.

Eisenhower lost his breakfast when he was going through Ohrdruf. I remember the stench of death I experienced at Buchenwald could certainly cause you to throw up.

The generals made the townspeople in Weimar walk through the camp of Buchenwald to see what had happened. As a result, the mayor and his wife went home and slit their wrists.

About this same time, the 90th Division stumbled upon an underground cache of the last of the Reich gold reserves. It was hidden in the salt mines about 2,500 feet below ground and represented a billion dollars of gold bullion. A guard at the facility told Gens. Eisenhower and Patton that it was needed to pay the Army payroll, to which their reply was, they didn't think the German Army was going to need too many more payrolls. Several pieces of art stolen by the Nazi government were also located in that underground cave, but its cool, dry environment had not deteriorated their quality.

On April 17th, Gen. Bradley asked Patton to be present at his headquarters in Weisbaden to announce a big shift in the table of organization of the 12th Army Group.

A rumor was circulating that there was a redoubt being formed by the German Army in Austria. The German Army had placed large reserves in the southern part of Germany and in Austria. They were placed there to be the defender, and/or to go on an offensive from that particular area.

The 3rd Army was to make a 90-degree shift in its direction to the south, and the other armies would adjust to the 3rd Army's movements. As a result, the 1st Army, which was to our left flank on the north, also did a 45-degree right flank to the southeast, entering Czechoslovakia.

The meeting between Bradley and Patton was to set up this movement. It was also noted that the Chemnitz area was very stubborn, and there was still some resistance there. The 12th Army Group had assigned the 1st Army to forge ahead and meet the Russians at the preassigned Elbe River.

In this change of objectives, the 3rd Army lost its VIII Corps to the 1st Army and picked up the III Corps as well as the XVII Airborne Division. The 3rd Army was to move south to pick up the 13th Armored from the 7th Army along the way and maintain contact with the XII Corps to its left. In the meantime, the 70th Infantry Division and its attached troops continued to secure the installations on the Rhine River until it could be relieved by the 15th Army. The 471st Infantry Regiment continued to be guard troops around 3rd Army headquarters at Hersfelt. What all this meant to the 565th was that it was going to be relieved of its mission at Weimar and begin a long, quick move to the south. (An advance party from Bn HQ already had scouted the Chemnitz area.)

Late in the day on the 17th, we were informed that we were going to move to the vicinity of Nurnberg the next day. On April 18th, we were packed by early morning, and at 4 p.m. Headquarters Battery moved to the airport at Weimar where the "B" and "C" Batteries had been set up, and we all began our trek toward Nurnberg.

We got within 30 miles of Nurnberg and set up headquarters the following morning at 6:00 a.m. The XX Corps, in the meantime, had turned over to the VIII Corps the area it had occupied to the north. The 1st Army move and our move was all coordinated to the south. In other parts of the Army, the Ruhr pocket had been reduced to 317,000 prisoners, which was the entire German 15th Army. The final count of prisoners taken in the Ruhr was 370,000. The 3rd Army had reached the Czechoslovakian border, and the 9th Army had reached Magdeberg.

On April 21, Pvt. James Vann shot down a German Me 109 with a .50 caliber ring mount.

A few days earlier we lent 112 Group headquarters a 2-1/2-ton truck; that is, Headquarters Battery had lent it, and it was being driven by Harvey Cornelius. Cornelius relates the story of how somebody else in Group Headquarters took that truck, and as the driver was proceeding south in the direction of Bamberg, he made a left turn to the east as opposed to a right turn. The truck was blown up. We, of course, knew that the area immediately east of that autobahn had not yet been cleared. But whoever was driving that truck did not.

On April 20th, "A" Battery got a new officer by the name of Lt. Schmall. Also, "A" and "D" Batteries, which had been operating to the south of Headquarters Battery, were reattached to the 565th. Thus, we were a complete battalion again. It is also interesting to note that they had been attached to the 38th Brigade and subsequently attached to the VIII Corps. We in the north had been attached to the XX Corps. It was generally assumed that the 565th could wear either 3rd Army patches or XX Corps patches. In effect, Headquarters Batteries "B" and "C" were qualified to wear XX Corps patches, while members of "A" and "D" Batteries were authorized to wear VII Corps patches. "C" Battery moved to Hollfeld and "B" Battery moved to Baiersdorf.

On April 21st, rumors were circulating around the Battalion Headquarters that we were about to move, this time to the vicinity of Nurnberg. Staff Sgt. Sam Thomas, the supply sergeant from "A" Battery, had come to Headquarters Battery as the acting 1st Sergeant.

"D" Battery's reconnaissance party left the battalion for the purpose of going to the headquarters of the 7th AAA Group, which was assigned to the mission of protecting the Lucky Forward Headquarters at Erlangen. In the meantime, "C" Battery remained at Hollfeld and "B" Battery was at Baiersdorf.

Meanwhile, the 3rd Army was well underway in the last of its campaigns, having taken Regensburg and Straubing, where we were to travel in the not too distant future. XIX TAC had flown about 350 sorties on April 21st, and the VIII Corps, which was on the north flank, was now transferred to the 1st Army.

There were some Type A rations available, but it was difficult to distribute them once we had them in hand because of the great distances between our batteries. The order of battle of the 3rd Army now was that the XII Corps was on our north flank, the XX Corps in our center flank and the III Corps on our south or right flank. There were 134,000 displaced persons housed in the 3rd Army area.

Early in the morning on April 22nd, we left Breitengressbach and set up our Battalion CP in Nurnberg. On April 22nd, "C" Battery moved to Lauf, a suburb of Nurnburg.

It's interesting to note the many moves that were made and then finally being together as a complete battalion again. We found that "A" Battery was at Neustad, "B" was at Baiersdorf, "C" was at Lauf and "D" was at Reichelsdorf. We were still operating under the 112th Group, which we had joined when we had made our move from the Rhine River northeast to the Eisenach area.

On April 23rd, "D" Battery had been attached to the 7th AAA Group and had been guarding 3rd Army Headquarters at Erlangen and attached to the 129th AAA Battalion for food and operations. That day, "D" Battery was relieved of its defensive of 3rd Army Headquarters and attached to the 16th AAA Group, whose headquarters was in Nuestadt, and the 2nd platoon was assigned to a mission to defend a bridge at Reichelsdorf. The 1st Platoon was assigned to defend III Corps Army Headquarters, southwest of Nurnberg, at Schwabach. "C" Battery had been relieved of its mission at Hollfeld and assigned a new mission providing AAA Defense of a supply depot at Lauf. On this same day, the Lucky Rear Echelon moved to Erlangen, which was probably the reason that some of our AAA Defense was moved there. It is also noted on this day that "C" Battery had expended 59 rounds of 40mm and 2,460 rounds of .50 caliber ammunition. The action involved two planes in separate raids that had strafed the "C" Battery area. No results were claimed, although the plane was identified as a JU88.

On April 25th, we received a couple of new missions. "B" and "C" Batteries were to protect a bridge crossing in the vicinity of Lauf, and "C" Battery was to protect a bridge crossing at Poikam, near Regensburg. These airfields were canning areas. In other words, this was where gasoline was arriving in bulk and was put in cans to be distributed to the front.

Railroads now began operating as far as Wurzburg into Germany, which was a great stride as far as supply was concerned. It is also interesting to note that a Lt. Craig from the 1st Army met a cavalry unit from the Russian Army at about 4:45 p.m. that day.

A jeep left the 565th Battalion Headquarters with Cpl. Harris Dake, Tech Sgt. Luther Sheldon and Warrant Officer Guy F. Boyle for the purpose of authenticating an aircraft kill, which had involved a death of a full colonel, that occurred while we were still at Weimar. They were to testify in an inquiry there. They were captured just outside Chemnitz. They were the only members of the 565th to be captured. In the last 10 days of the war, the Germans only captured about 100 Allied prisoners, and three of them were from the 565th.

On April 26th, Battalion Headquarters moved to Hemau, due west of Regensburg about 12 miles. Here we set up headquarters in an old hotel, which was very nice. The weather was beginning to get warm and very pleasant. There were 465 sorties flown by the XIX TAC, and the first crossing of the Austria border took place. Ingolstadt, north of Munich, had been captured. On this day 1,129,675 gallons of G80 gasoline was used, the largest amount ever consumed in a single day.

Regensburg, which we were to visit in just a few days, was captured on April 27th. The 1st Army began to move to the right just slightly, taking over some of the left flank of the 3rd Army. We were alerted that we should have gas masks readily available because of an alert that the Germans might use it as a last resort. At this time, "B" Battery was defending a pontoon bridge for the 71st Infantry, and "C" Battery had a similar mission with the 65th Infantry. On this particular day, "D" Battery engaged a single JU88 flying very low over a bridge area. The enemy aircraft made no attacks on the area and "D" Battery made no claims, however, they did expend 17 rounds of 40mm ammunition and 1,200 rounds of .50 caliber ammunition.

The 2nd Platoon of "D" Battery was relieved of its position and moved to a bridge near Belilnries. The 1st Platoon remained in the current position with the 71st Division, as did "C" Battery, remaining with the 65th Division. Straubing was cleared by the 71st Division, which was going to be our last stop in the days ahead before we reverted to the army of occupation. The 71st Division continued policing the area south of Regensburg. "B" Battery did claim a Category 3, or a JU88, when a 40mm hit a wing of the aircraft.

It was expected that headquarters was going to move very shortly. We weren't sure whether it was going to be on April 29th or the following day.

In the meantime, "B" Battery CP was moved to Mainburg near Schweinfurt, and "C" Battery was moving both of its platoons to different bridges. There was an assault boat crossing the Isar River.

On April 30th, the Battalion Command Post was moved to Straubing, which was a fairly large city southeast of Regensburg. It moved again within the same city to better quarters on the 3rd.

The battalion's assigned mission at this time was to defend the Danube Crossing for the Corps Zone and be relieved of this present mission whenever the 3rd Army chose to do so. In the meantime, crossings were made at Pelsting and Willersdorf on the Isar River immediately to the south of Straubing.

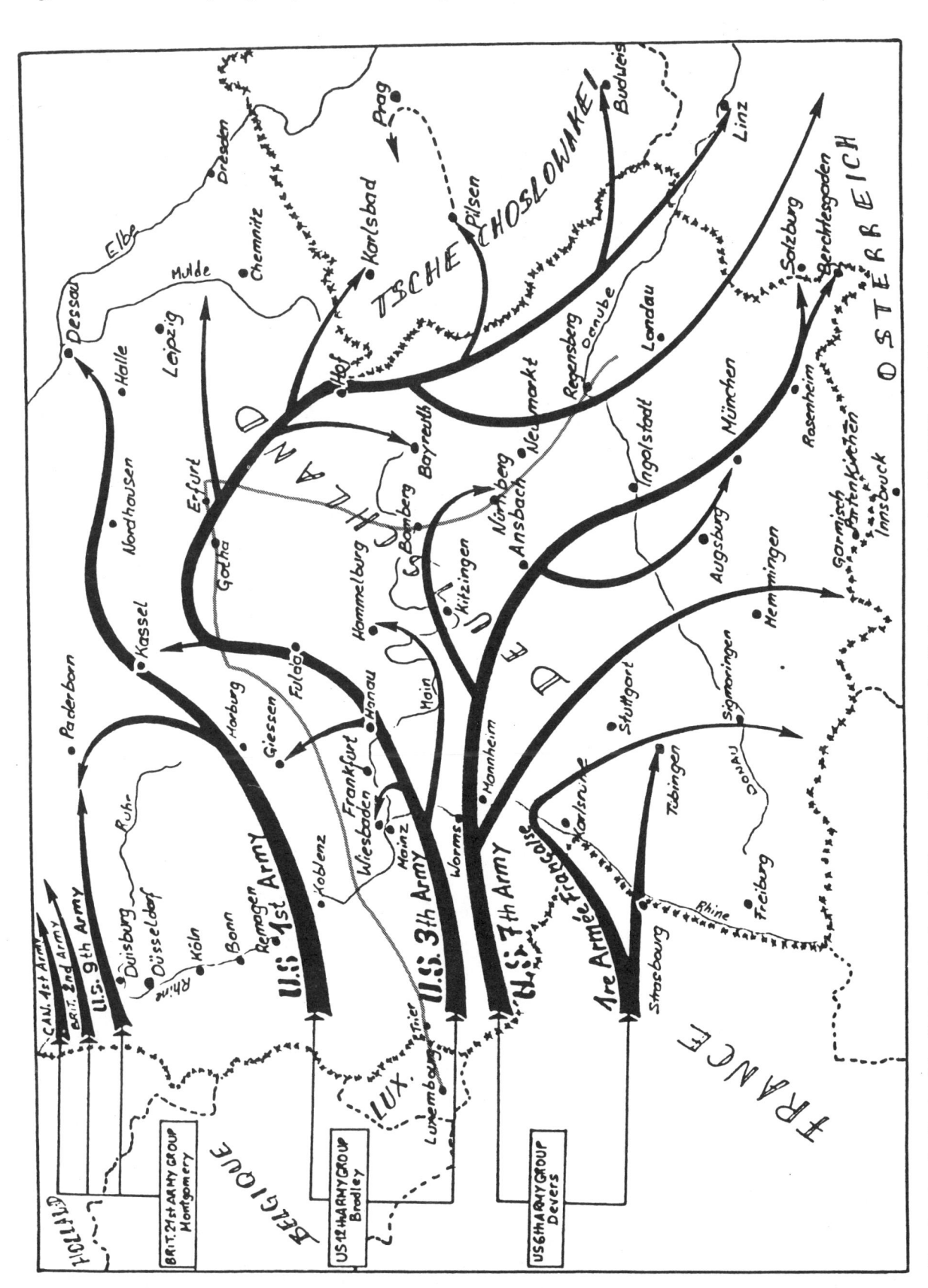

Map showing the Battle of the Rhineland and central Europe, Jan. 17 to May 8, with the general route of the 565th overlaid.

Chapter 10
(May 1-8, 1945)

On May 1st, "D" Battery was given a new mission to cross the Isar River with the 71st Infantry Division. Upon removal of the Treadway Bridge across the Danube, "C" Battery was assigned the mission of crossing the Isar River in the 80th Division Sector. "C" Battery was to move to the Isar River crossing until relieved by the 3rd Army, and "B" Battery's mission changed to AAA defense of an airstrip in the vicinity of Straubing. Two of our batteries were assigned to the 71st and the 80th Infantry Divisions. Both of these divisions had an antiaircraft battalion assigned to them, but because of the rapid movement and the dozens of bridges and airfields to protect in the area, we supplemented their efforts.

On May 2nd, we moved to a much larger hotel in the center of Straubing. There was also more movement within the batteries. The 1st Platoon of "D" Battery and the Battery CP moved from the III Corps Headquarters in Deilngries, and the 1st Platoon was moved to Mainburg. "C" Battery was being relieved by the 455th AAA "A" Battery on May 3rd. Upon relief, they were to be detached from the XX Corps and revert to the control of the 38th AAA Brigade in Erlangen, north of Nurnberg. They were to send an advanced party to the 38th Brigade as soon as possible. Our "B" Battery was to remain in position at the airfield until properly relieved by the 38th Brigade.

This was also a significant day because this was the day that Hitler died; it was also a day that I shall not forget too quickly. On this day I got a flashburn -- a flash from an electric welder which you get without the aid of a welder's eye protection helmet. The only aid I had to this point was a set of Polaroid goggles that were used by the gunners on M51s. The welder was one the battalion motorpool had constructed. While rather primitive, it did a good bit of work. With flashburn, little blisters form on the ball of your eye, and the eyeball becomes highly irritated. I suffered with that for several hours.

On this day, a test train was driven into Nurnberg; trains were also operating in Wurzburg, Bamberg and Nurnberg. Supplies were coming in with relative ease by train, and they were repairing track to Regensburg, which was close to us at Straubing.

May 3rd was a bit cool, but it was a great one for us. Knowing the war was nearing its end, we were able to catch up on many things. We, the battalion motorpool, also ran into a bunch of Australian soldiers that had been captured at Dunkirk. They had been liberated from a prison nearby and had liberated a couple of German cars in the area. The cars needed air in the tires, gasoline, some radiator hoses and batteries, so we spent most of the morning fixing them so they could head for the coast in Holland. To express their thanks, they invited us into the house they had appropriated and were treating us to some "white lightning." Fortunately, by the time it was my turn to toast the occasion, I only needed to touch my lips to the glass. That stuff was hot! We also came away with dozens of rolls of film and other neat items. They, of course, were very happy to be heading home.

Looking at some notations that I found in the "3rd Army After Action Reports," I came upon some interesting information worth repeating. It deals with the activities of the 565th. Under Chapter 12 of "May Operations," it says, "...By May 1 activities of the Luftwaffe had been reduced almost entirely to armed reconnaissance. Such hit and run tactics here and there throughout the army area at targets of opportunity still constituted a threat to supply lines and concentration of troops. But the need for troops to handle law and order in the vast areas overrun by the 3rd Army grew so urgent that it became necessary to divert some of the Anti Aircraft troops from their primary missions for this task."

Plans were made to relieve the headquarters in Headquarters Battery of the 38th Antiaircraft Artillery Brigade, along with the 7th Antiaircraft Artillery Group, 129th Antiaircraft Artillery Gun Battalion, the 457th and the 565th Antiaircraft Artillery Automatic Weapons Battalions, were to become responsible for law and order and protection of lines of communication in the vicinity of Erlangen. Units were to be released for this mission by May 5th, at which time the scale of antiaircraft artillery in the 3rd Army would be reduced to one antiaircraft group, one gun and one automatic weapons battalion per corps and two groups, three gun battalions and four automatic weapons battalions for Army antiaircraft artillery. In addition, a 433rd Antiaircraft Artillery Automatic Weapons Battalion, attached to the 70th Infantry Division, was to remain temporarily under the control of the Army.

The 207th Antiaircraft Artillery Group, with the 119th Antiaircraft Gun Battalion, 456th, the 399th and the 433rd Antiaircraft Artillery Automatic Weapons Battalions and one searchlight platoon, were to cover installations in the southwestern portion of the Army area. The 24th Antiaircraft Artillery Group, along with the 411th and 120th Antiaircraft Artillery Gun Battalions, the 567th and the 815th Antiaircraft Artillery Automatic Weapons Battalion and one searchlight platoon, were to protect installations to the northwestern portion of the Army area.

Thus, when "C" Battery got march orders to Schwarzenberg on May 3rd, it came as no surprise to the battalion. On this date, "B" Battery fired five rounds of 40mm at an HE111K, which was the new German jet, however it came in at approximately 60 feet elevation and they had little chance of scoring a hit.

On May 4th, Headquarters Battery and "B" Battery moved to its new location at Schwarzenberg, which was a big old castle near Sheinfelt. "A" Battery also left for the assembly area there. "C" Battery had moved out the day before and it wasn't until May 6th that "D" Battery actually joined the rest of the battalion. We were all to move into the castle at Schwarzenberg in the near future, but were held in a field for a couple days pending our actual move into the castle. According to 565th Unit Reports, our goal was to maintain a civil and military order, control traffic, and guard the lines of communication and other assigned installations. Initially, we all came right into that big old castle in Schwarzenberg and within a couple of days moved out to take over guard duty.

On May 5th, the U.S. 7th Army made contact with the U.S. 5th Army, which had come up by Italy, and the new German Fuehur Doenitz was negotiating the surrender of all the German armies. Our assembly at Sheinfelt was the first time the 565th had been together since it had left England in October 1944.

On May 7th, the lettered batteries moved out to their respective guard areas, and on May 8th we celebrated VE Day. The Schwarzenberg Castle was an interesting place,

Chet Krause with an electric welder built by the headquarters motor pool.

one that most of us that served there shall never forget. The castle was on one end and the supply buildings were on other either side. A gate was to the north. Vats of beer were stored in the basements of one of the supply areas, and the enlisted men would go downstairs and drink the cool beer in excess. When they would come up and hit the warm air, their equilibrium would be challenged! Many had a hard time getting to their barracks or to the castle. I'm sure some of that beer found its way into the officers' quarters as well, but we would never admit to that.

Before our arrival, somebody descending the stairway probably got scared and fired a machine gun because one of the vats had sprung a leak, and there were about six inches of beer on the floor.

It is noted that orders required all people on guard duty to wear steel helmets. Of course, that was not warmly accepted because when the war was over, helmets were the first things we would have shed.

Chapter 11

(May 9 to July 10, 1945)

On May 11th, we got a message that all our batteries were to be relieved of the duties of protecting bridges, and we were looking forward to another move. At this particular time, we were still carrying our full supply of ammunition, which was 10,728 rounds of 40mm, 173,031 rounds of .50 caliber, 12,600 rounds of .45 caliber, 55,416 rounds of .30 caliber of 30.06, and 8,800 rounds of .30 caliber carbine ammunition. The battalion commander also requested some of the guard posts on abandoned railroads and insignificant spots be removed. In effect, we were guarding nothing.

We received 50 new men on May 12th. I imagine they were in replacement depots, and they had to be assigned somewhere. Also on the 12th, "A" Battery was relieved by the "A" Battery 457th AAA. The BN CO asked for a member of the CID to come into the battalion to discuss a rape case that had taken place at Wilhermsdorf (west of Furth/Nurnberg).

On May 13th, we received word from the 38th Brigade that we had been completely relieved of all our guarding missions in the area and that we were to move to an assembly area in the vicinity of Forchein Kreis, north of Nurnberg.

On May 15th, we had received a letter from Lt. Nelson, who had been wounded in Luxembourg City, saying that he was being returned to the United States. It was now May 17th, and we still had not moved to Forchein. We finally got permission from the 16th AAA Group that we could move two batteries, and we would move another couple batteries tomorrow. Thus, on May 18th, we were all in the Forchein area and had left the Schwarzenberg Castle behind.

It is recorded that on May 21st, the battalion became operational and the mission was security of the western portion of the Forchein Kreis area. That included five bridges in Forchein and the traffic control in Forchein, including two motorpools. We also had two foot patrols, two highway checkpoints, two guard posts at the APO and an MP detachment of 63 men and two officers.

On May 23rd, all executive vehicles were collected and turned in. I'm not quite sure whether they were some of our excess jeeps or civilian cars that had been collected along the way. I know that in the course of the war, it was a habit to pick up nice civilian cars. Officers and enlisted men would drive around in them. They were a great source of irritation to higher command because they were constantly using gasoline, as well as drivers, who should have been doing something else.

On May 24th, we moved out of the field and into the city of Forchein into better quarters. I'm not sure if that included all the lettered batteries or just headquarters. I can speak for headquarters; we moved into two or three homes that were just about a block from the railroad station. We in the motorpool set up our motorpool on the backside of the railroad station.

Recipients of bronze stars were notified and awards were to be made at a future retreat parade.

On the Pacific front, the U.S. Chief of Staff had completed a plan for the invasion of Japan. Of course, there were a lot of rumors floating around in our area that our unit or some other units were headed for the South Pacific theater of operation.

Apparently, our guard units at the various bridges had built some temporary shacks, and orders came down that these were to be removed and that nothing of significance should be present at a guard post.

It is also noted that Batteries "A," "B" and "C" all moved into some new command posts. Why they moved is unknown, but the reason was probably the same one headquarters used when it moved -- they got better billeting. "B" and "C" were also in Forchein. "A" CP was located at Hallerndorf. "D" was at Heroldsbach northwest of Forchein.

On May 29th, records indicate that we were forwarding some courtmartial cases to the 3rd Corps and the XX Corps. I don't know if we had fallen back into their command or whether this was something that had happened under their command. Also, there's an interesting note that 250 prisoners of war were going to arrive on May 30th, and apparently, it was going to be our duty to guard them. On the 29th, "D" Battery moved their command post. On the 30th we did receive 251 enlisted men and 16 German officers as POWs, and they were placed in a stockade. Guards were relieved at the postal regulating station because it had now been fenced.

On June 1st, Major Charles V. Frye, who had been our S3, the operations officer, was preparing for his departure and we were to have a retreat parade for him. Also included were M/Sgt. Conroy, the head of personnel, along with Sgt. Frank Katricak, the battalion communications sergeant, on the 16th Group Parade Field at 4:00 p.m. The entire event went off without error. It was quite an impressive ceremony. "C" Battery was judged to be the best in its formation with respect to the 565th. Special remarks were made during the retreat parade by Lt. Col. Martin, the executive officer of the 16th AAA Group.

Captain Moss was detailed to the S3, replacing Major Frye, and Captain Russell was detailed as S2, replacing Captain Moss. Sgt. Conroy and Sgt. Katricak were presented the bronze star for their efforts in the war. This award was dated May 21st, 1945. Word was also received that Cpl. Dake and Sgt. Sheldon were alive and well after their capture. We had previously heard that Warrant Officer Boyle was alive, and thus the three missing in action were accounted for (see appendix for further detail of this event by Harris Dake).

S3 Section was quite depleted of the ranks that had been with us all during the war because Major Frye, Warrant Officer Boyle, Sgt. Gravenstein and Sgt. Sheldon had all gone.

Light duty was performed by members of the lettered batteries, which furnished guards at railroad, as well as road, bridges to guard against sabotage as well as to pick up displaced persons.

June 4th was a Sunday, and there was a USO show in Nurnberg. Many of the organizations attended. It is also noted on this day that 533 enlisted men and 13 officers from the POW camps that were detailed for various types of work were under guard by members of the 565th. Approximately 100 POWs from the stockade were assigned to each battery each day.

The Third Riech's bombed-out retreat at Berchtesgaden.

It is indicated that on June 5th, the POWs' stockade had been moved to Pautzfeld. We were to establish a new dump south of the old one and to clean up the dump that had been in existence.

The Allies agreed on that day to divide Germany into four occupation zones and that Berlin be jointly occupied by all the major powers.

June 6th was the first anniversary of D-Day on the beaches in France. We recognized that day with a retreat parade. It is noted that on June 7th, Capt. Russell became the new S2 officer. The weather was warm and recommendations for the bronze star were sent out. Several of the enlisted men from the battalion's supply office were reduced to privates because they were caught intoxicated; they were transferred to lettered batteries.

On June 8th, Captain Russell was relieved as S2 and assigned to headquarters as its battery commander, with additional duties as claims officer and bomb reconnaissance officer. Lt. Olsen was relieved as commanding officer of headquarters and was assigned as S4 with additional duties. Captain Martin was relieved as S4 and assigned, without duty, to headquarters battery. Lt. Doremus was relieved of Battery "D" and assigned to headquarters as S2. Apparently, Captain Carter Martin of the Battalion Supply Office S4 was involved with the enlisted men who were caught intoxicated, and he was asked to resign.

Papers had been prepared in that regard and had been forwarded on to Group. We were gradually being relieved of the guarding of bridges on both railroads as well as roads. On June 10th it was announced that we were to have another retreat parade on June 13th at 4:30 p.m. Letters on bronze star awards were done over and three new men reported to the battalion and were assigned to the lettered battery. The number of POWs in our compound now was 544.

The retreat parade that had been scheduled for the battalion this week was cancelled because Group had called, and we were going to have an entire group parade as opposed to a parade for just the 565th. (Remember that a group is made up of three battalions.)

On June 13th, Sgt. Kallin was to go to Lucky Forward to take a test for warrant officer. A recreation trip was leaving soon to go into Czechoslovakia. The travelers would be gone several days using our own vehicles as transportation.

As June progressed, we began to get fewer men in the stockade. It's interesting to note that on one day we discharged 197 enlisted men and 10 officers, a total of 207 men. We received some new ones into the stockade as well. Gradually, these men were being processed out of stockade areas and released back into German society.

On June 17th, records indicate, "Word was received this date that the unit is Class 4 Category." I'm not sure what that means, but I suspect it means we didn't have a high priority for discharge and we didn't have a high priority for being considered for Pacific duty because of our average number of points per man in the battalion or the great mark we made in shooting down enemy airplanes in the course of the war. Eventually, we became inactivated, which occurred on Oct. 6th, 1945.

The men who had come into our battalion supply office (S4) received some promotions to replace the men who had been reduced in rank and transferred to the lettered batteries. It's also indicated that this would be the last promotions that would be received by this unit.

On June 22nd, there is a notation that says that there would be another trip to Czechoslovakia scheduled soon. The first trip had gotten off the ground and this was the second one. I was on that first trip and we got into four or five 2-1/2 ton trucks and went southeast into Czechoslovakia, then on to Hitler's home and Berchtesgaden.

A group of folk dancers at Pilsen, Czechoslovakia, performed for one of the postwar tours to that city.

We did not get up into the eagle's nest on top of the mountain, but just saw the mountain retreat at its base.

I'll never forget the beautiful mountain lake called "Konigssee" where we rested. We all wanted to go swimming. None of us had swimming suits, but we were told that we could proceed around the edge of the lake, go into a wooded area and jump into the lake in our shorts. Not realizing the temperature of the water, we all disrobed very quickly and made one mad dash to the lake and dove in. We suddenly realized the water was about 40 degrees and immediately lost our breath. While it had been our intention to swim out to a float about 50 feet at the end of a dock, we were lucky to make the dock and to get back to shore and dry off.

Our retreat did take us back to Pilson in Czechoslovakia, where at night they were having a folk festival. There was street dancing and a generally happy event in progress. It was a great relief for those of us who were able to go on that particular trip and get away from camp for a while.

You must understand that from the time we hit Luxembourg City in December until the war was over for us and we pulled back into Schwarzenberg in early May, we were under continuous duty, more or less. Then all of a sudden there was nothing for us to do. A trip like this was a stress reliever, as well as a way to see some country that we had never seen before. It is noted on the June 23rd a group left for Paris Detail at 7:30 -- another rest and relaxation event.

On June 24th, it is again noted that 190 POWs were released, which considerably cut down the number that was under our control. The next day shows that we had 131 of them left.

A second convoy to Berchtesgaden and Czechoslovakia left on June 25th. The first one arrived back on the 26th. It is also noted that Chaplain Bird and 19 men returned from Nancy, France from a rest and relaxation trip. Also during that same time, there were people going and coming from Paris. We were getting rest and relaxation. The month of March in the city of Luxembourg certainly wasn't a demanding one for us. This was a great relief from the boredom of having nothing to do in June after being very active in April and May.

Churchill was defeated, the Labor party won the elections and Attlee became the Prime Minister of Great Britain. I don't know if we GIs hated Churchill more than we hated Montgomery, but nonetheless, there certainly wasn't any love lost for either one of them. This was probably a day that we celebrated rather than feeling sorry for a defeated leader.

A report was received on the 27th that Pvt. Frank Orlandella of "A" Battery was killed in an accident in Czechoslovakia. He had been on a second trip to Berchtesgadon and Czechoslovakia.

At this particular time, we were assigned to the XII Corps; I'm not just sure when we passed from control of the 3rd Army. (I guess that means everyone in the 565th could wear the XII Corps patch, too.) It was also indicated that Capt. Martin was relieved of his assignment on June 27th, and on June 28th was going to leave for England for the 11th replacement depot.

Arrangements were made for Pvt. Orlandella's funeral at "A" Battery before having his body sent back to the United States.

The battalion was authorized three bronze stars, which were placed on service records as soon as possible. There's no indication of to whom those stars were assigned. Apparently, that was at the CO's discretion, or perhaps it meant that we were all authorized three battle stars on our ETO ribbon.

On June 29th, Battery "B" 565th replaced the 634th Battery "A" as security guard on Displaced Persons camp #3 and Displaced Persons camp #1, and that they were to keep one man on duty 24 hours a day.

We also received word that the 565th as a unit should be prepared to leave for La Harve, France on July 5th. We received an order that on July 1st, we would turn in all our primary armament, our 40mm as well as our M51s; we would convoy them to Butzbach, which is northwest of Frankfurt; and that we would move in two convoys five minutes apart via Nurnburg and Frankfurt.

July 1st saw the beginning of the depletion of the officers who had served the 565th, when Captain Russell was transferred to the 443rd Battalion and Lt. Farnsworth and some men from headquarters in "C" Battery were transferred to the 467th AAA Battalion.

We also received word that we probably would be going back to France or to La Harve, but our trip was merely being delayed, not cancelled. We also received word that Capt. Franklin, who was the battalion dentist, would probably be transferred sometime soon, but we had not received orders at this particular point.

On July 3rd, we found out that Lt. Wennen had been assigned to the 353rd Battalion and that our departure date from Forsheim for La Harve would now be July 10th. On July 5th, we found 11 enlisted men, including Sgt. Thomas, Sgt. Katricak, Sgt. Diegelman, Sgt. Fantauzzo and other enlisted men, were being transferred to the 91st AAA Group.

On July 6th we learned that another 40 men would be transferred to Group; these were all high point men who would be going home. Many of these were the key non-commissioned officers from headquarters and the lettered batteries. Lt. Doss was assigned to Nancy for duty in the recreation center there. Sgt. Drozd of our battalion supply office was lost at the AAA section of the 3rd Army.

July 7th was really a banner day for having key people depart the 565th. Orders were received transferring everybody but Maj. Pentecost, Capt. Moss, Capt. Olson, Lt. Clark and Hester and Mr. Dreeland to the 777th Automatic Weapons Battalion. In return, we received 12 officers from the 777th and three from the 353rd Searchlight Battalion. Only one of the latter reported. On this same day, 21 enlisted men were transferred to the 353rd Searchlight Battalion. Again, many of these men who were key men with high points would be sorely missed by the battalion. We also received road clearance to move to La Harve on July 10th and were notified that the 565th would be relieved of security duty at Forcheim by the 531st AAA Battalion. From this date forward, the 565th was under the command of Maj. Pentecost, who had been the executive officer since joining us in Camp Stewart, Georgia. Our new S1 officer was Lt. Saulbury.

On July 8th, we departed for La Harve, although no official records indicate the July 10th departure was moved up. Apparently, after everybody had departed from the headquarters, this type of record was abbreviated.

Chapter 12
(July 10 to Oct. 1, 1945)

We started our departure to La Harve about 1:30 p.m. and passed through Erlangen and Nurnburg first, then Neustadt, stopping in Aschaffenberg for the night. The next morning we were up and on the road by 5:30 a.m. and passed through Darmstadt, crossed the Rhine River at Mainz and proceeded along the west bank to Bingen and then through the mountains. We arrived at Trier about 3:00 p.m. and stayed in the bivouac area near the Moselle River for the night. In the meantime, our advanced party had arrived in La Harve and reported to the headquarters of the 16th Port Battalion. The next morning we got started early at 5:30 a.m. and went on through Luxembourg City, the country of Luxembourg and into France. We passed through Reimes and stayed at a camp in Soissms that evening. Our advanced party was told to report to the Provost Marshall in Rowen, more particularly, the 16th Sub. Port.

Again, the next day we departed at 5:30 a.m. and arrived about noon. Upon arrival, we received word that our new command unit would be Chanor Base of the Communications Zone. ("Chanor" was a contraction of the Channel and Normandy areas.) Rowen was just a few miles inland from La Harve.

When we came across the channel in December, we landed at La Harve and then convoyed into Rowen to the Red Horse assembly area where we got our act together before moving on to Luxembourg. There was a lot of work for us to do when we got to Rowen. Maj. Pentecost didn't even have time to cut a stencil assuming the command of the organization. (It is common practice in the Army that when someone leaves, nothing is said, but when someone comes in to assume command, they merely cut an order saying they are now in command. He then, as commander, cuts a stencil that details who is assigned to various tasks, and with all the turmoil in the officer ranks, there was a lot of that to do.)

On July 12th, we found out Maj. Dremen had joined us as executive officer as of July 8th. There were also orders cut assigning the officers that had come to us in the 777th to the various batteries.

Our new APO was now 567th, but it was subject to change because we probably were not designated to stay in the Rowen area too long as our mission there was rather light.

The 565th AAA Battalion relieved the 494th Port Battalion of the mission of guarding a pipeline, a Shell refinery, a petroleum dump and a railroad bridge. "C" Battery guarded the petroleum dump, "B" Battery guarded a power station, and "D" Battery guarded a bridge and storage tank along with some mobile patrols. These were our missions until something new came along.

I cannot find a list of officers that joined us from the 777th, so I can't detail them here.

On July 15th, a whole set of general orders (#4) were cut with details on how we were to guard each and every one of the posts that were assigned to us.

By July 16th, we had received orders to purge the files of unnecessary paperwork. Our files were to be checked for excess papers and eliminated. That work continued on into July 17th. The old papers were burned. All that would remain of the records of the 565th were the battalion commander's diary, the unit reports and the daily logs, which we received from the archives in Washington and which were reprinted about three years ago. This information is the basis of this history.

Articles of war were read to the men. Apparently, that was something that had to be done periodically. Once heard, the articles could be entered into the person's personal service record. Also, forms for passes to go into Rowen were being cut, and the Battalion Supply Office was looking for boxes to store our excess files, which were going into Belgium for storage.

On July 19th, Capt. Quillin reported from the 353rd and was assigned to headquarters as Battalion S2. Orders were cut on July 20th for a lot of enlisted men going to an educational school at Charleroi, Belgium, and Lt. Salzbury went to Brussels to Chanor Base to see if he could get information on what our assignments would be after our move to northern Belgium.

On July 21st, the battalion CO met with the first three grades and other non-commissioned officers with the thought of starting a non-commissioned officers club. This did become a reality after we reached Antwerp.

Records from July 26th reached a few more new names that we haven't before seen on the records. A Lt. Pretegaard was transferred to "C" Battery and a Cpt. Denver was made headquarters battery commander.

On July 27th, in the battalion commander's diary, there was no answer to a letter sent to Chanor Base on mechanics to be transferred to the 3rd Army. Apparently, some mechanics who had followed the whole convoy back into Rowen were needed back in Germany and were being transferred back there. Kelton Herndon, whom I worked with all through basic training and during our service in Europe, was one of those transferred.

It is indicated on the 27th that a truck went to Chanor Base to pick up a load of enlisted men who had been going to school there. Another truck went into Paris to pick up officers returning from school there. A new group to 3rd Army transfer would leave on Monday morning. Apparently, there were unlisted men, besides mechanics, who were being asked to go back into the area from whence they came.

In late July, the bylaws for the NCO club were approved, and on Aug. 2nd, the club came into being. It was doubtful that it would ever open for business. On Aug. 5th, the men that had been sent to the 3rd Army were returned with no particular reason. However, on Aug. 6th, a telegram advised us to transfer these replacements to replacement depot #2 in Namur, Belgium. It's also indicated that it was only mechanics and drivers who were being transferred. Also that there were some 15- and 72-hour passes issued for Paris.

On Aug. 8th, "D" Battery was relieved of its guard duty at Rowen, and the advanced party departed for Courcelles, Belgium. The main body of the battery was to depart on Aug. 10th to report to the commanding officer of the Signal Depot at Courcelles.

On Aug. 9th, the atomic bomb was dropped on Nagasaki.

On Aug. 10th, we received a request for anybody who had any experience in railroad. The entire railroad system in

Route of Liberty marker near the 1st Battalion headquarters. The route or road runs from Paris to the German border and leads through the center of Luxembourg City.

Europe had been destroyed and was being put back into use, and many of the civilians that were used to running railroads had become displaced persons or died in the course of the war. There was also an order requesting anyone with radar experience. We also received a request for some men to go to Berlin on temporary duty, which would be eight to 10 days.

By Aug. 13th, "D" Battery had already arrived in Belgium, and the battalion had received word that it was going to follow them there on Aug. 15th, with "A" Battery going up into Holland. On the 14th, we were busily packing that which remained, although our stay in Rowen had greatly reduced the amount of luggage we were carrying with us. Another new name that was picked up in the records was a Capt. Demet.

On Aug. 15th, we departed for Antwerp at 6:00 a.m. under cloudy skies. We passed through Charleroi and Mons and arrived in Antwerp, Belgium about 9:00 p.m. The Battalion's "B" and "C" Batteries were quartered in Lachttai barracks. "A" Battery continued north into Holland. It was V-J Day in the Pacific. The ETO continued to clean up what had happened during the war and returned men to the Zone of the Interior (U.S.A.). Once settled in Antwerp, we learned that our duties would be as guards on the docks and that it would take about all the men we had to do that. But passes and leaves continued as usual. Guard duty began on Aug. 17th.

By Aug. 20th, Chanor Base was inundating us with much of their paperwork. Some men had left for Barietz for training and Capt. Schell, our battalion surgeon, had left for school as well. He had not had opportunity to do that for a long time, and this was probably long overdue. Another person we picked up probably had come from the 777th; he was Lt. McConnel. We received orders on Aug. 21st that he was to be returned to the Zone of the Interior.

During the past several days, we had a lot of inclement weather, but this wasn't unusual for this part of the world. Some of the men who were on leave went to the United Kingdom. On Aug. 28th, all the men over 38 were sent to the 13th Port Battalion for return to the Zone of the Interior.

On Aug. 30th, we received a call from Chanor Base stating that Lt. Salsbury, Capt. Quillin and Capt. Demet were to be returned to the Zone of the Interior. On Aug. 31st, Maj. Dreman received the same orders. Nothing of particular importance happened on Sept. 2nd in Chanor Base, but it is noted that the Japanese surrender document was formally signed aboard the battleship "Missouri."

On Sept. 5th, Capt. Olson assumed command of headquarters battery, and new passes and furlough lists were not out yet, but apparently these were something that were offered in large quantities. Furloughs were generally to England or Paris and passes were into Brussels.

Another new name that I hadn't seen before, a Lt. Newby, was to go to school in England. The high point men from "D" Battery were being sent to the 16th reinforcement depot at Campugne for return to the United States.

We also received orders on Sept. 10th that Sgt. Jenisch was to return to the United States. Men were going on passes and furloughs all the time, and the chaplain and his furlough party returned on this particular date. Three men went to Oberammergau, Germany for school. They left on Sept. 13th.

On Sept. 17th, we received word that the battalion was going to move to Camp Top Hat, a port of debarkation where men were processed for return to the United States. We were going to be leaving our fine quarters to help in the processing of GIs heading home. We moved on the 20th.

On Sept. 24th, we were given notice that the battalion was to be deactivated, but no particular date was given. Passes and furloughs had been cancelled on the 25th pending this deactivation.

The last note in the battalion commander's diary was dated Oct. 1st, 1945. All it said was, "The files were packed this date. As soon as others come in, shipments will be made." We do know that the formal deactivation was dated Oct. 6, 1945.

It was behind this building that Willie Ford, a cook from headquarters battery, was struck with a spent .50 caliber bullet. (Photo taken 1989)

Hitler's house, 1933.

The Nest.

Hitler's house with the big window.

The entrance to the elevator, the only way to Hitler's house.

Hitler's house, 1947.

Bormann's house; Hitler's house.

Hitler's house as seen from Bormann's house.

Sherman tank at the entrance to the Diekirch (Luxembourg) Historical Museum (1989).

Veterans' memorial at American Military Cemetery at Hamm, Luxembourg.

Cemetery in Hamm, Luxembourg.

Gen. Patton's grave in the American Veterans Cemetery in Hamm, Luxembourg (1992).

Another view of the cemetery in Hamm (1989).

Guns, Bombers and New De Sotos

A Frank Statement of Policy by the President of De Soto Motor Corporation.

IT'S ONLY NATURAL *that people all over the country are asking questions like these:*

"Just what is happening behind the scenes in Detroit these days?"

"Will there be new models this fall?"

"Can the manufacturer turn out the new car I need, and meet defense demands, too?"

We'd like to answer those questions—so far as De Soto's plans are concerned.

By BYRON C. FOY, President

As YOU READ THIS, De Soto is already rolling on a two-point production program for the coming year.

First, as part of Chrysler Corporation's Number One Job —National Defense—we are building:

Parts for one of the world's finest anti-aircraft guns.

Parts for an already world-famous bomber.

Second, and *only to the extent the growing defense program permits*, a line of motor cars that are the finest De Sotos we've ever built.

We look upon each phase of this program as vital. The need for guns and more guns...bombers and more bombers...is urgent.

And everybody knows that the automobile has far outstripped its early days as a luxury purchase, and has become a vital necessity without which we would suffer severe dislocations in the day-to-day life and transportation system of the country.

More than half of the total car mileage covered and three-fourths of all trips made are *necessary* to earning a livelihood.

In our business activities, we wear out and replace more than 2,000,000 cars annually.

It is important that men and machines be kept busy at this normal task of fulfilling civilian requirements until such men and machines are needed and can be absorbed in expanding defense production.

That's why we undertook to meet our share of the country's civilian needs for transportation with this finest of De Soto cars, which was designed and tooled *before* the present need for defense production became apparent.

Frankly, we do not know how many of these great De Soto cars we will produce in the coming year, for with us the building of materials for the defense of our country will always come first. But we do know that every car we build (within the limits of our curtailed schedule) will be the finest we know how to produce...finest in engineering...finest in workmanship...finest in materials...finest in design.

The new De Sotos will be on display at your nearby De Soto dealer's showroom early in October. Watch for them—they're well-worth seeing.

If it is going to be necessary for you to replace your present car in 1942, it isn't too soon to start telling your De Soto dealer just what your needs will be. He'll do his best—within the limits of curtailed production—to help you.

Byron C Foy

PRESIDENT, DE SOTO MOTOR CORPORATION
DIVISION OF CHRYSLER CORPORATION

P.S. May I suggest that right now, when we face a possible shortage of new cars, a good used car honestly reconditioned by a De Soto dealer offers any man a lot of good unused transportation at bargain prices and diverts no material or needed man-hours from the essential task of arming our republic.

A period advertisement that appeared in a 1944 issue of Life magazine.

Order of Battle

<u>12th ARMY GROUP:</u>	General Omar N. Bradley
<u>U.S. 9th Army:</u>	Lieutenant General William H. Simpson
XIII Corps:	Major General Alvan C. Gillem Jr.
35 Infantry Division:	Major General Paul W. Baade
84 Infantry Division:	Major General A. R. Bolling
102 Infantry Division:	Major General Frank A. Keating
XVI Corps:	Major General John B. Anderson
29 Infantry Division:	Major General Charles G. Gerhardt
75 Infantry Division:	Major General Ray E. Porter
79 Infantry Division:	Major General Ira T. Wyche
95 Infantry Division:	Major General Harry L. Twaddle
XIX Corps:	Major General Raymond S. McLain
2 Armored Division:	Major General Isaac D. White
8 Armored Division:	Major General John M. Devine
30 Infantry Division:	Major General Leland S. Hobbs
83 Infantry Division:	Major General Robert C. Macon
<u>U.S. 1st Army:</u>	General Courtney H. Hodges
78 Infantry Division:	Major General Edward P. Parker Jr.
VII Corps:	Lieutenant General J. Lawton Collins
3 Armored Division:	Brigadier General Doyle O. Hickey
9 Infantry Division:	Major General Louis A. Craig
69 Infantry Division:	Major General Emil F. Reinhardt
104 Infantry Division:	Major General Terry M. Allen
VIII Corps:	Major General Troy H. Middleton
6 Armored Division:	Brigadier General George W. Read Jr.
76 Infantry Division:	Major General William R. Schmidt
87 Infantry Division:	Major General Frank L. Culin Jr.
89 Infantry Division:	Major General Thomas D. Finley
<u>U.S. 3rd Army:</u>	General George S. Patton Jr.
4 Infantry Division:	Major General Harold W. Blakeley
70 Infantry Division:	Major General Allison J. Barnett
III Corps:	Major General James A. Van Fleet
14 Armored Division:	Major General Albert C. Smith
99 Infantry Division:	Major General Walter E. Lauer
V Corps:	Major General Clarence R. Huebner
9 Armored Division:	Major General John W. Leonard
16 Armored Division:	Brigadier General John L. Pierce
1 Infantry Division:	Major General Clift Andrus
2 Infantry Division:	Major General Walter M. Robertson
97 Infantry Division:	Brigadier General Milton B. Halsey
XII Corps:	Major General S. LeRoy Irwin
4 Armored Division:	Major General William M. Hoge
11 Armored Division:	Major General Homes E. Dager
5 Infantry Division:	Major General Albert E. Brown
26 Infantry Division:	Major General Willard S. Paul
90 Infantry Division:	Major General Herbert L. Earnest
XX Corps:	Lieutenant General Walton H. Walker
13 Armored Division:	Major General John Milliken
65 Infantry Division:	Major General Stanley E. Reinhart
71 Infantry Division:	Major General Willard G. Wyman

80 Infantry Division:	Major General Horace L. McBride
U.S. 15th Army:	Lieutenant General Leonard T. Gerow
66 Infantry Division:	Major General Herman F. Kramer
106 Infantry Division:	Major General Donald A. Stroh
XXII Corps:	Major General Ernest N. Harmon

---

17 Airborne Division:	Major General William M. Miley
94 Infantry Division:	Major General Harry J. Malony
XXIII Corps:	Major General Hugh J. Gaffey

---

28 Infantry Division:	Major General Norman D. Cota
6th ARMY GROUP:	General Jacob L. Devers
U.S. 7th Army:	Lieutenant General Alexander M. Patch
12 Armored Division:	Major General Roderick R. Allen
63 Infantry Division:	Major General Louis E. Hibbs
45 Infantry Division:	Major General Robert T. Frederick
100 Infantry Division:	Major General Withers A. Burress
XXI Corps:	Major General Frank W. Milburn

---

101 Airborne Division:	Major General Maxwell D. Taylor
36 Infantry Division:	Major General John E. Dahlquist
XV Corps:	Lieutenant General Wade H. Haislip

---

20 Armored Division:	Major General Orlando Ward
3 Infantry Division:	Major John O' Daniel
42 Infantry Division:	Major General Harry J. Collins
86 Infantry Division:	Major General Harris M. Melasky
VI Corps:	Major General Edward H. Brooks

---

10 Armored Division:	Major General W. H. Morris Jr.
44 Infantry Division:	Major General William F. Dean
103 Infantry Division:	Major General Anthony Mc Auliffe
Ire Armee francaise:	General d'Armee Jean de Lattre de Tassigny

---

21st ARMY GROUP:	Field Marshall Sir Bernard L. Montgomery
Canadian 1st Army:	General Henry D. Crerar
British 2nd Army:	Lieutenant General Sir Miles C. Dempsey
XVIII Airborne Corps:	Major General Matthew B. Ridway

---

5 Armored Division:	Major General Lunsford E. Oliver
7 Armored Division:	Major General Robert W. Hasbrouck
82 Airborne Division:	Major General James M. Gavin
8 Infantry Division:	Major General Bryant E. Moore

Reserves:

1st Allied Airborne Army:	Lieutenant General Lewis H. Brereton
13 Airborne Division:	Major General Elbridge G. Chapman Jr.

Antiaircraft Artillery Units Serving in the ETO

I Antiaircraft Artillery Brigades
---

31 AA Bde
34 AA Bde
35 AA Bde
38 AA Bde (Luxembourg 08.02.45)
44 AA Bde
47 AA Bde
49 AA Bde
50 AA Bde
51 AA Bde
52 AA Bde
54 AA Bde
55 AA Bde
56 AA Bde
74 AA Bde

II Antiaircraft Artillery Groups
----
1 AA Gp
2 AA Gp
5 AA Gp (Luxembourg (19.03.45)
7 AA Gp
8 AA Gp
9 AA Gp
11 AA Gp
12 AA Gp
16 AA Gp (Luxembourg (22.10.44 04.02.45)
17 AA Gp
18 AA Gp
19 AA Gp
21 AA Gp (Luxembourg (28.03.45)
22 AA Gp
23 AA Gp
24 AA Gp
26 AA Gp (Luxembourg (06.10.44)
27 AA Gp (Luxembourg (22.12.44)
29 AA Gp
30 AA Gp
31 AA Gp
32 AA Gp (Luxembourg (19.12.44)
34 AA Gp
38 AA Gp
45 AA Gp
68 AA Gp
71 AA Gp
80 AA Gp
91 AA Gp
92 AA Gp

103 AA Gp
118 AA Gp

207 AA Gp (Luxembourg (04.02.45)
213 AA Gp

III Antiaircraft Artillery Battalions
----
62 AAA Gun Bn (Mobile)
67 AAA Gun Bn (Mobile)
68 AAA Gun Bn (Mobile)
72 AAA Gun Bn (Mobile)
73 AAA Gun Bn (Mobile)
74 AAA Gun Bn (Mobile)
87 AAA Gun Bn (Mobile)

103 AAA AW Bn (Mobile)-att. 1ID
106 AAA AW Bn (SP)-att. 45ID
107 AAA AW Bn (Mobile)
108 AAA Gun Bn (Mobile)
109 AAA Gun Bn (Mobile)-att. 3 Army
110 AAA Gun Bn (Mobile)
112 AAA Gun Bn (Semimobile)
113 AAA Gun Bn (Semimobile)
114 AAA Gun Bn (Semimobile)
115 AAA Gun Bn (Mobile)-att. 3 Army
116 AAA Gun Bn (Mobile)-att. 30ID
118 AAA Gun Bn (Mobile)
119 AAA Gun Bn (Mobile)
120 AAA Gun Bn (Mobile)
124 AAA Gun Bn (Mobile)
125 AAA Gun Bn (Mobile)
126 AAA Gun Bn (Mobile)
127 AAA Gun Bn (Mobile)
128 AAA Gun Bn (Mobile)
129 AAA Gun Bn (Mobile)
131 AAA Gun Bn (Mobile)
132 AAA Gun Bn (Mobile)
133 AAA Gun Bn (Mobile)
134 AAA Gun Bn (Mobile)

135 AAA Gun Bn (Mobile)
136 AAA Gun Bn (Mobile)
141 AAA Gun Bn (Mobile)
142 AAA Gun Bn (Mobile)
143 AAA Gun Bn (Mobile)-att. 1 Army
167 AAA Gun Bn (Semimobile)
184 AAA Gun Bn (Mobile)
195 AAA Gun Bn (SP)-att. 2AD
197 AAA AW Bn (SP)

203 AAA AW Bn (SP) -att. 7AD
204 AAA AW Bn (Semimobile)
214 AAA Gun Bn (Mobile)
215 AAA Gun Bn (Semimobile)
216 AAA Gun Bn (Mobile)
217 AAA Gun Bn (Mobile)-att. 3 Army

376 AAA AW Bn (Mobile)
377 AAA AW Bn (Mobile)-att. 4ID
379 AAA AW Bn (Mobile)
385 AAA AW Bn (Semimobile)
386 AAA AW Bn (Semimobile)
387 AAA AW Bn (SP)-att. 5AD
390 AAA AW Bn (Semimobile)-att. 26ID
391 AAA AW Bn (Semimobile)
397 AAA AW Bn (Semimobile)
398 AAA AW Bn (SP)-att. 44ID-14AD

400 AAA AW Bn (Semimobile)
405 AAA Gun Bn (Semimobile)
406 AAA Gun Bn (Semimobile)
407 AAA Gun Bn (Semimobile)
409 AAA Gun Bn (Semimobile)
410 AAA Gun Bn (Semimobile)
411 AAA Gun Bn (Mobile)
413 AAA Gun Bn (Mobile)-att. 9ID-3AD
414 AAA Gun Bn (Semimobile)
430 AAA AW Bn (Mobile)
431 AAA AW Bn (Mobile)-att. 42ID
433 AAA AW Bn (Mobile)-att. 70ID
436 AAA AW Bn (Mobile)-att. 63ID
437 AAA AW Bn (Mobile)
438 AAA AW Bn (Mobile)
439 AAA AW Bn (Mobile)
440 AAA AW Bn (Mobile)-att. 75ID-106ID
441 AAA AW Bn (SP)-att. 3ID
443 AAA AW Bn (SP)-.att. 36ID
444 AAA AW Bn (Mobile)-att. 97ID
445 AAA AW Bn (Mobile)-att. 8ID
446 AAA AW Bn (Mobile)-att. 28ID-86ID
447 AAA AW Bn (Mobile)-att. 28ID
448 AAA AW Bn (Mobile)-att. 30ID-35ID
449 AAA AW Bn (Mobile)-att. 5ID
450 AAA AW Bn (Cld) (Mobile)
451 AAA AW Bn (Mobile)-att. XII Corps
452 AAA AW Bn (Cld) (Mobile)
453 AAA AW Bn (Mobile)-att. 83ID
455 AAA AW Bn (Mobile)
456 AAA AW Bn (Mobile)-att. 3 Army
457 AAA AW Bn (Mobile)-att. XII Corps
459 AAA AW Bn (Mobile)-att. 29ID-30ID-35ID
460 AAA AW Bn (Mobile)
461 AAA AW Bn (Mobile)-att. 69ID
462 AAA AW Bn (Mobile)-att. 2ID
463 AAA AW Bn (Mobile)-att. 79ID
465 AAA AW Bn (Mobile)-att. 94ID
467 AAA AW Bn (SP)-att. 8AD
468 AAA AW Bn (SP)-att. 20AD
473 AAA AW Bn (SP)-att. 83ID-84ID-94ID-95ID-102ID-8AD
474 AAA AW Bn (SP)
480 AAA AW Bn (Semimobile)
481 AAA AW Bn (Semimobile)
482 AAA AW Bn (SP)-att. 9AD

486 AAA AW Bn (SP)-att. 3AD
489 AAA AW Bn (SP)-att. 4AD
491 AAA AW Bn (Semimobile)
494 AAA Gun Bn (Semimobile)
495 AAA Gun Bn (Semimobile)

519 AAA Gun Bn (Semimobile)
530 AAA AW Bn (Mobile)-att. 71ID
531 AAA AW Bn (Mobile)
533 AAA AW Bn (Mobile)
534 AAA AW Bn (Mobile)
535 AAA AW Bn (Mobile)-att. 99ID
537 AAA AW Bn (Mobile)-att. 90ID
542 AAA AW Bn (Mobile)-att. 97ID
546 AAA AW Bn (Mobile)-att. 65ID
547 AAA AW Bn (Mobile)-att. 95ID
548 AAA AW Bn (Mobile)-att. 102ID
549 AAA AW Bn (Mobile)
550 AAA AW Bn (Mobile)-att. 89ID
551 AAA AW Bn (Mobile)
552 AAA AW Bn (Mobile)-att. 78ID
553 AAA AW Bn (Mobile)
554 AAA AW Bn (Mobile)-att. 29ID
555 AAA AW Bn (Mobile)-att. 104ID
556 AAA AW Bn (Mobile)-att. 102ID
557 AAA AW Bn (Mobile)-att. 84ID
558 AAA AW Bn (Mobile)
559 AAA AW Bn (Mobile)-att. 87ID
562 AAA AW Bn (Mobile)
563 AAA AW Bn (Mobile)-att. 106ID
564 AAA AW Bn (Mobile)
565 AAA AW Bn (Mobile)-att. 3 Army
566 AAA AW Bn (Mobile)
567 AAA AW Bn (Mobile)-att. 101A/BD
568 AAA AW Bn (Mobile)
569 AAA AW Bn (Mobile)
571 AAA AW Bn (SP)
572 AAA AW Bn (SP)-att. 12AD
573 AAA AW Bn (SP)
574 AAA AW Bn (SP)-att. 13AD
575 AAA AW Bn (SP)-att. 11AD
597 AAA AW Bn (Mobile)
599 AAA AW Bn (Mobile)

601 AAA Gun Bn (Semimobile)
602 AAA Gun Bn (Semimobile)
605 AAA Gun Bn (Semimobile)
633 AAA AW Bn (Mobile)-att. 80ID
634 AAA AW Dn (Mobile)-att. 106ID-82A/BD
635 AAA AW Bn (Mobile)-att. VIII Corps
639 AAA AW Bn (mobile)

740 AAA Gun Bn (Semimobile)
749 AAA Gun Bn (Semimobile)
716 AAA AW Bn (Semimobile)
777 AAA AW Bn (SP)-att. 6AD
778 AAA AW Bn (SP)-att. 76ID
784 AAA AW Bn (Semimobile)
787 AAA AW Bn (Semimobile)
788 AAA AW Bn (Semimobile)
789 AAA AW Bn (Semimobile)
791 AAA AW Bn (Semimobile)
792 AAA AW Bn (Semimobile)
794 AAA AW Bn (Semimobile)
794 AAA AW Bn (Semimobile)
795 AAA AW Bn (Semimobile)
796 AAA AW Bn (SP)-att. 10AD
798 AAA AW Bn (Mobile)
815 AAA AW Bn (Mobile)
838 AAA AW Bn (Mobile)
839 AAA AW Bn (Mobile)-att. 86ID
863 AAA AW Bn (Semimobile)
893 AAA AW Bn (Mobile)
894 AAA AW Bn (Mobile)
895 AAA AW Bn (Mobile)
896 AAA AW Bn (Semimobile)
897 AAA AW Bn (Semimobile)
898 AAA AW Bn (Mobile)
899 AAA AW Bn (Semimobile)

910 AAA AW Bn (Mobile)

IV Airborne Antiaircraft Artillery Battalions
----
80 Abn. AA Bn.- 82 A/B D
81 Abn. AA Bn.-101 A/B D
153 Abn. AA Bn.- 13 A/B D
155 Abn. AA Bn.- 17 A/B D

V Antiaircraft Artillery Searchlight Battalions
----
225 AAA S/L Bn.
226 AAA S/L Bn.
231 AAA S/L Bn.
353 AAA S/L Bn.
357 AAA S/L Bn.

VI Antiaircraft Balloon Battalions
----
320 AA Balloon Bn, Very Low Altitude (Cld)

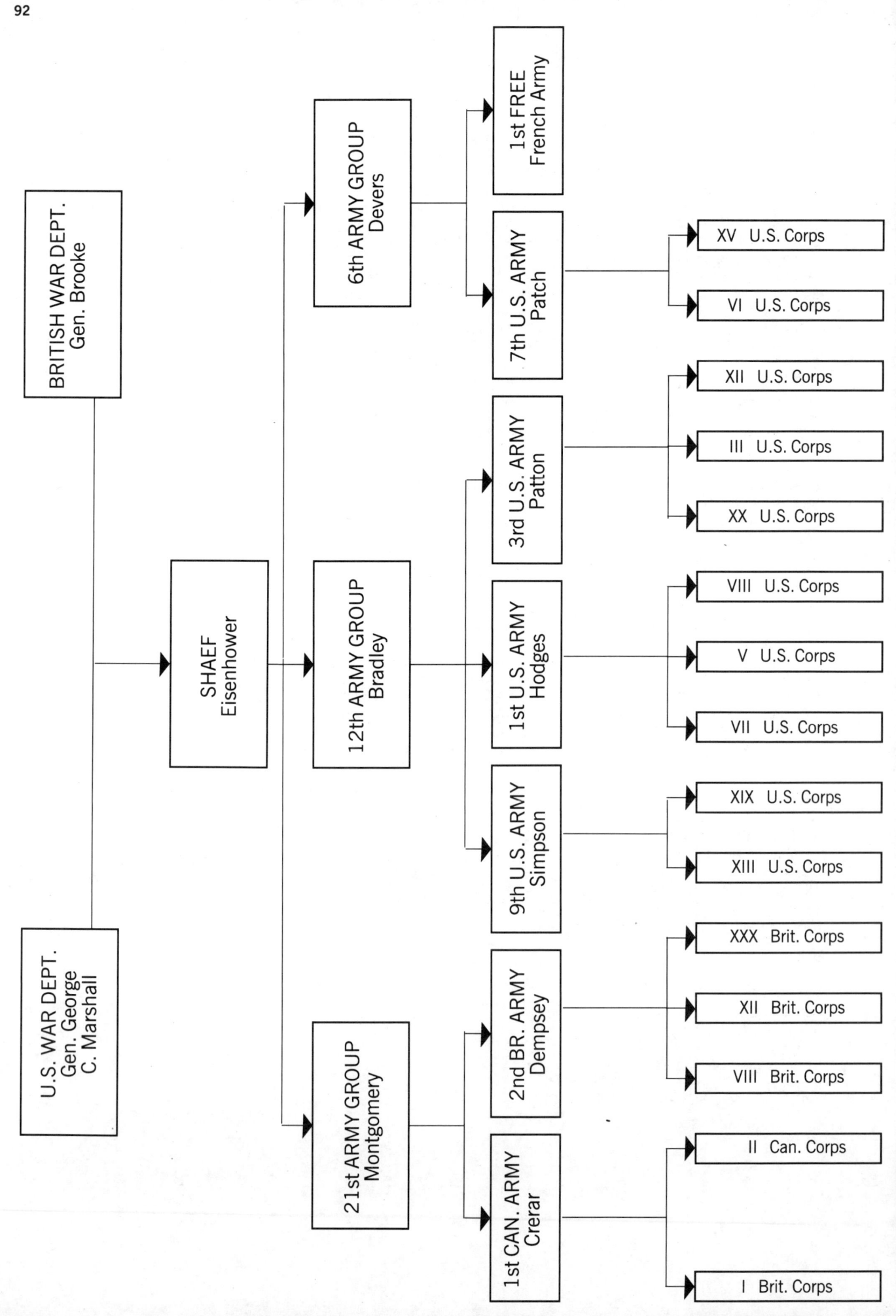

```
U.S. WAR DEPT.                                          ┌─ 1st FREE French Army
Gen. George          ┌─ 6th ARMY GROUP ─┤
C. Marshall          │   Devers         │               ┌─ XV  U.S. Corps
                     │                  └─ 7th U.S. ARMY┤
                     │                     Patch        └─ VI  U.S. Corps
BRITISH WAR DEPT.    │
Gen. Brooke          │                                  ┌─ XII U.S. Corps
                     │                  ┌─ 3rd U.S. ARMY├─ III U.S. Corps
       │             │                  │   Patton      └─ XX  U.S. Corps
       ▼             │                  │
    SHAEF ──────────►│── 12th ARMY GROUP┤               ┌─ VIII U.S. Corps
  Eisenhower         │    Bradley       ├─ 1st U.S. ARMY├─ V    U.S. Corps
                     │                  │   Hodges      └─ VII  U.S. Corps
                     │                  │
                     │                  └─ 9th U.S. ARMY┌─ XIX  U.S. Corps
                     │                      Simpson     └─ XIII U.S. Corps
                     │
                     │                                  ┌─ XXX  Brit. Corps
                     │                  ┌─ 2nd BR. ARMY ├─ XII  Brit. Corps
                     └─ 21st ARMY GROUP─┤   Dempsey     └─ VIII Brit. Corps
                        Montgomery      │
                                        └─ 1st CAN. ARMY┌─ II Can. Corps
                                            Crerar      └─ I  Brit. Corps
```

92

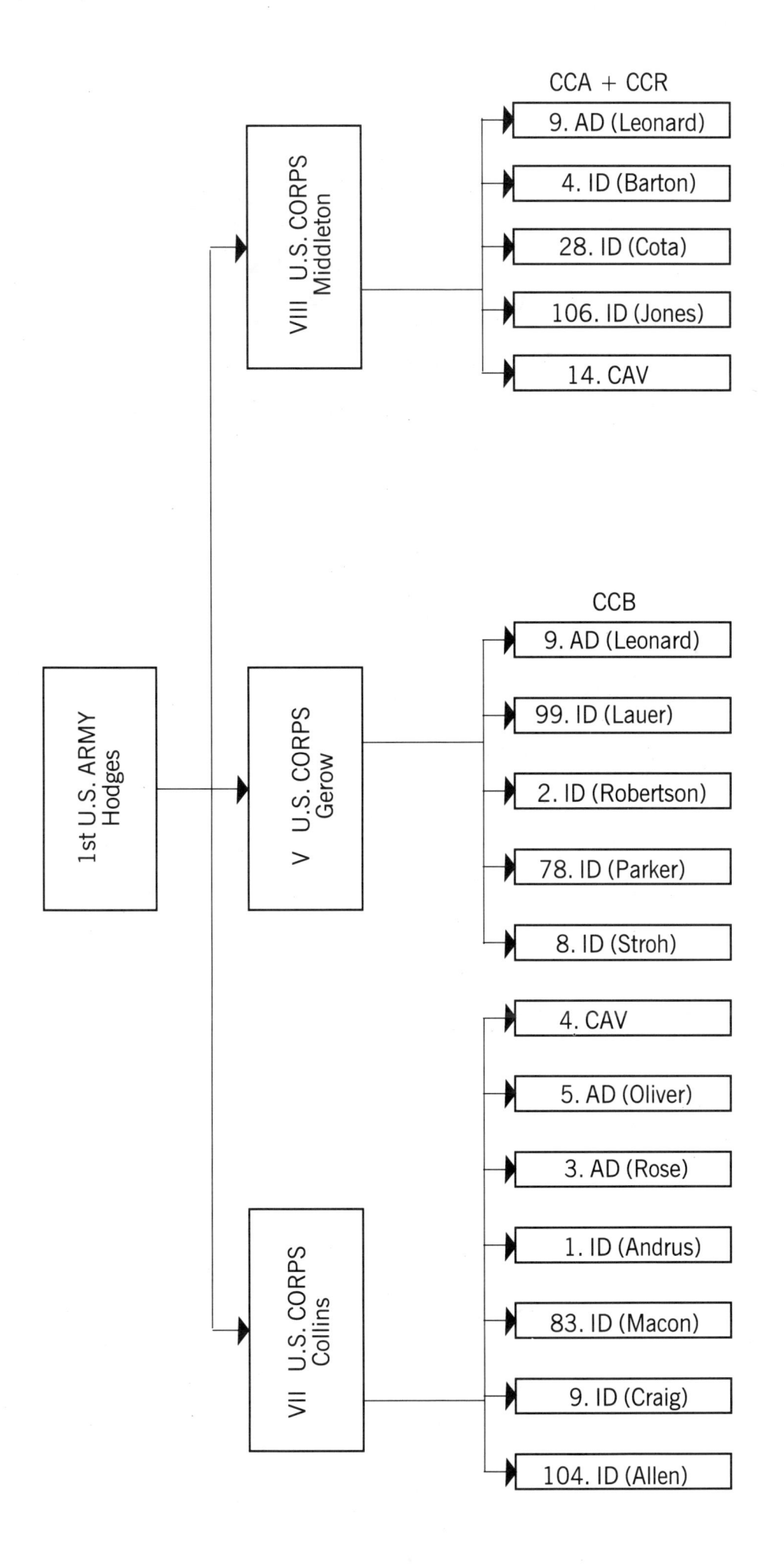

```
1st U.S. ARMY
Hodges
├── VIII U.S. CORPS Middleton
│   ├── 9. AD (Leonard)        [CCA + CCR]
│   ├── 4. ID (Barton)
│   ├── 28. ID (Cota)
│   ├── 106. ID (Jones)
│   └── 14. CAV
├── V U.S. CORPS Gerow
│   ├── 9. AD (Leonard)        [CCB]
│   ├── 99. ID (Lauer)
│   ├── 2. ID (Robertson)
│   ├── 78. ID (Parker)
│   └── 8. ID (Stroh)
└── VII U.S. CORPS Collins
    ├── 4. CAV
    ├── 5. AD (Oliver)
    ├── 3. AD (Rose)
    ├── 1. ID (Andrus)
    ├── 83. ID (Macon)
    ├── 9. ID (Craig)
    └── 104. ID (Allen)
```

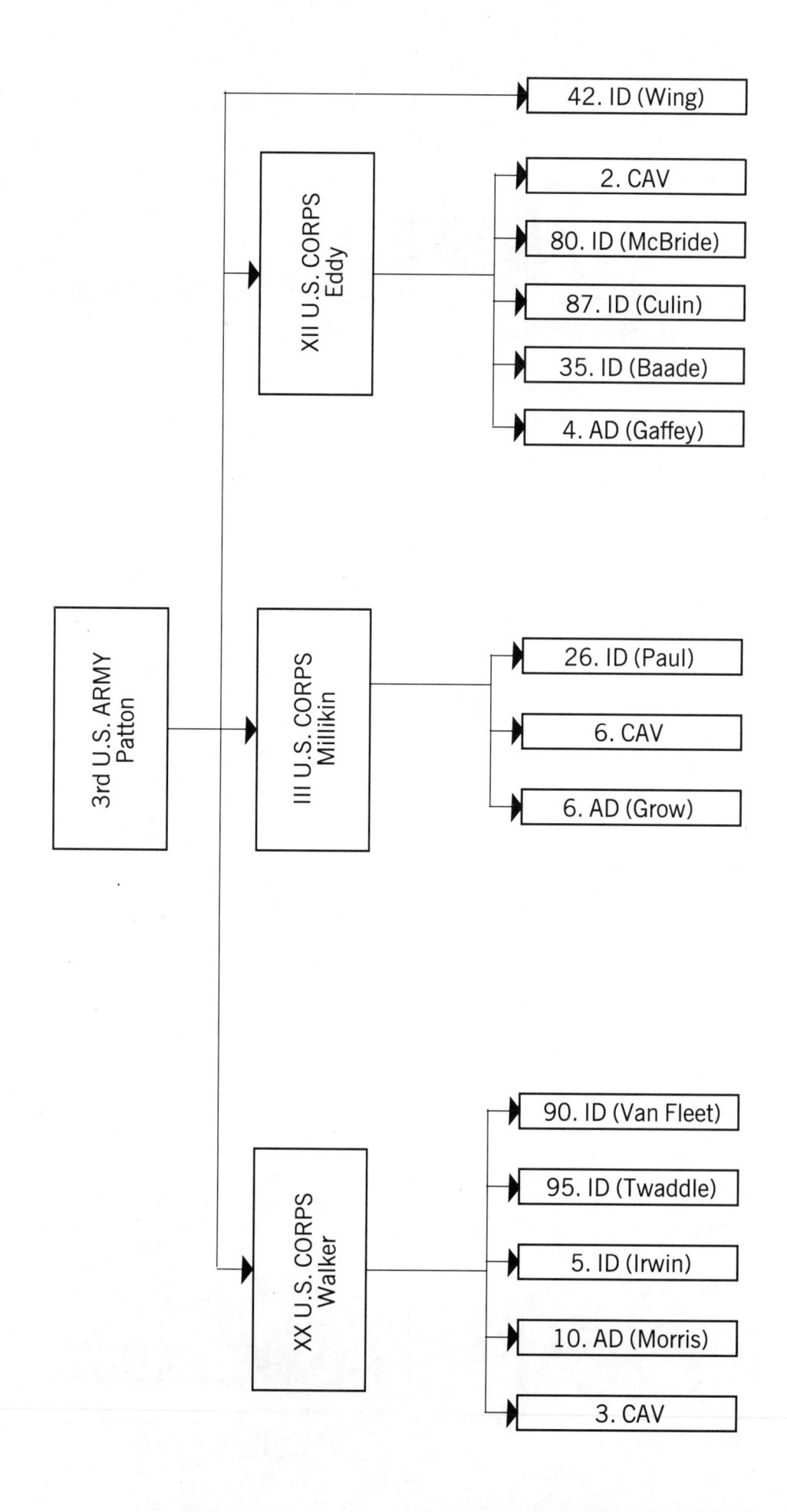

```
3rd U.S. ARMY
Patton
├── XII U.S. CORPS — Eddy
│   ├── 42. ID (Wing)
│   ├── 2. CAV
│   ├── 80. ID (McBride)
│   ├── 87. ID (Culin)
│   ├── 35. ID (Baade)
│   └── 4. AD (Gaffey)
├── III U.S. CORPS — Millikin
│   ├── 26. ID (Paul)
│   ├── 6. CAV
│   └── 6. AD (Grow)
└── XX U.S. CORPS — Walker
    ├── 90. ID (Van Fleet)
    ├── 95. ID (Twaddle)
    ├── 5. ID (Irwin)
    ├── 10. AD (Morris)
    └── 3. CAV
```

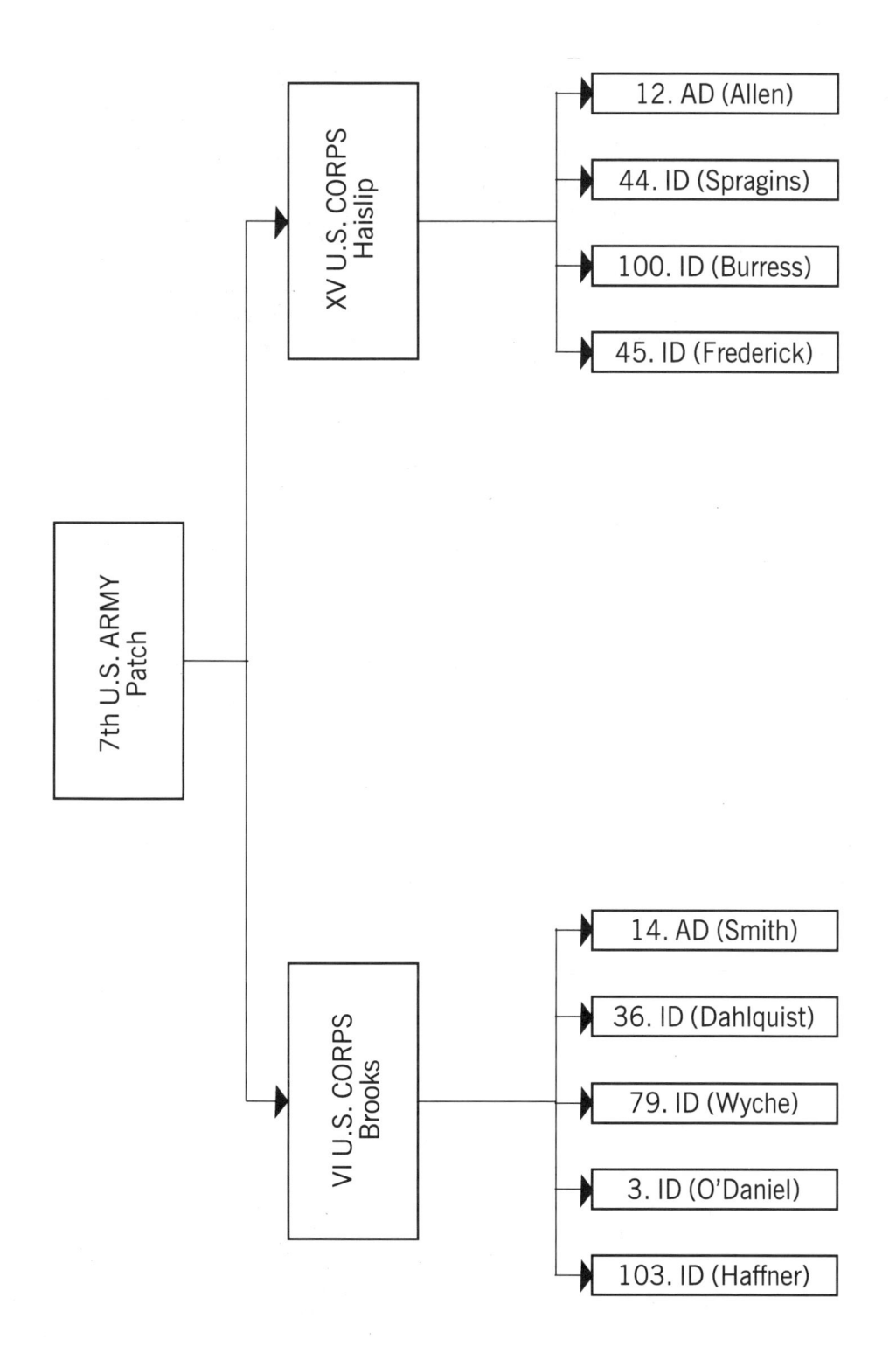

```
                                    ┌─────────────────────┐
                                 ┌─▶│ 12. AD (Allen)      │
                                 │  └─────────────────────┘
                                 │  ┌─────────────────────┐
               ┌──────────────┐  ├─▶│ 44. ID (Spragins)   │
            ┌─▶│ XV U.S. CORPS│──┤  └─────────────────────┘
            │  │ Haislip      │  │  ┌─────────────────────┐
            │  └──────────────┘  ├─▶│ 100. ID (Burress)   │
            │                    │  └─────────────────────┘
            │                    │  ┌─────────────────────┐
┌──────────┐│                    └─▶│ 45. ID (Frederick)  │
│ 7th U.S. ││                       └─────────────────────┘
│ ARMY     │┤
│ Patch    ││                       ┌─────────────────────┐
└──────────┘│                    ┌─▶│ 14. AD (Smith)      │
            │                    │  └─────────────────────┘
            │                    │  ┌─────────────────────┐
            │  ┌──────────────┐  ├─▶│ 36. ID (Dahlquist)  │
            └─▶│ VI U.S. CORPS│──┤  └─────────────────────┘
               │ Brooks       │  │  ┌─────────────────────┐
               └──────────────┘  ├─▶│ 79. ID (Wyche)      │
                                 │  └─────────────────────┘
                                 │  ┌─────────────────────┐
                                 ├─▶│ 3. ID (O'Daniel)    │
                                 │  └─────────────────────┘
                                 │  ┌─────────────────────┐
                                 └─▶│ 103. ID (Haffner)   │
                                    └─────────────────────┘
```

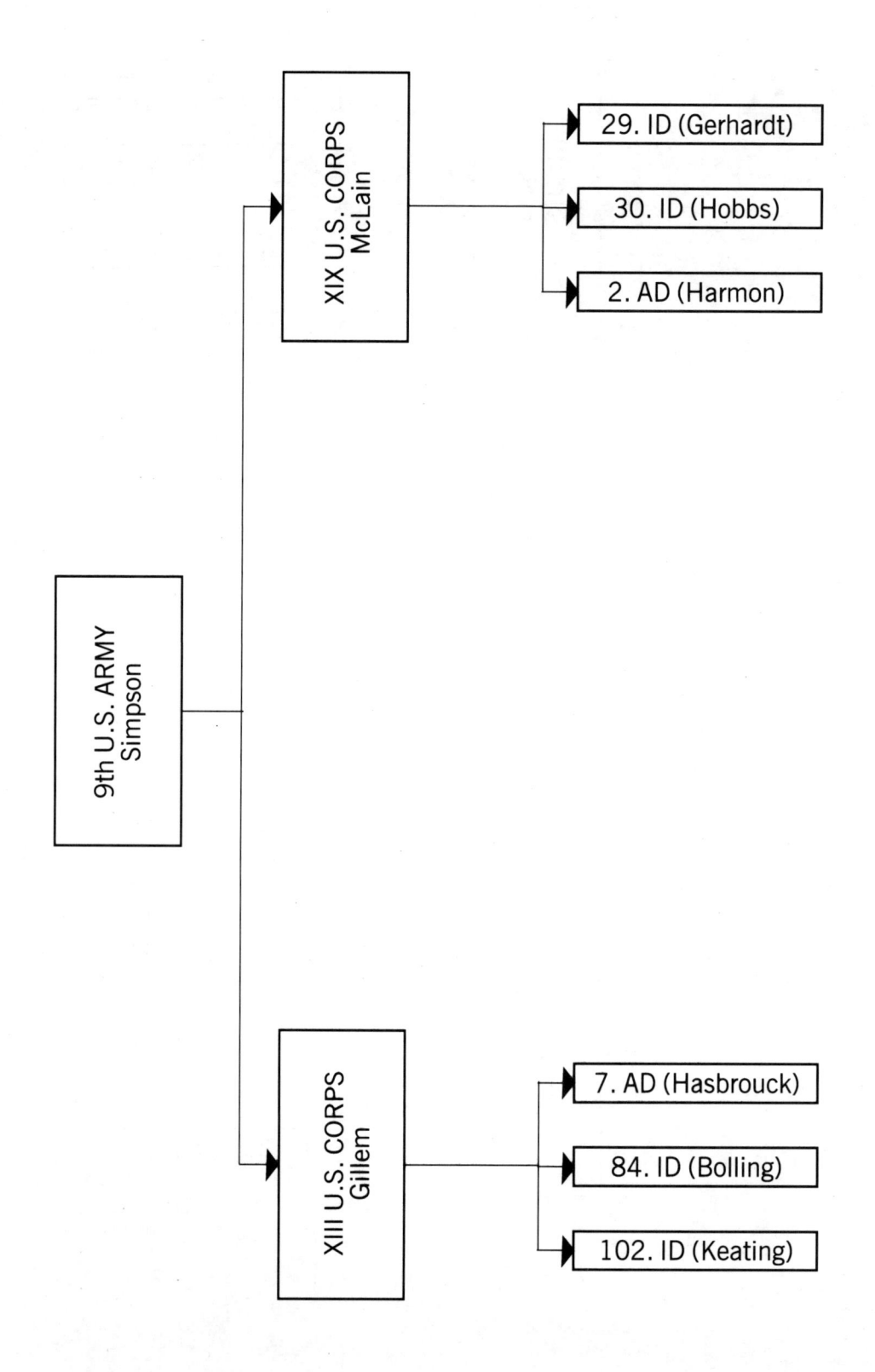

```
9th U.S. ARMY
Simpson
├── XIX U.S. CORPS McLain
│   ├── 29. ID (Gerhardt)
│   ├── 30. ID (Hobbs)
│   └── 2. AD (Harmon)
└── XIII U.S. CORPS Gillem
    ├── 7. AD (Hasbrouck)
    ├── 84. ID (Bolling)
    └── 102. ID (Keating)
```

Monthly Operations Reports

Reprinted from the 3rd Army After Action Reports

Chapter 7
December Operations

The 32nd Antiaircraft Artillery Group which was assigned to Third US Army on 22 November, arrived in the vicinity of Joudreville (U5978) on 2 December and was attached to the III Corps. Plans were made to attach additional Antiaircraft units to the corps on the normal scale, pending availability of units.

By 3 December, the advance of the Third US Army on Saarlautern (Q2981) indicated that this city would fall within a few days. Two batteries of the 119th Antiaircraft Artillery Gun Battalion were moved therefore from Thionville (U8685) to the vicinity of Saarlautern (Q2981) to protect the vital bridge across the Saar River which had been seized intact. The other two batteries remained at Thionville (U8685).

The advance on Sarreguemines (Q5257) was likewise progressing satisfactorily and the 115th Antiaircraft Artillery Gun Battalion was moved forward to the vicinity of Puttelange (Q4151) pending the clearance of Sarreguemines (Q5257) which would be the focal point of communications on the south flank of the army. Arrangements were made to establish this city as an Inner Artillery Zone effective 7 December.

On 6 December, IX Air Defense Command took over complete responsibility for Antiaircraft defense of Verdun (U5978) and consequently the two batteries of the 120th Antiaircraft Artillery Gun Battalion were moved forward to Pont-A-Mousson (U7735). Two batteries of the 411th Antiaircraft Artillery Gun Battalion were relieved at that crossing and moved north to reinforce the Antiaircraft gun defenses at Metz (U8858).

To the north, the two batteries of the 119th Antiaircraft Artillery Gun Battalion, still at Thionville (U8685), were moved forward for the defense of Saarlautern (Q2981) and the 38th Antiaircraft Artillery Brigade took over from XX Corps responsibility for defense of the crossing at Thionville (U8685) and vicinity.

By this time it had become apparent that all Saar River crossings in the XX Corps zone would be south of Merzig (Q2195). The Inner Artillery Zone which had previously been requested for that city was therefore cancelled on 10 December.

On 9 December, the 87th Infantry Division recently assigned Third US Army, began to move from Metz (U8858) to the XII Corps zone to relieve the 26th Infantry Division. Protection for movement and assembly of this initial division element was provided by Army Antiaircraft units until the 549th Antiaircraft Artillery Automatic Weapons Battalion arrived and was attached to the Division.

The new 90mm fuse PD T74E6, known as the Pozit fuse, was released for use on the continent as of 15 December. Initially, notification to higher headquarters was required prior to use of this fuse in each Inner Artillery Zone. On 16 December its use was authorized in the Saarlautern (Q2981) Inner Artillery Zone and shortly thereafter it was authorized for use in all other existing Inner Artillery Zones.

For the first fifteen days in December, enemy air activity had been very light. Only sixteen enemy aircraft appeared over the Third US. Army area, two of which were shot down.

Gun defenses had been established on 6 December, at the city of Metz (U8858) but at the request of the XIX Tactical Air Command for a corridor across the Saar River which would avoid restricted areas, an Inner Artillery Zone had not been set up until another such zone could be cancelled along the river line. By 18 December the importance of Metz (U8858) as both a supply area and crossing point justified the cancellation of the Restricted area at Pont-A-Mousson (U7735) in order that one could be established at Metz (U8858).

On 17 December, two batteries of the 120th Antiaircraft Artillery Gun Battalion from Pont-A-Mousson (U7735) and two batteries of the 546th Antiaircraft Artillery Automatic Weapons Battalion from Nancy (U8511) established an Antiaircraft defense for St. Avold (Q2557) since the Third US Army Command post was scheduled to move there within a few days.

The remaining two batteries of the 411th Antiaircraft Artillery Gun Battalion defending this crossing were relieved of this mission, released from attachment to the 38th Antiaircraft Artillery Brigade, and attached to the XII Corps. These batteries were to be used by the XII Corps to fire a flak line in conjunction with a planned attack which included close air support and preliminary bombardment by bombers. This flak line to be used by the Air Force for the purpose of orientation was to be fired by these two batteries and two additional gun batteries which had previously been attached to the corps for this purpose.

The German break-through, in the First US. Army area on 16 December delayed the move however and by 19 December, the German thrust had gained such momentum that plans for movement to the east were discontinued. Instead the Third US Army wheeled to the north.

The wheeling movement made necessary great shifts in troops and supplies and in order that these movements back across the Moselle River and then to the north could be made with the greatest possible speed, all crossings over the river were utilized and Antiaircraft defense of these crossings assumed a high priority. The Antiaircraft Artillery previously sent to St. Avold (Q2557) being available, the two gun batteries were moved to augment the Antiaircraft defense of the Thionville (U8685) crossings and the two Automatic Weapons Batteries were moved to establish Antiaircraft defense of the Pont-A-Mousson (U7735) crossings, as well as two supply points east of the river. Gun protection was furnished for the Pont-A-Mousson (U7735) crossing by detaching from XII Corps, the two batteries of the 411th Antiaircraft Artillery Gun Battalion which had been attached for the flak line mission, now no longer required due to the change in Army mission. The already established Antiaircraft defenses at Metz (U8858) and Nancy (U8811) crossings were considered adequate.

The change in mission for the Third US Army brought about a major shift of Antiaircraft Artillery units The situation at the beginning of the move northward is indicated in **Figure 10.**

Since the crossing at Pont-A-Mousson (U7735) would be important only until the initial transfer of units to the west and north could be accomplished, it was not desired to establish an Inner Artillery Zone in this area. Without such a restricted area however, the guns were greatly handicapped in their mission of defending the crossing at night since they could not open unseen fire until after a hostile act had been

FIGURE 9

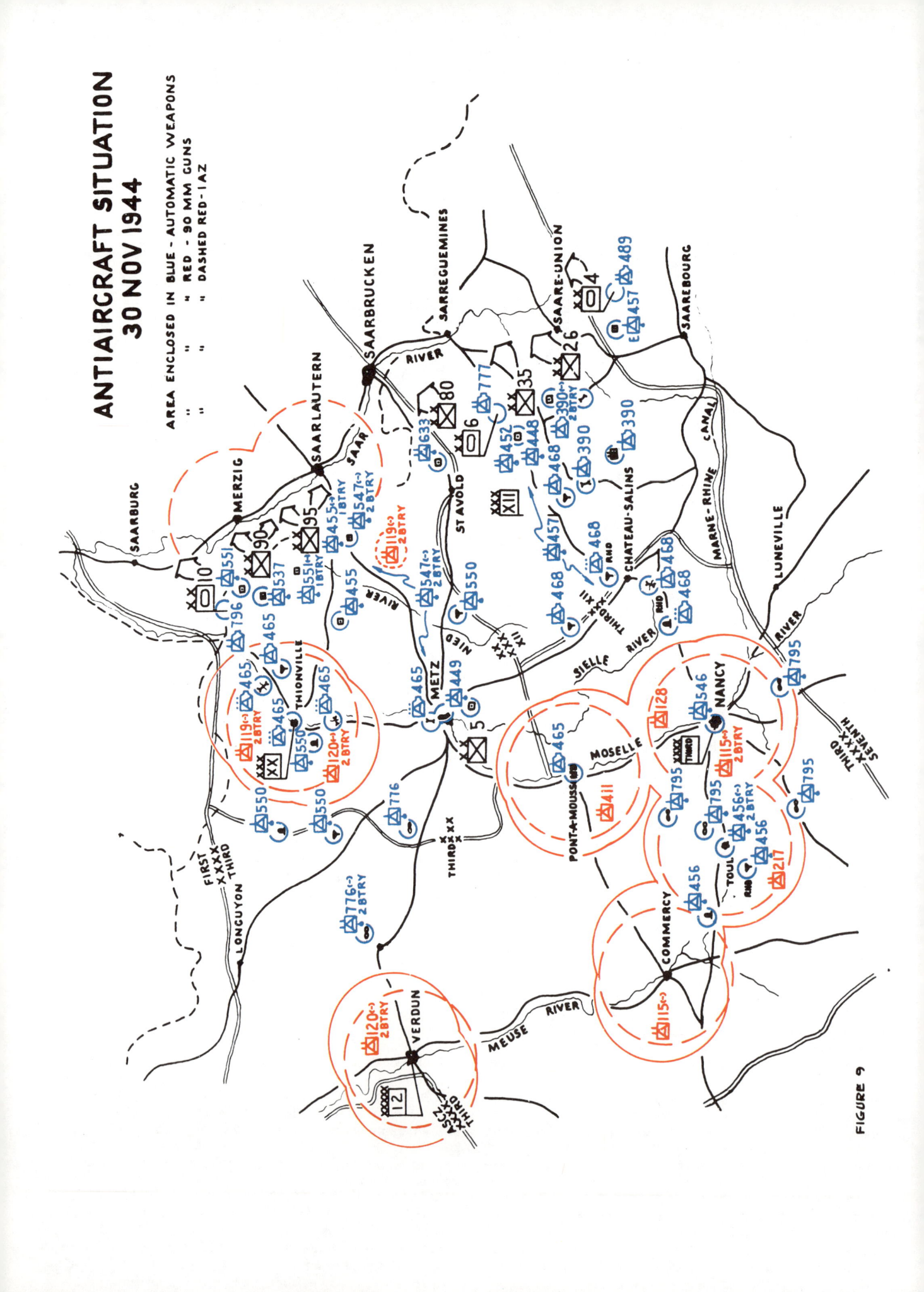

FIGURE 10

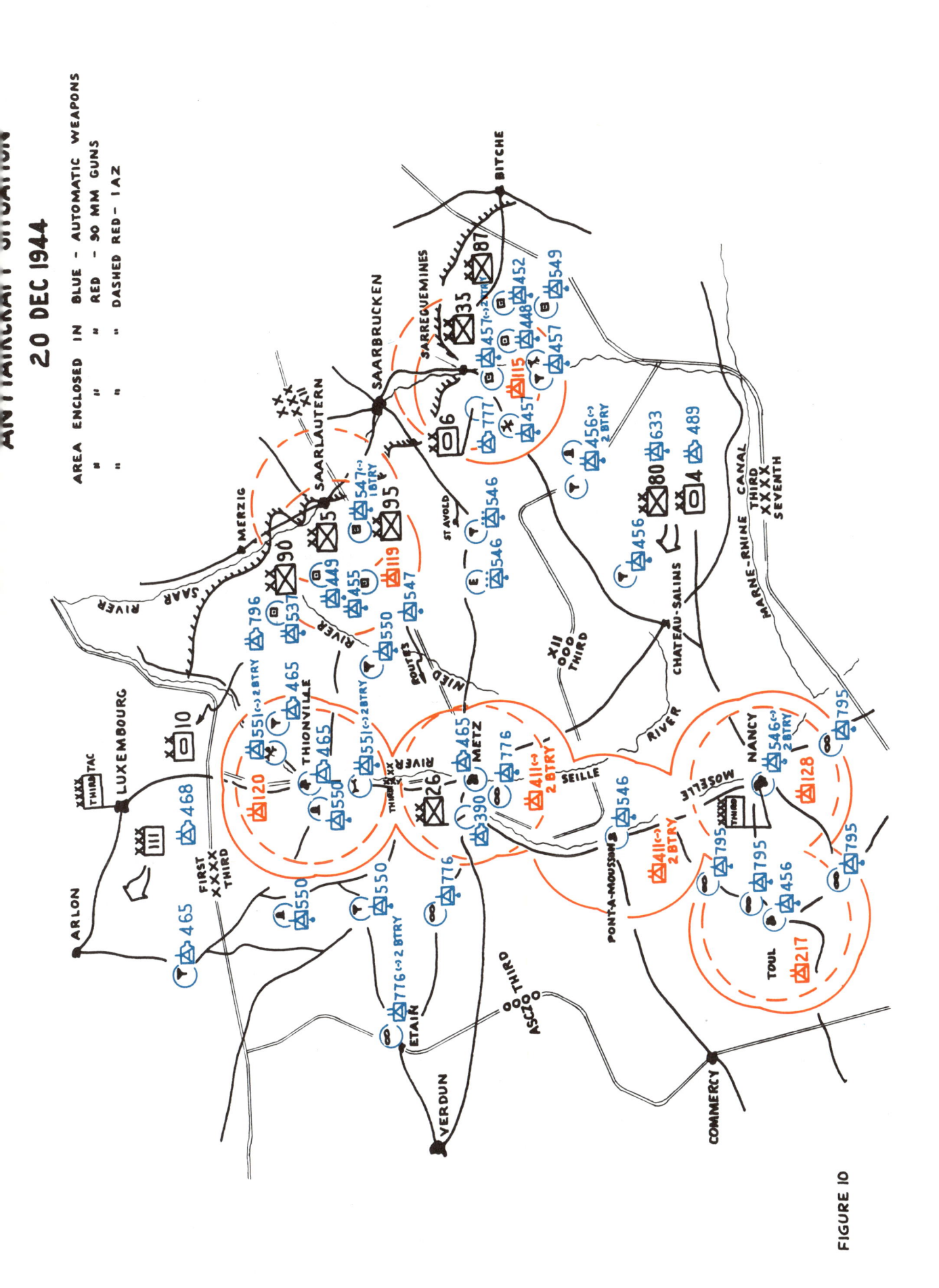

committed. Arrangements were made therefore with the XIX Tactical Air Command for their controller at the Fighter Control Center to authorize unseen firing by the 90mm guns when he knew that no friendly aircraft were in the vicinity at that particular time. This was to be known as "Blank Check" area and became effective 22 December.

The launching of the German counterattack had been accompanied by large scale Luftwaffe attacks in the First and Ninth US Army areas. In the Third US Army area enemy air activity had shown only a moderate increase. On the 17th of December sixteen raids were made by seventeen aircraft, five of which were shot down and four more claimed as probably destroyed. But for the next three days, enemy air activity fell off considerably.

The German thrust had cut off a number of elements of the First US Army, resulting in a new Army boundary, which ran approximately through the center of the break-through area. All First US Army troops located south of this new boundary were assigned or attached to Third US Army. On the 21st of December, the following units were attached or assigned as indicated below:

16th AAA Group — assigned First US Army attached Third US Army (Army)

109th AAA Gun Bn — assigned Third US Army (Army)

113th AAA Group — assigned Third US Army (Remained attached VIII Corps)

129th AAA Gun Bn — assigned Third US Army (Army)

377th AAA AW Bn — assigned Third US Army (Remained attached to 4th Inf Div)

447th AAA AW Bn — assigned Third US Army (Remained attached to 28th Inf Div)

467th AAA AW Bn (SP) — attached Third US Army (Remained assigned to First US Army)

482d AAA AW Bn — assigned Third US Army (Remained attached 9th Army Div)

565th AAA AW Bn — assigned Third US Army (Army)

635th AAA AW Bn — assigned Third US Army (Remained attached VIII Corps)

Btry A, 792d AAA AW Bn (SM) (Army) — attached Third US Army for operations only, remained assigned Communications Zone.

The major changes resulting from the above assignments were the assumption of the defense of the city of Luxembourg (P8414), the Steel Mill at Differdange (P6604), the Radio Station Luxembourg located at Junglinster (Q9325), and airfield A97. The 115th Antiaircraft Artillery Gun Battalion was relieved from its attachment to the XII Corps and moved forward to the city of Luxembourg (P8414) on 22 December to increase the defenses there to two gun battalions **and two automatic weapons batteries.** Two batteries of the 129th Antiaircraft Artillery Gun Battalion which had been employed in the defense of Luxembourg (P8414) were moved to Differdange (P6604), increasing the defenses there to one gun battalion and one automatic weapons battery.

As Third US Army troops struck into the south flank of the German salient, the Luftwaffe made a desperate effort to halt the tide of men and supplies which were rapidly flowing north. On the 21st of December 39 planes were sent over the Army area in a series of raids, from which eleven did not return. On the following day, eighty-nine planes participated in seventy-eight raids. Of this number Antiaircraft Artillery claimed eight as destroyed and one as probably destroyed. On 23 December more than 100 planes strafed and bombed installations and troops in the Army area. Eighteen of those raiding planes were shot down and six more claimed as probably destroyed.

By 24 December supply installations at Metz (U8858) had been increased to such an extent that it became necessary to augment its defense by moving two gun batteries of the 119th Antiaircraft Artillery Gun Battalion from Saarlautern (Q2981). Other supply installations further to the north had also expanded and automatic weapons for their defense became available from supply installations to the south which had been taken over by Seventh US Army upon the change in the Army lateral boundary. The disposition of Third US Army Antiaircraft Artillery on 25 December after the change in boundaries is shown in **Figure 11.**

Strafing and bombing by the enemy had continued to increase in the Third US Army area. On 24 December, the largest number of planes, since the German break-through occurred, had attacked installations, traffic, artillery and other targets. Ninety-four raids consisting of 145 planes made up the total for the day. Seventeen of the planes were chalked up as destroyed and six more were claimed as probables.

In view of the enemy strafing and bombing along the highway between Metz (U8858) and Thionville (U8685), Automatic Weapons protection was provided along the route by XX Corps.

On 25 December the violence of the German Air Force activity decreased somewhat from that experienced on the previous day, however, fifty-two raids were made by 103 planes. Antiaircraft fire accounted for eleven destroyed and eleven probably destroyed.

The 778th Antiaircraft Artillery Automatic Weapons Battalion (self-propelled) which had been assigned to Third US Army on the 19th of December, arrived in the Army area on 25 December and was placed under control of the 16th Antiaircraft Artillery Group for operations.

Anticipating that the German Air Force might attack forward airfields which, with planes stacked wing to wing presented a profitable target, the 9th Air Force instructed the IX Air Defense Command to double the scale of protection on all XIX Tactical Air Command airfields. Third US Army concurred and three additional Automatic Weapons batteries were attached to the Army for this purpose.

On 26 December the German Air Force struck with a violence not experienced since Avranches (T2915) and the river crossing at Mantes-Gas-Sicourt (R6959) early in the campaign. 145 separate raids consisting of 234 planes of practically all types available in the German Air Force, were made against communications, supply routes and installations, and against traffic particularly at points of congestion. Antiaircraft Artillery rose to the occasion and had a field day, shooting down twenty-six of the attacking aircraft and claiming twenty-one more as probably destroyed. For the next two days enemy air activity decreased sharply. Only eighty-four planes appeared over the Army area of which three were destroyed and eight probably destroyed.

The movement of supplies to the north permitted the reduction of defenses at Toul (U6410) and Nancy (U8511) from four gun batteries each to two gun batteries each. On 30 December the 217th Antiaircraft Artillery Gun Battalion was moved north, and attached to VIII Corps for the defense of Bastogne (P5558), the center of the vital road network which had been denied the enemy in his thrust to the west.

Since it had been noted that many unidentified planes were flying at night, just above the Inner Artillery Zone ceiling of 10,000 feet, Twelfth US Army Group was requested to approve an Inner Artillery Zone for Bastogne (P5558) with a ceiling of 15,000 feet. The Twelfth US Army Group modified this request and gave approval for a ceiling of 12,000 feet. This restricted area became effective on the night of 31 December.

On the 29th of December, the German Air Force appeared in strength with eighty-eight planes which participated in sixty-one raids over the Third US Army area. Antiaircraft shot down ten of these planes and claimed seven probables. The following day, enemy planes restricted their activities mostly to reconnaissance. Two were brought down and three additional planes probably destroyed.

The 567th Antiaircraft Artillery Automatic Weapons Battalion was assigned Third US Army on 30 December and was earmarked for attachment to the 38th Antiaircraft Artillery Brigade as soon as it closed in the Army area. On 31 December the 894th Antiaircraft Artillery Automatic Weapons Battalion (self-propelled), assigned to the Seventh US Army, arrived in Third US Army area to take over defenses at airfields A-90, 95 and 96 in the Toul (U6410) — Nancy (U8511) area since these fields were being used by the Tactical Air Command of Seventh US Army. In accordance with Twelfth US Army Group policy, the unit was attached to Third US Army for operations and was placed under operational control of the 38th Antiaircraft Artillery Brigade.

The last day of the month was another day of heavy enemy air action. Sixty-four raids, consisting of eighty nine planes, struck at installations throughout the area. Three of the raiding planes were destroyed and four additional planes probably destroyed.

The disposition of Third US Army Antiaircraft Artillery on 31 December, supporting the lightning attack on the southern flank of the German bulge, is shown in **Figure 12**.

SUMMARY OF ENEMY AIR ACTIVITY FOR THE MONTH OF DECEMBER.

The month of December saw enemy air activity increased almost ten-fold over activity of any previous month, excluding August when 3213 enemy planes were overhead. Although the first three weeks of December brought almost no activity, the enemy air effort from 22 December on was such that by the month's end 729 raids by 1090 enemy aircraft had been tallied, as compared with November's seventy-eight raids by 138 enemy aircraft.

As Third US Army regrouped and moved north to strike at the flank of the German counter-offensive piercing its way through Belgium and northern Luxembourg, the skies cleared and the pent up fury of the German Air Force, hitherto so closely husbanded, was unleashed in its full strength. Attacks by as many as 250 enemy aircraft in one day were made.

At the outset, supply installations and traffic moving northward along highways were the main targets. Most attacks were by night. But later, attacks came by day as the German pilots took advantage of the first bright sun in weeks to dive down out of it, bombing and strafing. Most attacks were from low altitudes, some so low that gun battalion radars failed to detect the approaching aircraft, so that automatic weapons played the major defensive role for Antiaircraft.

As the lines became more tangible, target priorities changed and heavy attacks were made upon artillery, troops, vehicles and such other targets as opportunity presented. Tactics were keyed to harass and hinder, rather than to forestall or destroy entirely. Airfields were frequently attacked by one or two aircraft, flying in low at night to bomb and strafe. Command Posts were lightly attacked, and vehicles parked in fields were frequent targets.

Despite the weight of the effort, however, little damage was done. A few vehicles were destroyed, some men were killed and wounded. But compared with the size of the effort, results obtained were insignificant. The exception to this was the strafing of a Class III dump near Mancieules (U6677) where 100,000 gallons of gasoline, some jerricans and boxcars were lost. This was the sole instance where objectives protected by Antiaircraft Artillery were destroyed or even seriously damaged. In most cases, the protection afforded was most successful. And in the course of their engagements, Antiaircraft Artillery claimed 115 enemy planes destroyed and seventy-five probably destroyed, with innumerable others undoubtedly damaged.

For further information the Weekly Intelligence Reports covering the month of December are enclosed as Annex 7.

Member of the 217th Antiaircraft Gun Battalion in the alert for enemy planes outside Bastogne, Belgium during the battle for Bastogne.

Gun crew of the "Black Widow," a 90mm gun of the 217th Antiaircraft Gun Battalion standing by to fire on an enemy plane approaching the city of Bastogne, Belgium.

Chapter 8
January Operations

The savage attacks by the Luftwaffe, in the attempt to slow down Third US Army's drive, reached their peak on 1 January when more than 308 hostile aircraft were over the area in 133 raids during the twenty-four hour period. Attacks were heavy in the XX Corps zone but the heaviest single attack of the day was on an airfield southwest of Metz (U8858). Here twenty five aircraft came in from all directions at low level and strafed the parked P-47's, twenty of which were destroyed and seventeen damaged. Of the twenty five enemy aircraft attacking however, sixteen were shot down by Antiaircraft Artillery and one more was claimed as probably destroyed.

Other targets most frequently attacked in the Third US Army area were supply installations, traffic, and field artillery and although no material success was achieved by these attacks, the enemy paid heavily. During the twenty four hour period, sixty-three planes were shot down and seventeen more were claimed as probably destroyed by Antiaircraft Artillery. The 445th Antiaircraft Artillery Automatic Weapons Battalion, which was defending artillery in the XX Corps zone, turned in the highest tally for the day. Fire units of the battalion claimed sixteen Category I's and six Category II's, which included ten out of a flight of twenty-five FW 190's.

The arrival of the 567th Antiaircraft Artillery Automatic Weapons Battalion in the Army area on 1 January increased Army Antiaircraft Artillery sufficiently to permit coverage of all installations considered vital at this time. In addition the Army was able to take over from the Corps the Antiaircraft defense of two bridges in the vicinity of Thionville (U8685) and the supply point at Arlon (P6323).

Plans of the XII Corps for an attack across the Our River included preliminary close support bombing by medium bombers. Two batteries of the 119th Antiaircraft Artillery Gun Battalion were therefore attached to Corps to draw ammunition and compute necessary data for the firing of a flak line. Arrangements were made to attach an additional gun battalion since the flak line requested would require six gun batteries.

The heavy attacks at Y-34 brought about the strengthening of Antiaircraft Artillery defenses on the following day to the scale of three Automatic Weapons batteries. One battery of Automatic Weapons from Army was used to augment the two batteries of attached IX Air Defense Command Antiaircraft already at this field.

Enemy air activity continued to be heavy on 2 January but did not equal the violence of the previous days' attacks. Fifty-five raids were made by eighty-six planes. Attacks on supply installations had dropped off, and traffic and Field Artillery appeared to be the principal targets. For the day, Third US Army Antiaircraft claimed seven kills and an equal number of probables.

The 28th Infantry Division had been hit hard in the breakthrough and it became necessary to pull the division out of the line. The combat efficiency of its attached Antiaircraft Artillery Automatic Weapons Battalion, the 447th, was considered satisfactory, however, and in view of the Antiaircraft Artillery shortage the unit was relieved from attachment to the division on 3 January and attached to VIII Corps for defense of installations in the Corps area. One battery was used to augment the 155th Antiaircraft Artillery Automatic Weapons Anti-tank Battalion of the 17th Airborne Division.

The attack by XII Corps had been postponed and the two gun batteries which had been attached for the flak line mission became available for use in their primary role. To the west, Arlon (P6323) had been the target for repeated attacks and on 4 January the two batteries were moved to III

FIGURE II

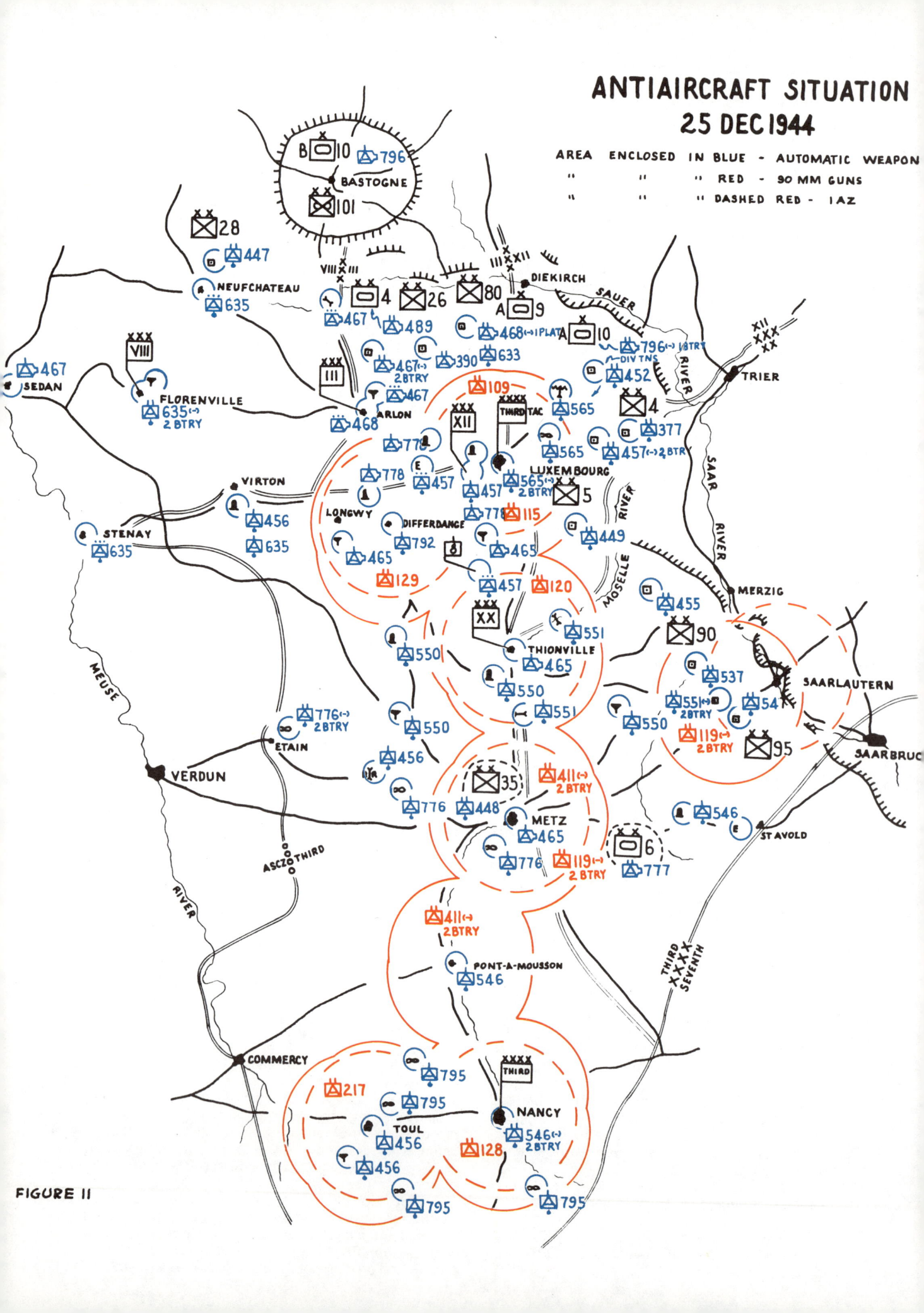

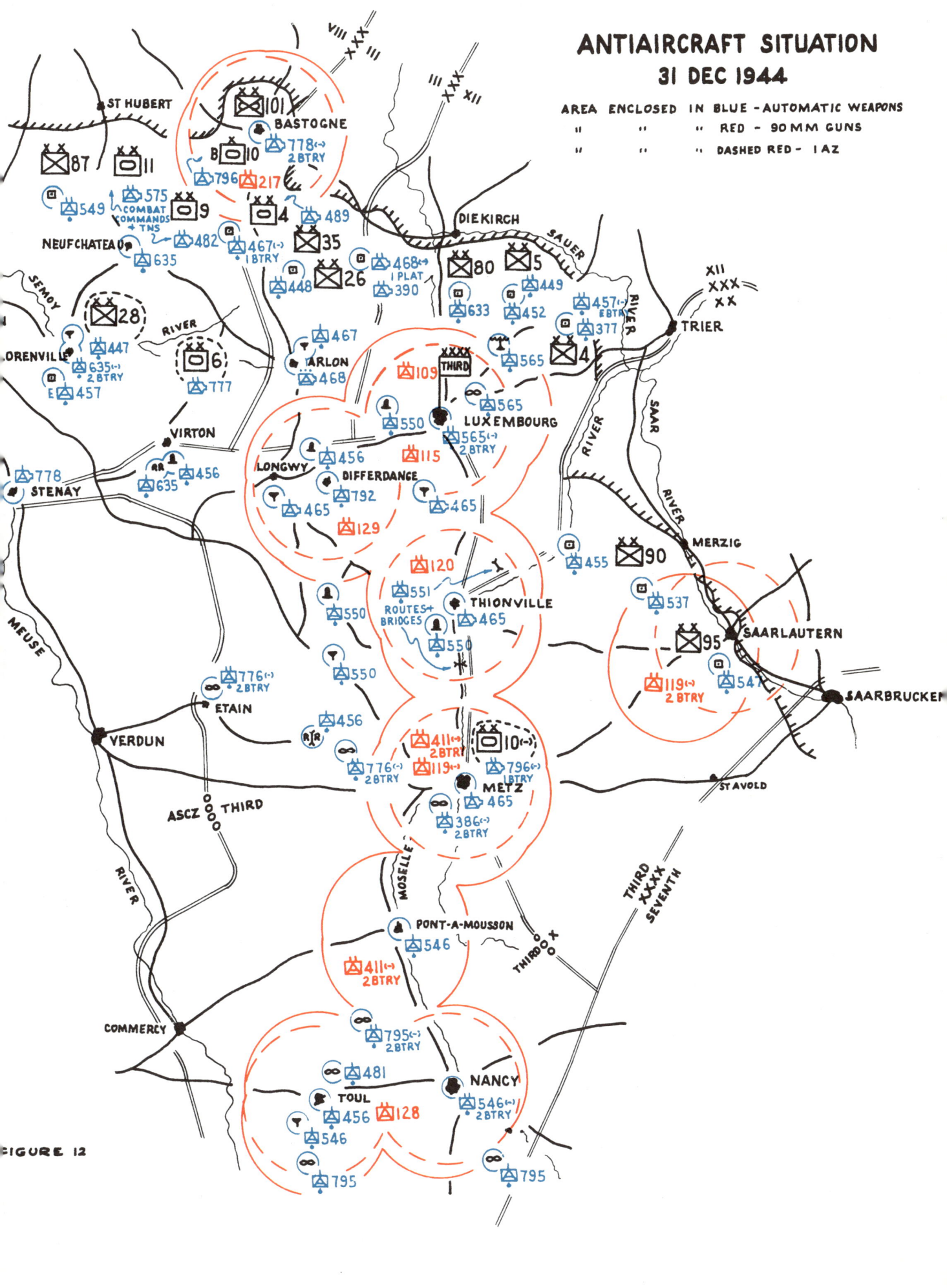

ANTIAIRCRAFT SITUATION
31 DEC 1944

AREA ENCLOSED IN BLUE - AUTOMATIC WEAPONS
" " " RED - 90MM GUNS
" " " DASHED RED - IAZ

FIGURE 12

SECRET

Corps for the defense of this city. In order to give the Air Force as much freedom as possible to operate on the Ardennes bulge, an Inner Artillery Zone was not requested for Arlon (P6323). Instead, arrangements were made with the XIX Tactical Air Command to allow the 90mm guns to fire at unseen planes at night upon authorization from the controller at the Fighter Control Center. This arrangement, called a "Blank Check" area, had previously been used in defenses along the Moselle River at Pont-A-Mousson (U7735).

On 4 January one battery of the 792d Antiaircraft Artillery Automatic Weapons Battalion (Semi-mobile), which had been included in the Antiaircraft Artillery defense of the steel mill at Differdange (P6604) reverted to IX Air Defense. Command and one battery of Automatic Weapons from Army was moved to relieve the outgoing unit. This loss of Antiaircraft Artillery from units available to cover supply points and other installations in the Army area was increased on 6 January, when the 94th Infantry Division arrived in Third US Army without an automatic weapons battalion. To furnish this division with a unit, it was necessary to relieve the 465th Antiaircraft Artillery Automatic Weapons Battalion (Self-propelled) from its mission under 38th Antiaircraft Artillery Brigade.

Since 2 January, enemy air activity had been negligible but the force with which it could strike was not underestimated, and every effort was made to provide adequate Antiaircraft Artillery for all vital points. The retention of the 482d Antiaircraft Artillery Automatic Weapons Battalion (Self-propelled) by the VIII Corps, when the 9th Armored Division was pulled out of the line for refitting on 8 January, assisted materially in this respect since the deep zone of the VIII Corps included many far flung bridges and installations.

Movement of the 94th Infantry Division into the XX Corps zone on 6 January strengthened the front considerably, but no major elements were on the line east of Luxembourg (P8414). The pressure in the Ardennes bulge, especially southeast of Bastogne (P5558) occupied most of our forces. This together with the fact that a number of German divisions were still unlocated, drew considerable attention to the possibility of a German thrust toward Luxembourg (P8414) or as far south as Metz (U8858). Plans were made therefore to employ Antiaircraft in anti-tank and field artillery roles, if such a threat should materialize. The 16th Antiaircraft Artillery Group, which controlled the defense of Luxembourg (P8414), coordinated its anti-tank and field artillery plan with the XII Corps. In the Metz (U8858) area, the 38th Antiaircraft Artillery Brigade planned the use of Antiaircraft Artillery for similar missions, coordinating with the XX Corps.

On 9 January, the 894th Antiaircraft Artillery Automatic Weapons Battalion (Semi-mobile) minus one battery, was attached to Third US Army for operational command. This was a Seventh US Army unit which was being employed in defenses at airfields A-90, 95 and 96 in the Nancy (U8511) and Toul (U6410) areas, all of which were used by the Tactical Air Command supporting Seventh US Army.

The failure of the German Air Force to sustain the scale of attacks set earlier in the month indicated that their violent effort to stop Third US Army's drive had been at least temporarily abandoned. Consequently, the defenses at airfield Y-34 near Metz (U8858) were reduced to the normal scale of two automatic weapons batteries in order that one battery of Army Antiaircraft Artillery could be made available to cover a Class III reserve at Landres (U6082).

Return of the 9th Armored Division to the Third US Army area on 11 January without Antiaircraft Artillery made it necessary to relieve the 482nd Antiaircraft Artillery Automatic Weapons Battalion (Self-propelled) from VIII Corps for reattachment to the division. Antiaircraft Artillery available to Third US Army for protection of vital points was further reduced by the arrival of the 8th Armored Division minus an Antiaircraft Artillery unit. The 467th Antiaircraft Artillery Automatic Weapons Battalion (Self-propelled) was relieved from the III Corps and attached to XX Corps for this division. This change reduced the Automatic Weapons of the III Corps to a single battalion and a readjustment was made in the Automatic Weapons units attached to III and VIII Corps so that the III Corps would have at least one and one half battalions to cover installations in the Corps zone.

With good weather, the German Air Force ventured out on 14 January to attack targets in the XIII and XX Corps. Of the eleven planes taking part in these raids, one was destroyed and two additional planes probably destroyed.

Two Antiaircraft Artillery units were lost by the Third US Army on 16 January when divisions were moved into Sixth US Army Group area where the Germans were applying considerable pressure at this time. The 796th Antiaircraft Artillery Automatic Weapons Battalion (Self-propelled) was moved with the 10th Armored Division and the 447th Antiaircraft Artillery Automatic Weapons Battalion went with the 28th Infantry Division, the unit moving on 18 January. Loss of the latter unit which had been attached to VIII Corps required an additional adjustment of Antiaircraft Automatic Weapons between the III and VIII Corps in order that each Corps could protect high priority installations in its area.

Still another unit was lost by Third US Army on 18 January when one more Automatic Weapons Battalion, the 567th, was ordered attached to Sixth US Army Group. Even though Antiaircraft defenses were readjusted, only those installations most vital to the Army were protected since sufficient Antiaircraft Artillery was not now available to cover all the important installations.

The swing of the Third US Army to the north had drawn to that area the bulk of supply installations and the supplies which had been formerly stored in the Nancy (U8511) and Toul (U6410) area had been depleted. Antiaircraft defenses at these two cities were therefore discontinued on 20 January and the units furnishing defense for these two points were moved to the city of Metz (U8858) which had become an important supply center.

The German "Bulge" had been reduced by 21 January and availability of roads in that area reduced the importance of Bastogne (P5558) which previously had been at the center of the only available road net. The Inner Artillery Zone at the city was therefore cancelled in order to allow maximum freedom for night operation in that area by the air force.

On 21 January the 76th Infantry Division arrived in the Third US Army area without an Antiaircraft Artillery unit and it became necessary to further reduce the Antiaircraft Artillery which was available to cover supply installations and other vital points in the Army area in order to provide the 778th Antiaircraft Artillery Automatic Weapons Battalion (Self-propelled) for the division.

As a result of a change in the Army boundary on 23 January, air fields covered by the units of the 795th and 894th Antiaircraft Artillery Automatic Weapons Battalion (Semi-mobile) were outside of the Third US Army area therefore operational command of these units was relinquished.

In accordance with instructions from Supreme Headquarters Allied Expeditionary Forces, arrangements were made on 29 January to establish a new boundary in the Army area which was to be known as the Army Group Rear Air Boundary. Antiaircraft defense of installations forward of this line was to be the responsibility of the Army. Antiaircraft defense of installations to the rear of this line was to be the responsibility of the IX Air Defense Command. The location of this boundary was to be determined by mutual agreement between the Army Group Commander and the Air Force Commander. The initial boundary agreed upon excluded from the areas of Army responsibility the Ordnance installation and the airfield at Etain (U4770) as well as the airfield east of Conflans (U6765) and airfield Y-34 southwest of Metz (U8858). Antiaircraft units of the IX Air Defense Command which had been defending these fields and had been attached to Third US Army for operational command, were relieved when IX Air Defense Command took over responsibility for defense of the airfields. Third US Army was to continue to exercise operational control over all Antiaircraft units inside the Army area.

During the month, Luxembourg (P8414) had been subjected to artillery fire of a strange type on several occasions. Information gathered indicated that the projectile was finned and traveled at a very high velocity. At the request of the Artillery Section, an attempt was made to use radar to locate the source of the firing. One radar set (SCR-584) was set at an estimated azimuth furnished by the Artillery Section, and at an angular height of 175 mils in order to avoid ground echos and reflections. The plan was to determine an approximate range and then run the narrow gate out to this range, if possible, to try and lock the radar on the projectile in automatic. If this were successful, readings were to be taken at the computer and at the tracking head to give range, azimuth and angular height of the projectile at specified times.

The above experiments were carried on during several shelling attacks. At the initial angular height, several "flicks" were seen which appeared to correspond with the landing of shells in the city but the radar was unable to "lock-on". The angular height was then lowered to fifty two mils in an attempt to pick up the projectiles nearer their source, but flicks then began to appear which were believed due to friendly artillery fire. These flicks appeared for a period of less than one second and did not show any noticeable travel in range which would give an indication of incoming or outgoing direction. No information was secured as a result of these experiments which was of any value in locating the source of enemy fire.

Copies of Weekly Intelligence Reports for the month of January are attached as Annex 8. It will be noted that after 2 January the German Air Force made no appearance in strength and only came over on infrequent reconnaissance flights.

The disposition of Third US Army Antiaircraft units is shown in **Figure 13**. The Ardennes breakthrough had been erased and Third US Army installations had been moved to support the drive through the Siegfried line.

Chapter 9
February Operations

Normal lines of communications and supply had been reopened and arrangements were made to relieve some Antiaircraft units which had been temporarily attached to the Third US Army at the time of the breakthrough. The 16th Antiaircraft Artillery Group and the 109th Antiaircraft Artillery Gun Battalion which had been employed in the defense of Luxembourg (P8414) reverted to First US Army control on the 3rd and 5th of February respectively.

The 38th Antiaircraft Artillery Brigade took over the responsibility of the defense of Luxembourg (P8414) as soon as the elements under its control could relieve the 16th Antiaircraft Artillery Group and the 109th Antiaircraft Artillery Gun Battalion. In order to maintain the two gun battalion scale of defense at Luxembourg (P8414), the 411th Antiaircraft Artillery Gun Battalion was released from its mission in the defense of Metz (U8659) and moved to Luxembourg (P8414) on 5 February.

Although impeded by melting of deep snows, and the weather which prevented air support, Third US Army troops were pushing deeper into Germany in the area of the German-Belgium-Luxembourg borders, and further to the south Third US Army troops were advancing favorably. Although Third US Army advances continued, the main effort was assigned to the First and Ninth US Armies, and troops were shifted north in preparation for an offensive. On the 1st of the month the 35th Infantry Division was moved to the Ninth US Army area, taking with it its attached 448th Antiaircraft Artillery Automatic Weapons Battalion. On 2 February the 467th Antiaircraft Artillery Automatic Weapons Battalion attached to the 8th Armored Division was relieved from attachment to Third US Army when this division also moved to the First US Army. Continuing the build-up of troops on 5 February, the 95th Infantry Division and its attached 547th Antiaircraft Artillery Automatic Weapons Battalion moved into the Ninth US Army area.

In October plans had been made for the use of searchlights in the crossing of the river Rhine. As a result, one battery of the 226th Antiaircraft Searchlight Battalion arrived in the Third US Army on 31 January. These searchlights were incorporated in the Antiaircraft defense of Luxembourg (P8414) until requested by Corps for battlefield illumination for infantry troops.

Searchlights were first used in a ground role in the Third US Army area on the night of 4 February, in a familiarization mission in the XII Corps area. Since the ground troops were not accustomed to night combat under artificial moonlight, a sector was chosen in which no major operation was underway.

A position overlooking the enemy lines along the Moselle River was chosen for first employment of searchlights for battlefield illumination. Two lights were emplaced in defiladed sites near the village of Canach (P9813) to throw a beam over the Moselle River in the direction of the German lines. At that time, outposts were established in the town of Ehnen (L0312). The hostile shores were illuminated sufficiently to discern objects on the far shore. The 284th Combat Engineer Battalion, which was supported by the searchlights, furnished communication for control. No artillery fire was drawn during the three day period these lights were in operation.

On the second night of the XII Corps attack over the Sauer and Our rivers in Luxembourg (P8414), the 5th Infantry Division requested Antiaircraft Artillery Searchlights for battlefield illumination. Two lights were sited in the 11th Infantry sector of the 5th Division for this purpose. The first night the lights were used only ten minutes as too much light was provided, revealing infantry assault boats making the crossing. Necessary adjustments in siting were made the following day and on the second night the lights were used for eight hours. The first reports stated the infantry did not like the illumination. However, after becoming accustomed to the effect of the lights, they requested additional lights. A total of six lights were employed with the 5th Infantry Division by 15 February.

During the hours of darkness progress on bridge construction was slow. Since the bridges were normally under direct observation it was impractical to employ local direct illumination. Indirect lighting provided by Antiaircraft searchlights was more diffused, comparing to the light of a three quarter moon. Our troops were able to see well enough to work, without being observed by the enemy who faced the light reflecting directly upon them from the low hanging overcast. Illumination for bridge construction in the 5th Infantry Division sector was furnished on the night of 13 February at the request of the engineers who reported a material increase in the amount of work accomplished.

During 10, 11 and 12 February, troops of the 26th Infantry Division, in the XX Corps sector to the south, first experienced working with searchlights under battle conditions. The division held a bridgehead over the Saar River and occupied several blocks of buildings in the town of Saarlautern (Q2980), Roden (Q2882) and Fraulautern (Q3081). Enemy troops occupied buildings directly across the street. Any movements during the hours of darkness drew small arms, automatic weapons and mortar fire. The S-3 of the 104th Infantry Regiment requested the assistance of searchlights on the night of 10 February to assist our patrols in occupying the outer fringe of enemy held houses which the enemy habitually vacated at night and reoccupied the following morning.

On the night of 11 February the lights were again employed all night at the request of Task Force "A" of the 101st Infantry, which was on the left flank of the 104th Infantry. Having objected to the use of lights on the previous

FIGURE 13

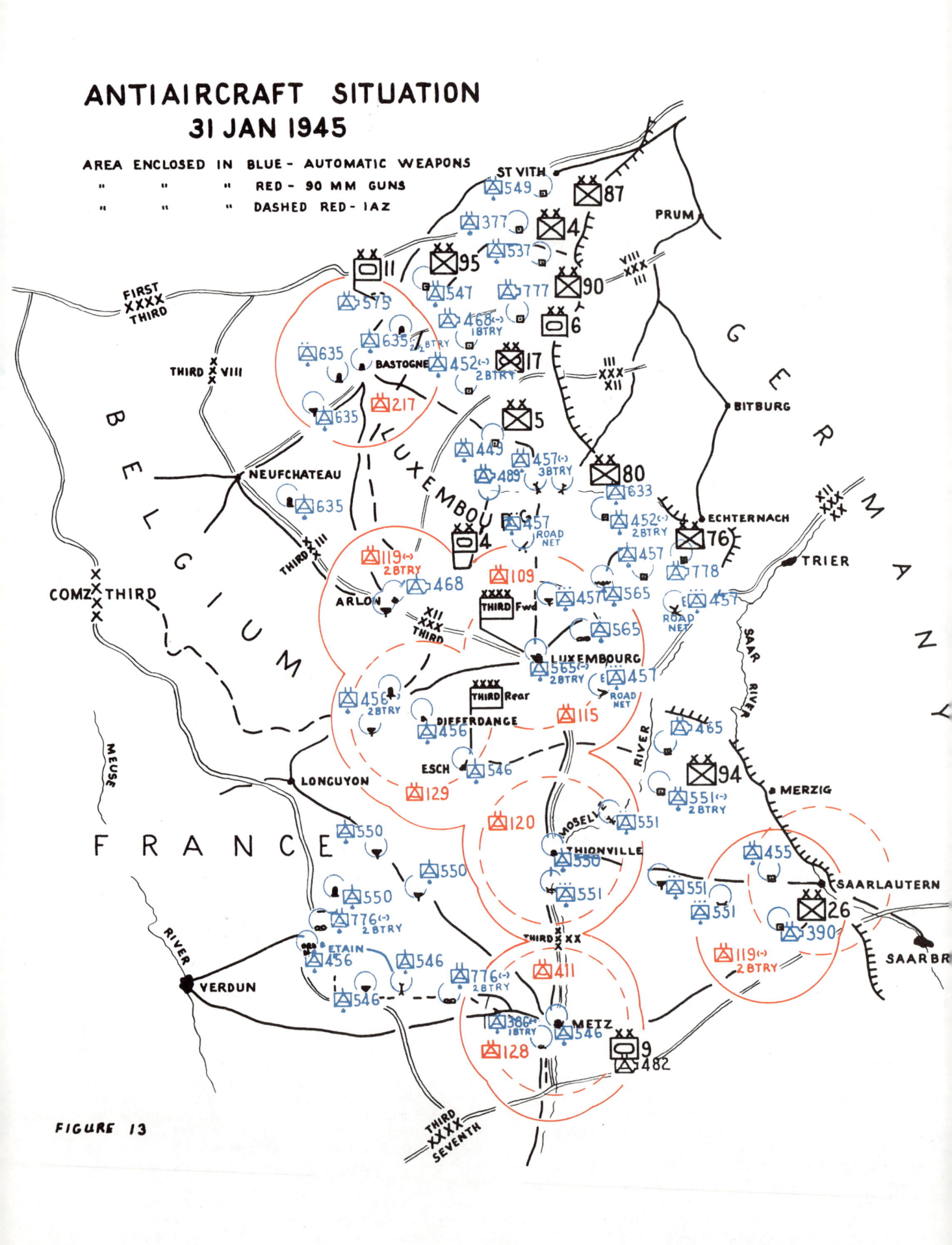

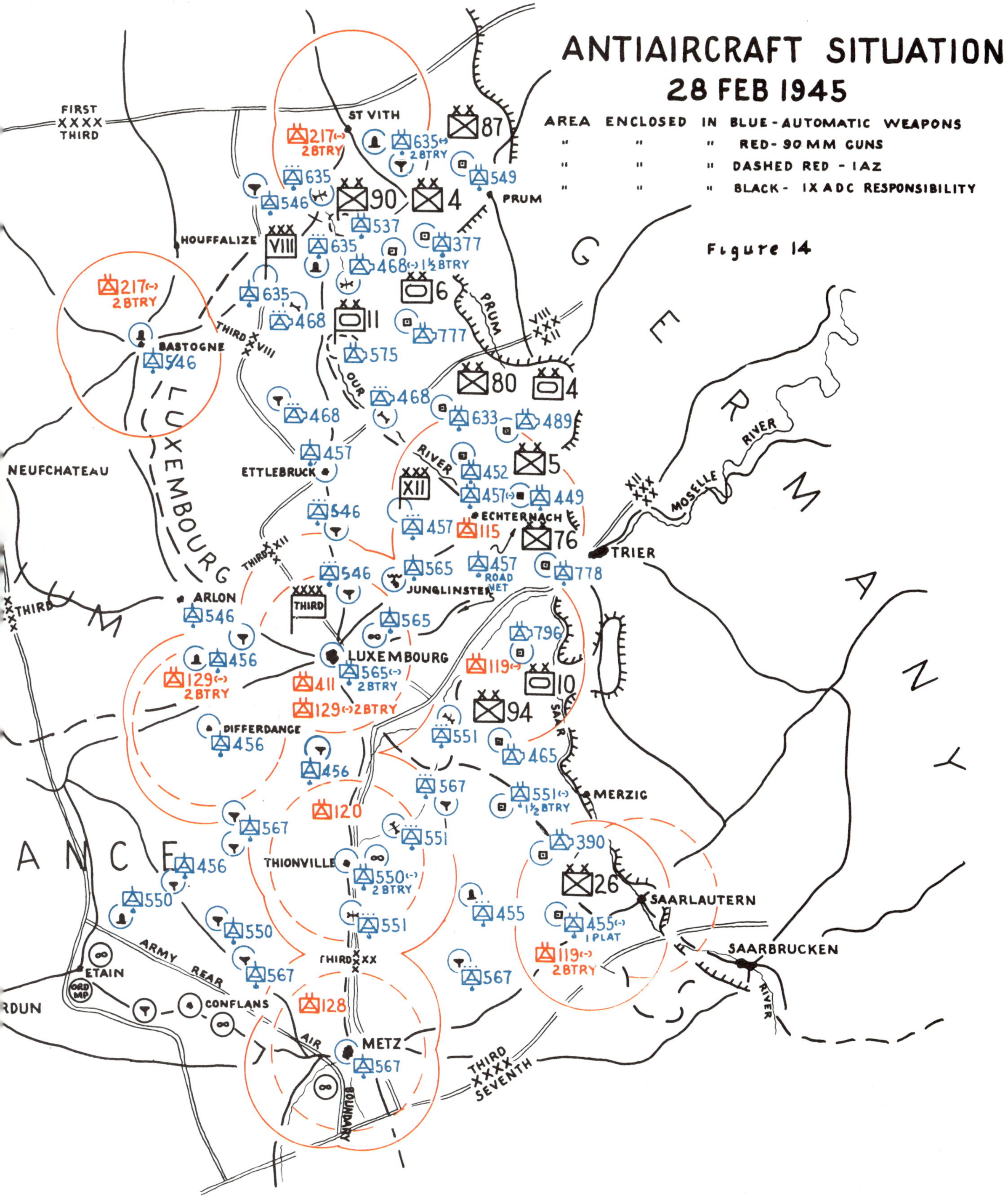

ANTIAIRCRAFT SITUATION
28 FEB 1945
AREA ENCLOSED IN BLUE - AUTOMATIC WEAPONS
" " " RED - 90 MM GUNS
" " " DASHED RED - IAZ
" " " BLACK - IX ADC RESPONSIBILITY
FIRST
XXXX
THIRD
ST VITH
PRUM
HOUFFALIZE
BASTOGNE
NEUFCHATEAU
ETTLEBRUCK
ECHTERNACH
TRIER
JUNGLINSTER
ROAD NET
ARLON
LUXEMBOURG
DIFFERDANCE
MERZIG
THIONVILLE
SAARLAUTERN
SAARBRUCKEN
ETAIN
CONFLANS
METZ
RDUN
ORD MP
ARMY REAR
AIR BOUNDARY
THIRD XXXX SEVENTH
THIRD XX
THIRD XXII
THIRD XXVIII
VIII XX XII
XII XX XX
GERMANY
LUXEMBOURG
ANCE
PRUM
OUR
RIVER
MOSELLE RIVER
SAAR
RIVER
XXX VIII
XXX XII
XXXX THIRD
XX 87
XX 90
XX 4
XX 6
XX 11
XX 80
XX 4
XX 5
XX 76
XX 10
XX 94
XX 26
217(-) 2 BTRY
635(-) 2 BTRY
635
549
546
537
635
377
468(-) 1½ BTRY
635
468
777
575
468
468
633
489
457
452
457(-)
449
546
457
115
546
565
457
778
546
565
456
129(-) 2 BTRY
411
565(-) 2 BTRY
129(-) 2 BTRY
796
119(-)
456
456
551
465
567
551(-) 1½ BTRY
120
567
551
456
550(-) 2 BTRY
390
550
550
551
455
455(-) 1 PLAT
119(-) 2 BTRY
567
567
128
567

Figure 14

night, they were now accustomed to them and believed they could better conduct mortar fire and motorized patrols.

The 104th Infantry was completely relieved by the 328th Infantry on 12 February during the hours of darkness with searchlights facilitating the relief of troops.

Searchlights were continued in operation on the night of 13 February. However, they were not used on the next two nights as clear skies failed to adequately reflect the light beams.

In the Saarlautern (Q2980) area, a number of night counter-attacks had taken place and on 17 February such an attack was launched against one of the battalions of the 328th Infantry. Searchlights were used and sufficiently penetrated the heavy mist to contribute to the halting of this counter-attack. It was observed that fine adjustment of mortar fire was possible under illumination.

Battlefield illumination by Antiaircraft searchlights was well received by units with which they were employed in the Third US Army area. A typical comment, by the 104th Infantry, is quoted below:

"The experimentation of this regiment with artificial moonlight was highly successful. The results obtained have exceeded expectations. All individuals interrogated from squad leaders to battalion commanders were very favorably impressed with the employment of artificial moonlight. The American soldier will fight anything he can see. This type of illumination lifts the doughboy from a blind groping ineffective, to an efficient, confident and aggressive soldier."

Although generally agreed on the assistance of Antiaircraft lights, Combat Commanders also observed certain limitations. The most serious objection offered was that, when located in buildings or in trenches, enemy troops could observe the movement of friendly troops in the open.

To ascertain the reaction of the enemy, PWs were interrogated regarding the use of searchlights. Generally speaking, PWs had been enjoying a number of the advantages from the lights that our own troops received, but patrol activity by the enemy had been greatly reduced.

As Third US Army Infantry and Armor continued to drive into the Siegfried line east and southeast of St Vith (P8588), the net work of roads leading from the city bore heavy movement of supplies and troops. The mud and slush from melting snow impeded traffic. St Vith (P8588) became a logical target for the German Air Forces. The Bastogne (P5558) road junctions having assumed a more normal status, its Antiaircraft defense was reduced to two gun batteries; an Antiaircraft defense of two gun batteries was accordingly set up at St Vith (P8588) on 9 February. On 12 February the 38th Antiaircraft Artillery Brigade took over from VIII Corps the responsibility for Antiaircraft defense of Bastogne (P5558) and added an Automatic Weapons Battery to the two gun battery defense.

The bridgehead over the Our River at Echternach (L0536) was being expanded and, when progress permitted it was planned to establish gun defenses of Our River bridges in that vicinity. Two batteries of the 115th Antiaircraft Artillery Gun Battalion, relieved by two batteries of the 119th Antiaircraft Artillery Gun Battalion from Arlon (P6222) in the Antiaircraft defenses of Luxembourg (P8414), were moved forward to the vicinity of Echternach (L0536) on 8 February. The 129th Antiaircraft Gun Battalion was divided between the steel mill at Differdange (P6604) and Arlon (P6222), with two batteries at each point.

On the night of 10 February, memories of a past campaign were revived when Third US Army Antiaircraft shot down an enemy mail plane bearing mail for German troops in the beleaguered ports of St Nazaire (H5663) and Lorient (G7521). These two cities formed the remaining pockets of German troops which the Third US Army had bottled up prior to driving eastward in its sweep across France.

On 10 February Third US Army regained control of the 10th Armored Division and the attached 796th Antiaircraft Artillery Automatic Weapons Battalion (Self-propelled). These units were moved to the vicinity of Metz (U8659) and attached to the XX Corps.

A request was received from the Ninth Air Force for protection of a large maintenance depot to be set up at Airfield Y-33C in the vicinity of Thionville (U8685). Defense of the above installation was established with one Automatic Weapons Battery, withdrawn from a supply point of relatively low priority, on 12 February.

Antiaircraft Artillery gun defense of Echternach (L0536) was established on 14 February with the two gun batteries which had been attached to the XII Corps on 8 February. Although it had been the policy of the Third US Army to establish Inner Artillery Zones at vital river crossings, it was felt that air superiority at this particular time was such that complete restrictions of flying in this area was not justified. With concurrence of the Commanding General XIX Tactical Air Command, a Blank Check area was established to permit Antiaircraft guns to fire at unseen aircraft when the Fighter Control Center could inform them that no friendly planes were in the area.

The offensive in the XX Corps was progressing and the Saar Moselle triangle was being cleared. This resulted in the movement of two batteries of the 119th Antiaircraft Artillery Gun Battalion from the defense of Luxembourg (P8414) into the XX Corps sector for Antiaircraft defense in the vicinity of Saarburg (L1412) on 23 February. The desired scale of gun defenses at Luxembourg (P8414) was maintained by taking the two batteries from Arlon (P6222), no longer a vital communications center.

With good weather continuing, the drive in the XII Corps was expanding its bridgehead and build-up of troops across the river. To insure adequate gun defenses for the river crossing in Echternach (L0536), the two remaining batteries of the 115th Antiaircraft Artillery Gun Battalion were moved forward to this crossing on the 22nd and 24th of February respectively, reducing the scale of gun defense of Luxembourg (P8414) to six batteries.

The 567th Antiaircraft Artillery Automatic Weapons Battalion which had been temporarily attached to the Sixth US Army Group was returned to the Third US Army on 27 February. Automatic Weapons defenses of installations in the Army area were adjusted to furnish maximum protection. The addition of this Antiaircraft unit permitted a general regrouping of Automatic Weapons units.

The German Air Force flew no sizable sorties in the area and was content with sporadic reconnaissance flights.

No new tactics were reported. No jet-propelled planes were sighted over the Army area.

Antiaircraft Artillery units claimed three category I's and six category II's. Since the number of enemy planes engaged was a few less than the thirty-two reported, these nine claims equal about thirty-three percent destroyed or probably destroyed of all enemy aircraft reported.

With the decline in activity of the Luftwaffe an increasing number of ground support missions were fired by Antiaircraft Artillery Automatic Weapons Battalion attached to Division.

Figure 14 indicates Antiaircraft disposition as of 28 February.

Copies of Weekly Intelligence Reports for the month of February are attached as Annex 9.

Chapter 10
March Operations

The assignment of the 65th Infantry Division to the Third US Army without an Antiaircraft Artillery Battalion made it necessary to furnish a unit from the 38th Antiaircraft Artillery Brigade. On 2 March, the 546th Antiaircraft Artillery Automatic Weapons Battalion was attached to the division. A second unit was withdrawn from Army Antiaircraft Artillery on 5 March, when the 550th Antiaircraft Artillery Automatic

Weapons Battalion was attached to the 89th Infantry Division which had also been assigned to Third US Army without Antiaircraft Artillery.

Due to limited activity of the German Air Force and the lessening of the threat to vital areas, it was felt that restrictions to flying of friendly aircraft over these areas were now unwarranted. Therefore the Antiaircraft Officer initiated action to have all Inner Artillery Zones within the Third US Army area cancelled effective 5 March. Inner Artillery Zones were to be again requested upon resumption of activity by the German Air Force. Blankcheck areas were substituted at all points defended by 90mm guns.

Having penetrated the Siegfried Line, the Third US Army advanced rapidly along the north portion of the front and by 2 March had expanded its Saar River bridgehead south of Trier (L2129). By 5 March the 10th Armored Division had pushed into Trier (L2129) and the 217th Antiaircraft Artillery Gun Battalion which had been employed at St Vith (P8588) and Bastogne (P5558) was moved forward in the XX Corps zone for the defense of this city. On 6 March when the city had been sufficiently cleared, gun defense was established.

The shortage of Antiaircraft Artillery which had been created by the arrival of the above Infantry Divisions was alleviated by the assignment of the 599th Antiaircraft Artillery Automatic Weapons Battalion and the 815th Antiaircraft Artillery Automatic Weapons Battalion to Third US Army on 5 and 7 March respectively. With these two additional units it was possible for the 38th Antiaircraft Artillery Brigade to readjust defenses and make a more complete coverage of important Army installations which were building up to support Third Army's drive toward Koblenz (L9095).

Between 8-10 March the 377th Antiaircraft Artillery Automatic Weapons Battalion and the 777th Antiaircraft Artillery Automatic Weapons Battalion (Self-propelled) were relieved from attachment to the Third US Army when control of the divisions to which they were attached passed to the Sixth US Army Group. On 12 March the 574th Antiaircraft Artillery Automatic Weapons Battalion (Self-propelled) arrived in the Army area and was attached to the 38th Antiaircraft Artillery Brigade to cover missions in the Corps and Army area.

Advantage was taken of the lull in enemy air activity to make available special tracking missions in the Army area and in the rear of the Corps area. Through the cooperation of the XIX Tactical Air Command, "battle weary" P-47's flown by replacement pilots simulated low level diving and strafing attacks on Automatic Weapons units. Missions were scheduled and flown with marked success whenever weather conditions permitted.

On 14 March the 32d Antiaircraft Artillery Group was given the task of reconnoitering for a suitable Antiaircraft Artillery Automatic Weapons firing range site and making necessary preparations to operate the range. The loss of the 32nd Antiaircraft Artillery Group to the Fifteenth US Army on 29 March together with the reappearance of the German Air Force in strength necessitated postponement of these plans.

A change in lateral boundaries excluded the city of Metz (U8659) from the Third US Army area. The 128th Antiaircraft Artillery Gun Battalion which had been defending this city was relieved of the mission on 16 March and prepared to move forward to the vicinity of Koblenz (L9095) where it was to defend the Rhine River crossing planned for this area. Arrangements were completed to establish a Blankcheck area to permit unseen firing at night when the defense was established.

On 16 March the 447th Antiaircraft Artillery Automatic Weapons Battalion was attached to Third US Army with the 28th Infantry Division. On 18 March the 574th Antiaircraft Artillery Automatic Weapons Battalion (Self-propelled) was released from the Third US Army in order to make available an Antiaircraft unit for the 13th Armored Division which had been assigned to the Sixth US Army Group.

During the initial phase of the drive toward the Rhine River, the German Air Force had failed to appear in strength. Antiaircraft units had therefore been employed extensively in a ground role. On 17 March elements of the 390th Antiaircraft Artillery Automatic Weapons Battalion (Self-propelled), supporting a task force of the 26th Infantry Division, pushed through the town of Buprich (Q3591) spraying enemy troops while under heavy fire and silencing sniper and machine gun fire to capture a bridge intact. The defense of the bridge was quickly organized and it was held intact until tanks, tank destroyers and infantry arrived to take over. Other Antiaircraft units contributed to the Third US Army push by their execution of ground role missions.

The 115th Antiaircraft Artillery Gun Battalion was relieved of its mission at Echternach (L0536) on 17 March and moved forward to the XII Corps zone. The 129th Antiaircraft Artillery Gun Battalion was relieved from its mission at the steel mill at Differdange (P6604) on 18 March and the defense of Luxembourg (P8413) and moved forward to the XII Corps zone to be available immediately for defense of planned Rhine River crossing. Temporarily they were given the mission of defending river crossings over the Nahe River in the vicinity of Bad Kreuznach (M0938).

On 18 March the Third US Army drove across the Nahe River capturing a bridge intact at Bretzenheim (M1242). A Blankcheck area was established at this point. Gun Battalions under control of XII Corps set up its Antiaircraft defense. Bridges were built across the river further southwest at Bad Kreuznach (M0938) and Bad Munster (M0835) and were immediately covered by automatic weapons battalion attached to Corps and Divisions.

The German Air Force, active over First US Army's Remagen bridgehead, displayed relatively little activity over Third US Army during the first sixteen days of March. As XII Corps continued its advance, however, enemy planes attacked fiercely. Columns of the 4th Armored Division, spearheading the Corps attack, were subject to heaviest attack. On 17 March, Antiaircraft shot down seventeen planes and probably destroyed sixteen more. During the following two days the scale of the enemy air attack lessened, although eight planes were shot down and ten more claimed as probables.

On the south, XX Corps' columns, rolling up the Siegfried Line and destroying German static positions, drew equal attention from the Luftwaffe. When it appeared that Rhine bridges might be captured, the Antiaircraft Officer of the XX Corps requested a gun battalion be made available at the earliest possible date. The 120th Antiaircraft Artillery Gun Battalion, which was divided between Differdange (P6604) and Thionville (U8685) had been alerted for movement on short notice. Upon being relieved by units of the 51st Antiaircraft Artillery Brigade Differdange (P6604), the 120th Antiaircraft Artillery Gun Battalion was moved forward on 22 March to the vicinity of Alzey (M2728), where large quantities of ordnance and engineer equipment were expected to accumulate. Under the control of the 38th Antiaircraft Artillery Brigade, the 120th Antiaircraft Gun Battalion and other Antiaircraft units which were moving forward in preparation for the river crossing were given the temporary mission of protecting the equipment.

By 23 March, armored spearheads of the Third US Army had driven deep into the Seventh US Army zone. As a result, the 10th and 12th Armored Divisions and their attached 796th and 572d Antiaircraft Artillery Automatic Weapons Battalions (Self-propelled) were attached to the Sixth US Army Group. On the same date the 777th Antiaircraft Artillery Automatic Weapons Battalion (Self-propelled) reverted to Third US Army control from Sixth US Army Group. The Antiaircraft situation as of 23 March is shown in **Figure 15.**

When Oppenheim (M4441) was chosen for the site of the river crossings for the XII Corps, a Blankcheck area was initially established to allow unseen fire at night. Because of the importance of this crossing, a request was immediately made for an Inner Artillery Zone with a ceiling of 15,000 feet and a radius of 15,000 yards through which the flight of friendly aircraft would be prohibited at night.

Figure 15

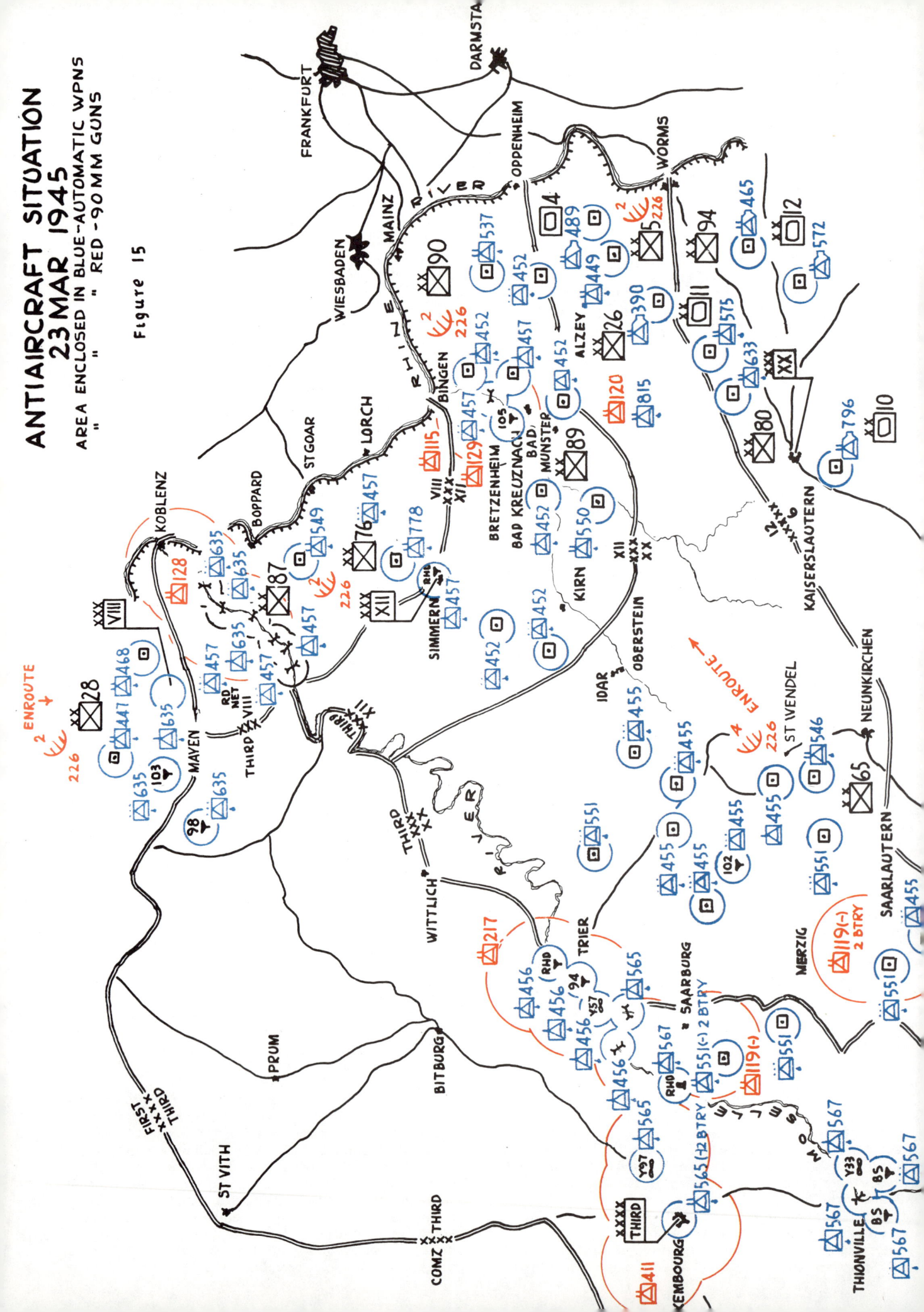

ANTIAIRCRAFT SITUATION
23 MAR 1945
AREA ENCLOSED IN BLUE-AUTOMATIC WPNS
" " " RED - 90 MM GUNS

Figure 16

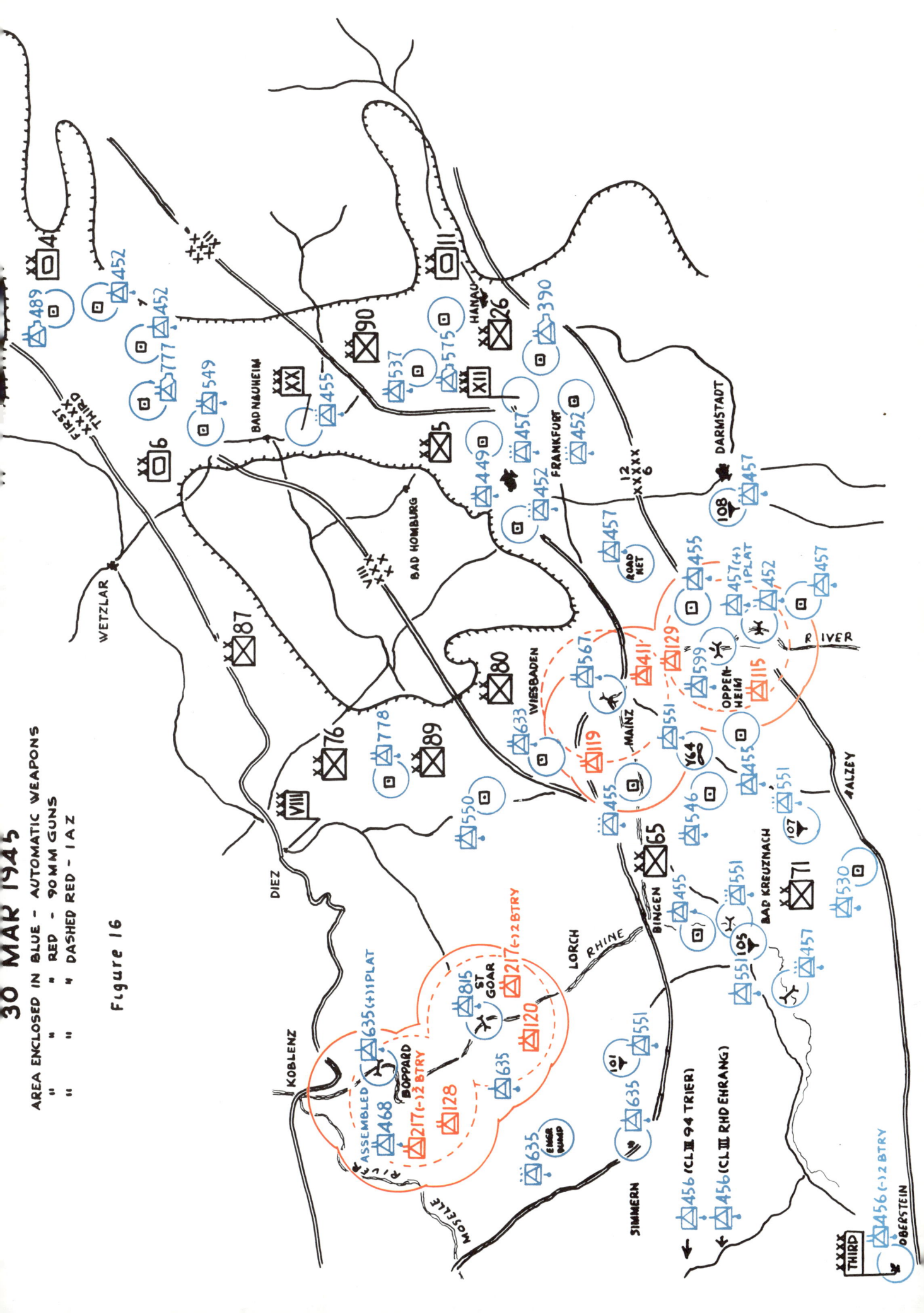

30 MAR 1945

AREA ENCLOSED IN BLUE — AUTOMATIC WEAPONS
" " RED — 90MM GUNS
" " DASHED RED — 1 AZ

On the 20th, the enemy made the heaviest air attacks experienced by Third US Army troops during the entire campaign. Attacks were made against the bridge in the vicinity of Bretzenheim (M1242), Bad Munster (M0835) and against elements of the 4th Armored and 90th Infantry Divisions. Many types of enemy aircraft, including jet-propelled Me-262s participated in bombing and strafing attacks. A total of 314 aircraft made sixty one raids in the XII Corps zone. Antiaircraft, successfully defending troops and installations, shot down twenty-five attacking planes and claimed eleven more as probably destroyed.

On the night of 22 March troops of the 5th Infantry Division began moving over the Rhine River at Oppenheim (M4441). An additional Automatic Weapons Battalion, the 599th, had been attached to XII Corps for the bridgehead. Both heavy and light Antiaircraft, which had been held ready for this crossing, quickly established antiaircraft defenses. The crossing apparently achieved tactical surprise. The Luftwaffe made no attacks during the first twenty-four hours; then it struck in force at the bridges. Of 154 attacking enemy aircraft, eighteen were shot down and fifteen more were probably destroyed. Bridges remained intact. Two additional enemy planes were shot down by XX Corps Antiaircraft gunners when attacks were made against the 12th Armored Division and Field Artillery Battalions.

On 24 March the German Air Force continued to concentrate its efforts against the crossing in the XII Corps zone. Again Antiaircraft scored heavily when it shot down twenty-six of the 138 attacking planes and probably destroyed six additional planes. On the following day, the heaviest attacks yet made on the bridgehead took place when 230 aircraft struck at bridges, troops and installations. Antiaircraft Artillery destroyed twenty-nine of the raiding planes and claimed twenty-three probably destroyed. Attacks were unceasing and around-the-clock. They were made from altitudes of twenty feet to 15,000 feet. Strafing followed each bombing attack. Only three planes appeared over the remainder of the XII Corps zone, one of which was destroyed and another probably destroyed. These losses to the German Air Force, combined with the loss of its fighter fields which had been overrun by Third US Army's advancing armor and infantry, reduced the threat to the bridgehead which had now been firmly established. The Inner Artillery Zone with a radius of 15,000 yards and a ceiling of 15,000 feet established for the Oppenheim (M4441) Crossing aided considerably in the defense.

Following close behind the establishment of the bridgehead at Oppenheim (M4441) the VIII Corps sent troops of the 87th Infantry Division across the Rhine River at Boppard (M9081) on 24-25 March. Troops of the 89th Infantry Division made crossings at St Goar (L9872) on 25-26 March. For use at these crossings the 120th and 217th Antiaircraft Artillery Gun Battalions and the 551st and 815th Antiaircraft Artillery Automatic Weapons Battalions, all Army units, had been attached to Corps to supplement Antiaircraft Artillery of the Corps and divisions. Inner Artillery Zones were established at both crossings on the night of 25 March. The ceiling of these Inner Artillery Zones was 10,000 feet, a 15,000 feet ceiling having been refused by higher headquarters.

Enemy Air Force efforts at Boppard (L9081) and St Goar (L9872) was confined to less than thirty planes of which four were shot down and three probably destroyed during the first five days of the operation.

The Third US Army forward Command Post was moved from Luxembourg (P8413) to Oberstein (L7123) Germany on 27 March and an Automatic Weapons defense established there with two batteries of the 456th Antiaircraft Artillery Automatic Weapons Battalion.

A fourth crossing of the River Rhine at Mainz (M3950) was made by the XX Corps on 27-28 March by troops of the 80th Infantry Division. Army units, the 119th and 411th Antiaircraft Artillery Gun Battalions and the 567th Antiaircraft Artillery Automatic Weapons Battalion, had been attached to the XX Corps for this crossing. A Blankcheck area was established there effective the night of 28 March until an Inner Artillery Zone became effective. Enemy air activity over this bridgehead was very light.

Third US Army's sweep across the Rhine toward the heart of Germany had produced supply problems similar to those which existed after the Avranches (T2718) breakthrough in August. Lines of communication were extremely long and every available truck was needed to move supplies forward and prisoners of war to the rear. A large number of trucks were made available for twenty-four or forty-eight hour trips and thousands of tons of badly needed supplies were moved by Antiaircraft Artillery units.

On 30 March the 468th Antiaircraft Artillery Automatic Weapons Battalion (Self-propelled) was relieved of its missions under VIII Corps and assembled in preparation for its transfer to Fifteenth US Army on 1 April. The Antiaircraft Artillery situation as of 30 March is shown in **Figure 16**.

The attachment of the bulk of Army Antiaircraft Artillery to the Corps for the Rhine River crossings left undefended many important installations in the Army area. Some of these in the rear of the Army area were taken over by Antiaircraft units of the IX Air Defense Command. Others remained undefended. The vulnerability of the bridges and bridgeheads and also the belief that the Luftwaffe would mass its strength there, justified the risk which was taken.

By 31 March the 38th Antiaircraft Artillery Brigade had taken over from the Corps the mission of protecting all crossings of the Rhine River as well as important installations west of the Rhine. Corps Antiaircraft Artillery Groups, moving forward, set up defenses along the Main River for airfields on which gasoline was being landed by the Air Transport Command and for other important installations.

The arrival of the 70th Infantry Division provided an additional Antiaircraft ArtilleryAutomatic Weapons Battalion which was placed under operational command of the 38th Antiaircraft Artillery Brigade on 31 March. Under an existing directive this battalion could only be employed on the west bank of the Rhine River. The 70th Infantry Division was charged with ground security to the west of the Rhine River, including the crossings, and all Antiaircraft Artillery on the river, including radar and searchlights employed in river surveillance, was coordinated with the Division Plan.

The month of March marked the first appearance of jet-propelled aircraft over Third US Army area in any numbers as Me-262s and Ar-234s became commonplace. Flights as large as six and larger flights of mixed jet and standard type aircraft were encountered.

Copies of Weekly Intelligence Reports for the month of March are attached as Annex 10.

Gunners of an Antiaircraft battery supporting the 90th Infantry Division with Third US Army on alert during preparation of emplacement.

Chapter 11
April Operations

At the beginning of the month the enemy decreased his efforts to interrupt traffic over the Rhine and Main rivers. Instead, frantic efforts were made to brake the advance of the 4th, 6th, and 11th Armored Divisions, all of which were thrusting prongs deep into the center of Germany. The change in enemy tactics proved costly as evidenced by the 2 April reports of the 489th Antiaircraft Artillery Automatic Weapons Battalion (Self-propelled) which claimed thirty-five enemy planes destroyed and five probably destroyed during the twenty four hour period. In the entire Army area, sixty-seven enemy planes destroyed and twenty-three probably destroyed were claimed for the same period.

The abandonment of the Boppard (L8983) crossing, and the expected opening of the bridges at Lorch (M0560) and Bingen (M1353) necessitated the reorganization of defenses

on the Rhine River. On 3 and 5 April the entire defense of the Boppard (L8983) crossing was discontinued and the units moved to establish the defense of the Lorch (M0560) crossing at a scale of one gun battalion and one automatic weapons battalion. On 4 and 5 April, two gun batteries from the Oppenheim (M4441) crossing were moved to the Bingen (M1353) crossing and on 4 April this gun defense was augmented by two automatic weapons batteries. Inner Artillery Zones were established at the Bingen (M1353) crossing on 6 April, and at the Lorch ((M0560) crossing on 4 April. The zone at Boppard (L8983) was cancelled on 3 April. Two automatic weapons batteries were moved from Oppenheim (M4441) to the Mainz (M3956) crossing on 5 April to balance defenses between these two major crossings.

On 5 April, the 574th Antiaircraft Artillery Automatic Weapons Battalion (Self-propelled) which had been defending supply points and installations in the Army area was released to the 13th Armored Division and the 551st Antiaircraft Artillery Automatic Weapons Battalion, which had just been relieved of defense of bridges at Bad Kreuznach (M1040) by the IX Air Defense Command, was placed under control of the Provost Marshal, Third US Army. Although there were many installations at which use could be made of the 551st Antiaircraft Artillery Automatic Weapons Battalion, the need for additional troops to provide security was urgent enough to make the change necessary.

As the 4th Armored Division drove through the Thuringia Forest and the other armored divisions continued their rapid progress, uninterrupted delivery and supply of gasoline became a matter of great concern. The defense of the airfield terminals constituted an important part of the Antiaircraft activities throughout April. The 5th Infantry Division, being temporarily on a security mission, its Antiaircraft unit, the 449th Antiaircraft Artillery Automatic Weapons Battalion, was placed under operational command of the 38th Antiaircraft Artillery Brigade on 6 April and assigned the mission of protecting airfields. On 8 April the 5th Infantry Division moved north out of the Third US Army area and the antiaircraft artillery battalion was released from its mission. Defenses on the Rhine at Mainz (M3956) and Oppenheim (M4441) were decreased by two automatic weapons batteries each in order to replace the battalion on the airfields.

The importance of giving protection to airfields used by C-47 transports carrying gasoline was illustrated on 10 April when enemy planes attacked C-47s coming in to the Langensalza (J0484) airfield. Two C-47s were attacked and destroyed while they were out of range of the antiaircraft protecting the airfield. As the flight of transports came closer, the attacking fighters were engaged by the antiaircraft unit protecting this field and were driven off, thereby preventing further damage.

Further reduction of the defenses on the Rhine River was necessary on 8 April to provide antiaircraft units for several new missions. **Two gun batteries and one automatic weapons battery were required for the Forward Third US Army Command Post which was scheduled to move from Frankfurt (M6768) to Hersfeld (H4053) in a few days.** Two gun batteries and one automatic weapons battery were required for river crossings at Eisenach (H8068). Third US Army troops had discovered a mine in the vicinity of Merkers (H6850) where gold and art treasures were stored; two gun batteries and one automatic weapons battery were necessary for this defense. Antiaircraft units furnished a task force on 15 and 17 April which provided protection for movement of the gold and art treasures out of the mine to the rear area. To provide these organizations, the gun defenses at Oppenheim (M4441) and Mainz (M3956) were each decreased by two gun batteries; this change left a full gun battalion at Oppenheim (M4441) and six gun batteries at Mainz (M3956). **The gun defenses at Lorch (M0560), consisting of four gun batteries and four automatic weapons batteries, were decreased fifty percent as it became apparent that the approaches to the bridge were inadequate, and the crossing would be abandoned.**

On 10 April, the defenses at Lorch (M0560) and St Goar (L9873) were discontinued and the Inner Artillery zones at these points were cancelled. Four gun batteries so released were placed under control of XX Corps and two were used to augment defenses at Merkers (H6850) under XII Corps. **Two automatic weapons batteries were released to VIII Corps.**

On 16 April, the defense at Merkers (H6850) was placed under the control of the 38th Antiaircraft Artillery Brigade. When the defense at Merkers (H6850) was discontinued on 18 April, the gun battalion so relieved was released to XII Corps.

During the period 12-16 April while the 6th Armored Division was driving southwest of Liepzig (E3020) and the 4th Armored Division smashed east and southeast to clear Wiemar (J5070) against ineffective resistance, **antiaircraft operations consisted chiefly of rapid movement in order to protect the airfields and Class III Supply Points which were being established on airfields as soon as they were overrun.**

On 16 April, the Third US Army started its shift southeast to drive on the area reported to be the German National Redoubt. This change presented to antiaircraft artillery the problem of protecting the heavy movement of troops and supplies down to the area occupied at that time by the Seventh US Army. To provide this protection, the defense of bridges on the Autobahn Highway A-4 was discontinued on 17 April releasing one gun battalion and one automatic weapons battery. One gun battalion and **two automatic weapons batteries were detached from the VIII Corps on the same date.** These units were used to establish a highway defense in the vicinity of Coburg (O-3090). The gun batteries were placed at 20,000 yard intervals on Highway 4 north and south of Coburg (O-3090). The automatic weapons were used to reinforce the defenses at critical points along the route. Another important road net was in the vicinity of Schweinfurt (N7964). **Units for defense of this area were obtained by reducing the defense of Forward Command Post, Third US Army and the Mainz (M3956) crossing by two gun batteries each.** Two automatic weapons batteries were obtained from Merkers (H6850) and from a Class III Supply Point in the vicinity of Menningen (H9122). The plan for defense of this area was the same as that for the Coburg (O-3090) area.

Antiaircraft defenses were also established on Route 8 east and west of Wurzburg (N5935) on 20 April with five gun batteries and two automatic weapons batteries which had been relieved by IX Air Defense Command at Mainz (M3956) and Bingen (M1353). By 26 April much of the troop movement had taken place and the Third US Army was poised for its drive southward. The disposition of Antiaircraft Artillery units at that time is shown in **Figure 17.**

On 24 April a readjustment of the road defenses was made. The main north-south road through Coburg (O-3090) had decreased in importance. One gun battalion was relieved of its mission in this area and assigned the mission of protecting Route 8 and the railroad line between Wurzburg (M5935) and Aschaffenburg (N0154). The units already in this area were redeployed to protect the highway southeast of Wurzburg (N5935) to Nurnberg (T4399).

The army move southward also necessitated shifting automatic weapons batteries to cover new Class III Supply Points and airfields. On 17-18 April, supply points at Wurzburg (N5935) and Bamburg (O-2749) were covered. A unit of the Seventh US Army was relieved at airfield R-6, vicinity of Kitzingen (N7831) on 18 April.

On the night of 18-19 April, the highway in the vicinity of the Army Forward Command Post at Hersfeld (H3953) was strafed and bombed. On the three previous nights, this area had been strafed. **The defense consisting of two gun batteries and one automatic weapons battery was augmented by the addition of one automatic weapons battery** and the entire defense was planned to take advantage of the consistent northeast-southwest course flown by the enemy. Six

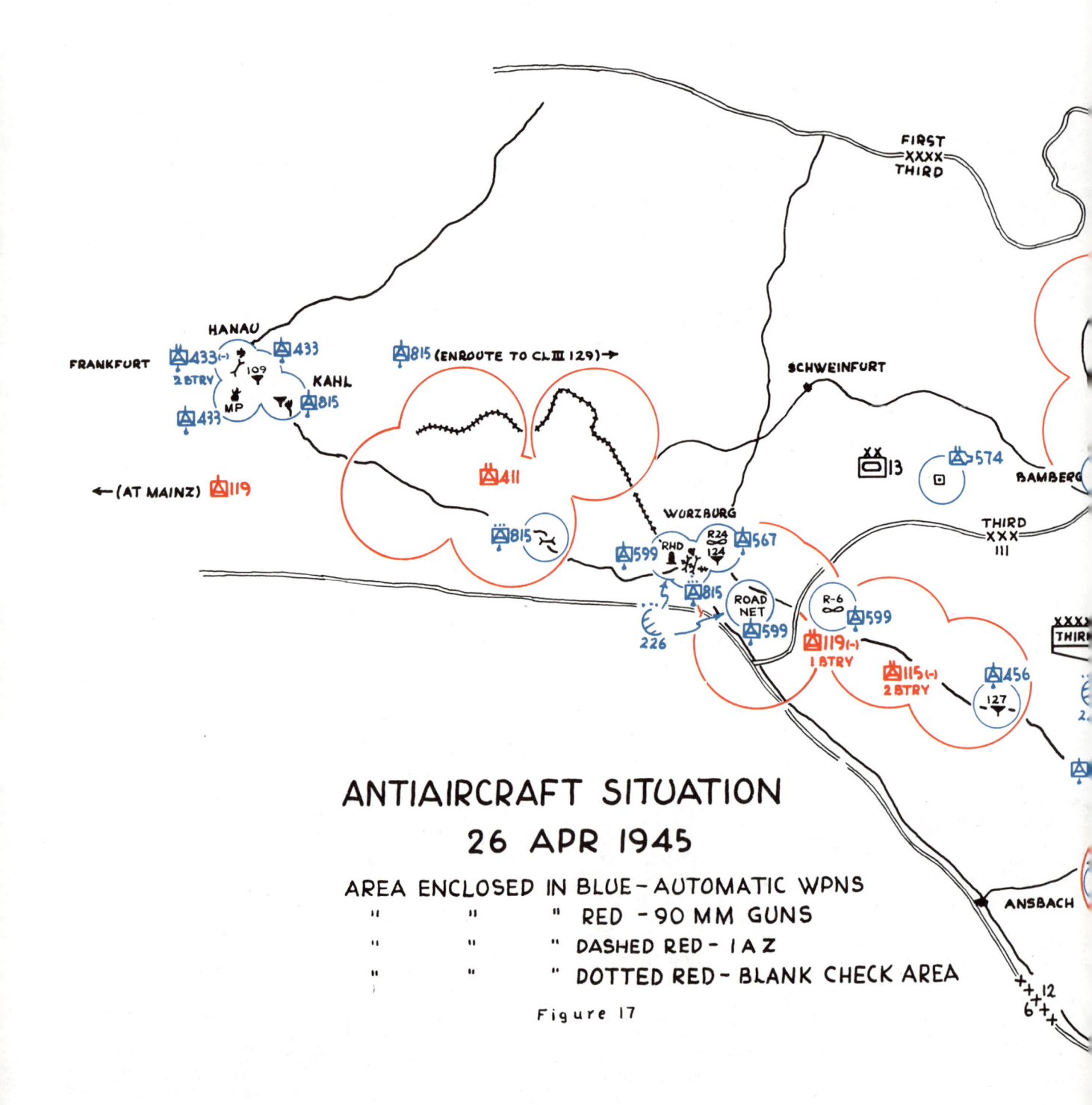

ANTIAIRCRAFT SITUATION
26 APR 1945

AREA ENCLOSED IN BLUE — AUTOMATIC WPNS
" " " RED — 90 MM GUNS
" " " DASHED RED — IAZ
" " " DOTTED RED — BLANK CHECK AREA

Figure 17

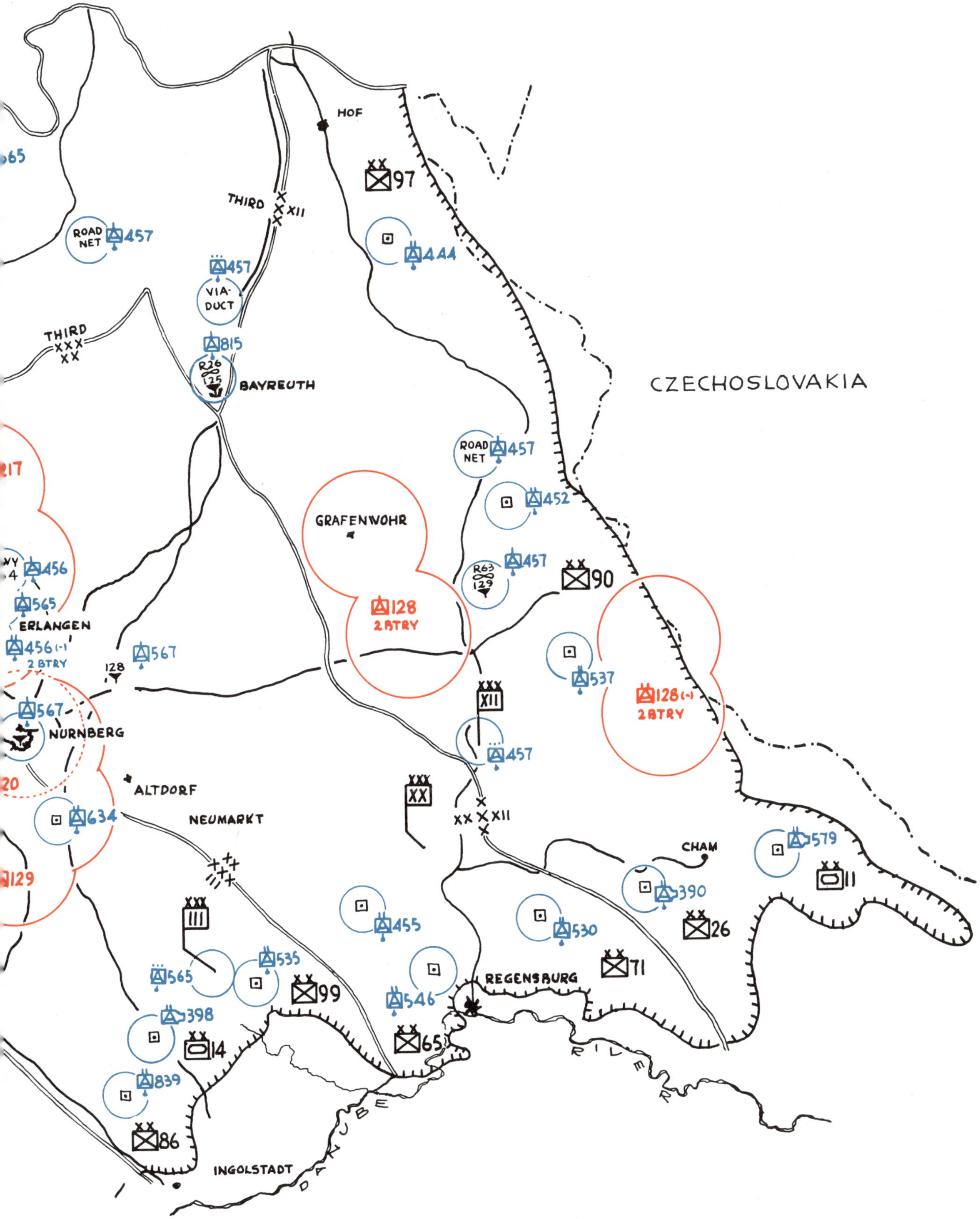
HOF
THIRD
XII
ROAD NET
457
444
97
VIA-DUCT
815
THIRD
BAYREUTH
CZECHOSLOVAKIA
GRAFENWOHR
128
2 BTRY
452
90
456
565
ERLANGEN
456 (-)
2 BTRY
567
537
128 (-)
2 BTRY
XII
NURNBERG
ALTDORF
XX
NEUMARKT
634
129
CHAM
579
390
455
530
26
11
III
535
565
99
546
REGENSBURG
71
398
14
65
RIVER
839
DANUBE
86
INGOLSTADT

searchlights were brought into the area to illuminate low flying craft. **The defenses in the area were placed under the direct operational control of the Antiaircraft Section, Headquarters Third US Army.** An Inner Artillery Zone was established on 20 April.

On 26 April, the defenses on the road between Coburg (O-3090) and Nurnberg (T4399) were discontinued and the two gun batteries released were sent south of Nurnberg (T4399) to protect the road net in that area. Nurnberg (T4399) was becoming more and more important as a supply base and communications center. Throughout the remainder of the month, defenses in the Nurnberg (T4399) area were augmented as the Quartermaster and Ordnance supply points there increased in size. The relief of Third US Army units in the rear area by IX Air Defense Command made units available for these missions.

The 120th Antiaircraft Artillery Gun Battalion which had been employed by XX Corps to protect installations in the vicinity of Nurnberg (T4399), was moved to an assembly area on 23 April in readiness for the Danube River crossings. On 23 and 24 April, the 129th Antiaircraft Artillery Gun Battalion was attached to the III Corps for Danube River crossings. **A Blankcheck area at Regensburg (U1956) was established for the XX Corps on 27 April.** On 29 April, Blankcheck areas at Ingolstadt (T7325) and at Marching (T9332) were established for III Corps. **By 30 April, Corps had already moved forward to the Isar River.** Defenses on the Danube were taken over by the 38th Antiaircraft Artillery Brigade, and the 411th Antiaircraft Artillery Gun Battalion was attached to XX Corps and the 119th Antiaircraft Artillery Gun Battalion to III Corps for the Isar River crossings.

Antiaircraft Artillery gunners during the month of April took heavy toll of the Luftwaffe, turning in a new record. 316 Category I's and 172 Category II's — a total of 488 claims — were made for the month, surpassing even the claims for August, 1944. An estimated 1,327 enemy planes operated over the area in a series of 470 raids, of which 36.7% failed to return to their home bases as a result of Antiaircraft Artillery action.

One reason for the high losses claimed was the tactics of the Luftwaffe which attacked almost entirely during daytime and at altitudes ideal for engagement by automatic weapons. Although there was activity almost every day of the month, most of it occurred during the first half when spearheading armored divisions were continually under attack, as were forward elements of the infantry and artillery mopping up behind. Targets of opportunity such as highway traffic and convoys, troop assemblies, artillery and Antiaircraft Artillery positions were the main objectives, though airfields loading Class III supplies, Class III supply dumps, bridges, Command Posts and miscellaneous targets also were bombed and strafed. There was little activity behind Corps rear boundaries until the latter half of the month when small scale sorties were flown at night to harass headlighted traffic in the rear areas. Even reconnaissance missions behind Corps lines were infrequent, though many such missions were flown over forward elements of divisions.

Overruning of airfields, capture of crews and planes, gasoline shortages and attendant disruption of organization caused rapid reduction in the enemy air effort and, at month's end, the Luftwaffe tactical threat was ended. Indicative of this was the increased use of the ragtag planes heretofore kept in the background for training and liaison purposes, which were now tactically employed for reconnaissance and possibly for agent-dropping missions. Such odd planes as Me-108s, Bu-181s, Arados and other trainers were shot down, including several "pick-a-back" planes which were even used for strafing missions. The end was definitely in sight and the once feared, once unequaled Luftwaffe was rapidly on its way toward oblivion as the month drew to a close.

During the month three instruction teams had been placed on temporary duty with the Third US Army. Two of the teams were specially trained on automatic weapons and the other on 90mm guns. Schedules were arranged for both Corps and Army units to receive instruction in gunnery, maintenance, and operation of equipment.

An Antiaircraft radio net incuding the Antiaircraft Section, Headquarters Third US Army, 38th Antiaircraft Artillery Brigade, 51st Antiaircraft Artillery Brigade, 27th, 112th, and 113th Antiaircraft Artillery Groups became operational on 17 April. Just after the net became operational, the 113th Antiaircraft Artillery Group was transferred with the VIII Corps to the First US Army, and the 16th Antiaircraft Artillery Group attached to the III Corps took the place of the 113th Antiaircraft Artillery Group. The Antiaircraft Section, Third US Army operated the net control station with an SCR-399 radio set. All other stations used the SCR-177. The net proved useful in maintaining communications with Antiaircraft units during the rapidly moving situation.

During April, ten corps and division automatic weapons units finished conversion from M-51 quadruple .50 caliber machine gun trailer mounts to type M-16 half track mounts. The objections to the M-51 trailers were that they were not suitable for use in a ground role because of their weight, low clearance which made them an easy prey for bad roads, and the fact they could not be fired to the front. Sixty four type M-16 half tracks complete with type M-45 quadruple machine gun turrets and 39 type M-2 half track vehicles were made available. The type M-45 turrets were removed from the M-51 trailers and mounted in the M-2 half track vehicles. These converted vehicles called M-16B and the type M-16 half tracks were enough to equip each of ten battalions with sixteen tracked vehicles which replaced the same number of M-51 trailers. M-51 mounts made excess by the M-16 mounts were reissued to gun battalions.

Weekly Intelligence Reports for the month of April are included as Annex 11.

Chapter 12
May Operations

By 1 May, activities of the Luftwaffe had been reduced almost entirely to armed reconnaissance. Such "hit and run" tactics here and there throughout the army area at targets of opportunity still constituted a threat to supply points and concentrations of troops. But the need for troops to handle law and order in the vast areas overrun by Third US Army grew so urgent that it became necessary to divert some antiaircraft troops from their primary mission for the task.

Plans were made to relieve Headquarters and Headquarters Battery, 38th Antiaircraft Artillery Brigade, which, with the 7th Antiaircraft Artillery Group, 129th Antiaircraft Artillery Gun Battalion and the 457th and 565th Antiaircraft Artillery Automatic Weapons Battalions, was to become responsible for law and order and protection of lines of communication in an area in the vicinity of Erlangen (O-3816). Units were to be released for this mission by 5 May at which time the scale of antiaircraft artillery in the army would be reduced to one antiaircraft artillery group, one gun and one automatic weapons battalion per corps, and two groups, three gun battalions and four automatic weapons battalions for Army Antiaircraft Artillery. In addition, the 433rd Antiaircraft Artillery Automatic Weapons Battalion, attached to the 70th Infantry Division, was to remain temporarily under operational control of Army. The 207th Antiaircraft Artillery Group with the 119th Antiaircraft Artillery Gun Battalion, 456th, 599th, 433rd Antiaircraft Artillery Automatic Weapons Battalions, and one searchlight platoon was to cover installations in the southwestern portion of the Army area; the 24th Antiaircraft Artillery Group with the 411th and 120th Antiaircraft Artillery Gun Battalions, 567th and 815th Antiaircraft Artillery Automatic Weapons Battalions and one platoon of searchlights was to protect installations in the northeastern portion of the Army area. See overlay number one.

Third US Army's drive to the south and southeast had continued and on 1 May, Blankcheck areas were established to protect Isar River crossings at Nd Humel (Z0690) and Landshut (U2502), in the III Corps zone, and at N. Poring (U7525) and Nied Viehbach (U4212), in the XX Corps zone. The 119th Antiaircraft Artillery Gun Battalion had already been released to the III Corps and the 411th Antiaircraft Artillery Gun Battalion to the XX Corps for these crossings.

By 2 May, the Third US Army area had become so long that it was difficult to exercise control over Antiaircraft units defending installations in the rear. A change was made therefore in the rear air boundary and units of the 51st Antiaircraft Artillery Brigade relieved Third US Army on a Class III Supply Point, a Class III Decanting Point, an Ordnance Motor Pool and a railroad bridge, all in the vicinity of Hanau (M8470). Two of the four batteries so relieved were used to defend the railroad bridge being completed vicinity of Bamberg (O-2452) and a Class V Railhead in the Nurnberg (T4399) area which had become important upon the completion of the rail line from Wurzburg (N5935) to Nurnberg (T4399). **The other two batteries relieved units at Third US Army Rear Command Post at Erlangen (O-3916) for use forward in the army area.**

Movement of the Third US Army forward Command Post to Regensburg (U1956) on 2 May necessitated a readjustment of defenses there to include a platoon of searchlights. The blankcheck area already in effect was changed several days later to an Inner Artillery Zone.

As during the month of April, the protection of airfields being used by gasoline carrying planes continued to be one of the most important missions for antiaircraft artillery. The rapid movement forward continued to emphasize the importance of relieving Corps Antiaircraft Artillery units on these airfields as soon as possible. **By 3 May, Army Antiaircraft Artillery had taken over airfields in all Corps zones as far to the front as Ingolstadt (T7819), Straubing (U5438) and Cham (U5880).**

In order to relieve the 129th Antiaircraft Artillery Gun Battalion for its security role, it became necessary to reduce gun defenses along the Danube River. On 3 May the defenses at Regensburg (U1956) were reduced by two Gun Batteries which moved to relieve the 129th Antiaircraft Artillery Gun Battalion at Ingolstadt (T7819). **The two automatic weapons battalions which had been designated for the security mission were Corps units and were also being relieved to make them available on 5 May.**

By 4 May, use of the original assault crossings in the XX Corps was discontinued. New crossings had been established at Platting (U7832) and Landau (U6420). The 411th Antiaircraft Artillery Gun Battalion was redeployed and blankcheck areas were changed to cover the new crossing. On 5 May, responsibility for antiaircraft defenses of the Isar River crossings in the XX Corps zone was taken over by Army and the 411th Antiaircraft Artillery Gun Battalion reverted to Army control. XX Corps units were now at the Inn River and the 217th Antiaircraft Artillery Gun Battalion which had been attached to XX Corps on 3 May was now establishing defenses at Hagenau (Z9878) and Kirchdorf (V1081) where blankcheck areas had been set up on 4 May.

To the west in the zone of the III Corps, responsibility for Antiaircraft Artillery defense of the Isar River crossings was taken over by Army on 5 May; the 119th Antiaircraft Artillery Gun Battalion reverted to Army Control. The 115th Antiaircraft Artillery Gun Battalion had been attached to III Corps to cover the Inn River crossing and was moving south to an assembly area.

V Corps was placed under control of Third US Army on 5 May. Attached to the 115th Antiaircraft Artillery Group, operating under V Corps, were the 467th Antiaircraft Artillery Automatic Weapons Battalion (Self-propelled) and the 460th Antiaircraft Artillery Automatic Weapons Battalion. Attaching the Corps brought also the 103rd, 444th and 462nd Antiaircraft Artillery Automatic Weapons Battalions attached to the 1st, 97th and 2nd Infantry Divisions and the 571st and 482nd Antiaircraft Artillery Automatic Weapons Battalions (Self-propelled) attached to the 16th and 9th Armored Divisions.

Until V-E Day, 8 May, Third US Army continued to surge forward to the southeast into Czechoslovakia and Austria. During the period, an estimated 110 enemy aircraft were over the area in a series of approximately ninety raids with the Luftwaffe reluctant to remain on the ground until the final day. Of these, nearly all planes were engaged in reconnaissance missions. Only four attacks were reported. A Bu-181 reconnaissance craft dropped two small anti-personnel bombs (perhaps hand grenades) in the 80th Infantry Division area; two Me-109s strafed in the 26th Infantry Division area; and on the final day — 8 May — fifteen enemy aircraft strafed in the vicinity of Passau (Q2212) and Deggendorf (U8338). In the strafing attack on Passau (Q2212), two reconnaissance type ships used machine pistols fired out of the cockpit. Many were shot down and a number of pilots and passengers killed. In all, Antiaircraft claimed forty-seven aircraft destroyed and twelve probably destroyed.

Some of the reconnaissance ships shot down were loaded with explosives and detonating caps intended for use of pilot saboteurs who were to land behind our lines. This fairly large scale plot aborted.

As the last day of the campaign entered the pages of history, Third US Army Antiaircraft Artillery reported 6192 enemy planes over the area in 2463 raids since 1 August 1944. Of these 1084 were claimed as destroyed and 564 more as probably destroyed.

AAA Weekly Intelligence Report Number 41 covering the period from 040600B May to 090001B May is included as Annex 12.

Chapter 13
Lessons Learned & Conclusions

Tactics

1. **Employment.** With relatively few exceptions, enemy tactics were to make small-scale hit and run attacks on targets of opportunity throughout the area. In most instances a relatively light concentration of Antiaircraft Artillery fire was sufficient either to destroy or drive off the attacking aircraft. Where targets of vital importance presented themselves, however, attacks by enemy planes were made in large numbers and were pressed regardless of casualties. Where the enemy is not aggressive and has shown a disinclination to launch large scale attacks, defenses may be lightened to cover many objectives. A few batteries under such circumstances will be adequate to drive off light attacks. On the other hand, where objectives are of vital importance, sufficient concentration must be provided to meet intensified attacks.

2. **Automatic Weapons Fire On Unseen Targets.** Firing of automatic weapons at unseen targets was wasteful of ammunition and had no apparent deterrent effect on attacking planes. In addition, the tracer streams disclosed the gun position and outlined the target area. No barrage fire was employed by Third US Army Antiaircraft Artillery units. With the present equipment, automatic weapons are of little value unless the target can be seen.

3. **Ground Combat.** During the campaign many Antiaircraft Artillery units engaged in close combat with enemy ground or mechanized troops either in its own defense or while in an offensive supporting mission. Such engagements occasionally resulted in excessive casualties and loss of equipment due to lack of training for this type of combat. Greater emphasis should be placed upon training of Antiaircraft Artillery personnel for ground support missions and in the role of an infantry soldier. The training required is not so much in shooting as in moving into and occupying positions.

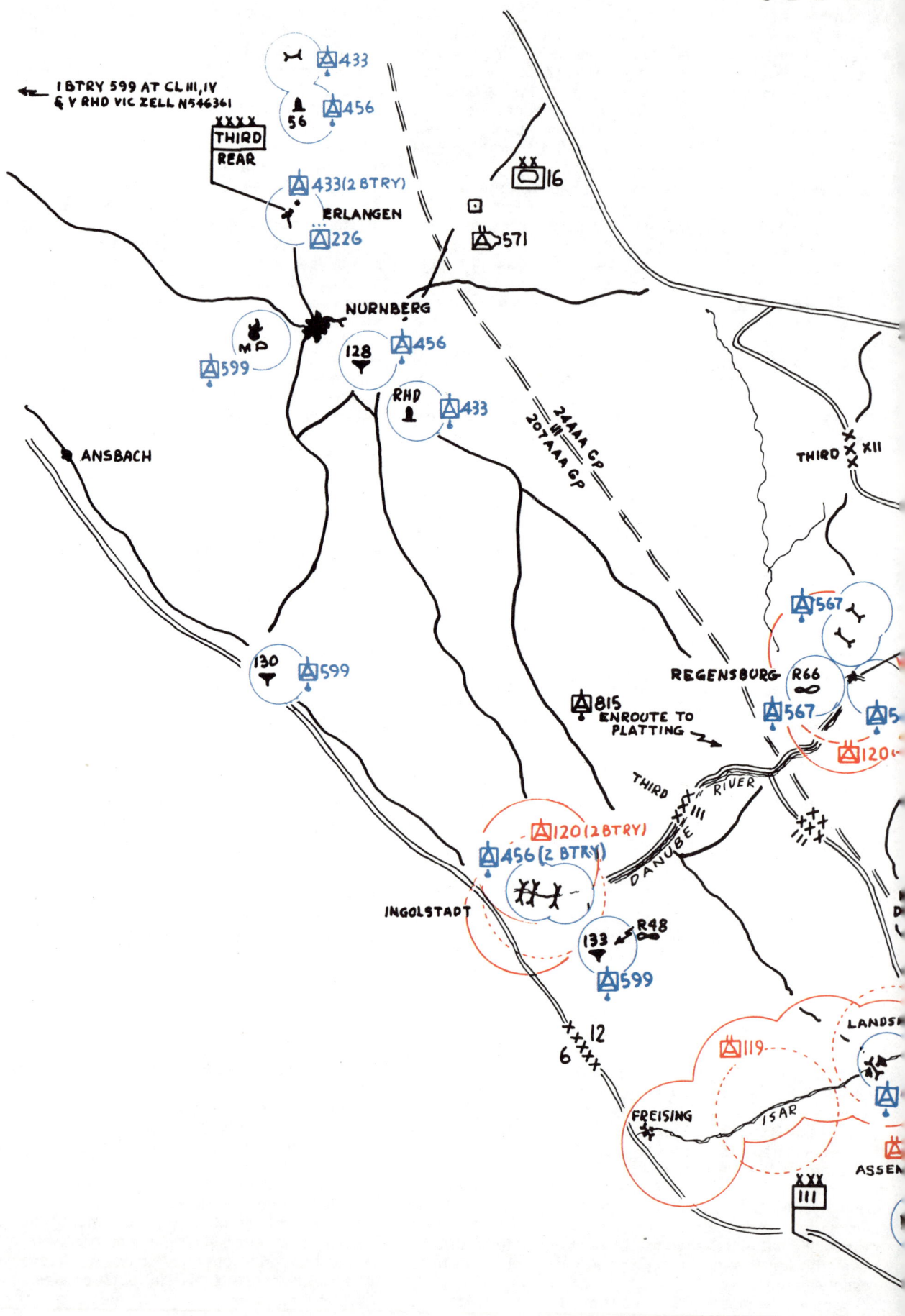

SECRET

MUNICH

ANTIAIRCRAFT SITUATION
4 MAY 1945

AREA ENCLOSED IN BLUE – AUTOMATIC WPNS
"   "   "   RED – 90MM GUNS
"   "   "   DASHED RED – IAZ
"   "   "   DOTTED " – BLANK CHECK AREA

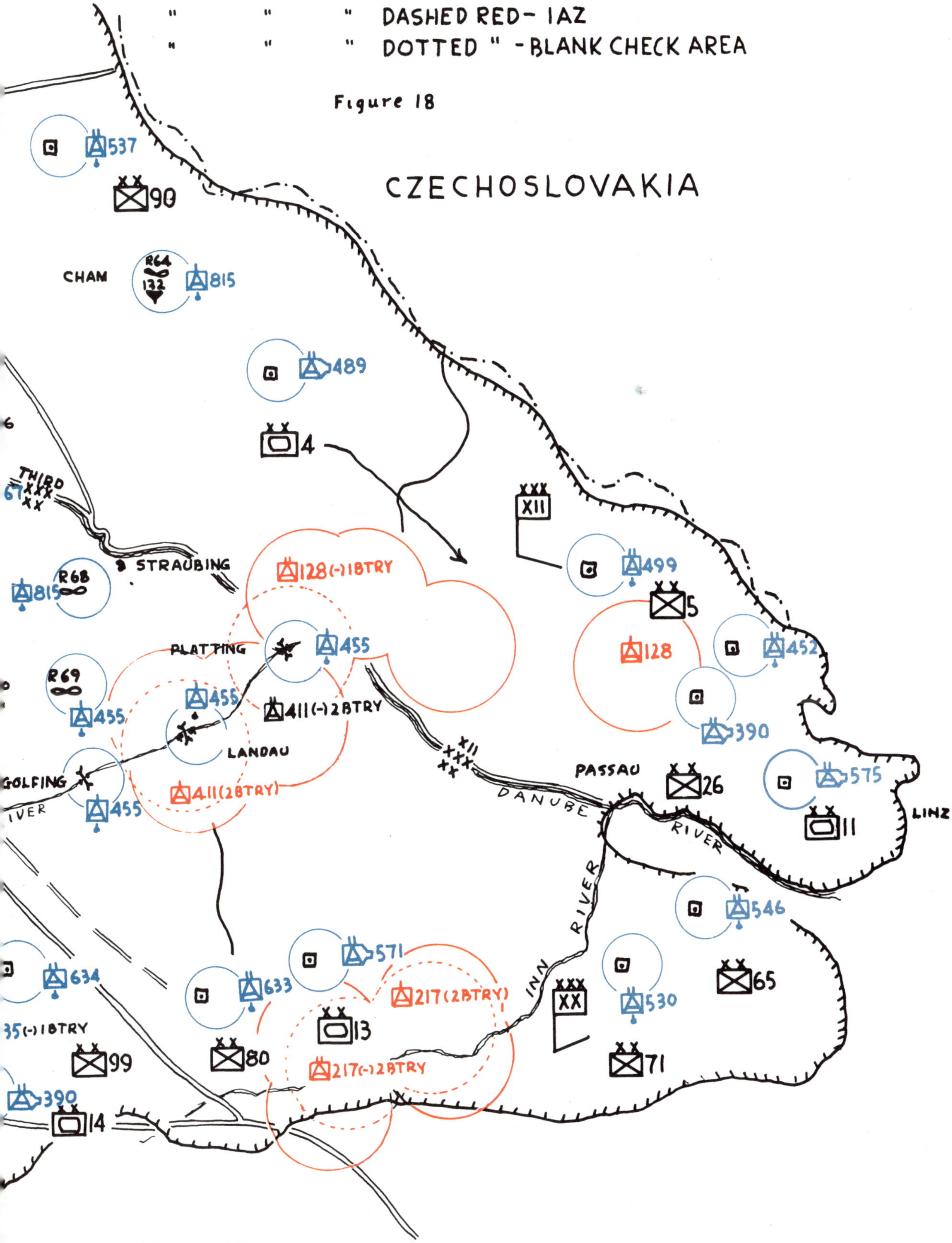

Figure 18

Antiaircraft Artillery Intelligence Service

Two methods of indentification were provided, i.e., IFF (Identification Friend or Foe) and identification through flight plans or liaison officer. Neither proved successful, many targets being carried as unidentified. Frequently the IFF equipment was not used by friendly aircraft. Communications provided for the dissemination of Air Warning by Antiaircraft Artillery units was inadequate. Transmission of warning was accomplished with equipment supplied in excess of Tables of Organization and Equipment by the Air Force and Army Signal Officer. Early warning would not be necessary for antiaircraft units except to alert gun crews, if a satisfactory means of identification for guns and automatic weapons units were provided. Units lacked training in establishment of local Antiaircraft Artillery Intelligence Service nets, and procedures evolved in the field differed considerably, often making difficult the coordination of Antiaircraft Artillery Intelligence Service between adjacent units. Mutual identification between aircraft and ground units is vital to efficient operation of the Air Force and Antiaircraft Artillery. Communication equipment for the dissemination of air warning should provide two-way radio communication for the exercise of operational control. Antiaircraft Artillery Intelligence Service training should be standardized. Nets for transmitting this information should be specified and personnel indoctrinated and trained accordingly.

Automatic Weapons

1. **Mine Detectors.** Antiaircraft units normally occupied positions not previously swept for mines by Engineer units and each gun section had to clear its own area of mines. Mine detectors should be provided for each automatic weapons fire unit.

2. **Security And Observation.** The normal disposition of automatic weapons in the field was such that each halftrack, 40mm gun and type M51 mount had to provide its own security and perform its own observation. Bazookas and field glasses should be provided for each 40mm gun, type M51 mount and halftrack.

3. **Fire Units.** In the majority of situations the towed automatic weapons mounts were greatly handicapped in furnishing convoy protection and in occupying positions. The separate fire control equipment which required orientation and frequent adjustment proved to have distinct disadvantages. Fire control equipment proved unsatisfactory for coping with normal seen targets. No provision was made for unseen fire or to illuminate targets.

Throughout the campaign, automatic weapons were employed for both offensive and defensive missions in a ground role. Difficulty in this role was encountered due to the unsuitability of fire control equipment for direct and indirect fire plus the inability of antiaircraft weapons to depress below zero degrees in elevation, and fire in travelling position to the front. All automatic weapons should be Self-propelled. A more effective built-into-the-carriage system of fire control is required. Provision should be made for fire during darkness. Automatic weapons should be designed to perform useful and necessary secondary ground missions. Sufficient armor and mobility to perform such a role as well as scales and sighting equipment for indirect fire should be provided. Weapons should be designed to fire below zero degrees through 360 degrees.

Ordnance

Mixed lots of 90mm ammunition were common and required continual planning on the part of Battery Commanders to insure availability of a sufficient number of rounds of the same lot for check fire and engagement of aircraft. Provisions should be made for ammunition to reach ammunition supply points with a minimum of lot numbers. Supervision must be exercised by antiaircraft officers to insure the fewest possible lot numbers at each battery position.

Equipment

1. **Radar.** The type SCR 584 radar was not fully dependable for detection of enemy aircraft, particularly low flying targets. It was necessary to take the set off search to make circuit checks. Supply of spare parts for the SCR 584, especially spinner motors and T-R tubes, proved entirely inadequate. Search feature of SCR 584 requires modification or redesign to provide better search coverings against low flying targets. Built-in test equipment to enable checks during search operation would be advantageous. More adequate supplies of spare parts should be provided.

2. **Height Finders.** Height finders of 90mm batteries were not used by Third US Army units during operations on the continent. They should be eliminated from Tables of Organization and Equipment.

3. **Type M-7 Generators.** Supply of spare parts for type M-7 Generators proved entirely inadequate to permit the required hours of operation. The additional load resulting from the energizing of the remote control systems of one or more guns, frequently caused the output voltage to fluctuate to such an extent that the radar went off the air and the target was lost. Supply of spare parts for type M-7 Generators, especially piston rings, valves and over size pistons should be increased. Facilities should be provided for reboring cylinders. Voltage regulators should be modified of redesigned.

4. **Type M-4 Tractors.** Type M-4 Tractors proved unable to maintain traction under conditions of icy roads and packed snow. Attachments should be provided for tracks of type M-4 tractors to enable them to maintain traction under icy conditions.

5. **Communications Equipment.** Due to rapidly changing situations, radio proved to be the primary means of communication, with wire used infrequently. Radio equipment provided by Tables of Organization and Equipment however, proved inadequate in quantity and performance. The type SCR 593 radio was totally unsatisfactory; it was difficult to tune and lacked satisfactory provision for maintaining power. The range of the type SCR 543 radio proved insufficient to meet normal needs. The type SCR 177 radio was found difficult to keep on frequency and its range was frequently inadequate. Wire communication was used where possible. The fact that Tables of Organization and Equipment of Self-propelled units made no provisions for wire or telephone proved a distinct handicap in communication with supported elements. Radio is the primary means of communication for antiaircraft units in the field and more dependable radio equipment with longer range should be provided in sufficient quantity to maintain command and intelligence nets. Adequate telephone equipment should be provided each Self-propelled unit for wire communications with headquarters of supported elements.

Weekly AAA Intelligence Reports

Reprinted from the 3rd Army After Action Reports

Secret

**Headquarters
Third United States Army
Antiaircraft Section
APO 403**

Secret
Auth: CG, Third US Army
Init: FRC
Date: 19 December 1944

19 December 1944
AAA Weekly Intelligence Report No. 20
Period:
080600A to 150600A

1. Summary of Action

a. German air activity this week was negligible, but 6 E/A being overhead, one on high altitude reconnaissance and the remainder flying at low and medium altitudes. No attacks were made upon ground targets. Four of these A/C were observed over Saariautern, one at Pont-A-Mousson and one over 35th Div Arty. AAA engaged 5, resulting in claims for 2 Category Is by an AAA Gun battalion. Two PACs were observed, but neither crashed in the area.

b. Totals for the week, and to date from 1 August 1944, are as follows:

	Raids	No E/A	Cat I	Cat II
Week	6	6	2	0
To Date	1,482	2,924	333	160
	PAC Over Area	**PAC Engaged**	**Cat A**	**Cat B**
Week	2	0	0	0
To Date	100	23	0	0

2. GAF Tactics Notes
No new tactics were reported.

3. Miscellaneous Notes

a. At the request of a Cavalry Ron Sq Commander, 4 halftracks of the 796th AAA AW Bn (SP) — attached 10th Armd Div — this week performed a special road-clearing mission, firing into woods, at houses, emplacements and personnel. 117 rds 37mm and 2,300 rds .50 cal ammunition were expended, resulting in destruction of 3 houses, a machine gun emplacement, 2 small ammunition dumps, some mines, and causing an undetermined number of enemy casualties.

b. The same battalion was singled out for commendation by the Commanding General, 10th Armd Div, for the low rate of trench foot cases reported during the past month.

c. Reference radar interference reported in paragraph 3 d, AAA Weekly Intelligence Report No. 17, the Signal Section of Twelfth Army Group has advised that it probably was a case of "Squittering IFF", caused by maladjustment of the transponder in the aircraft. Procedure has been established so that the pilot may be quickly notified and his IFF equipment adjusted to prevent further occurrences.

/s/ F.R. Chamberlain, Jr.
/t/ F.R. Chamberlain, Jr.
Colonel, CAC, Antiaircraft Officer.

Distribution:
"A" & "H"

SECRET
28 December 1944
AAA Weekly Intelligence Report No. 21
Period:
150600A to 220600A

1. Summary of Action

a. It was not until mid-afternoon of December 17th — 36 hours after the German counter-offensive began — that the Luftwaffe visited the Third US Army zone. One strafing attack was reported that afternoon and a flurry of reconnaissance flights was reported over XII and XX Corps zones, as great interest in troop movements in those areas was evinced. Thereafter, hostile air activity declined until December 21st, when the first indication was given of the large-scale activity to follow. 39 E/A were over the area on that day. 10 strafing attacks were made during the week but no bombings were reported by AAA units, though other sources reported bombing of troop concentrations and the dropping of butterfly bombs in XX Corps area. One unconfirmed report of rocketfiring was received. Most attacks were during hours of darkness with only two made by daylight. All attacks were by single A/C, whose missions apparently were to harass convoys and other road traffic. Field artillery was also strafed and, for the first time since Third US Army became operational, airfields in its area were attacked. No damage from the attacks was suffered by any AAA-protected installation or unit. Most reconnaissance, likewise, was flown at night as improved visibility and use of lights by vehicles aided this mission. Areas mainly covered were highways along the river leading north from Metz to Thionville, where photographic flares were dropped, the Saarlautern and Sarreguemines areas, and a few flights reported over Nancy and Luxembourg. 2 PAC (a V-1 and a V-2) were reported observed from the Saarlautern Iaz. Neither is known to have crashed.

b. Totals for the week, and to date from 1 August 1944, (Corrected) are as follows:

	Raids	No E/A	Cat I	Cat II
Week	74	75	.15	7
To Date	1,556	3,999	348	167
	PAC Over Area	**PAC Engaged**	**Cat A**	**Cat B**
Week	2	0	0	0
To Date	100	23	0	2

For the same period, Ninth US Army reported 259 raids and 415 E/A, and First US Army showed 167 raids by 444 E/A.

2. GAF Tactics Notes

a. A tendency of E/A to hug the ground, even during night sorties, has been noted in recent days. This probably is in furtherance of attempts to escape giving early warning through radar sources and to hinder engagement by 90mm guns and has, to some extent, been successful in terrain favorable to such tactics, such as country of long, winding valleys affording masked lanes of approach.

b. "Window" has, with increasing frequency, been reported in the area, as would be expected. No difficulties in radar tracking have occurred.

c. Flares were frequently reported, but only infrequently preceding an attack, as most concern evidently was for photo reconnaissance, rather than harassment.

3. Miscellaneous Notes

a. During the recent period of heavy rains, a large number of the slow-moving targets frequently detected by gun radars were picked up by the 119th AAA Gun Bn. Once identified, they are easily distinguished from E/A. To add to the data already known concerning these phenomena, the 119th AAA Gun Bn submitted the following findings made in the Saarlautern area:

(1) Signal was weak and at times would disappear in the range scope. This occurred at slant ranges as close as 4,000 yards.

(2) The speed was determined, in most cases, to approximate 40 miles per hour.

(3) The targets proceeded in all directions, though the majority moved south or west.

(4) Altitudes varied from 300 yards to 4,000 yards. The large majority, however, were from 300-600 yards.

(5) The following meteorological conditions prevailed on two occasions:

30536	4391706	30536	4370904
0150406	5401706	0230404	5400904
1300406	6411905	1240804	6440903
2330906	7441905	2271104	7491103
3381506	2200	3301104	1800

(6) Gun batteries could locate these targets by relocation as they were broadcast over the unit AAAIS.

(7) It was noted that on all nights the phenomena occurred, air density was extremely high, being as much as 5%-6% above normal.

(8) Normal targets may be tracked without confusion.

b. In shooting, unusual not only for exceptional results but also because all engagements were with unseen targets (all firing data being furnished by radars and M9 directors), the 120th AAA Gun Bn claimed 4 Cat I's and 1 Cat II out of 9 E/A engaged during a 45 minute period in the Thionville Iaz, one night this week.

c. Hitting power of the 90mm gun used in a ground role is amply shown by examination of fortifications and positions against which it was used. A PW recently taken from one of these stated that the 150mm steel doors on a medium sized bunker (20 man bunker complement) was completely pierced by 90mm shells. He had been informed of the caliber weapon used against them by a US officer present at the time of his capture, who was aware of the employment. Concrete walls of 1.50m to 2.00m thickness were damaged, but not pierced, by the 90mm fire. (Source: Third US Army, G-2 Periodic Report No. 188).

/s/ F.R. Chamberlain, Jr.
/t/ F.R. Chamberlain, Jr.
Colonel CAC, Antiaircraft Officer.

Distribution:
"A" & "H"

**SECRET
HEADQUARTERS
THIRD UNITED STATES ARMY
Antiaircraft Section
APO 403**

SECRET
AUTH: CG, THIRD US ARMY
INIT: FRC
DATE: 3 Jan 45

3 January 1945

AAA WEEKLY INTELLIGENCE REPORT NO. 22

Period:
220600A to 290600A

1. Summary of Action.

a. As the regrouped Third US Army started its attack on the southern flank of the enemy salient the Germans unleashed the striking power of their air forces, hitherto so closely husbanded. 751 enemy airplanes were counted during the week in a series of 493 raids over the Army zone. Largest number of E/A reported for any single day was 234 for the period 26-27 December. Most attacks were made against lines of communication, supply routes and installations. Traffic passing along main roads, and particularly at points of congestion—such as in the vicinity of the bridge at Uckange and the road nets surrounding and inside of Nancy, Pont-A-Mousson, Conflans, Metz, Thionville and Arlon — was attacked time and time again. Ammunition dumps at Sivry and Audunle-Roman were bombed and strafed, supply dumps (particularly Class III) were attacked with a loss at one, via Mancieulles, of 100,000 gallons of gasoline, 3,000 jerricans and 8 boxcars. Likewise attacked were railroads and railheads at Conflans, Sedan and Florange. Attacks upon Field Artillery were numerous and AAA units also were subjected to several attacks. In addition, bombing and strafing attacks upon airfields continued, some 18 being made in all. Other than the loss of gasoline, not much damage was caused by these efforts, and personnel casualties were inconsiderable. Jet-propelled A/C attempted to bomb a division CP from low altitude, with no success. Reconnaissance flights were numerous and covered the entire Army area, night and day.

b. 3 PAC were engaged and one was hit and caused to crash. All others passed over the area.

c. Totals for the week, and to date from 1 August 1944, are as follows:

	Raids	No E/A	Cat I	Cat II
Week	493	751	83	56
To date	2,049	4,750	431	223
	PAC Over Area	PAC Engaged	Cat A	Cat B
Week	25	3	0	1
To Date	125	26	0	3

2. GAF Tactics Notes

a. With the weather clear and bright sun prevailing this week, much use was made of the sun's blinding effect and many attacks, both bombing and strafing, were made with the sun behind the attacking aircraft.

b. Noticed again was the continuing tendency of E/A to attack from very low altitudes. However, this was far from being an exclusive tactic and in many instances bombs were released from medium and even from high altitudes. Whenever engaged from the ground by AAA, few bombing runs were completed and, in most cases, bombs were apparently released haphazardly with the pilot more intent upon escape than upon accurate bombing, as the results achieved show.

c. Some AAA Gun Battalions have cited increasing instances of German A/C, (which ordinarily take continuous avoidance tactics in flying across IAZs), flying a straight-line course at altitudes only a thousand feet over IAZ top limits. This has led to their conclusion that German pilots, well aware of the restrictions imposed on AAA gun fire, feel secure in flying at slightly above the IAZ ceilings.

d. In an attack upon artillery and other targets, a flight of 75 E/A of mixed types approached at noontime at an altitude of 18,000-20,000 feet. When over the target area, they broke formation and approximately 30 of them, in groups of two, began a circling descent to 5,000-6,000 feet, from which altitude they began a dive-bomb and strafing attack lasting some time.

e. E/A were overhead at all hours, both day and night, so that no time seemed to be preferred for attack or reconnaissance.

f. In an attack upon targets in Neufchateau, 7 jet-propelled Me-262's, attacked at noontime from altitudes of 300-5,000 feet. These A/C first bombed at the end of a long, shallow dive and then came low to strafe targets of opportunity.

3. Miscellaneous Notes

For a period of 14 days, from 4 December to 18 December, the 547th AAA AW Bn (M) furnished antiaircraft protection to the bridge crossing the Saar River into Saarlautern. The bridge had been captured intact on 3 December by elements of the 95th Inf. Div. who wished AAA protection given to this vital crossing. Battery "A" was assigned the mission and at 0930, ? December, the 1st platoon was given March Order, to proceed to an assembly point, via Oberfeisberg, Germany, preparatory to occupying positions in defense of the bridge.

A Ron party went forward to select gun sites and upon arrival at Saarlautern found the town to be under intense enemy small arms, sniper and artillery fire. The S-3 of the 379th Inf Regt suggested not bringing in AAA at this time because of the uncertainty of a counterattack. However, it was decided to continue as planned and the Ron party completed the selection of positions on foot.

The guns were brought up and while Sec #4 was building revetments, a heavy concentration of enemy artillery fire forced members of the crew to take cover. Shortly thereafter, enemy MG fire harassed the position and an EM, who had elected to remain at his M-51, fired 200 rds .50 Cal ammo from his exposed position, silencing the enemy MG nest. In order to emplace the M-51 at Sec #2, it was necessary to build a revetment and then back the M-51 into position. An EM, with assistance, built three sides of the revetment while lying on his side, then backed the mount into position, disconnected the truck, and completed the revetment. Sniper fire originating from a church steeple located about 150 yards from the gun section, forced members of Sec #3 to take cover on several occasions. Bazooka fire was ordered on the steeple and an EM fired 9 rds of bazooka ammo from an exposed position in the middle of the street. Later on, at the request of an Inf lieutenant, 24 rds 40mm AP ammo were fired into the tower and sniper fire from this source ceased.

About 1200 hours, 6 December, "A" Btry Commander was directed to move two gun sections across the river. Accompanied by the 2nd Platoon Commander, he made a reconnaissance on foot and selected the two gun sites, Gun sections #7 and #8 moved across the bridge and occupied positions under heavy artillery fire. Wire communications were established between the battery and all gun sections.

During the first 36 hours that the platoon occupied positions, all gun sections were under extremely heavy enemy artillery fire, averaging 200 rds per hour. After that time and until 0600, 18 December, at which time the Bn was relieved of this mission, approximately 31,050 rds of enemy artillery landed in the bridge area.

During the period of the defense of the Saarlautern bridge a director, a power plant, a truck and an M-51 quadruple machine gun mount were destroyed by enemy artillery fire, in addition to the loss of 10,255 rds .50 Cal ammo and some 40mm ammo. The M-51 was destroyed by two direct hits at 2030, 4 December 1944. No casualties were suffered and the gun was replaced on the morning of 5 December 1944. The position was changed and the M-51 was emplaced in an open casemate which was blown by the engineers. Other equipment, including 4 trucks and one M-51, was also damaged by artillery. Personnel casualties were 1 EM killed, and many wounded.

The period was highlighted by individual achievements and acts of heroism, for which 2 officers and 6 enlisted men received Silver Stars, 4 officers and 14 enlisted men received Bronze Stars and 14 men were awarded Purple Hearts for wounds received.

/s/ F.R. Chamberlain, Jr,
/t/ F.R. Chamberlain, Jr.
Colonel, CAC
Antiaircraft Officer.

DISTRIBUTION;
"A" & "H"

7 January 1945

AAA WEEKLY INTELLIGENCE REPORT NO. 23
Period:
0600A, 29 Dec 44 to 0600A, 05 Jan 45

1. Summary of Action

a. Continuing the pace of the previous week for the first five days of the present one, the Luftwaffe was over in force until bad weather grounded its ships. Flying more day than night sorties, it struck savagely at ground targets and — except in one instance — failed in material success. The scale of attacks reached its peak New Year's Day and night, when 343 hostile aircraft were reported in raids approaching but never quite equalling the air attacks on this Army in Normandy. Targets most frequently attacked were highway targets vehicles and field artillery, with a lessening in number of attacks upon supply installations. Highways from Metz to Luxembourg were strafed by jaggles of up to 20 A/C, and vehicles and bridges were strafed or bombed in and near Pont-A-Mousson, Metz, Thionville, Neufchateau, Sedan, Arlon, Bastogne, Martelange, Trentange, Arsdorf, Longwy, Wecker, Florenville and other cities and villages. An Ordnance dump via Boulay was strafed and bombed; railheads and railroad installations at Sedan Mancieulles, Toul, Esch and Latour, Class I or III dumps at Sivry and Arlon, and parked vehicles and tanks at various places, including Rambrouch, all were attacked. Artillery was frequently attacked and in XX Corps zone, flights as large as 50 E/A fired machine guns, rockets and cannon at gun sites. 57 E/A attacked Bastogne on New Year's night. The damage from all these attacks was slight in comparison with the scale of the effort. A few vehicles were damaged and some personnel casualties were caused. An attack on the airfield near Metz, however, had more success though at great cost to the enemy. There, E/A bounced the field to strafe and destroy 20 closely-parked P-47's and damage 17 others. Of the 25 E/A attacking, 16 were shot down by AAA in the Metz area defense, and another was probably destroyed. Many other E/A covered the army zone on reconnaissance and there were few AAA units that did not sight and engage some hostile A/C.

b. 46 PAC were sighted over the area, of which 4 were engaged without result. One crashed in an open field, causing no damage.

c. Totals for the week, and to date from 1 August 1944 (corrected) are as follows:

	Raids	No E/A	Cat I	Cat II
Week	336	647	86	38
To date	2,392	5,427	516	259
	PAC Over Area	PAC Engaged	Cat A	CAT B
Week	46	4	0	0
To date	172	30	0	3

Ammunition expenditures on AAA firing for the week (check and test fire expenditures included) are as follows:

90mm	40mm	37mm	.50 Cal
3,014	7,461	3,255	241,513

2. GAF Tactics Notes

a. In attacking Metz airfield at 0920 New Year's morning, the German aircraft approached from the north at altitudes ranging from 1,500 feet down almost to ground level, and speeds of 250-300 mph. Near the field, they split into elements of three which circled the field to attack from the four points of the compass and, as the attack progressed, these split up and the planes attacked individually. Those still flying then departed to the north, hedge-hopping and strafing Moselle River bridges on the way out.

b. Dive-bombing was a tactic more frequently employed than heretofore, though other approaches were used, as well. The A/C frequently attacked from out of the sun. Accuracy was rather poor, however. Near Rambrouch a plane attempted to bomb vehicles dispersed in an open field but, instead, hit a church, demolishing it.

c. Strafing often was done from extremely low altitudes and in attacking field artillery, strafing with machine gun and cannon and rocket-firing were almost exclusively the methods used.

e. A jet-propelled Me-163 was engaged via XII Corps Artillery while cruising at 250 mph. In avoidance of AAA fire, it was reported to have accelerated to approximately 500 mph in a short space of time.

f. The AAA Gun Battalion in Saarlautern IAZ reported that E/A passing through, upon one occasion dropped "window" in such large quantities that radars could not stay on target, nor could the targets be carried through on remote.

g. Increasing efforts to create momentary confusion among AAA gun crews by the dropping of flares has been noted. Various colors and combinations of flares have been dropped, but there is no reason to believe recognition codes have been compromised.

h. In one strafing attack upon field artillery by approximately 15 E/A, the bulk of the planes created a diversion on one side of the area to allow a single Me-109 sneak in from the other side and strafe.

3. Miscellaneous Notes

a. Many of the battalion engagements these past two weeks have been outstanding. On 26 December, a total of 36 E/A attacked the artillery with the 26th Inf Div and a division bridge crossing of La Sure River. The 390th AAA AW Bn, a self-propelled unit, engaged 25 of these, claiming 15 Cat Is and 3 Cat IIs. The attacking A/C came in at speeds of 250 to 300 mph, and at altitudes of 100 to 1,000 ft — so low that almost all Cat Is claimed crashed within view of the firing units. To vary the pattern, 2 gun sections protecting the bridge crossing, besides shooting down several A/C, lowered their sights to fire at mortar-observation, machine gun and sniper positions across the river, accounting for 15 enemy casualties and materially assisting the advance of the infantry.

b. Located well within artillery range and taking an occasional pounding, the 217th AAA Gun Bn is in Bastogne, where it has been almost constantly firing throughout several nights, using both 90mm and .50 cal weapons. On the night of 1 January, it had 57 engagements between 1825 and 0604 hours, with most activity concentrated between 2200-0100 hrs. The E/A came in singly and in pairs at altitudes averaging 4,500 ft, but on occasion as low as 900 ft. Radars performed well despite liberal dropping of "window". Target pick-ups were made at 900 ft altitudes while the A/C still were well outside the Iaz, and none were lost because of any radar failures. Little damage was caused by the raids, despite bombing and strafing attempts. Enemy artillery fire twice cut battery telephone lines during the night. The battalion claimed 10 Cat Is for the night's firing, mostly as a result of unseen fire, using radars.

c. On the morning of 1 January, between the hours of 0804-1030, great numbers of E/A attacked targets in the XX Corps area. Corps Artillery, AAA positions and targets of opportunity were worked-over at low altitudes by aircraft which fired rockets and strafed. A few casualties, but little other damage was caused. The 455th AAA AW Bn (M), protecting Corps Artillery, was in the thick of things and had many engagements, claiming 17 Cat Is and 5 Cat IIs for its efforts. Two actions were of particular interest. An Me-109 strafed one AAA gun position twice. It was shot down on the second run-up and crashed 200 yds from the gun position which engaged it. After crashing, the pilot seemed still full of fight and was shot by nearby FA personnel after he exhibited considerable hostility. Another plane crashed when .50 cal hits caused the motor to conk out. The pilot, likewise, was apparently unhurt. Quitting his ship he started a dash for the woods, but was delayed when 2 rounds of 40mm tracer were fired across his bow, and he thought it better to sit down and wait for his captors to catch up with him. Following this, 2 more Me-109s, curious about their fellow A/C, flew low to inspect the crash and were both shot down and crashed nearby. The 455th AAA AW Bn feels it was a lovely day. In all the 112th AAA Gp reported 33 Cat Is and 12 Cat IIs for activities during the day by the AAA units within XX Corps zone.

d. Preliminary to the action at Metz airfield, units under control of the 24th AAA Gp (38th AAA Brig) had established a defense for all Metz, including the airfield. The CO, 411th AAA Gun Bn, was designated area defense commander and for his defenses had 4 batteries of guns, 1 battery of the 465th AAA AW Bn (SP) and 2 batteries of the 386th AAA AW Bn (SP), attached to Third US Army for operational control from the 51st AAA Brigade (the ADC Brigade supporting XIX TAC). Only the 386th AAA Bn was in direct defense of the airfield, alone, and its first engagements with enemy aircraft gave it 8 Cat Is from the 15 targets it engaged. Batteries of the 411th Gun Bn used .50 cal fire exclusively, with the exception of one course fired by its 90mms, to garner 7 Cat Is, and the 465th Self-propelled Bn, firing at the flight only as it approached and departed to the North, got a Cat I and Cat II. Several of the hit E/A crashed on the field, or blew up over it, spraying parts for many yards around. Most of the other carcasses already have been found.

e. Battalions bothered by frozen solenoids in the present cold weather conditions have shown ingenuity in solving the problem. The 796th AAA AW Bn, a self-propelled unit, attaches a small hose to the exhaust of the turret generator motor and heats the solenoids with the hot exhaust gases. The 547th AAA AW Bn (M) has found that turning on the firing switch let enough current pass through the solenoids on M-51 mounts to warm them in 3-4 minutes. Machine gunners are instructed to open the top cover, point the guns to a safe field of fire, and turn on the firing switch, taking care that the trigger is not released.

f. The 635th AAA AW Bn (M) is experimenting with a method of conducting unseen ground fire by 40mm guns. Range and azimuth drums have been made by calibrating 90mm shell cases and fitting them to elevating and traversing mechanisms of a 40mm towed mount. Test firing to determine accuracy and practicability of the method is being conducted.

g. Under certain conditions, tracer ammunition has been used by M-51 and half-track mounts when employed in ground support roles. Ordinarily, this involves the hazard of drawing mortar and artillery fire as the source of fire, even when defiladed, is soon discovered. When used, however, tracers have proved of considerable value in bolstering morale of our own troops, who delight in the readily apparent spray of fire, and are sure of its direction. Now, from PW sources, comes a statement from the enemy.

"The defenders of Bastogne, in repulsing the attack of 3 PG Div in the early morning hours of 30 Dec, did so partly by a lavish expenditure of tracer bullets. All PW ascribe to them a considerable part in lowering morale. The lighting effect of the tracers made every soldier feel that he could not possibly go any farther without being spotted immediately. Secondly, the certain feeling that every tracer bullet comes straight onto the man, immobilized many of the enemy, especially inexperienced young Replacements, through sheer fear. Even such enemy personnel as had already some five years of warfare to its credit, men that have gone through the Stalingrad battle, commented on the frightening display of fireworks ("Feuerzauber"), more intense than anything they had previously experienced." (Source: Third US Army G-2 Periodic Report No. 208)

/s/ F. R. Chamberlain, Jr,
/t/ F.R. Chamberlain, Jr,
Colonel, CAC, Antiaircraft Officer.

Distribution:
"A" & "H"

16 January 1945

AAA Weekly Intelligence Report No. 24
Period:
050600A to 120600A

1. Summary of Action
a. Clouds, snow and haze halted most air activity during the week. In Third US Army area, a total of 4 raids by 5 enemy aircraft were observed in efforts which, following upon the heavy raids of the previous two weeks, were anticlimatic. 2 single E/A which made no attacks were observed near Batogne, and a flight of 2 other E/A attempted to strafe and bomb a task force in the same general area. One E/A flew over Luxembourg, apparently on reconnaissance. All 5 A/C were detected during hours of darkness. Other A/C, believed to be hostile, were detected by radars. AAA engaged 3 of the 5 reported E/A, making no claims.

b. 6 pilotless aircraft were observed over the area, 3 of them crashing without causing any reported damage. All but one of these were observed during hours of darkness.

c. Totals for the week, and to date from 1 August 1944, are as follows:

	Raids	No E/A	Cat I	Cat II
Week	4	5	0	0
To Date	2,396	5,432	516	259
	PAC Over Area	PAC Engaged	Cat A	Cat B
Week	6	0	0	0
To Date	178	30	0	3

2. GAF Tactics Notes
No new tactics were reported.

3. Miscellaneous Notes
a. The Air PW interrogation unit with Ninth Air Force has furnished information of considerable value and interest, recently obtained from German Air crewmen shot down by our AAA. In particular, a Ju-88 pilot criticized our light AAA by saying it often opens fire with tracer at such long ranges that it was frequently possible for a pilot to locate the firing section and swing out around it in a circle, thus never coming into really effective AAA range.

b. Of encouraging nature is information from the gunner of an Me-110, shot down by AAA near Saarburg just after midnight, 27 December. He stated that the turn-over in his unit, in both flying personnel and aircraft, was very heavy due to the toll of our AAA. One Me-110 had returned to base, a week before his capture, with 84 medium caliber perforations in wings and fuselage.

/s/ F.R. Chamberlain, Jr,
/t/ F.R. Chamberlain, Jr,
Colonel, CAC, Antiaircraft Officer.

21 January 1945

AAA Weekly Intelligence Report No. 25
Period:
120600A to 190600A

1. Summary of Action
a. Clearing skies allowed a slightly increased air effort this week, and raids by a total of 87 A/C were reported. While some flights were flown for reconnaissance, the majority of aircraft made attacks upon ground targets. Field Artillery received most of these, some 16 strafing and bombing attacks by a total of 34 A/C being made. Vehicles, and troops along highways were frequently strafed and bombed, notably vic Laumesfeld, St Marguerite, Evendorf, Nothum, Halstroff, Fels and Bouzonville and AAA positions were twice included as targets. Few attacks were apparently preplanned. Targets of opportunity were the main objectives as no supply installations, large communications centers, bridges or like targets were attacked. some casualties were reported although the total number wounded or killed was small, and several vehicles were damaged. On the whole, missions seemed intended to harass, rather than to disrupt or seriously impede our ground efforts. Instances of reconnaissance were scarce, although flares were dropped 11 miles east of Thionville, apparently for photographic purposes.

b. 8 PAC, both V-1 and V-2, were observed over Third US Army zone, 2 of which crashed without doing any reported damage. One of these was reported as a V-2, but the report is unconfirmed at this date.

c. Totals for the week, and to date from 1 August 1944, are as follows:

	Raids	No E/A	Cat I	Cat II
Week	27	87	3	9
To Date	2,423	5,519	519	268
	PAC Over Area	PAC Engaged	Cat A	Cat B
Week	8	0	0	0
To Date	186	30	0	3

2. GAF Tactics Notes
No new tactics were noted. A/C attacked out of the sun when possible. Upon occasion, attacks came from several directions simultaneously, the attackers then climbing into the sun in avoidance of AAA fire. A/C frequently dove to the attack at angles of 45°-60°, from altitudes of 1,000-2,000 ft, pulling out at very low altitudes.

3. Miscellaneous Notes
a. Summarizing the over-all story of recent German air activity on the western front, XIX TAC's A-2 has gathered interesting information in a small tract entitled "Thirty-one Days with the GAF in the West". Figures given include claims of both air and ground forces, made in beating the GAF to its knees.

"10. in summarizing the GAF activity on the Western Front during the period covered by this report (17 December 1944 to 16 January 1945), it may be said that:

a. The enemy flew an average of 275/300 sorties daily in the Western battle area.

b. Total claims of Allied units, as reported, are 1740 enemy aircraft destroyed, 208 probably destroyed, and 380 damaged.

c. The 1740 enemy aircraft reported as destroyed represents about 20% of the sorties flown.

"11. To appreciate the recuperative powers of the GAF, the following estimates on production of their single-engine fighters may be of interest:

a. The enemy single-engine fighter aircraft production for October 1944 is estimated to have been 850 Me-109s and 650 FW-190s.

b. It is believed that the total number of new Me-109s and FW-190s produced in November was about 50 less than in the previous month.

c. Estimates for December are not yet available, but indications lead to the belief that production during this month should at least equal that of November.

"12. The single-engine fighter strength of the German Air Force, based in Germany (not including fighter aircraft employed on the Russian front) 16 December 1944 to the 16th of January 1945 is estimated as follows:

Date	W Germany (S of 11°)	E Germany (E of 11°)	Total
16 December	1350	650	2000
23 December	1250	550	1800
2 January	1000	375	1375
9 January	1005	405	1410
16 January	1000	450	1450

"14. Of the 1,000 enemy single-engine fighter aircraft on the Western Front, there are approximately 600 considered as operationally serviceable. Of the 600 serviceable aircraft, there are 250/275 within range of XIX TAC (and Third US Army) installations.

"15. d. With reinforcements from NE and NW Germany, the GAF is capable of doubling his single-engine fighter forces in range of the Third US Army.

e. Up to 150 night fighters may be employed on harassing attacks...

f. The enemy can make dive-bombing attacks, at night...using formations of up to 50 aircraft (Ju-87s)."

b. The CG, XII Corps Artillery, has advised that fire by Battery C of the 115th AAA Gun Bn, used in a ground role for the period 16-21 December, was of considerable help, thickening the fires of artillery with the Corps and in at least one instance being instrumental in averting a threatened enemy tank attack. The battery fired 1,200 rds of 90mm ammo during the period.

c. The 2d platoon of the 390th AAA AW Bn's "B" Battery recently was called upon to fire a ground mission in support of infantry. The enemy was located in a wooded area bounded by two roads, between Wiltz and Nothum. A foot reconnaissance was made by the Platoon Commander as a result of which he decided to back his four half-tracks along the road up to the area, using fire from the tracks alternately so that continuous fire could be delivered. As a weapon moved forward, or completed fire and was pulled out, its movement was covered by fire from the other tracks. On a succeeding day the same mission was repeated, fire being delivered this time from the other road. Small arms fire from very close range was encountered, but armor on the tracks afforded good protection against it. Heavy mortar and artillery fire fell upon the road and nearby road junction soon after this second firing mission was completed, so the half-tracks were quickly moved out. Only one casualty, resulting from small arms fire, was suffered. Infantry which swept the area reported 30 enemy were killed and 16 wounded, mostly as result of the fire, and 20 PWs were taken from the area.

Firing could not be done from a distance as the surrounding area was wooded. The Battalion Commander recommended that half-tracks should not normally be used in a ground role which involved taking them into enemy-held territory not providing adequate cover. However, since in this instance a foot reconnaissance was made and there were no indications either of enemy tanks or TDs in the vicinity, it was concluded the employment was feasible and the results satisfactory.

d. From the 633d AAA AW Bn comes another report of ground firing by M-51 (quad .50 cal) mounts. Weather limited visibility to 50 yards, but this had been foreseen and aiming stakes had been emplaced for each mount, indicating the azimuth to the selected target. Range had been computed and elevation was set by gunners' quadrant using firing table data.

e. From the same battalion comes report of an unusual casualty. An 88mm shell struck a house and, without detonating, passed through its foot thick wall, went across a room and thru another wall 4 inches thick, where it struck the ankle of soldier who was walking up some stairs. The shell continued through the stairway and into another room where it struck another wall and finally exploded.

f. In the interests of improving air-ground recognition, a discussion had with Army's G-3 (Air) and a representative from Ninth Air Force brought out the fact that in relatively few cases are amber flares fired from the ground seen by pilots in the air. While realizing the difficulties and even hazards involved, it was suggested that every effort be made to fire the flares so that they burst somewhere ahead, along the line of the plane's line of flight. Other units in the area which observe such attacks should also fire flares, keeping in mind that a flare must be fired intelligently if it is to be seen by the pilot.

g. Also attached are airplane silhouettes which it is planned to make a regular addition to this publication.

/s/ F.R. Chamberlain, Jr.
/t/ F.R. Chamberlain, Jr.
Colonel, CAC, Antiaircraft Officer.

1 Incl
  Incl No 1 — Aircraft Recognition — Tempest II and Tempest V.

Distribution:
  "A" & "H"

28 January 1945
AAA Weekly Intelligence Report No. 26
Period:
190600A to 260600A

1. Summary of Action

a. The GAF, licking its woods as a result of recent drubbings, bothered by bad weather, and undoubtedly called for duty more pressing on the Eastern front, this week set a record for inactivity over Third US Army zone. One raid, by one, lone aircraft in the Bastogne area was all that was reported. It was a quiet week.

b. 11 PAC were reported over the area. One of these is reported to have crashed in a heavily wooded spot via Luxembourg. No damage is believed to have been caused. All others passed without falling.

c. Totals for the week, and to date from 1 August 1944, are as follows:

	Raids	No E/A	Cat I	Cat II
Week	1	1	0	0
To Date	2,424	5,520	519	268
	PAC Over Area	PAC Engaged	Cat A	Cat B
Week	11	0	0	0
To Date	197	30	0	3

2. GAF Tactics Notes
No new German tactics were reported.

3. Miscellaneous Notes

a. Crews of 90mm guns will be happy to know that they no longer carry a simple thing like a 90mm gun but, instead, are T/O hostlers of a "Ratschbum". This is a nickname devised by the Germans for American 90's and expresses, according to PW recently interrogated, the sound made by the gun when fired at them as ground artillery. Rrrrratsch — bum!

b. German antiaircraft gun densities are usually much heavier than those of the Allies and the Allied Air Forces fly deep into Germany in large, massed formations. Nevertheless, figures of the Ninth Air Force for loss and damage caused by German flak are of considerable interest to Antiaircraft Artillerymen. (Source: 9th AF Int Sum No 114):

"Flak, the most formidable foe of the Ninth's fighters and bombers . . . is the primary cause of loss and damage to (aircraft) of this command.

"During the period covered by this report (1 June — 30 Nov):

Bombers
(1) Flak caused 58% of all bomber losses.
(2) Enemy aircraft caused about 9% of all bomber losses.
(3) Flak caused about 97% of all bomber damage.
(4) Enemy aircraft caused about ½% of all bomber damage.

Fighter-Bombers
(1) Flak caused 53% of all fighter losses.
(2) Enemy aircraft caused 27% of all fighter losses.
(3) Flak caused 88% of all fighter damage.
(4) Enemy aircraft caused about 1% of all fighter damage.

"An analysis of bomber loss by type of mission shows that medium altitude visual bombing sustains the highest rate of loss, followed in order by blind bombing, and by miscellaneous, which included window and leaflet dropping. When atmospheric conditions make blind bombing necessary, the Flak gunners must rely on non-visual methods of fire control, which are less accurate than visual methods.

"An analysis of fighter loss by type of mission shows that:

(1) Fighter bombing missions have by far the highest rate of loss. This results from the increased exposure to Flak incident to the low "dropping" altitude and the vulnerable "pull-out", well within the effective ceiling of light Flak fire. The rate of loss for this type mission has increased 60% during the last three months covered by this report, so it is particularly imperative that fighter pilots check constantly with their Intelligence Officers on the location of Flak, the best approach to particular targets, and the best evasive tactics to use.

(2) Escort missions have the smallest rate of loss. This is as it should be, what with the higher altitude and the fact that the aircraft being escorted would be the primary targets of the Flak defenses.

(3) Armed reconnaissance, area support, and fighter sweep missions are more than twice as hazardous as escort missions, but only about two-thirds as hazardous as bombing missions.

"In summary it is seen that in the case of both fighters and bombers Flak is responsible for almost all the damage and approximately half of the losses. Also it is seen that bomber losses due to enemy aircraft represent an almost negligible proportion of the total losses, and that enemy aircraft account for only about one-fifth of the combat losses of fighter planes."

c. Though no unit can be singled out to credit, the following happening may be of interest to those AAA units who participated in the Bastogne battle (Source: USSTAF Air Int Sum No 62):

"It sounds like a sequence from a Laurel and Hardy comedy, but the radio-operator of a Ju-88 night-fighter insists it's the reason he became a prisoner.

"The plane . . . was flying a standing patrol in the Bastogne area on 27 December, and the radio operator was minding his own business when American AA started popping at it. The pilot took violent evasive action, including a steep dive, which lifted the radio man from his seat and conked his head against the roof. Before he knew what was happening, the plane was pulling out of the dive and he was going in the opposite direction — so fast that he hit the floor, knocked open the escape hatch, and sailed right out into space.

"After that all he had to do was pull the ripcord and surrender to ground troops."

d. If doubt ever existed that the AAA units with the infantry face many of the hazards faced by the units they defend from air attack, the following announcement may suffice. The CO of the 377th AAA AW Bn (m), attached to the 4th Inf Div, has just received the 2d Oak Leaf Cluster to his Purple Heart, for wounds received in action in Luxembourg 3 January 1945.

e. Below is a tabulation of the formal claims submitted and formal awards made to battalions for planes shot down while such units were attached to Third US Army. Awards by other armies are not tallied, therefore some units have more Categories credited to them than shown below.

(1) Brigade and Groups:

	Confirmed Claims	
	Cat I	Cat II
16th AAA Group	14	1
23d AAA Groups	95	27
27th AAA Group	41	16
32d AAA Group	20	6
112th AAA Group	46	27
113th AAA Group	98	18
38th AAA Brigade #	106	37
Total	20	132

---

* — No longer asgd Third US Army.

\# — Includes some for 27th AAA Group.

(2) Battalions:

	UNIT	Formal Claims Submitted			Claims Approved			TOTAL
		Cat I	Cat II	Cat III	Cat I	Cat II	Cat III	I & II
1.	411th AAA Gun Bn	48	8	0	41-5/6	11	1	52-5/6
2.	456th AAA AW Bn	33	11	0	30-1/2	13	0	43-1/2
3.	455th AAA AW Bn	34	22	0	26-1/2	15	9	41-1/2
4.	217th AAA Gun Bn	39	4	3	24	9	4	33
5.	463rd AAA AW Bn*	27	5	0	26	5	1	31
6.	120th AAA Gun Bn	33	3	0	24	6	4	30
7.	115th AAA Gun Bn	24	13	0	23	6	2	29
8.	390th AAA AW Bn (Sp)	19	7	0	17-5/6	7	0	24-5/6
9.	489th AAA AW Bn (Sp)	24	3	0	23-1/2	0	2	23-1/2
10.	445th AAA AW Bn*	24	1	0	20	2	1	22

Chart continued on next page.

* — No longer asgd Third US Army.

\# — Includes some for 27th AAA Group.

(2) Battalions:

		Formal Claims Submitted			Claims Approved		TOTAL
UNIT	Cat I	Cat II	Cat III	Cat I	Cat II	Cat III	I & II
11. 119th AAA Gun Bn	20	4		17-1/2	4	2	21-1/2
12. 777th AAA AW Bn (Sp)	21	2	1	18-1/4	2	2	20-1/4
13. 473rd AAA AW Bn *	14	4	0	13	4	0	17
14. 398th AAA AW Bn *	14	1	0	14	0	0	14
15. 452nd AAA AW Bn	13	4	1	10-7/12	2	3	12-7/12
16. 128th AAA Gun Bn	15	1	0	10	2	2	12
17. 386th AAA AW Bn	11	4	0	8-1/3	3	1	11-1/3
18. 465th AAA AW Bn(SP)	9	4	0	8-1/3	3	0	11-1/3
19. 547th AAA AW Bn	7	10	0	4	7	5	11
20. 551st AAA AW Bn	11	0	1	8-1/2	1	1	9-1/2
21. 457th AAA AW Bn	7	4	1	5-1/3	4	2	9-1/3
22. 537th AAA AW Bn	6	5	2	5-1/2	2	3	7-1/2
23. 448th AAA AW Bn	5	7	0	5-1/4	2	1	7-1/4
24. 129th AAA Gun Bn	7	0	0	5-1/3	1	0	6-1/3
25. 633rd AAA AW Bn	5	2	0	1/4	5	1	5-1/4
26. 387th AAA AW Bn *	5	3	0	2	3	0	5
27. 796th AAA AW Bn	3	2	0	4	1	0	5
28. 468th AAA AW Bn(SP)	5	0	0	4-1/2	0	0	4-1/2
29. 109th AAA Gun Bn	4	5	0	4	0	1	4
30. 635th AAA AW Bn	1	4	4	3	1	4	4
31. 449th AAA AW Bn	2	4	0	1	2	3	3
32. 546th AAA AW Bn	3	2	0	1	2	1	3
33. 550th AAA AW Bn	1	7	0	1	2	5	3
34. 776th AAA AW Bn	3	2	0	3	0	2	3
35. 467th AAA AW Bn(SP)	2	3	0	1/2	2	1	2-1/2
36. 792nd AAA AW Bn *	2	0	0	1-1/3	0	0	1-1/3
37. 22nd FTA (Fr.) *	1	0	0	1	0	0	1
38. 203rd AAA AW Bn *	2	2	0	0	1	0	11
39. 481st AAA AW Bn *	0	1	0	0	1	0	1
40. 549th AAA AW Bn	0	1	0	0	1	0	1
41. 559th AAA AW Bn *	1	0	0	1	0	0	1
42. 795th AAA AW Bn *	1	0	0	1	0	0	1
43. 778th AAA AW Bn (SP)	1	1	0	1/3	0	1	1/3
44. 447th AAA AW Bn *	0	1	0	0	0	0	0
45. 565th AAA AW Bn	0	1	0	0	0	1	0
Totals	506	168	14	420	132	66	552

* - No longer asgd Third US Army

/s/ F. R. Chamberlain, Jr.
/t/ F. R. Chamberlain, Jr.
Colonel, CAC,
Antiaircraft Officer.

---

1 Incl —
Incl No 1 — Aircraft Recognition — FW-190-D and FW-190.

Distribution
"A" & "H"

5 February 1945
AAA Weekly Intelligence Report No. 27
Period:
260600A to 020600A

1. Summary of Action

a. One lone plane, venturing into Bastogne under cover of darkness, was the sole bit of GAF activity reported in Third US Army zone. Once again, miserable flying weather and the urgencies of the Eastern front combined to restrict even normal intruder and reconnaissance missions.

b. Two PAC were observed. One crashed in a densely wooded area, but no damage was reported.

c. Totals for the week, and to date from 1 August 1944, are as follows:

	Raids	No E/A	Cat I	Cat II
Week	1	1	0	0
To Date	2,425	5,521	519	268
	PAC Over Area	PAC Engaged	Cat A	Cat B
Week	2	0	0	0
To Date	199	30	0	3

2. GAF Tactics Notes

a. To obtain a variety of viewpoints on recent German air tactics, the S-2s of Army AAA Brigade and of separate AAA Groups were canvassed for comments and conclusions. Lack of space prevents printing these in full, so that extracts, only, appear below.

38th AAA Brigade, S-2

"...Generally speaking, units of this command have been assigned principal missions of defending bridges, supply installations, rails, roadways and airfields in that area bounded by corps rear boundaries and the Army rear boundary and have discovered that these areas are attacked from the air only when conditions in the GAF and the army are such that planes must be committed to attain an important or desperate end.

"...In periods of attack by Third Army forces the missions defended by our units have rarely been attacked, the main activity noted by the AAA protecting them being an occasional reconnaissance mission flown at medium or high altitudes. During this same period of quietude, however, reports from corps AAA units indicate much low-level strafing and bombing of front line troops concentrations and movement.

"On the opposite and unusual side of the picture there is the recent period of German ground offensive, in furtherance of which German air plunged wholeheartedly. During the most active part of this offensive the GAF treated corps and Army areas very similarly. Practically every type of defended area was struck at least once during the offensive, with dumps and convoys as the principal targets, the one exception being the airfield attack on 1 January, near Metz.

"During this period, Me-109s were engaged by Brigade units more than any other type, although a few FW-190s and Ju-88s were reported in the raiding parties on occasion. It was especially interesting to note that the new jet-propelled aircraft were conspicuous by their absence from the Army area during this period.

"...The present Russian offensive has without doubt affected the disposition of the German air force by drawing planes to the East, while continual bombings by our strategic air force and overrunning of oil fields in the East has hurt the strength of the GAF by depriving it of its most vital supply, fuel.

"The loss of the initiative by the Germans on the West and their return to the defensive will surely result in a period of limited air activity in Army rear areas until Hitler becomes so desperate that he must commit the remainder of his air force to attack every target available to him no matter where it may be located."

16th AAA Group, S-2

(Since 22 October 1944, this Group has provided defense for the City of Luxembourg, Radio Luxembourg, steel mills at Differdange and airstrip 97. Until 17 December, air activity was light, consisting chiefly of reconnaissance missions. After that date, activity increased materially.)

"During the period of the German counter-offensive, the battalions attached to the Group engaged as many as 35 enemy flights, totally 39 E/A in twenty four hours, and a total of 193 enemy flights in the 18 days . . .

"Seldom has the GAF sent multiplane flights over the area in the past three months, and in only three instances were as many as three enemy planes encountered in one flight. Further, during the entire period in Luxembourg there have been but three ''seen'' engagements . . .

"Some bombing and strafing was experienced while the GAF was operating in force, although there seemed to be no specific objectives for the attacks . . . On numerous occasions targets engaged by 90mm guns dove to very low altitudes and utilized deep valleys, masked from radar coverage, as routes of escape.

"German pilots employed a ruse not previously experienced by units of the 16th AAA Group. When entering the gun defended areas at low altitudes, colored flares were dropped as soon as automatic weapons opened fire. This undoubtedly was intended to confuse AAA Gunners momentarily, giving aircraft an opportunity to maneuver out of range of the weapons. When fire did not cease, flares of different colors often were dropped . . .''

27th AAA Group, S-2 (III Corps)

"In studying GAF tactics (for the period 21 Dec to 1 Feb) two viewpoints were considered, namely that of AAA units in Divisional area and that of AAA units in Corps area . . .

"**Divisional area.** The GAF activity was limited to reconnaissance flights and attacks on Field Artillery positions. 75% of engagements were with E/A committing no hostile act and flying at 3,000 ft altitude. In each engagement E/A took evasive action and left the area. 25% of engagements were with E/A committing hostile acts upon Field Artillery and in each case upon being engaged the E/A left the area.

"**Corps area.** The GAF activity can be resolved into three categories: (1) Attacks on convoys and vehicle concentrations — 50%. (2) Reconnaissance flights — 40%. (3) Attacks on supply installations — 10%. Convoys were always attacked in the vicinity of traffic bottlenecks when vehicles tended to close up. Supply dumps attacked were in the vicinity of the Corps rear boundary. It is believed that there were no attacks on bridges only because there were no large bridges within the Corps.

"**Conclusions:**

(1) In Division areas the GAF was mainly concerned with reconnaissance.

(2) In Corps area the GAF was mainly concerned with vehicular traffic reported by reconnaissance flights.

(3) The GAF will not continue missions when accurate AAA fire is brought to bear upon them. In other words, 'They don't like it'.''

32d AAA Group, S-2 (III Corps)

"Most of the activity of the GAF during this period (3 December 1944 to 31 January 1945) was directed at harassing the front line troops and division trains. A few attacks were made upon rear installations in an apparent effort to knock out the railway and railroad underpass at Arlon.

"For the attacks on Arlon, the GAF used planes identified as Me-410s and Me-110s, bombing from low altitudes within range of AW fire. One attack made at Arlon during daylight hours took full advantage of low cloud cover to conceal approach and departure from target. In a strafing attack made on the Arlon-Luxembourg road . . . the GAF used several SEF with one E/A making a strafing attack out of the sun while the others circled providing cover and then followed in a strafing dive after the preceding attacking E/A had regained altitude.

"During this period there has been no report of any flights of heavy bombers over the III Corps area."

112th AAA Group, S-2 (XX Corps)

"...The Corps interrogation of several pilots points to the suggestion that the primary objectives of their effort (during the latter part of December) were grounded US aircraft.

"The E/A attacking front line troops would usually depart upon being engaged by AAA fire. However, on several occasions the GAF pressed the attack despite effective AAA fire . . . Divisional troops have reported that when E/A came in over the tree tops without motors; the sound resembles that of a Cub plane.

"...The attackers were obviously well informed on terrain, as they were able to fly at great speeds at a very low altitude. Numerous reports state that the attacks were made from 50 feet off the ground. This would indicate that the scattered sorties over the area earlier in the month had gathered sufficient information for a detailed study of terrain features as well as a general appreciation of various Field Artillery installations. It would also indicate that the Luftwaffe had considered an extremely low altitude attack advantageous inasmuch as AAA gunners would easily recognize the hazards of engaging below safe levels and perhaps experience some difficulty. In several instances, enemy planes approached along deep valleys and draws where Field Artillery positions were well defiladed. In many cases the tactical disposition of Antiaircraft defenses, well-sited for a 360° field of fire, precluded the possibility of engaging aircraft that took full advantage of terrain and flew low along these valleys and draws ... In one instance during the attack on January 1st, the 537th AAA AW Bn had placed on M-51 mount on the same level as the well defiladed Field Artillery positions. This mount was responsible for the destruction of an Me-109, who undoubtedly was overcome with surprise in finding his avenue of approach fully covered ... This incident suggests that although fields of fire would not be 360°, a small percentage of AAA fire power probably should be disposed on equal terrain levels with the Field Artillery to cover the approach of aircraft through the numerous valleys and draws peculiar to this zone of operations.

"Observers over the Corps front during recent action state a noticeable lack of the usual evasive action by aircraft engaged by AAA. Perhaps the daring behavior of the Luftwaffe is beginning to far outdistance the experience of its pilots."

113th AAA Group, S-2 (VIII Corps)

"...the majority of air attacks (in our area) during December, 1944 were directed at railroads, marshalling yards, bridges and critical road junctions.

"During the period 010001A January 1945 to 030821 January 1945, a total of 55 raids were reported by AAA units attached to VIII Corps. Types could not be identified in 27 raids. Twin-engined E/A (Me-410s, Me-210s, Ju-88s and Ju-188s) made up 24 of the raids. In all instances they attacked singly and generally bombed or strafed from altitudes below 1,000 ft. Twin-engined types observed during daylight hours were in level flight, at altitudes from 2,000 to 7,000 ft and were apparently employed for reconnaissance as no attacks were made.

"No definite conclusions have been drawn from the enclosed summary of enemy air activity ... Jet-propelled types as well as the 'old reliable' Me-109s and FW-190s were conspicuous by their absence.

217th AAA Gun Bn (M) — "On the night of 1 and 2 January . . . a very determined effort was made to get in the Bastogne area. Planes came in from all directions using no main approach, and at varying altitudes. Objectives seemed to be troop concentrations and gun positions rather than roads, bridges or other definite objective.

"On the same night, one German A/C came into the Iaz with landing lights on and caused a little confusion to machine gunners at first . . .

"Since the majority of engagements by this unit have been at maximum altitudes of 2,000 yds, it is believed that a close-in defense is the most desirable for the protection of a specified area. Unless the weather was clear with a bright moon, the enemy was never over in great strength.

"It has been the experience of this unit that, once heavy enemy air activity has ceased in an Iaz, the GAF makes no further attempts at heavy raids if 90mm AAA has been encountered. When heavy AAA is encountered by the GAF, no further effort is made to make a bomb run but, instead, they tend to jettison their bombs and take evasive action.

"Window is still employed by the GAF but it is not cut to our SCR 584 wave-length, nor is it used in sufficient quantities to disrupt tracking by radar.

"The first daylight attack this unit has ever experienced was at 0815, 2 January 1945 after a big night before."

"A" Battery, 635th AAA AW Bn (M) — "At 180353A December, Guns #4 and #13 . . . were attacked by one single-engine fighter strafing the positions from an altitude of 300-500 ft. The plane approached #4 Bofor position from the West at about 250 mph and very low and attacked from a shallow dive . . . Plane then leveled off and continued on a straight line to attack #13 (M-51) position. Activity occurred on a very dark night . . . However, pilot of the E/A apparently knew exactly where the two guns attacked were located . . . as he attacked on a direct extension of a straight line drawn between the positions."

537th AAA AW Bn (M) — "Following is a summary of observations of witnesses of GAF activity in the vicinity of Waldwisse (wQ-125915) and Oberesch (wQ-152893) at 0930 hrs, 1 January 1945:

"A number of Me-109s appeared simultaneously at **very low** altitudes, coming from several directions. The average height above the ground was less than 100 ft. These A/C flew down the valleys and barely skimmed over ridges in order to get down into the next valleys. One Me-109 at one point was reported coming up over a hill, flying about 5 ft from the ground. Because of these tactics, fire units could not engage targets because of the danger of firing into friendly troops and installations. From many positions the planes were below the horizon for almost entire courses. This shows the need for having some AAA weapons emplaced on lower levels down in the valleys, especially in the type of terrain where A/C can fly for some distance down a valley.

"The few two-motored enemy A/C seen recently flew generally on level flight just out of 40mm range or at higher altitudes.

"...A single FW-190 flew over a portion of our lines . . . apparently on a reconnaissance flight. When engaged the A/C dropped its landing wheels down and left a trail of black smoke. A few seconds later it was glimpsed again flying normally on a level course, with landing wheels up, and not smoking. The reason for this action could not be determined."

b. Below is a tabulation showing the number of actual attacks made against specified targets, and numbers of aircraft involved in making these attacks. By referring to figures previously given in earlier reports for enemy aircraft over the area, it will be seen that many enemy aircraft reported made no attack at all. Thus, for December, a total of 980 E/A were reported but, of these, only 412 were involved in attacks on ground targets. Percentages given are not figured on a basis of all aircraft observed during a month, but only on a basis of those aircraft making attacks.

	NOVEMBER		DECEMBER		JANUARY	
	Number attacks 15 Number E/A attacking — 30		Number attacks 195 Number E/A attacking — 412		Number attacks 53 Number E/A attacking — 276	
TARGET	% Attacks	% E/A Attacking	% Attacks	% E/A Attacking	% Attacks	% E/A Attacking
Airstrips	0.0	0.0	7.2	3.4	1.9	9.1
Ammo Dumps	0.0	0.0	4.1	1.5	0.0	0.0
AAA Positions	13.3	6.7	6.7	5.8	20.7	25.4
Armd Concentrations	20.0	20.0	0.0	0.0	1.9	1.1
Arty Observation Planes	13.3	26.7	0.0	0.0	0.0	0.0

Chart continued on next page.

	NOVEMBER		DECEMBER		JANUARY	
	Number attacks 15 Number E/A attacking — 30		Number attacks 195 Number E/A attacking — 412		Number attacks 53 Number E/A attacking — 276	
TARGET	% Attacks	% E/A Attacking	% Attacks	% E/A Attacking	% Attacks	% E/A Attacking
Bridges	0.0	0.0	1.4	4.9	3.8	0.7
Cities	0.0	0.0	9.2	24.8	11.3	4.3
Command Posts	6.7	3.3	4.6	1.5	0.0	0.0
Convoys and M/T	6.7	6.7	14.9	9.0	5.6	8.3
Engr and Ord Depots	0.0	0.0	2.6	1.0	0.0	0.0
FA Positions	40.0	36.6	7.2	26.2	16.9	21.4
Gasoline Dumps	0.0	0.0	2.6	0.7	0.0	0.0
Railroads and RR Yards	0.0	0.0	10.3	3.9	1.9	0.4
Troops & Concentrations	0.0	0.0	1.0	0.5	3.9	0.7
Target Unknown	0.0	0.0	28.2	16.8	32.1	28.6
	100.0%	100.0%	100.0%	100.0%	100.0%	100.0%

c. In the next table is tabulated the activities of **all** E/A over Third US Army area, whether attacks were made or not, from the time this Headquarters became operational. These have been broken down to show two periods. During the first period, from 1 August 1944 to 15 December 1944, the German army may be considered to have been continually on the defensive. During the second period, enemy air activity was almost entirely for the purpose of supporting the German counter-offensive and is therefore shown as an offensive period. It will be seen by glancing at the bottom line of the tabulation that most air activity during both periods was for reconnaissance. In order not to be misleading, however, it should be stated that the figures for reconnaissance also contains that percentage of E/A which passed over the person reporting and may have made an attack elsewhere, unknown to him, as well as those E/A which actually made an attack the target of which could not, by reason of terrain features, be seen by the observer.

d. In the following table column one gives altitudes and types of attack by percentages. The second column gives altitudes at which planes were observed which, however, made no attack so far as was known to the observer. (Covers only the months of November, December, January).

Type of Attack	Attack Made	No Attack Made
High Altitude (Bombing)	2.1%	.9%
Medium Altitude (Bombing)	3.0%	22.5%
Low Altitude (Bombing)	25.0%	71.8%
Dive Bombing	1.3%	
Strafing & Rocket-Firing	62.3%	
Unknown	6.3%	4.8%
	100.0%	100.0%

	FIRST PERIOD DEFENSIVE (1 Aug-15-Dec. 1944)		SECOND PERIOD OFFENSIVE (15 Dec. 44-1 Feb 45)	
	Percent of Attacks	Percent of E/A Attacking	Percent of Attacks	Percent of E/A Attacking
Airstrips	0.0	0.0	1.5	2.1
Ammo Dumps	0.3	0.8	0.7	0.3
AAA Positions	4.0	5.9	2.0	5.0
Armd Concentrations	0.2	0.1	0.1	0.2
Arty Observation Planes	0.5	0.4	0.0	0.0
Bridges	24.2	24.9	0.4	1.2
Cities	3.6	3.8	2.0	6.1
Command Posts	0.1	0.1	0.8	0.3
Convoys & M/T	11.3	16.2	2.7	3.2
Dams	2.3	1.7	0.0	0.0
Engr and Ord Depots	0.0	0.0	0.4	0.2
FA Positions	5.0	9.4	1.9	8.9
Gasoline Dumps	0.1	0.1	0.4	0.2
Railroads & RR Yards	0.0	0.0	1.7	0.9
Troops & Concentrations	1.1	1.9	0.3	0.2
	52.7%	65.3%	14.9%	28.8%
Targets unknown or no attack made, and Rec on Flights	47.3%	34.7%	85.1%	71.2%

3. Miscellaneous Notes

a. As an interesting example of the coverage given by the FCC-AAOR (Fighter Control Center-Antiaircraft Operations Room), an occurrence on the night of 27/28 January is illuminating. At 0320 hrs the FCC-AAOR detected an aircraft flying South from Liege toward Bastogne. It was plotted to the Bastogne area and then followed as it turned around and went back North. At 0436 hrs, an aircraft was detected near Metz flying South. This was followed until the track faded. But Seventh US Army, to the South, picked it up and broadcast the plots until it passed out of the Seventh's sector, when the First French Army picked it up and carried the plot almost to the Swiss border. Thus, intelligence on hostile aircraft covered a distance of almost 300 miles, from Liege, Belgium, to Switzerland.

b. For their outstanding performance in the defense of the airfield near Metz on the morning of 1 January, units concerned have been officially commended in General Orders No 23, this Headquarters, dated 25 January 1945, as follows:

"**Unit Commendation** — The following antiaircraft units are commended for their outstanding performance of duty:

	Batting Averages from 1 Aug 44 to date			Batting Averages from 15 Dec 44 to date			
	TOTAL	**NO. E/A**		**TOTAL**	**NO. E/A**		Relative
	I & II	**ENGAGED**	**AVERAGE**	**I & II**	**ENGAGED**	**AVERAGE**	Standing
1. 481st AAA AW Bn*	1	2	.5000	1	2	.5000	(2)
2. 386th AAA AW Bn*	11-1/3	24	.4722	11-1/3	24	.4722	(3)
3. 777th AAA SP Bn	20-1/4	66	.3068	1	5	.2000	(8)
4. 489th AAA SP Bn	23-1/2	102	.2304	0	1	.0000	(33)
5. 549th AAA AW Bn	1	5	.2000	1	5	.2000	(7)
6. 559th AAA AW Bn*	1	5	.2000				
7. 452nd AAA AW Bn	12-7/12	67	.1878	3	13	.2308	(5)
8. 390th AAA SP Bn	24-5/6	134	.1853	18	53	.3396	(4)
9. 455th AAA AW Bn	41-1/2	226	.1836	19-1/2	128	.1523	(10)
10. 776th AAA SM Bn*	3	17	.1765	3	17	.1765	(9)
11. 463nd AAA AW Bn*	31	190	.1632				
12. 120th AAA Gun Bn	30	194	.1546	12	87	.1379	(15)
13. 387th AAA SP Bn*	5	34	.1470				
14. 119th AAA Gun Bn	21-1/2	156	.1378	8-1/2	58	.1466	(11)
15. 448th AAA AW Bn*	7-1/4	55	.1318	2	4	.5000	(1)
16. 217th AAA Gun Bn	33	268	.1231	9	69	.1304	(16)
17. 445th AAA AW Bn*	22	179	.1229				
18. 411th AAA Gun Bn	52-5/6	434	.1217	11-1/3	80	.1417	(14)
19. 796th AAA SP Bn*	5	42	.1190	5	41	.1220	(18)
20. 456th AAA AW Bn	43	373	.1166	0	16	.0000	(36)
21. 128th AAA Gun Bn	12	105	.1142	1	28	.0357	(30)
22. 457th AAA AW Bn	9-1/3	84	.1111	2	20	.1000	(19)
23. 551st AAA AW Bn	9-1/2	88	.1080	5-1/2	38	.1447	(12)
24. 633rd AAA AW Bn	5-1/4	49	.1071	1	17	.0588	(27)
25. 547th AAA AW Bn	11	111	.0991	10	109	0917	(20)
26. 792nd AAA AW Bn*	1-1/3	16	.0833	1-1/3	16	.0833	(21)
27. 129th AAA Gun Bn	6-1/3	85	.0745	6-1/3	85	.0745	(24)
28. 795th AAA SM Bn*	1	14	.0714	1	13	.0769	(23)
29. 468th AAA SP Bn	4-1/2	73	.0616	4-1/2	64	.0703	(25)
30. 546th AAA AW Bn	3	50	.0600	2	10	.2000	(6)
31. 398th AAA SP Bn*	14	240	.0583				
32. 537th AAA AW Bn	7-1/2	136	.0551	2-1/2	16	.1263	(17)
33. 467th AAA SP Bn*	2-1/2	47	.0532	2-1/2	47	.0532	(28)
34. 465th AAA SP Bn	11-1/3	233	.0486	4-1/3	54	.0802	(22)
35. 109th AAA Gun Bn	4	86	.0465	4	86	.0465	(29)
36. 449th AAA AW Bn	3	70	.0428	2	14	.1429	(13)
37. 115th AAA Gun Bn	29	719	.0493	3	99	.0303	(31)
38. 203rd AAA SP Bn*	1	27	.0370				
39. 22nd FTA (Fr)*	1	33	.0303				
40. 635th AAA AW Bn	4	157	.0255	0	40	.0000	(38)
41. 550th AAA AW Bn	3	157	.0191	2	29	.0690	(26)
42. 778th AAA SP Bn	1/3	29	.0115	1/3	29	.0115	(32)
43. 453rd AAA AW Bn*	0	1	.0000				
44. 575th AAA SP Bn	0	3	.0000	0	3	.0000	(34)
45. 447th AAA AW Bn*	0	7	.0000	0	7	.0000	(35)
46. 377th AAA AW Bn	0	17	.0000	0	17	.0000	(37)
47. 565th AAA AW Bn	0	61	.0000	0	61	.0000	(39)
48. 473rd AAA SP Bn*	17	Unknown	Unknown				
Totals	552	5271		161	1505		

* — No longer under control of Third US Army

12 February 1945
AAA Weekly Intelligence Report No. 28
Period:
020600A to 090600A

1. **Summary of Action**

a. There were four enemy planes over Third US Army area this week, all during hours of darkness. Only one of these made an attack, strafing a jeep on the road at (P644614), near Moinet. The other A/C were observed via Metz, Luxembourg and the 90th Inf Div CP, apparently on reconnaissance missions. AAA engaged two of the four, with no claims resulting.

b. Four PAC were over the area. One of these, a V-1, crashed but caused neither damage nor casualties.

c. Totals for the week, and to date from 1 August 1944, are given below. There will be noted a reduction over totals stated in last week's report. This results from the adoption of a new policy under which raids and planes will henceforth be filtered by Army to eliminate duplications. In accordance with this, past records have been checked and duplications in previous reports eliminated with the result that totals have been reduced. In reporting raids and numbers of aircraft all E/A, whether within range of AAA weapons or not, will, as in the past, be reported.

	Raids	No E/A	Cat I	Cat II
Week	4	4	0	0
To Date	1,569	3,666	511	252
	PAC Over Area	PAC Engaged	Cat A	Cat B
Week	4	0	0	0
To Date	203	30	0	3

2. **GAF Tactics Notes**

   a. No new tactics were reported.

   b. Interrogation of a Ju-88 pilot recently downed developed that the purpose of GAF night strafing and bombing is to cause convoys to black out, thus making them slow down, as much as for any other reason. Although small frag bombs and six 50-kilogram anti-personnel bombs were carried by the A/C it was not anticipated that raids of this type would cause much serious damage. (Source: USSTAF AIS No 64)

3. **Miscellaneous Notes**

   a. The note in last week's report on the observed use by a FW-190 of the trick of dropping its wheels and emitting black smoke brings to mind the reminder that such tricks to simulate damage are common practice. FW-190s may easily create smoke by changing to a rich gas mixture and by using their emergency power. Gasoline, injected into the intake manifold after the supercharger as a coolant, will create smoke in burning. Me-190s have a somewhat similar system and in later models a cooling system using a water and alcohol injection produces the same results. AAA gunners should not be fooled by this trick and where rapid acceleration accompanies the smoking should be wary of too trustfully making a claim for damaging the A/C.

   b. Under General Orders No 31, this Headquarters, two AAA units were cited for their part in the battle around Bastogne, during which time they were under attachment to the 101st Airborne Division. These units are Battery "B", 796th AAA AW Bn (SP) and Battery "C", 482d AAA AW Bn (SP). The citation ran to the division and attached units as follows:

   "These units distinguished themselves in combat against powerful and aggressive enemy forces during the period from 18 December to 27 December 1944, by extraordinary heroism and gallantry in defense of the key communications center of Bastogne, Belgium. Essential to a large-scale exploitation of his break-through into Belgium and northern Luxembourg, the enemy attempted to seize Bastogne by attacking constantly and savagely with the best of his armor and infantry. Without benefit of prepared defenses, facing almost overwhelming odds and with very limited and fast-dwindling supplies, these units maintained a high combat morale and an impenetrable defense, despite extremely heavy bombing, intense artillery fire and constant attacks from infantry and armor on all sides of their completely cut off and encircled position. This masterful and grimly-determined defense denied the enemy even momentary success in an operation for which he paid dearly in men, material, and eventually morale. The outstanding courage and resourcefullness and undaunted determination of this gallant force is in keeping with the highest traditions of the service.

   By command of Lieutenant General Patton:

   c. Recently the 38th AAA Brigade has been fostering a series of aircraft recognition schools among the Groups under it. The 24th AAA Group has just finished giving such a course to 166 officers and enlisted men selected on a basis of 4 EM and 1 O per gun battery and 32 EM and 2 O per Automatic Weapons Battery. The duration of the course was two weeks, with the classes lasting 45 minutes each. A Renshaw projector, flashing pictures on a screen for periods of 1 to 1/100th of a second, was used with good results. From test records kept it was found that the average recognition ability of the students increased 20%, while at the same time image exposure-time was reduced from 1 to ½ second. As a special incentive Paris passes and monetary prices were offered to the three EM scoring highest in the course.

   d. Attached as inclosure No 1 is the aircraft recognition annex.

/s/ F.R. Chamberlain, Jr,
/t/ F.R. Chamberlain, Jr,
Colonel, CAC, Antiaircraft Officer.

1 Incl — Aircraft Recognition (Spitfire).

Distribution:
"A" & "H"

Unit	#	Unit	#
AA Sec, this Hq (for 38th AAA Brig and atchd units)	125	633rd AAA AW Bn	14
		5th Inf Div	2
G-1 (Capt Richardson)	1	449th AAA AW Bn	14
G-2 (Sit)	1	76th Inf Div	2
G-2 (Air)	1	778th AAA SP Bn	14
G-3 (Air)	1	4th Armd Div	2
G-3 (PAD)	1	489th AAA SP Bn	14
SHAEF, Air Defense Div	1	XX Corps	2
AAO, ETOUSA	12	112th AAA Gp	2
AAO, 6th Army Gp	1	119th AAA Gun Bn	6
AAO, 12 Army Gp	2	455th AAA AW Bn	14
AAO, 1st US Army	1	551st AAA AW Bn	14
AAO, 1st Allied Airborne Army	1	9th Armd Div	2
AAO, 5th US Army	1	482nd AAA SP Bn	14
AAO, 7th US Army	1	94th Inf Div	2
AAO, 9th US Army	1	465th AAA SP Bn	14
AAO, 15 US Army	1	26th Inf Div	2
AAO, Fwd Esch Com Z	1	390th AAA SP Bn	14
IX ADC	1	AAO, 64th Fighter Wing	
IX TAC	1	(Thru 7th US Army & XII TAC Msg Cen)	1
XII TAC	1		
XIX TAC	1	51st AAA Brig, Attn: Maj Colquit (Thru Spitfire Msg Cen)	1
A-3	1		
A-2 (Attn: Maj Vosburg, Maj Bass)	2	23rd AAA Gp (XV Corps)	1
		275th Ord Maint Co (AA)	6
XXIX TAC	1	281st Ord Maint Co (AA)	6
100th Fighter Wing	1	6th Armd Div	2
VIII Corps	2	777th AAA SP Bn	14
113th AAA Gp	2	11th Armd Div	2
32nd AAA Gp	2	575th AAA SP Bn	14
217th AAA Gun Bn	6	87th Inf Div	2
468th AAA SP Bn	14	549th AAA AW Bn	14
635th AAA AW Bn	14	90th Inf Div	2
4th Inf Div	2	537th AAA AW Bn	14
377th AAA AW Bn	14	299th Ord Maint Co (AA)	6
XII Corps	2	305th Ord Maint Co (AA)	6
27th AAA Gp	2	306th Ord Maint Co (AA)	6
452nd AAA AW Bn	14	Brig Gen R. E. Starr, Hq AGF, Army War College, Washington 25, D.C.	1
115th AAA Gun Bn	6		
457th AAA AW Bn	14		
80th Inf Div	2		

---

19 February 1945

AAA Weekly Intelligence Report No. 29

Period:
090600A to 160600A

1. **Summary of Action**

   a. After several weeks of almost complete inactivity, the Luftwaffe aroused itself to the extent of making several small raids. 15 E/A were over the area during the week of which 10, bent upon reconnaissance, appeared in XII Corps zone the morning of 13 February. One of these is reported to have done some strafing of unknown targets in the 76th Inf Div sector. No attacks other than this one were reported. Other enemy planes were detected during nighttime flying through the Thionville, Luxembourg, Differdange and Metz Iazs. One of these, flying across both Luxembourg and Differdange, was shot down by AAA Guns in the latter area and when found proved to be a He-111 carrying supplies and considerable mail to the enemy garrison at Lorient. Of the 15 E/A reported, 13 were engaged by AAA with results as shown below.

b. 3 PAC were spotted overhead, but all apparently passed over the area as no crashes were reported.

c. Totals for the week, and to date from 1 August 1944, are as follows:

	Raids	No E/A	Cat I	Cat II
Week	11	15	3	2
To Date	1,580	3,681	514	254
	PAC Over Area	PAC Engaged	Cat A	Cat B
Week	3	0	0	0
To Date	206	30	0	3

2. GAF Tactics Notes
No new tactics were reported.

3. Miscellaneous Notes

a. AAA Automatic Weapons units continue to be employed in diversified roles. The 449th AAA AW Bn this week used both 40mm Bofors and .50 cal quad-mounted machine guns to support the advance of the 5th Inf Div. Missions were fired in conjunction with artillery concentrations, or separately, as called for. When visibility permitted, fire was adjusted by infantry forward observers. Pillboxes, road junctions and troop concentrations on hills and down in draws were targets. 40mm tracers also were fired to designate targets for the infantry and to guide them to the targets.

b. At the request of engineers, objects floating downstream and endangering bridges under construction near Echternach were fired upon and destroyed by firing sections of the 457th AAA AW Bn. Apparently the uses of AW units are endless.

c. During the past week or so, beginning in XII Corps zone the night of 4/5 February, AAA Searchlights have been used in XII and XX Corps sectors to furnish night illumination for the infantry in the form of artificial moonlight. The big, 800 million candlepower lights have been used almost nightly as weather permitted, and, once accustomed to them, front line troops have found them to be of great help. Comments of troops and of AAA Group commanders are of particular interest.

d. In XII Corps, illumination was furnished to the 5th Inf Div in its attacks over the Sauer and Our Rivers in Luxembourg. Lighting was also furnished to engineers engaged in bridge-building operations. The Commanding Officer of the 27th AAA Group (XII-Corps) stated:

(1) The beam of light in the sky, aimed over their objectives, enabled the troops to keep their sense of direction.

(2) The resulting illumination made it possible for the troops to distinguish trees and obstacles in their path.

(3) The lights enhanced the morale of the troops by eliminating the feeling of "blundering in the dark". After the infantry learned to keep in the shadows produced by the illumination they felt they could see the enemy and not be seen themselves.

(4) During the river crossing of assault boats lights were doused after a ten minute trial as the boats were too strongly illuminated.

(5) When used to illuminate bridge sites for engineers, 5th Inf Division G-3 reported that it enabled them to do more than twice the amount of work, during hours of darkness, than had been possible under blackout conditions.

(6) A training period in a rear area is considered desirable so that the troops can become acquainted with the effect of the illumination and made to realize the amount of light provided. In all cases where the lights have been used, troops have expected more illumination than it is possible to obtain.

e. In XX Corps, lighting was furnished the 26th Inf Div for operations in the Saarlautern bridgehead area. Since these operations were confined almost entirely to street and village combat, the effect of lights upon such activity is of especial interest. The Commanding Officer of the 112th AAA Group (XX Corps), quoting infantry sources, stated:

(1) The city is heavily booby-trapped and mined. It was German practice at night to withdraw from several houses, leaving them thoroughly trapped and mined, and then to return the following morning. This tactic made it difficult to enter the vacated houses without sustaining casualties, and difficult to take prisoners. However, in one period of three nights' operations with lights not a single casualty was suffered by American patrols, though 2 enemy were killed and 5 PWs taken. In addition, one regiment relieved another coming out of the line, the relief being greatly facilitated by the lights. Furthermore, no casualties were suffered in process.

(2) Combat patrols maintained better control over their members and better direction of movement.

(3) Mined and booby-trapped areas were easily skirted.

(4) Transportation of supplies to forward elements and other installations was considerably aided.

(5) Best results were obtained when patrols were sent out before artificial moonlight was turned on.

(6) Observation and adjustment of artillery and mortar fire was improved.

(7) Vehicular accidents were decreased.

(8) Observation of the enemy's avenues of approach was improved.

(9) Enemy patrols were observed and recognized before they got into our positions.

(10) Observations of enemy vehicles was improved and enabled them to be brought under artillery fire with greater success.

(11) A counterattack by approximately a company of infantry operating in a single city block was halted, facilitated considerably by the use of lights which enabled finer adjustment of artillery and mortar fires than normally.

(12) One disadvantage noted was that the lights favored the enemy when he was located inside buildings and entrenchments, as lights disclosed friendly troop movements to him.

(13) Generally, individuals could be identified at approximately 50 yards.

(14) Vehicles were identified from 100 to 150 yards.

(15) Vehicles and small bodies of troops were observed but not identified from 200 to 300 yards.

(16) Movements silhouetted by illumination were observed at 1,000 yards.

(17) Observation in a direct line between observer and the source of light was of greater range than 1,000 yards.

(18) After the first night of employment, the troops learned to keep well in the shadow cast by the lights.

f. Prisoner of War interrogation has revealed at some divergence. For that reason, a cross-section of testimony is given below.

(1) Some PWs (16th Div Sector) claimed they liked the lights, as it facilitated their supply. In the matter of feeding, food brought up at night was not spilled, and they thereby got full rations. Food to them is a critical item. They said it also made eating more a pleasure as they could see what they were doing. Lights were further approved as it made our movements easier to detect.

(2) However, (26th Div Sector) lights were disadvantageous as they caused their own movement to be observed with a result that their own patrol activity was greatly reduced, as was movement behind the lines.

(3) In XII Corps zone, PWs held to similar opinions, with some additions. The general consensus was that light fell on their positions with an intensity of about half moonlight. However, it was considerably brighter when there was snow

on the ground.

(4) Neither officers nor men had ever seen any of our personnel silhouetted by the lights.

(5) All PWs interrogated wondered that their own artillery did not fire at the lights. They believed our lights were well-defiladed though one PW stated he had received the beam directly in the eyes and been temporarily blinded. One PW, an artillery officer, stated that artillery did not shoot at the lights as they served as a warning of impending action and helped them as much as they did us. He could see no reason for destroying something that helped them and took no effort on their part to operate.

(6) A few PWs did not dare leave their slit trenches so long as the lights were on for fear of being observed. One EM even used the light as a beacon to which he walked to desert.

(7) All PWs were a little amused by the use of lights and felt their own people would never have thought of using them in such a manner. (Apparently they were unaware of the German use of some kind of searchlight North of Bastogne, in January)

g. Other PWs were interrogated as to the effect upon them of AAA Automatic Weapons fire, with the following results:

(1) The volume of infantry fire (from AAA M-51, quadruple .50 cal mounts) was such that trench battle positions were untenable and they were forced to surrender. Their own fire was limited to un-aimed shooting in the general direction of our troops. PW taken from vic Biesdorf stated that the heavy machine gun fire delivered in that direction made traffic impossible and inflicted heavy casualties on troops of the 316th Volksgrenadier Regt caught in the open. (80th Inf Div G-2 (IPW) Periodic reports, thru 633d AAA AW Bn, which did the firing in support of the infantry attack)

(2) Other PW interrogated, (taken from XII Corps front) had all been in or near concrete bunkers. Four of six said the fire was too high, and they could easily walk around under it. They knew of only one man killed, and he was on his way with another man to take up a rifle position. The one escaping dropped flat and was able to crawl back to the bunker, though fire in this instance was only two feet off the ground. One EM in the bunker was slightly wounded when a slug penetrated a block of wood in one of the firing apertures.

(3) One EM a veteran from the Russian front, said the Russians frequently used tracer fire. This veteran welcomed tracer fire because it could be seen and avoided, and because its source could be seen and dealt with. He stated that tracer fire had little or no effect upon morale of seasoned men, and thought the fire would be more effective if no tracer were used.

(4) Most PW apparently were unseasoned, since the voluminous tracer fire had considerable effect upon their morale. Those inside bunkers did not dare to come out; those caught outside said their morale was "crushed".

(5) None of the PWs interrogated had knowledge of the effect of fire on slit trenches or foxholes since, in cases known, fire had either been grazing or had entirely overshot the positions. However, one PW considered himself quite safe from grazing fire when lying in a trench about 16 inches deep, though he did not dare raise his head so long as the fire was going on.

h. The following commendation has been received by the CO, 455th AAA AW Bn from the Commanding General, XX Corps:

"I desire to commend the 455th Antiaircraft Artillery Automatic Weapons Battalion for outstanding performance in action against the enemy on 1 January 1945. For 34 minutes during the morning of 1 January 1945, approximately 60 enemy aircraft relentlessly bombed and strafed the field artillery installations which your battalion was defending. High speed diving tactics were, in general, used by the enemy, and he frequently endeavored to distract the attention of the antiaircraft gunners by sending in one plane from a different direction. The lone plane would dive on or near the anitaircraft unit, thus hoping to reduce the effectiveness of the antiaircraft fire on the original target. The antiaircraft gunners remained cool and stood their ground, thereby warding off the enemy. When the engagements had ceased, it was found that neither the field artillery installations nor those of the antiaircraft had suffered any material damage. Although subjected to devastating and continuous fire from the high speed enemy planes, none of the personnel of the ground installations were killed and only minor casualties resulted. As a result of the engagement, 10 enemy planes were destroyed, 5 were probably destroyed and 3 were damaged. The success of these few minutes of action is a tribute to the alertness, keeness and efficient manner of performance of the officers and men of your battalion. I desire to express not only my personal thanks to the officers, warrant officers and enlisted men of the 455th Antiaircraft Artillery Battalion, but those of the entire XX Corps for their splendid accomplishment and devotion to duty.

/s/t/ Walton H. Walker
Major General, United States Army Commanding

i. The 633d AAA AW Bn for the instruction, as well as amusement, of its men publishes a weekly paper called the "Ack-Count". This is a well-planned, two to four page shoot making use of the silhouettes appearing in Etousa AAA Notes and other publications for the edification of all concerned. Silhouettes are presented in test form, with answers printed the following week, and are enlivened by various eye-appeal drawings. Such other items as booby-traps and mines are dealt with, and combat tips also are passed along. It is distributed down to every section.

j. Attached as an enclosure is the weekly aircraft recognition annex.

/s/ F.R. Chamberlain, Jr,
/t/ F.R. Chamberlain, Jr,
Colonel, CAC, Antiaircraft Officer.

24 February 1945

AAA Weekly Intelligence Report No. 30

Period:
160600A to 230600A

1. **Summary of Action**

a. For the first week since becoming operational at 1200B hours, 1 August 1944, there were no enemy aircraft over Third US Army area.

b. 16 PAC were observed passing overhead. None of these is reported to have crashed. I was engaged by AAA fire but was apparently unhit.

c. Totals for the week, and to date from 1 August 1944, are as follows:

	Raids	No E/A	Cat I	Cat II
Week	0	0	0	0
To Date	1,580	3,681	514	254
	PAC Over Area	PAC Engaged	Cat A	Cat B
Week	16	1	0	0
To Date	222	31	0	3

2. **GAF Tactics Notes**

No new tactics were reported.

3. **Miscellaneous Notes**

a. During the week the 377th AAA AW Bn (M) was called upon almost daily by the 4th Inf Div, to which it is attached, to furnish supporting fires for infantry attacks. Both 40mm and M16B half-track quadruple .50 cal mounts were used to fire upon village houses sheltering a forward CP and communications center, and enemy positions in woods, among other targets. Tracers were not used in any of the missions.

b. The 465th AAA AW Bn, a self-propelled unit, fired several missions supporting the 94th Inf Div's attack in the Saar-

Moselle River triangle area. Pillboxes, roads and enemy fire trenches were so successfully engaged by fire characterized as "devastating and searching" that the enemy fell back under cover of smoke and the infantry easily reduced an area which had previously appeared impregnable. Besides firing also upon village houses sheltering enemy troops and a CP, elements of the 465th were attached to the 94th Ron Troops and patrolled a Northern zone of the Division sector along the Leuk River valley SW of Saarburg. Two road blocks were blown up, three small towns were cleared, and two enemy were killed and ten taken prisoner.

c. 19 February 1945 marked the completion of 30 months' continuous overseas duty for the 633d AAA AW Bn (M). Originally the 1st Bn, 244th Coast Artillery when it embarked for Iceland on 19 August 1942, it became the 633d AAA AW Bn (M) shortly after arriving in the UK, after nearly a year in Iceland, and under that designation remained in England for 10½ months. The battalion has been on the continent a few days over 8 months. Of the original personnel, 10 officers, 2 warrant officers and 318 enlisted men are still with them. Three EM have been home during this period for rehabilitation; none of the rest have been home.

d. Attached as an enclosure is the weekly aircraft recognition annex.

/s/ F.R. Chamberlain, Jr,
/t/ F.R. Chamberlain, Jr,
Colonel, CAC, Antiaircraft Officer.

The bomb load is 20,000 lbs (internal) at maximum. Some typical loads are 4 x 4000 lb bombs, 12 x 1000 lb bombs or 8 x 2000 lb bombs.

2. **Designations of Reconnaissance (Photographic) Aircraft**

Designation	Description
F-2A Beech	Modified UC-45
F-3A Douglas	Converted A-20J
F-4 Lockheed	Modified P-38 D & E
F-5A, B Lockheed	Similar to P-38 F & G
F-5C, E Lockheed	Similar to P-38 H & J
F-6 North American	P-51, B, C & D
F-7A Consolidated	B-24J
F-8 Dehavilland	Mosquito
F-9A, B Boeing	B-17F and B-17G
F-10 North American	B-25
F-13 Boeing	B-29

3. An Air Force officer who accompanied a Naval Task Force on a recent strike, reports that at Saipan naval aircraft encountered a Japanese jet-propelled aircraft. So far as can be ascertained, this makes the first appearance of such Japanese aircraft in a combat theater.

The aircraft appeared quite similar to German jet-propelled planes. Its speed was estimated at approximately 500 miles per hour. No other information is available at the present time.

4. The following outline of Status of British aircraft is based on informal reports and comments made in the U.S. Navy Semi-Monthly News Letter to Staff Recognition Officers:

Spitfire: The VIII, IX and XIV are the important models. Stress should be on the IX and XIV at present, and on the new XXII when this bubble canopy model appears.
Typhoon: Still in use and considered important. Had a large past production. Will evidently be replaced by Tempest eventually.
Tempest: Tempest V is the mark of the present operational model. It closely resembles the Typhoon and Tempest II. It differs somewhat recognitionally from Tempest II and will probably be the more important of the two models.
Mosquito: High production expected to continue. Two important versions are the solid nose fighter-bomber and the attack bomber version with bulged bomb bay to accommodate a heavy bomb.
Buckingham: In limited production. Doubtful if it will become an important aircraft.
Lancaster: Quantity production will continue. Important current model is the III. Lancaster IV with 120 feet span, scheduled to appear soon, will replace earlier versions.
Halifax: Halifax III is important current production model. The I is obsolete and II is unimportant. Halifax VII will appear later, with same recognition features as the III.

Note: It is considered that types not listed above are obsolescent or unlikely to be seen in the Third US Army area.

(Source of above news: 9th AF Info Int Memos)

5 March 1945
AAA Weekly Intelligence Report No. 31
Period:
230600A Feb to 020600A Mar

1. **Summary of Action**

a. Small scale enemy air activity continued this week in Third US Army area. 14 E/A were reported of which 11 appeared in one day over VIII Corps zone. The 3 other E/A flew singly and were reported on separate days, 2 in the Luxembourg area and 1 reported by friendly A/C who observed it over the XX Corps zone. All but one of the planes flew at low altitudes, with reconnaissance apparently their primary mission. Only one attack against ground targets was reported, as a single plane was observed to strafe unknown targets vic Basbellain (P-7578) with damage, if any, unknown. AAA engaged 10 of the 14 airplanes, and claimed probable destruction of 5 as a result.

b. Contrails of 16 PAC (V-2s) were observed over the area. No crashes were reported.

c. Totals for the week, and to date from 1 August 1944 (Corrected) are as follows:

	Raids	No E/A	Cat I	Cat II
Week	9	14	0	5
To Date	1,589	3,695	514	261
	PAC Over Area	PAC Engaged	Cat A	Cat B
Week	16	0	0	0
To Date	238	31	0	3

2. **GAF Tactics Notes**

a. No new tactics were noted.

b. Though the Luftwaffe apparently is not at present to be committed in strength on the Third US Army front, ground activity to the North is drawing considerable of its attention. Of particular interest is the increased proportion of jet-propelled A/C reported by Ninth US Army. Me-262s are the most commonly observed, though He-280s and Ar-234s have also appeared. These aircrafts are flying in at altitudes low enough for engagement by automatic weapons fire, and AAA is taking full advantage of opportunities presented to score many claims.

3. **Miscellaneous Notes**

a. The 390th AAA AW Bn (SP), on 25 and 26 February, conducted practice firing at ground targets for crews of all M15 and M16 halftracks. "The targets were set up at a range of from 800 to 1,400 yds. The purpose of the practice was to demonstrate the problems involved in firing at ground targets at various ranges. Special attention was given to the amount of elevation required in order to deliver accurate fire with the first few rounds at targets at the various ranges, and to emphasize the need for accurate boresighting. As a result of the firing it was found that more accurate fire could be delivered on ground targets with the M15, both initially and for sustained firing. Also, neither the M6 nor the Mk 9 sight is adequate for accurate ground fire".

b. The 119th AAA Gun Bn, finding itself in a proper situation for such employment, recently sited its spare radar in a location for the detection of ground targets moving along roads behind the German lines during darkness. B and D Batteries were given a secondary mission of engaging such targets, their fire being controlled from an FDC at the radar, with communications to the Field Artillery for the securing of necessary clearances. Quite a few vehicles were spotted and engaged, with the result that traffic was stopped in every instance. Actual damage done is unknown, but German nerves must have been severely strained, upon several occasions.

c. Battery A, 482d AAA AW Bn (SP), recently received a unit citation under General Orders 44, this Headquarters, for its part in smashing the German breakthrough effort of December. The citation reads as follows: "During this period (from 17 December — 26 December 1944) Battery "A" was assigned the mission of furnishing ground support to infantry, artillery, and tank destroyer units defending positions against the strong enemy thrust into Belgium and Luxembourg. Facing overwhelming odds with outstanding heroism the Battery fought stubbornly over difficult terrain, inflicting heavy losses upon the enemy. At one time this unit held a sector alone, without immediate support of other arms. The indomitable fighting spirit, the courage and devotion to duty of the officers and men of this Battery are in keeping with the highest traditions of the military service."

d. Attached as an enclosure is the Weekly Aircraft Recognition annex.

12 March 1945
AAA Weekly Intelligence Report No. 32
Period:
020600A to 090600A
1. Summary of Action
a. A jet-propelled Me-262, seen flying North over Bleialf (P9683) at 20,000 ft altitude, was the only German plane noted during the week in Third US Army's area. It was sighted the morning of 2 March and because of its high altitude was not engaged by antiaircraft fire.

b. Pilotless plane activity also decreased as contrails of but two V-2s were observed. No crashes were reported.

c. Totals for the week, and to date from 1 August 1944, are as follows:

	Raids	No E/A	Cat I	Cat II
Week	1	1	0	0
To Date	1,590	3,696	514	261
	PAC Over Area	PAC Engaged	Cat A	Cat B
Week	2	0	0	0
To Date	240	31	0	3

2. GAF Tactics Notes
No new tactics were reported.

3. Miscellaneous Notes
a. While the German Air Force, like the German Ground Forces, is gradually dying it still is far from dead and, in fact, maintains a considerable and formidable striking force in the West. Recent events on the ground have caused hurried redisposition of units to airfields in the interior, and it is not to be wondered that no heavy air attacks were made during the week. In spite of their difficulties, the GAF mounted 84 raids against First and Ninth US Armies involving a total of 156 A/C in a week which say much weather unsuited for flying. XIX TAC estimates current air strengths in western Germany to be as follows:

	SEF	TEF	Jet A/C	
NW Germany	550	420	105	(Me-262s - 80 (Ar-234s - 15) (Me-163a - 10)
SW Germany	130	140	25	(Me-262s - 25)
Totals, western Germany	680	560	130	

This is a total of 1,370 first line, operational aircraft all capable of employment at one time against Third US Army, though this prospect, at present, is unlikely. More aircraft are in reserve and pilot personnel is being increased. (See: AAA Weekly Int Rpts Nos. 18 and 25 for previous estimates.)

b. PWs from various western front sectors have stated that many men drawn from the Luftwaffe last summer and autumn for duties with ground forces are being returned from front line units. One PW claimed to have seen a Top Secret German document, dated 24 Feb 1945, providing for return of former GAF pilots and wireless operators to flight status. PW expressed the belief that this anticipated retraining on jet-propelled A/C. (Source: 9th AF, Air PW Interrogation Unit.)

c. "A source listed as 'usually reliable' reports that a four-engined Ju-290 is being luxuriously equipped with armor plate, bulletproof glass, and guns fore and aft, at an airfield near Augsburg (Possibly Kirchham, V-1086). It has a capacity of 20-22 persons. Gen. Bauer, Hitler's pilot, is personally supervising the construction and practicing handling the plane, according to this report. Delivery was originally fixed for 28 Feb for Berchtesgaden but has been postponed to the middle of March and Hitler is greatly disturbed over the delay. The original plan called for construction of 3 such planes but because of material shortages only one was built." (Source: XIX TAC Daily Int Summary No. 208). This plane is listed as having a range of 2010 miles with a bomb load of 10,000 lbs. Without bombs, and with auxiliary drop tanks, it's range is??

d. Attached as an enclosure is the weekly aircraft recognition annex.

/s/ F.R. Chamberlain, Jr,
/t/ F.R. Chamberlain, Jr,
Colonel, CAC, Antiaircraft Officer.

19 March 1945
AAA Weekly Intelligence Report No. 33
Period:
090600A to 160600A

1. Summary of Action
a. As the northern front stabilized on the Rhine and the Remagen bridgehead slowly expanded, the deep thrusts of Third US Army's armor through country heretofore classified as nearly "impossible" began to draw scattered attention from the Luftwaffe, presaging increased air activity in this area. Enemy planes were overhead each day of the week as air reconnaissance, of necessity, replaced ground information sources isolated by the Rhine. Only 19 E/A were counted, in all, but the diversity of sources reporting them indicate a broad area was covered. These aircraft flew at low altitudes for the most part, and paid marked attention to forward elements of divisions, division and corps artillery positions and installations. Other E/A were reported as far back as Luxembourg and Thionville. Only 3 of the 19 E/A were over during hours of darkness, 2 of these making strafing attacks on different nights, one on field artillery positions and the other on an undetermined target. One Me-110 strafed AAA positions during daylight and sources other than AAA reported two bombs dropped vic Thur (L-673955), to complete the sum of daylight attacks. Very minor material

damage resulted and no personnel casualties were caused. 12 of the E/A were engaged by antiaircraft units, with results appearing below.

b. One pilotless aircraft (V-1) and 6 jet-propelled rockets (V-2) were observed, none of which crashed in the area.

c. Totals for the week, and to date from 1 August 1944 (PAC totals corrected to drop V-2s) are as follows:

	Raids	No E/A	Cat I	Cat II
Week	17	19	3	1
To Date	1,607	3,715	517	262
	PAC Over Area	PAC Engaged	Cat A	Cat B
Week	1	0	0	0
To Date	168	31	0	3

2. GAF Tactics Notes

a. An increasing number of jet-propelled Me-262s were used in the area. Ju-87s also appeared, as did FW-190s, Me-109s and Me-210s. Employment of outmoded Ju-87s in daylight reconnaissance missions furnishes a commentary on the status of the German Air Force.

b. An Me-262, flying low over the 4th Armd Div at an estimated speed of 500 m.p.h., was said to give out a whistling sound similar to that of a P-51, but louder. No exhaust from its motors was noted.

c. Evasive measures were the customary ones, A/C taking full advantage of cloud cover whenever possible.

d. German air tactics noted in Ninth U.S. Army zone are of interest for their novelty as well as instructiveness:

"b. What was apparently an instance of bomber-searchlight coöperation was noted on 7 March. A light placed well forward of the German lines went into action as German planes neared the front lines. Its beam was pointed vertical until the enemy aircraft were almost over our lines. The light would then be swung to the horizontal and pointed in the direction of our lines. The planes would bomb and strafe along the lines of the beam. Only one searchlight was so engaged and no attempt at intersection was made. This is possibly another German attempt to overcome the lack of proper navigation and bombing equipment in the night harassing force."

"c. In the XIX Corps zone a determined attack was launched against our air OP's on 5 March. Two were shot down in the morning and two in the afternoon by German planes that were obviously assigned that specific mission. The method of attack was for one German fighter to close on the Cub and two other fighters to follow, behind and below the first. When the Cub dove to avoid the first plane, the other two planes would press their attack." (Source: 9th US Army AAA Isum No. 25)

3. Miscellaneous Notes

a. Again demonstrating its versatility as an instrument of war, radar has come up with a new employment, this time on behalf of the CIC. Gun battalion radars, tracking aircraft entering the area from the East, notified the CIC when several low-flying A/C flew in. The CIC swept swiftly over the area in their wake, masking a record haul of saboteurs espionage agents who had parachuted from the planes in the darkness.

b. While activity increased against air targets, activity against ground targets leaped forward as more divisions found missions to exploit the tremendous fire power of AAA automatic weapons units attached to them. The 449th and 546th AW battalions and the 390th, 465th, 575th and 796th Self-propelled battalions all reported ground role activities in support of divisions. Towns, woods, trenches, pillboxes and other such targets were fired upon with effect at times called "devastating", contributing to the rapid advance of our forces. In addition, the 119th, and 217th AAA Gun battalions fired 1,836 rounds of 90mm ammo in counter-battery, harassing and interdiction missions, performing as field artillery. By using radar to detect movement at night along roads, railroads and paths, the 119th Gun battalion effectively halted all night movement in the area under surveillance.

c. Many PWs were taken by AAA units this week, including a Lt Colonel charged with the southern defenses of Trier, taken by the 796th AAA AW Bn (SP) attached to the 10th Armd Div.

28 March 1945
AAA Weekly Intelligence Report No. 34
Period:
160600A to 230600A

1. Summary of Action

a. It was no wonder that Third US Army's advance in the Palatinate triangle during the past week drew the full, frantic attention of the German Air Force. With the enemy facing a catastrophic envelopment of all his forces and defensive positions he threw a considerable number of the aircraft available on this front into attempts to slow our drives. Hostile air activity began moderately with attacks on the spearheads of XII Corps' 4th Armd Div. But when the Nahe River was reached and crossed, it increased considerably and remained at a comparatively high level throughout the week, with few exceptions. Artillery and installations supporting and aiding the advance received much attention, and bridges over the Nahe River at Bretzenheim, Bad Munster and Oberhausen and over the Moselle River at Hatzenport were bombed and strafed. XX Corps' advance along the South flank which rolled up the Siegfried Line and destroyed the entire German static positions drew equal attention the last two days of the period. Traffic on the Autobahn Highway N of Kaiser-Lautern was attacked, as were other targets of opportunity. Elements of divisions under both corps received many attacks. Jet-propelled planes were numerous for the first time in Third US Army area, as both Me-262s and Ar-234s made frequent appearances in a ground attack role. Despite the intensity of the air attacks, damage from them was slight. No bridges were hit, casualties were few. Most attacks were by daylight with no preference shown for a particular hour, as attacks came throughout the day. A considerable number of these attacks were from altitudes well above the effective range of AAA automatic weapons. However, enough E/A flew at low altitudes to give Antiaircraft gunners a good workout. 72 Cat Is and 45 Cat IIs were chalked up, 51 Cat Is and 40 Cat IIs of these being claimed by XII Corps AAA units, the remainder by XX Corps. In addition, many E/A were claimed to be damaged (Cat III).

b. Reports have not been completely screened for duplications, so that only estimated numbers of raids and E/A appear below. Totals for the week, and to date from 1 August 1944, are as follows:

	Raids	No E/A	Cat I	Cat II
Week	122	475	72	45
To Date	1,729	4,190	589	307
	PAC Over Area	PAC Engaged	Cat A	Cat B
Week	0	0	0	0
To Date	168	31	0	3

2. GAF Tactics Notes

No new tactics were noted. Formations sighted varied in size from lone A/C up to groups of 25. Jet-propelled A/C pursued no noteworthy tactics and sometimes flew in mixed formations with standard types so that their special capabilities were, perhaps, thereby somewhat restricted.

3. Miscellaneous Notes

a. Many of the actions by AAA units this week are deserving of mention. Of particular interest, however, is the report of the 489th AAA AW Bn (SP) which supported the 4th Armd Div's swift advances. Numerous bombing, strafing and rocket attacks were made on elements of the division, its installations and bridges it captured intact, and on the AAA gun sections protecting them. For the most part, E/A involved were Me-109s and FW-190s, with a sprinkling of Me-262s, and Ju-188s. Making the most of St Patrick's Day the 489th SP, known as "Murphy's Marauders", engaged 39 of the E/A attacking and claimed 12 Cat Is and 8 Cat IIs. In the three day period from 17 to 20 March, a total of 103 of the E/A attempting to thwart the advances were engaged, of which 25 were claimed destroyed and 19 probably destroyed for a total of 44 out of the 103 fired upon. Sole damage reported from these attacks was done to a one-quarter ton trailer. There were no personnel casualties reported.

b. The 452d AAA AW Bn (M) had, among other missions, the protection of XII Corps artillery units and did considerable firing at enemy aircraft which attacked their area. On 17 March, of 51 E/A observed by them, 30 Me-109s and 6 FW-190s were engaged at altitudes of 1,000 to 3,000 ft. Five were claimed destroyed and 7 probably destroyed. On the 18th, 4 more Cat Is and 2 Cat IIs were claimed out of 14 E/A engaged, giving the 452d a two-day total of 18 claims out of 50 E/A fired upon.

c. Some units saw jet-propelled A/C for the first time this week. In their first few engagements, the deceptively high speeds flown caused many gunners to allow insufficient leads and tracers trailed the targets. However, improvement was rapid and, in proportion to the number of jet planes over, a good many were claimed shot down.

d. AAA units in the advance were almost continually engaged in ground fire missions, as well as in air defense. One outstanding piece of action occurred when a composite platoon of the 390th AAA AW Bn (SP), attached to a 26th Inf Div task force, arrived at the town of Aussen to find a bridge there across the Prim River was blown. Word was received that the bridge in the town of Burpich, to the South, was intact. The platoon commander offered to take his half-tracks to Burpich and try to secure the bridge and the plan was accepted by the task force commander. The lieutenant's jeep and three half-tracks raced full speed for the town running machine gun and small arms fire, and dodging hand grenades. The two hindmost of the three half-tracks delivered covering fire, destroying 4 enemy vehicles and killing or wounding 25 enemy soldiers during the mad dash for the bridge. The bridge was reached and found intact. Intense enemy small arms and machine gun fire was directed at the half-tracks from houses across the river, and soon artillery fire fell in heavy concentrations. However, this lieutenant had radioed the task force to come down and secure the bridge and it was held until tanks and infantry reached it and effected their crossing, following which the tracks took cover among the buildings in town.

e. In an attack by the 65th Inf Div on the Siegfried Line city of Dillingen, 40mm guns of the 546th AAA AW Bn (M) were emplaced to deliver supporting fires. In order to secure a satisfactory field of fire, approximately 100 trees had to be cut down just prior to the time of the attack, at 0630 hours. Telephone communication was established with an Inf OP, and fire missions were requested from there by the Inf battalion commander. Four enemy guns and one machine gun position were located by their flashes and silenced by the 40mm's. Numerous pillboxes were also engaged and the entire mission was of such success that advancing infantry drew no fire from any positions in the area fired upon.

f. PWs were taken by everyone this week, it seems. AAA units contributed their share, also, and many prisoners were taken after short, sharp fire fights. Largest number so far reported taken was 500 taken by "A" Battery of the 796th AAA AW Bn (SP) in a few days' time, 300 being taken in one day. On 16 March, platoon elements of the 390th Self-propelled, assisted by 3 TDs, fired into some woods and took 300 PWs, killing in addition over 100 Germans, later found there by an I & R platoon.

g. With the rapid advances on the ground leaving the German populace shocked and frightened, there still remain behind "master race" members with the will to resist, either in or out of uniform. For these, AAA firing sections, isolated as they generally are in open fields and hilltops, should be particularly on the lookout. All gun crews should be thoroughly instructed in curfew and other restrictive measures placed on the German population so that they will know what to expect, and security and non-fraternization measures should be fully explained and properly emphasized. A reminder is also in order to be on the watch for mining and booby-trapping activities. An occurrence such as that of last December, when a Hq and Hq Btry of an AAA AW Bn billeted in St Avold was blown up by a time bomb, killing 19 and wounding 17 others, is not to be regarded as a present impossibility. In line with this, the following is quoted:

"c. Attention of all units is called to the danger of time bombs, booby traps and other secreted demolitions in buildings, on bridges, in culverts, at road junctions, etc. With the enemy withdrawing and desirable billeting and CP facilities limited, time-bombing and booby-trapping by the enemy is highly probable. That the enemy is employing these weapons in Third US Army zone has already been confirmed by PW. All units should be warned to take nothing for granted and to exercise every precaution against time bombs and booby traps." (Source: Third US Army G-2 Periodic Rpt. No. 282)

"d. **This is Enemy Territory.** At 0900A, 17 Mar 1945, 8 men were killed and 3 wounded near Elsdorf (F-1760) when members of a Bomb Disposal Squad lifted a box of TNT from a pile of 4 boxes of enemy explosives which had been inspected 15 Mar and found free of mines and booby-traps. **The box of TNT had apparently been booby-trapped since its previous inspection.** Casualties such as these will continue unless **all** troops realize that we are in hostile country, surrounded by people who are still our enemies. Our victory over them has only served to increase their animosity towards us. They will regard lack of vigilance on our part as a sign of weakness and will be quick to take advantage of it." (Source: First US Army, thru Third US Army G-2 Periodic Rpt. No. 282)

h. Attached as an inclosure is the weekly aircraft recognition annex.

/s/ F.R. Chamberlain, Jr,
/t/ F.R. Chamberlain, Jr,
Colonel, CAC, Antiaircraft Officer.

1 Incl — Aircraft Recognition (Jet-propelled He-280)
Distribution:
"A" & "H"

2 April 1945
AAA Weekly Intelligence Report No. 35
Period:
230600A Mar to 300600A Mar

1. Summary of Action

a. On the ground during the period, XII Crops' Oppenheim bridgehead over the Rhine became firmly established and expanded to such proportions that it no longer could be described by so limiting a term. VIII and XX Corps also crossed and the end of the period saw all Third US Army's units far past the Rhine and deep into Germany. The Oppenheim crossings were made under many attacks by the Luftwaffe which began last week and carried on into the first three days of the current period. Attacks occurred during early morning hours, but by far the larger number were made from dusk to 0230A hours in the morning. Flights of as many as 20 or more single and twin-engined E/A were involved, with jet-propelled planes used frequently at night to bomb and strafe. Many E/A appeared at altitudes under 6,000 to 15,000 ft, and at slant ranges up to 13,000 yds. Troop concentrations, highway traffic, dumps and artillery were frequent targets, but most numerous were attempts to strafe the bridges and hit them with rockets and bombs both by day and by night, with many flares dropped in aid of the bombing. AAA gun sites were attacked and, for the first reported time, a direct hit by an enemy rocket was made on a gun position, when a rocket struck inside a revetment, killing 3 men and severely wounding 3 others. Establishment of an exempted laz with ceiling at 15,000 ft permitted AAA to work at full effectiveness as testified by the number of planes destroyed. No bridges were touched, material damage was slight and casualties few. AAA gun battalions as well as Automatic Weapons units saw considerable action and were firing constantly through the night, scoring many kills. On 26 March, activity slackened and thereafter was almost negligible for the remaining four days of the period.

b. Screening of reports has not been completed so that only estimated numbers of raids and E/A appear below. Totals for the week, and to date from 1 August 1944, are as follows:

	Raids	No E/A	Cat I	Cat II
Week	185	340	79	46
To Date	1,914	4,530	668	353
	PAC Over Area	PAC Engaged	Cat A	Cat B
Week	0	0	0	0
To Date	168	31	0	3

2. GAF Tactics Notes

a. Nearly all E/A took violent evasive action both upon entry into a defended area and following engagement by AAA weapons, tactics fostered by the desire for self-preservation which, however, do not lead to bombing accuracy as their lack of effectiveness proved. Zig-zagging was common, but a most typical maneuver was to dive, then climb and circle. Diving turns also were used in avoidance.

b. Dive-bombing tactics were frequently attempted, usually at 45° angles of approach to bridges, and at diving angles varying from steep to fairly flat glide-bombing attempts. Skip-bombing by an Me-109 against objectives vic Geinsheim, near the Rhine, was reported.

c. The 599th AAA AW Bn (M) told of a novel strategem by an enemy photographic plane. It came in with lights on to attract AAA fire and then dropped magnesium flares, photographing the active AAA defenses below.

3. Miscellaneous Notes

a. Third US Army's AAA units this week scored their 1,000th enemy plane claimed destroyed or probably destroyed, for an average of better than four planes a day during the 241 days of operations this Headquarters completed on 300600A March.

b. The 129th AAA Gun Bn contributed materially to this accomplishment when, in one night's firing in an exempted laz this week, it claimed 17 knocked down and 4 probables and the next night claimed 10 more Cat Is and 4 Cat IIs, making a two-day total of 35 claims. Gun engagements were mostly after dark and at altitudes averaging roughly 6,500 feet, but there were many at altitudes of 10,000 feet and over. However, sufficient E/A flew at low altitudes to give their machine gunners good opportunities, too, and several Categories were claimed by them.

c. A well-placed German 20mm AAA Gun on the East bank of the Rhine above Rhens had held up the advance of elements of the 347th Inf for two days, after its initial river crossing. The position had a very low silhouette and was approximately 6 feet in diameter, so that it was hard to see or to hit. At the request of the 347th Inf's CO, the 635th AAA AW Bn engaged the target on 26 March, from the West side of the river. The range was 3,300 yards and the target so small and so placed that it could not be seen at that distance, even with binoculars. Indirect firing procedure was accordingly employed, with an Inf OP doing the adjusting. 40mm guns were laid on target, using map data and improvised range and azimuth drums devised by the 635th AW Bn. (See: Etousa AAA Notes No 22, and these reports, No 23). Sensings were given by the OP in terms as little as 5 yards range and 1 mil azimuth in attempts to get a direct hit. Single shots were used for adjustment, but fire for effect was done on auto-fire. A total of 88 rounds of 7 Sec 40mm (HE) ammo was fired, of which 9 were reported by the OP as hits, inflicting damage and casualties on the position. Actually, accuracy was higher as several of the rounds burst short of the target due to the tracer burn-out point.

d. Having just completed transporting troops of the 80th Inf Div, a driver of the 633d AAA AW Bn (M) was on his way back to a town in Germany to rejoin his unit, one night recently. Outside the town of Kusel he came upon a parked convoy of jeeps and started by them when vehicles were seen approaching from the opposite direction and he pulled into the jeep line to let them pass. The careening manner and odd blackout lights of the first vehicle attracted his attention and, as it went by, he saw it to be a German half-track towing a gun and filled with German soldiers. He immediately pulled out of the jeep line and across the road so that his trucked blocked the rest of the oncoming German vehicles. Jumping from his truck cab, he shouted at the occupants of the first truck to surrender, instead of which they grabbed their weapons and a few dashed for some nearby woods. He immediately opened fire over their heads with his tommy gun, which caused them to throw away their weapons and shout "kamerad" in a very convincing manner. His firing attracted some help from the personnel in the jeep convoy and, in all, approximately 300 prisoners were taken from the vehicles and surrounding territory.

/s/ F.R. Chamberlain, Jr.
/t/ F.R. Chamberlain, Jr.
Colonel, CAC, Antiaircraft Officer.

11 April 1945

AAA Weekly Intelligence Report No. 36

Period:
300600A Mar to 060600B Apr

1. Summary of Action

a. Enemy air activity showed no sign of abating this week and, in fact, increased considerably over last week's efforts. Improved flying weather permitted the Luftwaffe to react to our penetration of the Werra River defense line by striking repeatedly at armored spearheads, supporting units, and at bridges. Activity was at a comparatively low scale the first three days of the period, but on 2 April it spurted and a peak effort with approximately 180 planes was reported, dropping thereafter to daily averages of 60-70 E/A over the area. Me-262s were in much evidence the forepart of the period, bombing a bridge over the Main River via Grossauheim and strafing traffic on the Reichsautobahn via Alsfeld. After that they were seldom seen and Me-109s and FW-190s, with a light sprinkling of Ju-87s, Ju-88s and Me-410s, came out to attack elements of the 4th Armd Div and supporting units and forward elements of the 6th Armd Div. Quite a number of these passed up the armor to strafe Field Artillery, road convoys and other such targets farther back. Only 3 or 4 planes were seen in the rear of Corps boundaries, however. Below Kassel, assembly areas and artillery of the 80th Inf Div were attacked. AAA attached to other Infantry divisions also had many engagements, sometimes in self-defense as their gun positions were several times attacked. The enemy's air aggressiveness fell off sharply after 2 April and many flights appeared bent more on sight-seeing than anything else as, for example, when a flight of 30 E/A flew along over a convoy making no attacks and lingering in the area until driven off by a flight of friendly fighters. Most E/A flew at low altitudes (100-6,00 ft) making a field day for AAA automatic weapons units which, on 2 April, alone, claimed 72 planes destroyed and 32 probables, with many others damaged. Air attacks punctured two pontons of the bridge at Grossauheim and destroyed a treadway bridge over the Werra River at Creuzberg. An attempted bombing of a bridge at Gr Burschia over the Werra was unsuccessful. Some few casualties were caused and other material damage was slight.

b. Screening of reports has not been completed so that only estimated numbers of raids and E/A appear below. Totals for the week and to date from 1 August 1944 (corrected) are as follows:

	Raids	No E/A	Cat I	Cat II
Week	150	490	149	76
To Date	2,064	5,020	874	441
	PAC Over Area	PAC Engaged	Cat A	Cat B
Week	0	0	0	0
To Date	168	31	0	3

2. GAF Tactics Notes

a. Air tactics appeared standard for the most part, with nothing particularly novel emerging. Pilots indulged their penchant for attacking low from the East, out of the sun, in the morning hours and coming in somewhat higher to dive during noontime. Cloud cover was used whenever possible.

b. The 550th AAA AW Bn reported an attack by 12 FW-190s which came out of the clouds in three lines of four planes each to drop fragmentation and demolition bombs on Field Artillery positions. Despite AW fire they remained on their bombing course until bombs were released only after which did they head for the clouds.

c. In the jet-propelled attack on the bridge over the Main River via Grossauheim, Me-262s came in at 3,500 ft to dive at a 10° angle and speed of 450 mph, dropping anti-personnel bombs.

d. Another tactic not usually employed was reported by the 550th AAA AW Bn. Upon being engaged an Me-109 went into a vertical climb from 1,000 to 4,000 ft and disappeared in clouds. When last seen it was smoking badly, however, indicating this is not the best way to avoid AW fire.

3. Miscellaneous Notes

a. AW units had many intensive engagements with low-flying enemy planes as daylight strafing replaced last week's night and high-level bombing attacks. Of the 104 claims arising from engagements on 2 April, more than a third were made by the 489th AAA AW Bn (SP). Its fire units, deployed in protection of armored columns, CPs and bridges had their biggest day on record — perhaps the biggest of any AAA unit in the ETO — to claim 34 Cat Is and 6 Cat IIs. In addition, another E/A was claimed damaged (Cat III).

b. During a period highlighted by outstanding achievements, not the least outstanding among AAA units was the feat of the 546th AAA AW Bn in shooting down an Me-109 with one round of 40mm ammo. Weissight fire control was used and the plane, a "flamer", crashed a mile away, bearing out the adage that nothing succeeds like success.

c. Other units performed outstandingly and the 777th AAA AW Bn, a self-propelled organization, had many engagements with E/A attacking leading armored columns of the 6th Armd Div to which it is attached. Only slight damage and casualties resulted from these air efforts but the 777th, on the other hand, is able to boast taking a toll of 25 Cat Is, 19 Cat IIs and 11 other badly damaged.

d. On the ground, AAA units had many skirmishes with enemy foot troops, taking PWs and inflicting casualties. In one instance, half-track section No 220 (one M15 and one M16 track) of the 390th AAA AW Bn (SP) was attached, with other sections, to a task force of the 26th Inf Div having the mission of clearing out by-passed pockets of resistance in the rear of forward elements. The task force had just entered the town of Hitzkirchen and section 220 had occupied positions NW and S of there when a column of 200 jerry foot troops approached town from the NW and 300 approached from the S in an evident attempt to encircle and trap the task force. Section 220, having received permission, opened fire on the enemy as soon as they emerged from the woods and were well into the open. As a result, 200 to 300 enemy were killed and wounded and the attack stopped cold. The remainder were later mopped up by the infantry.

e. As further evidence that there is constant need for alertness, a few of the week's occurrences are cited. Civilians, taking advantage of the noise of anti-aircraft firing, used the opportunity to fire rifles at the gun crews nearby and caused several casualties. A firing section of the 455th AAA AW Bn, having just completed an all-day convoy, bedded down for the night in the vicinity of field artillery it supported. At 0400 hours, the guard challenged the source of a noise, which signalled an attack on the section by enemy small arms, machine guns, bazooka and mortar fire. The attack was beaten off but only after one crew member was killed and four seriously wounded and a 40mm gun damaged. A platoon of the 390th AAA AW Bn (SP) while traveling in convoy was ambushed by approximately 200 enemy troops firing small arms and throwing grenades from both sides of the road. One officer and six enlisted men were killed, two were wounded and six listed as missing (two of whom later escaped capture and returned). The half-tracks opened fire and killed 10 enemy and wounded 35.

f. Taking time from their duties of providing AAA defenses for various installations, men of the 551st AAA AW Bn helped the supply services recently by collecting 1,347 empty jerrycans in one day.

g. Variety is the Spice of Life Dept. In combing an area S of the 76th Inf Div boundary, men of the 778th Self-propelled Bn took 78 PWs, destroyed three 88mm gun positions and de-booby-trapped a searchlight position. The 567th AAA AW Bn: handled 4 Russian soldiers who escaped from a German labor camp; a Belgian, wanted for murder of a Belgian MP and who had been released from confinement by the Germans, was returned to allied custody; took a PW; expedited the needs of an enemy ambulance full of German soldiers and one woman who was about to have a baby.

h. Said the Commanding Officer of the 27th AAA Gp (XII Corps) to the Commanding Officer, 24th AAA Gp (38th AAA Brig), "we are now moving toward the Elbe River where we can share an IAZ with the Russians. Please sign a receipt for these bridges over the Rhine." So the 24th AAA Gp command gave a receipt as follows:

Oppenheim, Germany
270800 A March 1945

"Received from the 27th AAA Gp four (4) bridges across the Rhine, with bridges and approaches intact, and the mission fo providing AA protection for same."

i. (1) Periods of greatest air activity over Third US Army have always accompanied its periods of greatest advance. Static or slow-moving periods such as those occurring along the Moselle River were times of slight air activity. In August, December and March, however, during which months there were rapid advances, AAA communications were not only loaded with activity but stretched by distance to the point where wire communications were nearly impossible, a luxury for the slow. At one time, for example, Third US Army's zone stretched 650 miles from Brest to Verdun, perhaps the longest Army area in modern history.

(2) As a result, since Third US Army became operational upon the continent, the 38th AAA brigade and subordinate units and Corps and division units have relied on radio almost exclusively for command and air warning functions. This use of radio has not been confined alone to inter-unit work but has also been the primary means of communication within the various gun and automatic weapons battalions.

(3) It was in early October, when movement across France slowed down, that a period of trial and correction in AAA radio communications for early warning and AAAIS systems took place. The procuring of FM radios from the Fighter Control Squadron solved the long range voice radio problem and no problem existed within gun battalions with their SCR-543

radios or automatic weapons battalions with their SCR-543s and various FM sets. Since early December there has not been one roll of wire used for communications within the 38th Brigade except for wire run by AW platoons to their various gun sections and by gun battalions to their batteries when conditions permitted. The use of radio has proved itself invaluable in recent operations, such as when communications were continuously maintained between units deployed along the Rhine River and others far back in Luxembourg.

(4) Because the 38th AAA Brigade has, of necessity, relied on radio, it has become radio's staunchest supporter among AAA units on the continent. By emphasis on maintenance, proper sighting, proper procedure and security aspects of radio communication, radio has become the foundation of its entire operations.

j. Another AAA unit recently passed a milestone in its history, when the 635th AAA AW Bn (M), on 19 February 1945, completed its third continuous year of overseas duty. Eleven officers and 170 enlisted men left over from the original battalion departed from the U.S. on 19 February 1942 for Iceland as part of the 61st Coast Artillery (AA). After 18 months of hard, monotonous work on a 24 hour manning status with rare hostile air activity to enliven the time, the unit went to the UK where it was separated from the 61st CA Regt and reorganized as a separate battalion. Thereafter, it was trained on new equipment and placed under the ADGB in an operational status defending airfields of the Ninth Air Force. Gunners of the battalion claim some of the first, if not the first, Category As for shooting down buzz-bombs along the English coast. The unit landed in France with VIII Corps and under Third US Army, participated in the Normandy and Brest campaigns, and is still going strong.

/s/ F.R. Chamberlain, Jr
/t/ F.R. Chamberlain, Jr,
Colonel, CAC, Antiaircraft Officer.

1 Incl — Aircraft Recognition (Russian A/C)

Distribution:
"A" & "H"

Restricted
Aircraft Recognition

With this issue of Aircraft Recognition we introduce the Red Air Force. As the Allied advance into central Germany continues, Russian aircraft may be seen on an increasing scale. The standard national marking is a red star.

The two fighter bombers pictured below are currently operational in the Red Air Force. Basically the same in design, the most apparent difference is in the power units. The Lagg 3, which is the older, has an inline engine and a 20mm cannon which fires through the large spinner. The tail wheel is fixed.

The LA-5, powered by a radial engine, is in extensive use. It is said to be the USSR's answer to the FW-190 which it closely resembles. Care must be taken not to confuse the two.

Incl No 1 to Hq Third US Army AAA Weekly Int Report No 36.

16 April 1945
AAA Weekly Intelligence Report No. 37
Period:
060600B to 130600B

1. Summary of Action

a. No new trends were noted in enemy air efforts this week. As Third US Army's divisions thrust across central Germany the Luftwaffe, as in the previous week, launched sharp, small-scale attacks at armored spearheads, forward infantry elements, and at the bridges over which they moved, in efforts to harass and slow the advance. Most activity occurred in XX Corps zone where the 6th Armd and 76th Inf Divs drew considerable attention. E/A were over every day of the week in numbers averaging 50-60 per day. Tank and truck columns, field artillery, CPs and miscellaneous targets of opportunity drew attention as almost all aircraft flew by daylight in search of them. A Class III dump via (H7070) was attacked, bridges over the Werra River near Spichra (H7472) and Creuzburg (H7575), and over the Saale River via Kosen (J762885), were bombed and strafed. Several CPs were bombed and an airfield near Wenigenlupnitz (H9070) was attacked three days running. There was also an attack on a truck convoy of German PWs. A good many planes were over on reconnaissance, but infrequently penetrated deeper than Corps. In the rear areas, E/A were seldom seen and few attacks were made. FW-190s and Me-109s were in great majority of types observed, though a few He-111s, Me-110s and jet-propelled Me-262s were seen, a flight of 6 of the latter being reported and several smaller formations. In addition, a few odd, unrecognizable types were reported and one of them, a trainer bearing on the fuselage the lettering "Luftkriegs Schule 1 Dresden Tel 68441", was shot down by small arms fire. Damage from air attacks was not heavy. Two gas-laden C-47s coming in to land were attacked while still some distance from their field and shot down. Other attacks upon the field made within range of protecting AAA were driven off without further damage. Several vehicles were damaged and there were personnel casualties, including an undetermined number of the German PWs who were bombed.

b. Screening of reports has not been completed so that only estimated numbers of raids and E/A appear below. Totals for the week, and to date from 1 August 1944, are as follows:

	Raids	No E/A	Cat I	Cat II
Week	140	395	83	59
To Date	2,204	5,415	957	500
	PAC Over Area	PAC Engaged	Cat A	Cat B
Week	0	0	0	0
To Date	168	31	0	3

2. GAF Tactics Notes

a. In attacking the C-47s ferrying gasoline 10 Me-109s and FW-190s lying in wait at high altitude, dropped down to engage the slower cargo craft which were approaching the field to land. After shooting down two, they followed in to strafe A/C lining the field. This brought them within range of AAA, however, and they were driven off.

b. A summary of activity received from the 777th AAA AW Bn (SP) for the period 30 Mar-10 Apr gives interesting data on air tactics employed against the 6th Armd Div, to which it is attached. In part, it states: "The attacks . . . have been . . . directed mainly at columns and at forward troop assembly areas. Trains, dumps, bridges and CBs have been attacked very lightly. The damage has been slight considering the large numbers of aircraft involved. There has, of course, been some damage and there have been casualties, but much less than the damage that could have been caused by aggressive air force. Most of the attacks have consisted of only one pass, the aircraft employing hit and run tactics, and not pressing home a vigorous raid . . . Most of the flights have consisted of singles and pairs. A few large formations (12-20) have been over, but not many. Lately, there has been an increasing trend towards flights of 4-6 aircraft; most of these have been attacks. Most of the A/C have been Me-109s or FW-190s. There have been a few jets, both Me-262 and Me-163, and one Ju-87 was reported . . . The jets all operated singly, and have made attacks . . . The time of day has not mattered, as planes have been over from dawn to dark. However, the "peak" seems to have been mid-morning (0800-1100) and mid-afternoon (1400-1600). Very few attacks have been at dawn and dusk." (That the 777th has had ample chance to observe and counter Luftwaffe tactics is attested by the fact that, after screening, for the period mentioned formal claims for 38 Cat Is and 22 Cat IIs were submitted, as well as 8 Cat IIIs.)

3. Miscellaneous Notes

a. Once again, automatic weapons units enjoyed the larger share of activity as most raids occurred during daylight and at low altitudes, providing them with plentiful targets. The 778th AAA AW Bn (SP), attached to 76th Inf Div, demonstrated sharpshooting ability and during one 18 hour period, engaged 15 of 21 enemy planes scoring 5 Cat Is and 7 Cat IIs. No damage was occasioned to protected FA and Infantry and only one man was wounded despite intensive bombing and strafing. On the preceding day 6 Cat Is and 6 Cat IIs, plus 2 Cat IIIs were claimed in an equally successful defense.

b. In one five minute period from 1455 to 1500 hours on 10 April, the 390th SP Bn had activity over the 26th Inf Div area comparable to that which they experienced Southeast of Bastogne last December. 13 E/A attacked FA positions, Infantry, convoys and an Arty observation plane in sharp strafing attacks only to lose 7 planes which were seen to crash and 2 probables.

c. Reappearances of jet-propelled A/C this week, after almost complete absence last week recalls the many attacks by jets during the Nahe and Rhine River crossings and makes a glance at their tactics timely. Excerpts from a report of the 115th AAA Gun Bn covering the two crossings state: "In the late afternoon two Me-262s and one FW-190 were over the Bretzenheim crossing site for 15 minutes. The Me-262s dropped bombs in a 50 yd/sec glide from 2,500 ft; the glide began at 15,000 ft. Glides were not steady, but were characterized by rapid changes in course and speed. Speeds varied from 240 to 500 mph. When the jets made a rapid acceleration white smoke was seen to come from the engines for a second or two. The rate of climb was high. Heavy AA fire control equipment is fully capable of coping with the jet although jets are difficult to hit due to their ability to make very rapid changes in speed, altitude and direction. No damage was done at the crossing site . . . On 20 March the peak of enemy air activity over the Nahe crossing was reached. 2 Me-262s and . . . were destroyed. The jets were shot down in level steady flight at 15,000 ft . . . On 21 March 1 Ar-234 at 8,000 feet altitude, via 400 mph in a dive of 50 yds/sec was engaged and shot down by 90mm fire." The 115th Gun Bn employed its equipment well and in a 6 day period 16 Cat Is and 8 Cat IIs were claimed, most of them engaged at altitudes of 8,000 to 16,000 ft, once again demonstrating the adequacy of the SCR-584 radar and M-9 director to cope with and destroy enemy planes at higher altitudes than normally permitted.

d. An unusual occurrence of recent days has come to notice through the statement of a Chemical Company enlisted man, submitted in support of a formal claim for destruction of an enemy plane. "On the evening of . . . I was stationed at the Rhine River crossing at Oppenheim, Germany. The German Air Force came in early in the evening and dropped flares and attacked the bridge by strafing and bombing. Section No. 7 of Btry "D", 599th AAA AW Bn, was firing at a plane and after they hit it it began to fall looking like it was out of control. As it fell towards the ground another German plane came in under it and the two planes collided in the air. There was a big explosion and both planes fell to the ground, burning." A question: should the unit be granted one or two Cat Is?

e. In addition to such defenses as booms and nets, part of the defenses against waterborne demolitions, "Kampfschwimmer" (swimming saboteurs) and the like were provided to the Rhine River crossings at Mainz, while under Corps control, by Batry "A" of the 455th AAA AW Bn, under XX Corps AA. The Battery Commander was given operational control of 4 searchlights from the 226th AAA S/L Bn, 2 SCR-584 radars borrowed from gun battalions and charged with coordinating the waterborne defense with a platoon of light tanks assigned the same task. The equipment concerned was emplaced on the West bank as a safety precaution, and fields of fire were so laid out as to avoid endangering engineer personnel working in the vicinity of the bridge. All suspicious objects floating downstream towards the bridge were engaged and destroyed by gun fire. The 40mm gun was found to be especially efficient at this task. Eye-shooting with Stiffkey Stick sights was used with ranges set in, and never more than 3 rounds were required to hit and destroy waterborne targets. The light tanks mounted 75mm guns and employed ammunition with a very sensitive fuze. M51 mounts were not used due to the danger of ricochet. Small arms fire was employed against smaller targets. At night, the radars were used in conjunction with searchlights in picking up and illuminating waterborne targets. The switchboard at the battery CP had a line running to the radar and searchlights, which were on a hot loop, and another hot loop to the tanks with a third loop connecting all AAA fire units employed on the mission, an arrangement which facilitated control and expedited warning of floating targets.

/s/ F.R. Chamberlain, Jr,
/t/ F.R. Chamberlain, Jr,
Colonel, CAC, Antiaircraft Officer.

Distribution:
"A" & "H"

24 April 1945
AAA Weekly Intelligence Report No. 38
Period:
130600B to 200600B

1. Summary of Action

a. Hostile air activity slackened somewhat as an estimated 202 enemy aircraft flew over the area this week, about halving the effort of the previous period. While a considerable number of daylight attacks were made, the Luftwaffe began reversion to familiar night tactics, strafing lighted vehicles on highways and making other similar nuisance attacks using small flights of aircraft. Columns, assemblies and installations of nearly all Armored and Infantry divisions were bombed and strafed in daytime raids, and Corps Artillery units were several times attacked. With more effort devoted to these targets, there were still many other attacks made, both by day and by night. Class III supply installations via Meiningen, Herleshausen, Wurzburg and Burgjoss, bridges via Muhlau, Kronach, Hanau and other places, and highway traffic all through the area and as far separated as Hanau and Hersfeld, all were attacked. Night intruders passed through Corps rear boundaries to hit at targets far back. In addition, there was considerable reconnaissance activity. There were few large formations, and 12 FW-190s which strafed Corps Artillery was the largest reported. E/A of all types were seen, including jets, and Ju-52 transports probably used to evacuate personnel from the Ruhr pocket. Indicating the low estate to which the once-tough Luftwaffe has sunk was the appearance in front line missions of Arado training planes and composite, "pick-a-back" aircraft. One of these latter was even reported employed for a strafing mission. In one of the week's outstanding events, an AAA battalion motor sergeant shot down 3 Me-109s and badly damaged a 4th out of 5 engaged, using the single .50 cal machine gun mounted on the cab of his wrecker.

b. Screening of reports has not been completed so that only estimated numbers of raids and E/A appear below. Totals for the week, and to date from 1 August 1944 (corrected), are as follows:

	Raids	No E/A	Cat I	Cat II
Week	70	202	48	30
To Date	2,274	5,617	989	532
	PAC Over Area	PAC Engaged	Cat A	Cat B
Week	0	0	0	0
To Date	168	31	0	3

2. GAF Tactics Notes

No new tactics were reported. As usual, the enemy flew in small jaggles and at low altitudes, taking advantage of terrain and clouds and of the sun. At night the planes flew at altitudes so low that gun battalion radars had difficulty in picking them up and little heavy AAA fire could be thrown against them.

3. Miscellaneous Notes

a. With hostile air activity apparently once again on the wane, a short summary of the past month's activity seems not improper. In the thirty-one day period from 15 March through 14 April, Third US Army's Antiaircraft Artillery units engaged many planes, most of which made attacks upon ground targets. While some slight damage was caused and some casualties inflicted, in proportion to the air effort they were poor payment, indeed. In throwing back these many air attacks, AAA units claimed to have destroyed 455 enemy planes and probably destroyed 260, with many others damaged, for a total of 715 Category Is and IIs. Biggest day was 2 April when over 100 members of the Luftwaffe were claimed shot down. Biggest day, too, for any individual unit was the same 2 April when a single battalion claimed 40 planes shot down, with an additional one damaged. Ammunition expenditures for the period were as follows:

Caliber	No. rds.
90mm	7,255
Pozit (90mm)	857
40mm	44,185
37mm	29,465
.50 cal	1,573,532

b. Oh, Boy! What a Wonderful Day Dept. In a day of accomplishment as full as any yet reported for a single individual, Friday the 13th will probably long stand in the memory of the motor sergeant with Btry "C" of the 455th AAA AW Bn. On that day he was rolling in convoy toward Chemnitz when his wrecker was stopped by Engineers at the Reichautobahn outpass near Gera, requesting assistance of him and the .50 cal machine gun mounted on the roof of his wrecker. Two enemy vehicles had just come into view on a road leading South from the autobahn. The sergeant obliged and set both vehicles afire with his gun. He then reloaded the weapon and took off to catch up with his column. A bit farther along he came upon the Btry mess truck bogged down with a flat tire so stopped to help. While so engaged he heard a cry. "Hold onto your hats, boys, here they come," and, looking up, he saw five Me-109s bearing down upon him in single file and at low altitude, straight down the highway. The sergeant climbed once more into the ring mount in time to fire at the second of these aircraft, his gun still warm from the previous ground firing. The plane literally "flew down his gun barrel" and was immediately hit, and crashed within view of the wrecker. The other E/A, apparently uncertain as to what had happened, turned about and once again came down the highway. The foremost plane this time was hit, crashing 300 yds from the other, and, as the remaining three circled, a third, flying low across the road, was hit and crashed a kilometer away. The fourth plane fired at received hits in the motor and was smoking badly as it flew out of sight. The total ammunition expenditure was just a neat 225 rounds. The German belief in mythology and superstition must have been considerably strengthened by the day's occurrences.

c. German composite, or "pick-a-back", aircraft are not an entirely new development though not a great deal is known about them, most information having come from photo interpretation. However, it is believed that this week's occurrence was the first time one ever was reported in so unsuited a mission as strafing. Two and possibly three of these were shot down by automatic weapons units with forward elements of divisions but the destruction of each was so complete little could be told from the wreckage. Composite aircraft ordinarily consist of a Ju-88 surmounted by an Me-109 or FW-190. The Ju-88 is loaded with explosives and is released and guided towards the target by the fighter. While it may be that other twin-engined types than Ju-88s have been used, no other has been definitely identified.

/s/ F.R. Chamberlain, Jr.
/t/ F.R. Chamberlain, Jr.
Colonel, CAC, Antiaircraft Officer.

3 May 1945

AAA Weekly Intelligence Report No. 39

Period:
200600B to 270600B April

1. Summary of Action

a. Despite the mounting seriousness of his position on the ground, the enemy was able to launch but a lessening number of air sorties this week even the most illiterate member of the Luftwaffe must have seen that the writing on the wall spelled "kaput". An estimated 180 enemy planes flew over the area in approximately 80 raids, most of which occurred the last three days of the period. In the forepart of the week, activity was mainly at night and consisted of small-scale nuisance strafing raids against headlighted traffic along MSRs, particularly Highways 4 and 26 (Aschaffenberg-Schweinfurt-Bamberg-Nurnberg) and Highway 8 (Aschaffenberg-Wurzburg-Kitzingen-Nurnberg). Targets along these routes such as troop assemblies, Class III supply points and the like also received nuisance attacks, and there were several attacks near Lauf (O-565078) upon similar targets. In addition, three airfields used in landing supplies were strafed in nighttime efforts. The last three days saw activity jump sharply and on the final day of the period 80 E/A were over the area on bombing and strafing missions. Most of the latter attacks were along the left flank of the Army in XII Corps zone, the aircraft probably taking off from airfields located NE of there in the via of Prague. The 11th Armd and 26th Inf Divs and Corps Artillery bore the brunt of these attacks through several other divisions reported activity. And, indeed, throughout the week small flights of enemy planes appeared in all Corps sectors, reconnoitering troop movements and positions and in some instances making short, unaggressive attacks. Aircraft appearing were standard types for the most part. Ju-88s, Ju-188s, He-111s and Me-110s were frequently used at night and in the daytime Me-109s and FW-190s were used, with a sprinkling of Me-262s and such bottom-of-the-barrel types as Arado trainers, Bu-181s and others. Defended areas were undamaged and casualties reported were few, as accurate antiaircraft fire kept attacking planes generally at a respectful distance.

b. Screening of reports has not been completed so that only estimated numbers of raids and E/A appear below. Totals for the week, and to date from 1 August 1944, are as follows:

	Raids	No E/A	Cat I	Cat II
Week	80	180	38	18
To Date	2,354	5,797	1,027	550
	PAC Over Area	PAC Engaged	Cat A	Cat B
Week	0	0	0	0
To Date	168	31	0	3

2. GAF Tactics Notes

No new tactics were reported.

3. Miscellaneous Notes

a. Hostile activity was spread well over the area so that no individual battalion enjoyed such ample opportunities to score as existed in the previous few weeks. Elements of the 128th AAA Gun Bn were unusually employed in that they were attached to a combat command of the 11th Armd Div for antiaircraft protection, and in such employment had several engagements. From 0650 to 2325 hrs on 26 April, 16 E/A were engaged resulting in claims for 4 Cat Is and a Cat II. The 575th AAA Self-propelled, which is regularly attached to the 11th Armd Div, participated to a greater extent in the shooting and in a period from 240600B to 261830B Apr claimed 12 Cat Is and 4 Cat IIs materially deepening the dent in the Luftwaffe.

b. One recent afternoon, members of a gun section of the 633d AAA AW Bn idly observed several small German boys playing on an abandoned but intact 88mm gun in a section of the city of Nurnberg. Closer attention was paid when it became apparent the children not only knew how to operate the gun but were earnestly tracking a friendly P-47 overhead. As crew members dashed for the gun the children ran hurriedly off, leaving the gun, which was found cocked and in perfect operating condition and contained a live round in the chamber. It is good to remember these things. When temptation arises to give these "harmless German children" chocolate or gum, remember — you may feed a child secretly planning to blow your head off. It has happened.

/s/ F.R. Chamberlain, Jr,
/t/ F.R. Chamberlain, Jr,
Colonel, CAC, Antiaircraft Officer.

8 May 1945

AAA Weekly Intelligence Report No. 40

Period:
270600B Apr to 040600B May

1. Summary of Action

a. The rapid disintegration of the German Air Force was typified by the aircraft engaged this week. The stricken beast, writhing in the throes of death, raised its head for a last gasp that spewed up almost the entire aircraft recognition handbook. In addition to ordinary Me-109s and FW-190s, the following types were reported: Ar-69, Ar-234, Bu-181, DO-217, Fi-156, FW-44J, He-111, He-126, He-177, Ju-52, Ju-87, Ju-88, Ju-188, Me-108, Me-210, Me-262. With these specimens, the Luftwaffe flew a rather considerable number of sorties, however, and made several attacks. On the morning of 27 April, approximately 30 E/A flew across XX Corps to enter the III Corps area and bomb and strafe infantry and armored elements. In doing so, these planes passed over the Danube River bridgeheads, newly established, for a complete reversal of previous tactics which would have called for attempts on the bridges. Other attacks during the week were made upon a crossing of the Naab River, via Wernberg, Isar River crossings, an airfield and vehicle assembly via Cham, convoys and other similar targets. Reconnaissance was rather extensive and E/A were reported over most division and corps elements and installations, as well as in rear of corps boundaries. Flights of 6 and 8 E/A were noted, though most raids were composed of single or, at most, 2 planes. Almost all activity occurred during daylight, with some occasional night flights.

b. Screening of reports has not been completed so that only estimated numbers of raids and E/A appear below. Totals for the week, and to date from 1 August 1944, are as follows:

	Raids	No E/A	Cat I	Cat II
Week	54	110	35	5
To Date	2,408	5,907	1,062	555

	PAC Over Area	PAC Engaged	Cat A	Cat B
Week	0	0	0	0
To Date	168	31	0	3

2. GAF TACTICS NOTES

A summary of German air reactions as observed in XX Corps zone from 1 Feb to 25 Apr has been received from the 112th AAA Gp. It views air activity as falling into four distinct phases of ground operations by the Corps, the first of which, from 1 Feb to 16 Mar, is a semi-static period with the Siegfried Line from Saarlautern to the Saar-Moselle River confluence still to be overcome. Air activity at this stage of opertions was so meager as to merit no attention. As the offensive began, however, and the Siegfried Line was out flanked at Trier and rapidly rolled South to Kaiserlautern and beyond, a new stage (phase 2) of hostile air effort began with the GAF attacking convoys and leading tactical elements using 120 E/A in a period from 16-29 Mar. Enemy pilots were aggressive, but evasive when engaged by AAA. Clouds and haze were used to mask approaches and for evasion, violent aerobatics being resorted to on days with clear skies. Rhine River crossings were effected at Mainz and this phase of operations (phase 3, 29 Mar-3 Apr) saw activity almost double the previous period. GAF reaction was violent, not so much against bridges and bridge areas as against threatening advances of XX Corps armor and infantry. On 2 Apr, 183 E/A were reported over the Corps area. The final phase began 3 Apr with the drive N and E to a point W of Chemnitz, turning SE on 16 Apr to seize areas via Bamberg, Nurnberg and advancing to a point W of Regensburg. The Luftwaffe, no longer able to justify a policy of conservation, went into high gear and against the drive NE nearly trebled the sorties of the previous phase. E/A were overhead constantly, some forming large formations of planes. But hit-and-run tactics were used and there was no indication of the old college try, no do-or-die, in any of these attacks. Few, if any, attacks were pressed in the face of AAA fire and, once engaged, no planes returned for a second attempt. Indeed, a considerable number of pilots apparently flew only to acquire flight pay for sizable formations passed over good targets without dropping so much as a hand grenade. Jet-propelled A/C were used in larger proportions than before, but primarily in reconnaissance roles, with only occasional strafing. During none of these four phases was high altitude bombing reported.

3. Miscellaneous Notes

a. That all the odd type aircraft flown by the Germans were not as harmless as might appear, is indicated by the experience of the 128th AAA Gun Bn this week. Two Bu-181s shot down contained loads of explosives and detonating caps (as well as a dead SS officer in one). Such occurrences were not uncommon elsewhere as revealed in the following quote:

"b. **Airborne Sabotage.** Recurring reports from XII and III US Corps of the discovery of explosives, caps and slow-burning fuse in crashed enemy liaison or training-type planes, plus interrogation of captured German pilots, lays bare some of the details of a desperate last chance enemy plot to conduct organized sabotage in friendly areas by means of amateur airborne saboteurs.

"One German pilot captured by III Corps stated that his was the last of 40 planes flown by volunteer pilots, forming Kommando Wenstock, commanded by Col Herman, to take off from Ainring Airport (Z-8926), W of Salzburg on mission of sabotage. Pilots are said to carry papers stating that they are discharged from service upon completion of this mission. One pilot stated all planes were training-type Bueckers-181s with top speed of 160 km per hr . . . First US Army reported 3 May several pilots captured in rear areas central portion Army zone; 8 of these planes captured in past 2 days. Interrogation revealed that a unit called Kommando Vienenstock . . . had mission of destroying bridges and railroads in Allied rear areas. Explosives were carried and the pilots, some of whom had missions via their homes, were to proceed home when mission accomplished. According to PW, pilots may wear civilian clothes or GAF uniforms." (Source: Tusa G-2 Periodic No 327, 4 May)

b. With the foregoing black machinations furnishing sinister highlights, other doings of the training-plane pilots provide a romantic lustre bound to appeal to one and all:

"Reminiscent of World War I action was a claim recently awarded for a Fieseler Storch reconnaissance plane. An L-4 from the 71st Armd FA Bn . . . was flying over a column when they saw a Fi-156 flying at tree top level below them. Circling down on the German plane they (pilot and observer) cut loose with their pistols and hit the gas tank . . . then dove on the Storch, forcing it to the ground where it hit a fence and was demolished. The L-4 landed nearby and captured the two occupants, one of whom had been wounded by the firing." (Source: Ninth US Army AAA Isum No 31)

c. Yet another battalion has joined the ranks of those select few who shot down a plane with one round. At 0400 hrs on 3 May, a lone Ju-88 flying over positions of D Btry, 457th AAA AW Bn, circled and dove to strafe, heading directly for gun position No 8. The Chief of Section held fire until the range was short, then fired one round getting a direct hit that caused the E/A to burst into flames and crash nearby.

d. The 634th AAA AW Bn reported that 3 of their officers, missing in action since the Ardennes breakthrough of December, were located in an enemy PW camp near Moosburg.

e. As reported briefly last week, two Btrys of the 128th AAA Gun Bn, with a provisional Hq supervising, were attached to the 11th Armd Div in an unusual employment. By leapfrogging the Btrys, one was always giving AAA protection for the armor and Div CP while the other was left behind to defend supply and service units in the rear against air attack. In ten days' time, the two Btrys moved 325 miles for an average of 32.5 miles per day, with no vehicles out of action due to any mechanical failure.

f. Another notation appearing in the Ninth US Army AAA Isum quoted above is of some interest, as indicating what might have been expected from the Luftwaffe had it been able to stay off the ground:

"Certainly the most interesting of the various airplane factories and airfields uncovered by the XIX Corps was the underground plant manufacturing the complete fuselage for the He-162. This is a highwing, twin-tail fighter with a single turbo jet mounted above the wing. The crashed remains of one of these planes was located . . . although no claim was submitted nor was it seen in flight."

For the Antiaircraft Officer:

/s/ G.C. Dunn
/t/ G.C. Dunn,
Maj, CAC, Asst AA Officer.

1 Incl
Tabulation of Formal Claims
Submitted and Claims Granted to Bns.

Distribution:
"A" & "H"

SECRET

Following is a tabulation of the formal claims submitted and formal awards made to battalions for planes shot down while such units were attached to Third US Army. Awards by other armies are **not** tallied, therefore some units have more Categories credited to them than shown below. This does not represent the final tabulation as some late claims are still in process of preparation and have not been forwarded to this headquarters.

(1) Brigade and Groups:

	Confirmed Claims	
	Cat I	Cat II
38th AAA Brigade #	110	37
16th AAA Group	18	1
23d AAA Group *	95	27
27th AAA Group	280½	79
32d AAA Group *	20	6
112th AAA Group	218	81
113th AAA Group *	143½	34
Unatchd Gp or Brig	1	
TOTAL	886	265

* - No longer as gd Third US Army
\# - includes some for 27th Group.

---

(2) Battalions:

Unit	Formal Claims Submitted CAT I	CAT II	CAT III	Claims Approved CAT I	CAT II	CAT III	TOTAL I & II
1. 489th AAA AW BN (SP)	126	43	0	117½	8	32	125½
2. 455th AAA AW Bn	97	46	0	77⅓	31	22	108⅓
3. 777th AAA AW Bn (SP)	73	33	16	64 7/12	19	26	83 7/12
4. 452d AAA AW Bn	70	24	1	58 5/12	19	11	77 5/12
5. 411th AAA Gun Bn	48	8	0	41 5/6	11	1	52 5/6
6. 115th AAA Gun Bn	42	20	0	34½	16	4	50½
7. 390th AAA AW Bn (SP)	44	2	0	35 7/12	12	3	47 7/12
8. 456th AAA AW Bn	35	11	0	35½	13	0	45½
9. 217th AAA Gun Bn	40	4	3	26	9	4	35
10. 129th AAA Gun Bn	38	4	0	30 1/6	4½	2	34⅔
11. 537th AAA AW Bn	24	17	2	21¼	12	6	33¼
12. 633d AAA AW Bn	29	5	0	24¾	7	1	31¾
13. 546th AAA AW Bn	24	10	0	26	5	2	31
14. 463d AAA AW Bn	27	5	0	26	5	1	31
15. 120th AAA Gun Bn	33	3	0	24	6	4	30
16. 550th AAA AW Bn	16	22	0	17	9	10	26
17. 119th AAA Gun Bn	23	4	1	20½	4	2	24½
18. 465th AAA AW Bn (SP)	22	6	0	19⅓	4	2	23⅓
19. 457th AAA AW Bn	22	10	2	15 7/12	7½	6	23½
20. 445th AAA AW Bn	24	1	0	20	2	1	22
21. 449th AAA AW Bn	16	10	0	11	10	5	21
22. 778th AAA AW Bn (SP)	17	8	0	14⅔	5	1	19⅔

Chart continued on next page.

	Formal Claims Submitted			Claims Approved			TOTAL
Unit	CAT I	CAT II	CAT III	CAT I	CAT II	CAT III	I & II
23. 473d AAA AW Bn (SP)	14	4	0	13	4	0	17
24. 128th AAA Gun Bn	22	1	0	13¾	3	3	16¾
25. 572d AAA AW Bn (SP)	11	8	0	9	7	3	16
26. 398th AAA AW Bn (SP)	16	1	0	16	0	0	16
27. 575th AAA AW Bn (SP)	13	8	0	12¼	2	6	14¼
28. 386th AAA AW Bn	11	4	0	8⅓	3	1	11⅓
29. 547th AAA AW Bn	7	10	0	4	0	5	11
30. 635th AAA AW Bn	4	12	4	5	5	9	10
31. 551st AAA AW Bn	11	0	1	8½	1	1	9½
32. 796th AAA AW Bn (SP)	7	4	0	5	4	2	9
33. 448th AAA AW Bn	5	7	0	5¼	2	1	7¼
34. 599th AAA AW Bn	7	0	0	7	0	0	7
35. 387th AAA AW Bn (SP)	5	3	0	2	3	0	5
36. 468th AAA AW BN (SP)	6	1	0	5	0	1	5
37. 109th AAA Gun Bn	4	5	0	4	0	1	4
38. 776th AAA AW Bn (SM)	3	2	0	3	0	2	3
39. 467th AAA AW Bn (SP)	2	3	0	½	2	1	2½
40. 722d AAA AW Bn	2	0	0	1⅓	0	0	1⅓
41. 565th AAA AW Bn	1	1	1	1	0	2	1
42. 559th AAA AW Bn	1	0	0	1	0	0	1
43. 22d FTA Bn (Fr)	1	0	0	1	0	0	1
44. 795th AAA AW Bn (SM)	1	0	0	1	0	0	1
45. 634th AAA AW Bn	1	0	0	1	0	0	1
46. 203d AAA AW Bn (SP)	2	2	0	0	1	0	1
47. 481st AAA AW Bn	0	1	0	0	1	0	1
48. 549th AAA AW Bn	0	1	0	0	1	0	1
49. 567th AAA AW Bn	0	1	0	0	0	1	0
50. 447th AAA AW Bn	0	1	0	0	0	0	0
TOTALS	1,047	386	31	886	265	185	1,151

17 May 1945

AAA Weekly Intelligence Report No. 41
Last Regular Report

Period:
040600B May to 090001B May

	90mm	90mm POZIT	40mm	37mm	.50 cal
AAA Firing	56,314	1,531	91,628	63,254	3,797,127
Ground Firing	26,245	0	12,607	13,143	1,425,886
TOTAL	82,559	1,531	104,235	76,397	5,223,013

1. Summary of Action

a. The last few days of the war in Europe passed with no final show of strength by the Luftwaffe. Its Air Marshal a prisoner, most of its planes grounded, its Bed-check Charlies a thing of the past, the German Air Force lived out its final days in comparative inactivity, waiting for rigor mortis. Its planes flew over in twos and threes making occasional half-hearted attacks, or sometimes located our airfields and landed. Often they were escorted by allied fighter craft. Areas of two regiments of the 26th Inf Div were strafed and bombed and Danube River targets via Ingolstadt were strafed. On 8 May, FW-190s and Me-109s strafed Danube bridge areas via Deggendorf & Passau. In the latter attack enemy aircraft included two observation planes which, in a final gesture of defiance, fired "burp" guns at ground targets. Only damage reported from these attacks was a slight injury to AAA fire control equipment caused by strafing.

b. Screening of all reports has been completed. Final totals for Third US Army operations from 1 August 1944 through 8 May 1945 are as follows:

	Raids	No E/A	Cat I	Cat II
Week	61	88	22	9
To Date	2,463	6,192	1,084	564
	PAC Over Area	PAC Engaged	Cat A	Cat B
Week	0	0	0	0
To Date	168	31	0	3

c. Ammunition expended upon its primary mission and in ground firing roles totaled as follows (number of rounds):

2. GAF Tactics Notes
Nothing to report.

3. Miscellaneous Notes

a. In accumulating scores of 1,084 planes destroyed and 564 probably destroyed — a total number 1,648 — Third US Army's antiaircraft downed better than a fourth of all enemy aircraft observed over the entire Army area, for a percentage of 26.6%. In 281 operational days an average of 5.86 E/A were claimed each day. In addition to these many E/A were damaged.

b. It was on 1 August 1944 at 1425B hours — 2 hours and 25 minutes after Third US Army became operational — that AAA scored its first kill. The 445th AAA AW Bn attached to the 8th Inf Div opened fire on a flight of 15-20 Me-109s and knocked one down, the first of a long procession of planes to fall before AAA gun fire. To the 390th AAA AW Bn (SP) goes the distinction of shooting down the last. Three FW-190s were engaged at 2030B on May 8th — an hour and thirty-one minutes before hostilities officially ceased — as they flew over service elements of the 26th Inf Div. One smoked as the tracers caught it, then burst into flames and crashed.

c. In a notable occurrence of the week a chaplain captured a Lt General. While making arrangements to conduct mass in a local monastery the chaplain learned that the General, former CG of Wehrkreis XVII, was in hiding there. He promptly notified his CO and together they took the General prisoner. The chaplain is with the 633d AAA AW Bn.

d. For their many achievements antiaircraft units may well be proud. In particular it is most gratifying to record in these pages the official commendations of high commands for superlative work done in combat. It is noted with pride that of the AAA units serving with Third US Army, several have received a Presidential Unit Citation. For their heroic part in the defense of Bastogne under the direction of the 101st Airborne Div, "C" Battery of the 482d AAA AW Bn (SP) attached to Res Command, 9th Armd Div, and "B" Battery of the 796th AAA AW Bn (SP) attached to CCB of the 10th Armd Div were awarded the unit citation. In addition, the entire 489th AAA AW Bn (SP) has been recommended by the 4th Armd Div to participate in the unit citation already granted to that division.

e. Attached as an inclosure is a tabulation of the "batting averages" of battalions, based on engagements and claims accruing while such battalions were attached or assigned to this Headquarters. Since all claims have not been finally processed, these do not represent the final figures, but do show increases over last week's report.

f. Also attached as an inclosure is a record of day-by-day enemy air activity over the entire Army area from the beginning of operations to date. These figures represent the screened totals, all duplications in reports of enemy planes having been eliminated so far as possible.

/s/ F.R. Chamberlain, Jr,
/t/ F.R. Chamberlain, Jr,
Colonel, CAC, Antiaircraft Officer.

2 Incls —
Incl #1 — Battalion "batting averages"
Incl #2 — Day-by-day enemy air activity over Army area from the beginning of operations to date.

Distribution:
"A" & "H"

UNIT and relative standing	Batting Averages from 1 Aug 44 to date TOTAL NO. E/A I & II ENGAGED		AVERAGE	Batting Averages from 1 Feb 45 to date TOTAL NO. E/A I & II ENGAGED		AVERAGE	Relative Standing (1 Feb to date, only)
1. 444th AAA AW Bn	1	1	1.0000	1	1	1,0000	(1)
2. 481st AAA AW Bn	1	2	.5000				
3. 386th AAA AW Bn	11⅓	24	.4722				
4. 489th AAA SP Bn	126 1/12	507	.2501	102 7/12	405	.2533	(7)
5. 455th AAA AW Bn	111⅓	464	.2399	64 5/6	238	.2724	(5)
6. 546th AAA AW Bn	31	141	.2191	28	91	.3076	(3)
7. 574th AAA SP Bn	3	14	.2143	3	14	.2143	(11)
8. 549th AAA AW Bn	1	5	.2000				
9. 559th AAA AW Bn	1	5	.2000				
10. 839th AAA AW Bn	1	5	.2000	1	5	.2000	(12)
11. 129 AAA GN Bn	35⅔	186	.1918	29⅓	101	.2904	(4)
12. 390th AAA SP Bn	48 1/12	269	.1814	23¼	135	.1722	(14)
13. 776th AAA SN Bn	3	17	.1765				
14. 463rd AAA AW Bn	31	190	.1632				
15. 633rd AAA AW Bn	33¾	201	.1679	28½	152	.1875	(13)
16. 796th AAA SP Bn	9	57	.1579	4	15	.2667	(6)
17. 120th AAA Gn Bn	30	200	.1500	0	6	.0000	(37)
18. 119th AAA Gn Bn	24½	164	.1494	2	8	.2500	(8)
19. 777th AAA SP Bn	83 7/12	560	.1493	63⅓	494	.1282	(19)
20. 387th AAA SP Bn	5	34	.1470				
21. 599th AAA Gn Bn	7	48	.1458	7	48	.1458	(18)
22. 217th AAA Gn Bn	37	272	.1360	1	4	.2500	(9)
23. 452d AAA AW Bn	77 11/12	579	.1346	65⅓	512	.1276	(21)
24. 537th AAA AW Bn	33¼	252	.1339	25¾	116	.2220	(10)
25. 448 AAA AW Bn	7¼	55	.1318				
26. 445th AAA AW Bn	22	179	.1229				
27. 128th AAA Gn Bn	17¼	146	.1182	5¼	41	.1280	(20)
28. 411th AAA Gn Bn	52 5/6	448	.1179	0	14	.0000	(38)
29. 456th AAA AW Bn	45½	392	.1161	2	19	.1053	(24)
30. 547th AAA AW Bn	11	111	.0991				
31. 778th AAA SP Bn	19⅔	200	.0984	19⅓	171	.1130	(23)
32. 449th AAA AW Bn	21	214	.0981	18	144	.1250	(22)
33. 551st AAA AW Bn	9½	102	.0931	0	14	.0000	(39)
34. 457th AAA AW Bn	23 1/12	266	.0895	13¾	182	.0755	(29)
35. 550th AAA AW Bn	26	292	.0890	23	135	.1704	(15)
36. 465th AAA SP Bn	23⅓	267	.0874	12	34	.3529	(2)
37. 572d AAA SP Bn	16	188	.0851	16	188	.0851	(28)
38. 792d AAA AW Bn	1⅓	16	.0833				
39. 795th AAA SM Bn	1	14	.0714				
40. 575th AAA SP Bn	14¾	229	.0644	14¾	226	.0653	(30)
41. 468th AAA SP Bn	5	78	.0641	½	5	.1000	(25)
42. 398th AAA SP Bn	16	262	.0611	2	22	.0909	(27)
43. 115th AAA GN Bn	50½	944	.0535	21½	225	.0956	(26)
44. 467th AAA SP Bn	2½	47	.0532				
45. 634th AAA AW Bn	1	19	.0521	1	9	.0521	(31)
46. 635th AAA AW Bn	10	197	.0508	6	40	.1500	(17)
47. 530th AAA AW Bn	2	42	.0476	2	42	.0476	(32)

Continued on next page.

UNIT and relative standing	Batting Averages from 1 Aug 44 to date TOTAL NO. E/A			Batting Averages from 1 Feb 45 to date TOTAL NO. E/A			Relative Standing (1 Feb to date, only)
		I & II ENGAGED	AVERAGE		I & II ENGAGED	AVERAGE	
48. 109th AAA GN Bn	4	88	.0455	0	2	.0000	(34)
49. 203d AAA SP Bn	1	27	.0370				
50. 22d FTA (Fr)	1	33	.0303				
51. 565 AAA AW Bn	1	67	.0149	1	6	.1667	(16)
52. 453d AAA AW Bn	0	1	.0000				
53. 460th AAA AW Bn	0	1	.0000	0	1	.0000	(33)
54. 433d AAA AW Bn	0	3	.0000	0	3	.0000	(35)
55. 815th AAA AW Bn	0	5	.0000	0	5	.0000	(36)
56. 447th AAA AW Bn	0	7	.0000				
57. 377th AAA AW Bn	0	17	.0000				
58. 535th AAA AW Bn	0	23	.0000	0	23	.0000	(40)
59. 567th AAA AW Bn	0	27	.0000	0	27	.0000	(41)
60. 473d AAA SP Bn	17	Unknown	Unknown				
Totals	1,169	9,204		608	3,933		

Incl #1 to Hq Third US Army AAA Weekly Intelligence Report No 41, 17 May 45.

Day-by-Day Enemy Air Activity Over Third US Army Area
011200B Aug 1944 to 090001B May 1945

	August 1944				September 1944				October 1944				November 1944				December 1944			
Date	Raids	E/A	I	II	Raids	E/A	I	II	Raids	E/A	I	II	Raids	E/A	I	II	Raids	E/A	I	II
1	14	85	24	9	10	57	13	1	0	0	0	0	0	0	0	0	0	0	0	0
2	30	113	29	6	9	31	4	2	5	8	0	1	1	1	0	0	1	2	0	0
3	32	185	29	20	8	13	4	2	2	2	0	1	1	2	0	0	0	0	0	0
4	73	169	15	8	4	5	0	0	0	0	0	0	0	0	0	0	3	4	0	0
5	61	204	5	7	2	3	0	0	4	9	0	0	4	4	2	0	2	30	0	0
6	85	114	23	18	2	2	0	0	5	5	0	0	2	2	1	0	1	1	0	0
7	68	189	20	6	4	6	2	1	1	2	0	0	0	0	0	0	0	0	0	0
8	76	225	8	2	8	11	0	3	1	4	0	0	10	16	1	3	0	0	0	0
9	10	40	3	0	10	18	0	2	0	0	0	0	0	0	0	0	1	1	0	0
10	10	40	2	0	3	3	0	0	0	0	0	0	1	1	0	0	0	0	0	0
11	3	4	0	0	1	1	0	0	8	20	2	3	0	0	0	0	1	1	0	0
12	7	45	3	1	6	11	0	0	14	28	2	4	0	0	0	0	1	1	0	0
13	11	21	5	2	2	7	1	0	6	10	0	0	0	0	0	0	2	2	2	0
14	6	12	1	3	2	2	0	0	2	2	0	0	0	0	0	0	1	1	0	0
15	2	3	0	0	4	5	1	0	3	5	5	0	0	0	0	0	0	0	0	0
16	11	25	9	3	7	12	1	0	0	0	0	0	3	4	0	0	0	0	0	0
17	12	50	12	5	1	1	0	0	0	0	0	0	5	10	0	0	16	17	5	4
18	5	10	3	2	0	0	0	0	0	0	0	0	9	16	7	8	8	8	1	0
19	13	103	11	3	0	0	0	0	24	78	2	1	3	6	2	0	4	4	1	0
20	0	0	0	0	0	0	0	0	0	0	0	0	0	0	0	0	3	3	0	0
21	12	65	21	4	0	0	0	0	6	7	1	0	4	4	0	0	29	29	8	3
22	8	107	24	13	0	0	0	0	1	1	0	0	0	0	0	0	62	71	8	1
23	5	79	18	4	0	0	0	0	0	0	0	0	0	0	0	0	49	50	16	6
24	7	19	0	0	1	12	0	0	4	4	1	0	0	0	0	0	57	102	17	6
25	1	25	0	0	1	1	0	0	0	0	0	0	8	9	2	0	34	64	7	7
26	4	6	2	0	5	8	0	0	3	3	2	0	2	2	0	0	114	158	26	20
27	2	9	0	1	7	14	2	2	1	1	0	0	2	5	1	0	30	60	2	8
28	6	25	1	0	1	1	0	0	0	0	0	0	0	0	0	0	8	8	0	0
29	3	9	0	4	7	7	0	2	5	9	0	1	1	1	0	0	56	80	11	6
30	3	8	0	1	0	0	0	0	2	2	1	0	0	0	0	0	9	15	2	3
31	8	11	3	1					0	0	0	0					56	57	3	3
Total	588	2,000	271	123	105	231	28	15	97	200	16	11	56	83	16	11	548	742	109	67

Day-by-Day Enemy Air Activity Over Third US Army Area
011200B Aug 1944 to 090001B May 1945 (Cont'd)

	January 1945				February 1945				March 1945				April 1945				May 1945			
Date	Raids	E/A	I	II	Raids	E/A	I	II	Raids	E/A	I	II	Raids	E/A	I	II	Raids	E/A	I	II
1	125	243	63	15	0	0	0	0	1	1	0	1	8	14	0	3	6	8	5	0
2	29	48	7	7	0	0	0	0	1	1	0	0	63	289	68	32	17	22	14	2
3	1	1	0	0	4	4	0	0	0	0	0	0	16	73	17	5	9	11	6	1
4	0	0	0	0	0	0	0	0	0	0	0	0	43	150	39	21	8	14	5	4
5	2	3	0	0	0	0	0	0	0	0	0	0	36	137	15	10	2	2	1	0

Continued on next page.

Day-by-Day Enemy Air Activity Over Third US Army Area
011200B Aug 1944 to 090001B May 1945
(Cont'd)

Date	\multicolumn{4}{c}{January 1945}	\multicolumn{4}{c}{February 1945}	\multicolumn{4}{c}{March 1945}	\multicolumn{4}{c}{April 1945}	\multicolumn{4}{c}{May 1945}
	Raids	E/A	I	II	Raids	E/A	I	II	Raids	E/A	I	II	Raids	E/A	I	II	Raids	E/A	I	II
6	2	2	0	0	0	0	0	0	0	0	0	0	27	55	19	4	2	2	0	2
7	0	0	0	0	0	0	0	0	0	0	0	0	48	130	18	20	6	7	2	1
8	0	0	0	0	0	0	0	0	0	0	0	0	21	70	7	4	43	63	14	2
9	0	0	0	0	0	0	0	0	2	2	0	0	5	24	1	4				
10	0	0	0	0	2	2	1	0	3	3	0	1	16	64	18	12				
11	0	0	0	0	0	0	0	0	2	3	0	0	11	37	10	7				
12	0	0	0	0	0	0	0	0	1	2	0	0	8	20	8	0				
13	2	4	0	1	6	10	1	4	3	3	3	0	20	61	25	14				
14	6	11	1	2	2	2	0	0	4	4	1	0	14	60	7	6				
15	0	0	0	0	1	1	1	0	0	0	0	0	11	20	0	3				
16	1	1	0	0	0	0	0	0	3	7	0	3	10	34	11	3				
17	0	0	0	0	0	0	0	0	9	47	15	13	9	11	4	2				
18	0	0	0	0	0	0	0	0	13	60	11	7	5	16	1	2				
19	0	0	0	0	0	0	0	0	16	26	5	4	3	3	0	0				
20	0	0	0	0	0	0	0	0	42	235	43	23	8	9	0	0				
21	1	1	0	0	0	0	0	0	33	200	20	16	4	6	0	0				
22	0	0	0	0	0	0	0	0	9	20	7	1	1	1	0	0				
23	0	0	0	0	6	11	0	4	32	52	24	16	9	13	3	0				
24	0	0	0	0	1	1	0	0	16	62	32	9	11	17	6	2				
25	0	0	0	0	1	1	0	0	72	125	36	19	17	47	11	2				
26	0	0	0	0	0	0	0	0	14	66	3	2	27	80	18	14				
27	1	1	0	0	0	0	0	0	2	2	1	0	8	31	2	1				
28	0	0	0	0	0	0	0	0	0	0	0	0	1	1	0	0				
29	1	1	0	0					1	1	0	0	11	15	65	6	1			
30	0	0	0	0					13	18	2	3	3	4	2	0				
31	0	0	0	0					16	27	4	2								
Totals	171	316	71	25	23	32	3	8	308	967	207	120	474	1,492	316	172	93	129	47	12

Lessons Learned & Conclusions

Reprinted from the 3rd Army After Action Reports

FOREWORD

The "Lessons Learned and Conclusions" which follow are general enough in nature and wide enough in application to be those of the Command Section although they originated with the section indicated parenthetically after each item. The "Lessons Learned and Conclusions" applicable more specifically to the section as such are to be found at the end of each Section Report in Volume II.

ADMINISTRATIVE MEASURES. Throughout the campaign overemphasis was placed by all echelons on written confirmation by letter, message form or TWX orders orally issued for reassignment of personnel and enunciation of policies in administrative matters. This practice burdened an already over-taxed communications and message center system and added little, if any, effectiveness to the Army as a fighting unit. (G-1)

REINFORCEMENT DEPOTS. Interdependence between the Army and the Reinforcement Depot should be strengthened by a command relationship; the Reinforcement Depot should be commanded by the Army it services. (G-1)

TRANSPORTATION FOR REINFORCEMENTS. It was found that at least one truck company must be placed at the disposal of Army G-1 for the purpose of transporting reinforcements. Provisions must be made for stationing sufficient trucks at convalescent hospitals to transport discharged "Returns to Duty" promptly to the appropriate reinforcement battalions. (G-1)

PERSONNEL REQUISITIONING PROCEDURE. The fact that shortages existed in the divisions when there were stockages of reinforcements in the reinforcement battalions is evidence that the system of requisitioning for infantry - the bulk of personnel requirements - is too slow and cannot be controlled to the immediate needs of the combat units. If a division engaged in combat is actually short two hundred infantrymen, twice that number should be furnished. By the time they arrive in the line, in all probability two hundred additional casualties will have occurred. The solution is to make automatic allocation of infantry reinforcements to divisions in anticipation of losses. It would be impossible to make any bulk allocation of specialists or personnel in branches other than infantry. They could be requisitioned in the usual manner. (G-1)

HOSPITALIZED PERSONNEL RETURNED TO DUTY. A procedure of automatic return of hospitalized personnel to the former unit is essential to the successful operation of any major command with the least number of casualties and highest degree of morale. This eliminates much paper requisitioning and expedites return of casuals. A reasonable overstrength in a static situation is less alarming than an understrength of a similar number during heavy operations. Fifteen per cent overstrength is considered an adequate accumulation prior to anticipated heavy operations. (G-1)

EMERGENCY REASSIGNMENT FROM OTHER BRANCHES TO INFANTRY. Although there is no question as to the desirability of thorough training, a basically trained soldier in any arm or service can be fitted into an infantry unit if he is physically fit and has been instilled with the spirit of prompt, cheerful and automatic obedience. (G-1)

CHANNELS FOR REPORTS. Frequently units were assigned to this Army from other Armies but were not present in the Army area or in communication with Army Headquarters on the effective date of reassignment. Resultant was that G-1 reports for those units had to be estimated, often for several days. Reassigned units should report to the Army in whose area they are located until they have closed in the new Army area. (G-1)

BATTLEFIELD PROMOTIONS AND APPOINTMENTS. Battlefield promotions and appointments should be restricted to those individuals who have actually led troops in battle. Proper recognition should be given such cases in the form of a certificate indicating that promotion or appointment was made on the field of battle. (G-1)

LEAVES, FURLOUGHS AND PASSES. Considerable difficulty could be avoided if higher headquarters reserved a quota of passes to accommodate newly assigned units. An alternative solution would be to establish a policy whereby a unit once assigned a quota would retain that quota regardless of changes of assignment. (G-1)

HOLDING UNITS AT TRANSPORTATION CONCENTRATION POINTS. Before setting up an airfield or a railhead to accommodate troops on pass, a self-sustaining unit should be provided for the mission and responsibility of feeding and billeting such personnel. (G-1)

DISBANDMENT OF ENEMY FORCES. Disbandment of a defeated enemy must be anticipated by the conquering force without regard to enemy organization and must be accomplished with a minimum of administrative effort to be of maximum effect in returning needed manpower to their homes and normal occupations. Plans must be simple and practicable if they are to be effective in a period of confusion which follows a routed and destroyed enemy force. (G-1)

PLANNING PRIORITIES. It was the overall planning experience of the G-2 Section that, due to the operational lag as concerned operational commitment of Third U.S. Army on the Continent, Third Army requirements were in a low priority. In considering such priorities a basic time factor, which is a constant, exists. If the time lag for commitment of the Army operationally was to be 19 days, priorities should have been on a 19-day lag as well. Instead, certain items were postponed until such a date that they were incapable of fulfillment from the date of their inception. (G-2)

TACTICAL AND PHOTOGRAPHIC RECONNAISSANCE SQUADRONS. To perform all of the missions necessary for an Army consisting of three Corps, a minimum of three Tactical Reconnaissance Squadrons and one Photographic Reconnaissance Squadron should be available at all times.

Sufficient planes must be available to fly 40 missions per day to give adequate tactical reconnaissance coverage to a field Army where terrain and climatic conditions are similar to those in Western Europe. This number of missions is required by the Army itself and the Tactical Air Command. Should missions be assigned from higher headquarters, additional facilities must be provided. Artillery adjustment missions for medium (Corps) artillery are included in the overall total. (G-2)

TACTICAL RECONNAISSANCE COVERAGE. Tactical reconnaissance must be flown at least 150 miles in front of the line of contact and sufficiently far to either flank to locate threats to the Army. Narrow sectors of shallow depth and lack of overlap to flanks do not provide information of the movements of enemy troops which can be committed within 24 hours. This requires an availability of 40 missions per day in an Army with three Corps. (G-2)

GROUND LIAISON OFFICERS. Ground Liaison Officers attached to Air Squadrons of a Tactical Air Command cooperating with ground forces should be ground personnel assigned or permanently attached to such units. As the Squadrons are shifted the ground personnel should remain with the unit rather than revert to the ground headquarters as the ground headquarters has barely a knowledge as to who the individuals are or what their qualifications may be. (G-2)

BASIC PHOTOGRAPHIC COVER. Within the command framework existing in the European Theater of Operations, basic cover of strategic areas must be supplied by Army Group. Basic cover of tactical areas must be supplied by Army. Reasonable expectation of obtaining basic cover in formerly strategic areas will relieve the Army of concern when such areas suddenly become tactical in nature. A reasonable line of demarkation between the tactical and strategic areas can be drawn at a distance of 150 miles in front of the immediate line of contact. Basic cover should be supplied in sufficient quantities to provide initial distribution whenever the strategic area is reached by the imaginary line 150 miles to the front. (G-2)

INDOCTRINATION OF STAFFS WITH PHOTO INTERPRETATION POTENTIALITIES. A familiarization program with coordination and close liaison between the Photo Center and the Photo Interpreter Teams at lower echelons is desirable. The necessity of proving the importance of photo interpretation in the production of intelligence to newly arrived staffs within the theater was solved in most cases by exchanging the inexperienced Photo Interpretation Team from the unit for an experienced team from the Photo Center. This made immediately available to the G-2, personnel who were acquainted with Army policies and the capabilities and capacities of the Air Force units supplying air photos. (G-2)

G-2 AIR VERSUS ARMY AIR SECTION. Based on operational experience, though untested in this Army, it appears ill-advised to combine all air functions at the Army level in an Air Section. G-2 Air is concerned with reconnaissance, and its results. G-3 Air is concerned with the tactical operations of fighter-bombers and of medium bombers. Within the frame work employed in the Third Army, representatives of both G-2 Air and G-3 Air were present at the Tactical Air Command's Combined Operations. Appropriate results of reconnaissance were immediately given to G-3 Air for possible tactical use. Intelligence derived from the operations of the fighter-bombers was passed to the G-2 Air and from thence disseminated through intelligence channels to all interested units. At the Army Headquarters both G-2 Air and G-3 Air were integral sub-sections of the G-2 and G-3 Sections, respectively. This was a most efficient solution to the problem of providing reconnaissance and tactical coordination of fighter and bomber effort. (G-2)

PSYCHOLOGICAL WARFARE COMBAT LOUDSPEAKERS. Properly designed equipment to permit employment in the forward elements of our forces is essential to obtain maximum results from this weapon. A 200-watt output loudspeaker mounted on a tank proved to be the most effective employment of this type of Psychological Warfare. Equipment had to be improvised to provide this installation. A properly designed set of the smallest possible dimensions, suitable for mounting on a tank or any other tracked or wheeled vehicle, should be issued on a basis of not less than one per regimental combat team or armored combat command. (G-2)

ATTACHMENT VERSUS ASSIGNMENT OF SPECIALIST TEAMS. The advantages of assignment over attachment of various type specialist teams are that difficult administrative situations could have been eliminated, promotions could have been more equitable and just, and units to which personnel was placed on duty could more readily have exercised the desired control over team members. The fact that unqualified personnel appeared in some of the teams invariably resulted in relief and return to a headquarters in the rear, which, it appeared, evidently was to the liking of some of the individuals concerned. By assignment, qualified personnel could be interchanged within the organization without waiting for untried reinforcements. (G-2)

PERSONNEL. During an active operation, the After-Action Report requires personnel to maintain a continuity of the report. For the coordination at Army Headquarters a minimum of two officers and three enlisted men were on full time duty throughout, acting as an editorial board charged with style, reproduction, editing and lay-out. Inasmuch as these reports are provided for in Army Regulations, permanent trained personnel in this speciality should be attached or assigned for this duty. The Historical Section as such, functioning in Tables of Organization under G-3, has a mission which conflicts with the After-Action Report. (G-2)

LIAISON. A minimum of two liaison officers per corps headquarters is necessary at all times. One thus would be available at the Army Headquarters while the other is enroute or at his own headquarters. Daily staff visits by officers from Army to divisions were found to be of great value, not only in rapidly transmitting problems from division to Army, but also furnishing Army with the latest tactical front line information. Likewise, lateral liaison was maintained at Army level. (G-3)

BOMB LINES. Bomb lines were designated at Army level and coordinated with the corps. An effort was made to have the line follow objects visible from the air, often necessitating it being placed far in advance of friendly troops. It was found advisable to have the bomb line placed on estimated days advance in front of the troops and targets between the ground unit and the bomb line were attacked only on command of the ground controller. Targets on the far side of the bomb line were attacked by all aircraft. The factor most responsible for very effective employment of fighter bombers on Third U.S. Army front was the policy of scheduling aircraft in small flights briefed to check in with the ground controller of forward ground units. The controller directed the pilot to targets requested by ground units; this constituted "immediate" air cooperation during flyable weather. (G-3)

ARMY TRANSPORTATION SECTION. Field Manual 101-15 outlines the organization of a traffic headquarters in divisions and higher units but does not provide personnel to carry out these duties. Pertinent Tables of Organization should be ammended to provide for transportation sections in armies, corps and divisions sufficient to encompass highway, rail, air and, in landing operations, water, for the armies; for corps and divisions highway personnel is necessary. (G-4)

LINES OF COMMUNICATION AND SUPPLY. The Army Transportation Section, through its assigned Quartermaster Truck Group, should control the operation and administration of all Quartermaster Truck Companies. Railway construction and operating troops should be available in the army area and follow closely behind combat units to rehabilitate and put into operation rail lines with a minimum loss of time. Railway construction and operating troops, either attached or in direct support, should be available. Aviation construction engineers should be attached to an army and deployed behind corps, with the mission of closely following front line units in order to rehabilitate and mark airfields for supply and evacuation immediately after they have been uncovered. A battalion is considered ample. (G-4)

FISCAL. Purchasing and contracting appointments, down to and including at least the group or regimental level and, if necessary, to the battalion level, should be effectuated early in the build-up period. This will permit training of those personnel who will ultimately function as purchasing and contracting officers prior to the start of an operation. (G-4)

MISCELLANEOUS. Armored divisions should be provided with a ration breakdown section or similar unit. The personnel strength of the Quartermaster Company in the Infantry divisions is inadequate. Organic transportation should be authorized or provision made for attachment of Quartermaster Truck Companies on the basis of two to each Armored division and one to each Infantry division during mobile operations. (G-4)

REPORTS. Some reports are necessary for administration and historical purposes. All others should be cut to a minimum. The G-4 Periodic Report (Form 18, Section IV, Chapter 2, Field Manual

101-5) was impractical. The following report should be required daily from divisions and corps, forwarded by most expeditious means as of 1800 each day to arrive at army not later than 0900 the following morning:
   a. How many operational rations are on hand?
   b. Are gas tanks full?
   c. Are T/E gas cans full? Amount in excess.
   d. Are basic loads of ammunition complete? List shortages.
   e. Critical shortages of Class II and IV which will impede immediate operation. (G-4)

ELECTRIC POWER UNDER ENEMY CONTROL. Security was occasionally jeopardized when high tension lines from enemy territory continued to operate through the combat lines. Most high tension lines were provided with carrier operated telephone communications, so that communications were available as long as electric power continued to flow. Tactical forces should include specially trained personnel to disconnect but not destroy carrier communications systems. Censorship personnel should be available to be placed at key substations to safeguard security when power grids are repaired. (G-5)

MILITARY GOVERNMENT PERSONNEL. Scope of training for military government personnel should be widened to include military subjects of value in the field. Officers with general field experience should be selected for military government duties. (G-5)

MILITARY GOVERNMENT FINANCE PERSONNEL. The need for functional specialists in the fields of finance and property control became more acute in the occupation of enemy territories than it had been in the cases of liberated territories. In the cases of FRANCE, LUXEMBOURG, BELGIUM and CZECHOSLOVAKIA the advantages of being closely followed by a duly constituted and recognized governmental authority which was equipped to and did assume inherent responsibilities was quickly apparent. Additional fiscal and property control personnel should be assigned to staffs and detachments when dealing with occupied enemy territories. (G-5)

ORGANIZATION OF THE ADJUTANT GENERAL SECTION. In addition to the Personnel, Miscellaneous, Classification, Postal, and Executive Sections as normally organized for operations in the Zone of the Interior, it is necessary to have a Top Secret Section, a Forward Echelon Section, and a Battle Casualty Section during an Army's operational role. Additional equipment is necessary to accommodate these Sections. (AG)

OPERATIONAL ADMINISTRATION.
   a. It was found to be highly advantageous to by-pass corps headquarters with all possible administrative matters.
   b. Where many armies operate in juxtaposition to one another, and corps and divisions are frequently transferred from army to army, it would be highly advantageous to have an administrative standardization on a theater-wide scale to eliminate corps and divisions being required to modify their administrative procedures and adopt new systems and policies in the midst of operations.
   c. The postal regulating section should be located as closely as practicable to the Rear Echelon of the Army Headquarters because of the constant liaison which must be maintained to insure an even and steady flow of mail in both directions. Sub-postal regulating sections in the forward part of the army area are desirable so that division army postal units may not be required to travel great distances to obtain mail.
   d. Transportation of mail from the postal regulating section to the advance sub-postal regulating section should be an army responsibility. (AG)

ANTIAIRCRAFT FIRE UNITS. The antiaircraft fire units should be self-propelled. A more effective built-into-the-carriage system of fire control is needed with provision for fire during darkness. Weapons should be designed to fire below zero degrees elevation through 360 degrees and should have sufficient armor and mobility to perform a secondary ground role. Scales and sighting equipment for indirect fire should be provided. (AAA)

AIR GROUND IDENTIFICATION. Some means of providing mutual identification between aircraft and ground units must be developed to permit both the Air Force and the antiaircraft artillery to operate at maximum efficiency. Neither IFF (Identification Friend or Foe) nor identification through flight plans or liaison officer proved successful, many targets being carried as unidentified. (AAA)

CORPS PHOTO INTERPRETER TEAMS. A Photo Interpreter Team is needed at each corps artillery fire direction center. Only in this way can corps artillery accurately and quickly confirm sound and flash locations and targets reported through other sources. The team is likewise essential to the development of any corps fire plan which may be called for at any time. Although not absolutely a full time necessity, division artillery headquarters should have available on call the facilities of the Photo Interpreter Team at division headquarters. (Arty)

OPERATIONAL DATA. Artillery battalions should be placed in operation as soon as their shakedown period is completed to gain combat experience as rapidly as possible under the guidance of any headquarters already operational. A non-combat-experienced corps artillery headquarters can gain valuable experience in the capacity of a second fire direction center under an operating corps. (Arty)

ARTILLERY SUPPORTING CAVALRY. Supporting artillery attached to cavalry groups contributes immeasurably to the effectiveness of the cavalry group. There were times when cavalry groups, reinforced, were given zones or sectors comparable to those normally assigned a division. One or two field artillery battalions, preferably 105mm howitzer (self-propelled), should be attached to or placed in support of such cavalry groups. (Arty)

TIME FIRE OR POZIT AMMUNITION AS AN AID. The employment of time fire or Pozit ammunition to cover the approach to bridges in many cases proved a means of capturing bridges intact. The intention of the enemy to blow a bridge at the last moment is nullified by taking the bridge under fire in this manner ten to fifteen minutes before the arrival of tanks and thus enable friendly forces to seize the bridge intact. Damage to the bridges was found to be negligible and yet the enemy was prevented from placing demolitions or detonating ones already placed. (Arty)

ARMORED DIVISION 155MM HOWITZERS. In the light of experiences of the campaign, it is highly desirable to have a battalion of 155mm howitzers (self-propelled) as an organic part of an armored division. (Arty)

ARTILLERY AMMUNITION ALLOCATION. At certain critical periods during the operation it was found that some supervision of ammunition allocation was necessary, but only on a round-per-gun-per-day basis based on actual and forecast availability. Allotments of ammunition should be made to the several corps on a round-per-gun-per-day basis as the difference in mission between one corps and another is usually provided for by the artillery allocated to each corps. (Arty)

FLIGHT SURGEONS WITH GROUND FORCES. In view of the numbers of liaison artillery air observation posts and other aircraft operating within an army, a flight surgeon should be available at least one per Army Headquarters and preferably one per corps. (Arty)

MAINTENANCE AND SUPPLY FOR ARTILLERY AIRCRAFT. The Reclamation and Repair Squadron, which operated with this command as the higher echelon maintenance and supply agency for all field artillery aircraft, was an Air Force organization neither assigned nor attached to Army Headquarters, resulting in difficulties in obtaining supply, rations, services, etc. Such an agency should be assigned to the army and under direct supervision of the Army Artillery Officer. (Arty)

CHAPLAINS AT HOSPITALS. Combat conditions require the assignment of two chaplains, one Catholic and one Protestant, in Evacuation Hospitals during combat. One is now provided in Tables of Organization. (Chaplain)

MOBILE ACCOMMODATIONS. "Caravans" (trucks or trailers fitted as living quarters or offices) are the most satisfactory quarters and offices of senior officers and principal staff sections. These should be provided to assure continuity of function and eliminate pitching and lowering of heavy tentage. (Hq Comdt)

ADMINISTRATIVE PERSONNEL. The great number of permanent attachments to an Army Headquarters must be compensated for in housekeeping personnel and equipment within the headquarters proper. Although these attachments are generally known in advance, no Tables of Organization and Equipment expansion is provided for their accommodation. (Hq Comdt)

ELECTRIC GENERATORS FOR HEADQUARTERS. In addition to that provided, it was found particularly necessary to have on call three electric generators 50 KW, one 30 KW and three 15 KW. These are needed because of necessary dispersion of major installations within the headquarters proper. (Hq Comdt)

MEDICAL SERVICE. Reduction of trench foot can be accomplished from a preventive standpoint only. One method of prevention is through issuance of proper clothing to troops, for operations in cold, wet and muddy areas. Such clothing should include a loose-fitting, waterproof shoe with warm socks, preferably of the type used by the Russian Armies. The shoe pack is not the entire answer to this problem. Proper clothing combined with rotation of troops to avoid exposure for too long periods of time and strict foot discipline are the true determining factors. (Med)

NEUROPSYCHIATRY. It was definitely demonstrated that neuropsychiatric casualties must be given definite therapy in forward areas, preferably within sound of gunfire. Those patients returned to duty from battalion aid stations have less tendency to recur than those treated in rear areas. (Med)

WATER DISCIPLINE. Outbreaks of diarrheal diseases can almost invariably be traced to poor water discipline, i.e. usually drinking from unauthorized sources. This is a command function that is particularly difficult to enforce. (Med)

FIELD PRESS CENSORSHIP. Press censorship should be a function of the army as copy is censored primarily for security in conformity with policies and stops announced by higher headquarters, Army Headquarters is better equipped to evaluate the degree of security involved in any given situation. Press censorship at Army Group level complicates the clearing of information and necessitates a constant check on many details. (PRO)

INCEPTION OF COMMUNICATIONS ZONE ACTIVITIES. When landing on a hostile shore, an operations group of Quartermaster officers of the Advance Section, Communications Zone, should be attached to the staff of the commander of tactical troops. This group, operating under the tactical commander until a rear boundary is designated, should begin operations immediately upon landing, organizing beach dumps and being charged with the distribution of supplies from the very beginning. This will permit remaining in charge of beach dumps and gradually developing the inception of a communications zone. The Army Quartermaster should perform only his primary functions with regard to tactical troops, thus insuring a well organized, smoothly operating supply system before the initial army rear boundary is designated and before the situation becomes mobile. (QM)

SUPPLY SYNCHRONIZATION. The impetus of supply is from the rear; however, during rapidly changing situations, the supply agencies in rear of the army do not always possess a sufficiently complete picture to insure quick readjustment. The movement of these elements and installations must be closely synchronized with the army they are supporting. (QM)

RESERVE SUPPLIES. Reserves of Class I and III maintained in the army area depend considerably upon the rapidity of movement, the efficiency of the railway system and the amount of truck transportation available. In static situations, five days of Class I and III and fifteen days of Class II and IV are adequate; in mobile situations the stocks must be reduced and, at the same time, the agencies supporting the army from the rear must be speeded up. (QM)

WINTER COMBAT CLOTHING. Present type winter combat clothing is not entirely satisfactory. It is not sufficiently warm, wind resistant, water repellent or shrink proof, the material cloth is entirely too light in weight. The wide range of sizes makes it difficult to maintain balanced stocks in depots. Two depot companies are required for an army and each should have sufficient organic transportation to perform its function. (QM)

WIRE COMMUNICATIONS. The Tactical Air Command does not possess signal troops of the proper quantity and type to maintain a wire axis of its own behind rapidly advancing army. This places the burden of wire communications of supporting air units on the army, without proper facilities for this additional requirement. (Sig)

DEFENSIVE WEAPONS. Signal Corps troops should possess, as organic equipment, weapons of the proper type for antiaircraft defense and close-in defense of bivouacs and its isolated installations. (Sig)

CAPTURED ENEMY EQUIPMENT. The value of captured enemy equipment, particularly that of the Services, must be brought home to all troops during the training period. All personnel must be taught to report immediately the existence of such equipment when found and not to destroy items of unusual character or probable worth. (Sig)

TRACKS FOR VEHICLES. Although the M-18 was frequently the only combat tracked vehicle which could negotiate mud during the bad weather of the winter campaign, its tracks were found to be still not wide enough. Rubber tracks were found to be ideal for long distance movements and ordinary weather; cleated steel tracks are a "must" for icy weather. (TD)

Special Orders #1

HEADQUARTERS
565th CA Bn (AA (AW)
Camp Stewart, Georgia

SPECIAL ORDERS   April 10, 1943
No. 1

1. Captain Charles R. Griffin, O-346758, having reported for duty, is assigned as Commanding Officer, Headquarters Battery.

2. The following-named officers, having reported for duty, are assigned to Headquarters Battery:
2nd Lieutenant ROBERT B. CARR, 0-1053081
2nd Lieutenant WILLIAM E. SMILEY, 0-1053367
2nd Lieutenant CHARLES K. THIEBAUTH 0-1052997
2nd Lieutenant Melvin J. Berg, O-1053049
2nd Lieutenant MASON (NMI) TENAGLIA, 0-1052995

3. The following-named enlisted men having reported for duty are assigned to Headquarters Battery:
Tech Sgt. Randell J. Barnwell, 7004266
Tech Sgt. William J. Conroy, Jr., 20147705
S/Sgt. Murray M. Schwartz 32217515
Sgt. Michael (NMI) Gallagher, 6709509
Sgt. Michael T. Lesko, 6976299
Tech 4th Gr. Charles A. Dresland, 32158156
Tech 4th Gr. Millard P. Holcombe, 7083513
Cpt. Marcus G. Bosanic, Jr., 36114512
Tech 5th Gr. Marion L. Drozd, 6976836
Pfc. Joseph L. Diegelman, 32252405
Pfc. James H. Jones, 34099196
Pfc. Adelio (NMI) Revetti, 32252462
Pfc. Anton J. Fosolik, 32046739
Pvt. Herman C. Blanton, 32041174
Pvt. Edwin L. Gravenstein, 20939087
Pvt. Henry T. Hicks, 34319916
Pvt. George D. Hunt, 34319801
Pvt. Edward W. Levine, 34082594
Pvt. Stanley D. Majewski, 12015657

4. Captain JAMES T. COLLIER, 0-330346, having reported for duty, is assigned as Commanding Officer, Battery "A,"

5. The following-named officers, having reported for duty, are assigned to Battery "A":
1st Lieutenant JOHN M. CLARK, 0-1044196
2nd Lieutenant LEO W. STALL, JR., 0-1052981
2nd Lieutenant CLARENCE L. SLAGLE, 0-1053366
2nd Lietuenant CHARLES F. GILGUN, 0-1053613
2nd Lieutenant JOHN A. STAJDUHAR, 0-1053326

6. The following-named enlisted men having reported for duty are assigned to Battery "A":
S.Sgt. Richard L. Conner, 6067858
S/Sgt. Felix A. Jenisch, 20141429
Sgt. Harry E. Smith, 6879797
Tech 4th Gr. Albert J. Sladecek, 38030919
Cpl. Jacob M. Dellatorri, 33156050
Cpl. Louis V. Fantauzzo, 32038163
Cpl. Cecil A. Irwin, 36162039
Tech. 5th Gr. James H. Berry, 20441459
Pfc. David M. Blair, 33245292
Pfc. Robert J. E. Kodberg, 33276027
Pfc. Alvoid D. Huntley, 6154125
Pfc. Joseph E.A. Lamothe, 20155004
Pfc. Charles T. Wheatley, Jr. 37016782
Pvt. Cecil W. Garrett, 38078382
Pvt. Harvey E. Hunt, 6795625
Pvt. Ernest R. LaFayette, 20640291
Pvt. Louis (NMI) Lehman, 32115881

7. Captain MARION D. CHAPMAN, 0419934, having reported for duty is assigned as Commanding Officer, Battery "B."

8. The following-named officers, having reported for duty, are assigned to Battery "B":
2nd Lieutenant HOWARD W. STERNBERG, 0-1052984
2nd Lieutenant WARREN S. ELDREDGE, 0-1053576
2nd Lieutenant RUSSELL T. FARNSWORTH, 0-1053592

9. The following-named enlisted men having reported for duty are assigned to Battery "B":
S/Sgt. Joe B. Kuykendall, 18005296
Sgt. Timothy T. Athey, 6894192
Cpt. Frederick B. Burke, 6149782
Tech 5th Gr. Gerbert (NMI) Cone, 7004219
Tech 5th Gr. Harold A. Stephenson, 39018955
Tech 5th Gr. Zygmund J. Mroczkowski, 36110464
Tech 5th Gr. Anthony F. Zamborowski, 6980601
Pfc. Adelbert F. Danford, 12056096
Pfc. Raymond A. Hamann, 38090174
Pfc. Alexander G. Krull, 33269028
Pfc. Ray St. C. Matthews, 33076950
Pfc. Stanley P. Mazur, 36031326
Pfc. Frank P. Palmisano, 35046982
Pvt. Roy F. Dodge, 39018667
Pvt. Richard E. Sandstrom, 20624180
Pvt. Alberto R. Segura, 38077091
Pvt. Edward (NMI) Winters, 31057095
Pvt. Edward B. Woodbury, 37094802

10. Captain JAMES E. BOWRON, JR., 0-413187, having reported for duty is assigned as Commanding Officer, Battery "C":

11. The following-named officers, having reported for duty, are assigned to Battery "C":
2nd Lieutenant CARL A. TOMLIN, 0-1053001
2nd Lieutenant FREDERICK J. SZELES, 0-1052992
2nd Lieutenant MAURICE H. BERKOWITZ, 0-1053050
2nd Lieutenant MARK S. EATON, 0-1053571
2nd Lieutenant STANLEY H. FROISTAD, 0-1053609

12. The following-named enlisted men having reported for duty are assigned to Battery "C":
Sgt. John T. Swinford, 38069979
Tech 4th Gr. Isy (NMI) Arnow, 32020354
Tech 4th Gr. Antonio L. Penta, 11027119
Cpl. John B. Bodine, 20282931
Cpl. George (NMI) Souza, 39014515
Cpl. Fred A. Tartt, 20441803
Cpl. Alexander (NMI) Weiss, 6981064
Tech 5th Gr. Preston C. Ragsdale, 38046331
Pfc. Ralph J. Owens, 32252488
Pfc. Carl (NMI) Sprayberry, 14063734
Pfc. Charles B. Valdez, 38076508
Pvt. William A. High, 37120685
Pvt. Casimer A. Jozefowicz, 36310741
Pvt. Julius (NMI) Kiss, 31123843
Pvt. Jose C. Roybal, 38076659

13. Captain ROBERT B. NESBITT, JR., 0-390857, having reported for duty, is assigned as Commanding Officer, Battery "D."
1st Lieutenant WILLIAM W. EVARTS, 0-1043620
2nd Lieutenant RICHARD F. SPECNER, 0-1052976
2nd Lieutenant JAMES M. STOKES, 0-1052987
2nd Lieutenant FRANCIS R. FAHRINGER, 0-1053896
2nd Lieutenant NATHANTEL P. WILEY, JR., 0-1-53875
2nd Lieutenant Richard F. Spencer, 0-1052976
2nd Lieutenant James M. Stobes, 0-105-2987
2nd Lieutenant Francis A. Fahringer, 0-1053896
2nd Lieutenant Nathantel P. Wiley, Jr., 0-1058875
1st Lieutenant William W. Everts, 0-1043620

14. The following-named officers, having reported for duty, are assigned to Battery "D".

15. The following-named enlisted men having reported for duty are assigned to Battery "D":
Sgt. Ray E. Hadley, 6543131
Cpl. John M. Epps, 38077373
Tech 5th Gr. Joseph N. Ahmen, 36230884
Tech 5th Gr. Jesse L. Andrews, 14018651
Tech 5th Gr. James E. Ervin, 37046815
Pfc. Werner F. Ruopp, 36305383
Pfc. George W. Somershoe, 33050928
Pfc. Ralph W. Wright, 33045077
Pvt. Buck D. Baggett, 18023583
Pvt. Tracy C. Burns, 18085987
Pvt. Alvin L. Farris, 37047832
Pvt. Sidney (NMI) Glaser, 12007174
Pvt. William (NMI) Kolbensen, 32228742

Pvt. Paul W. McRae, 38054719
Pvt. Ralph E. Medling, 6999676
Pvt. William R. Moxley, 33269216
Pvt. Julius J. Timar, 33265426
Pvt. Charles H. Walton, 12017221

15. 2nd Lieutenant WILLIAM E. SMILEY, 0-1053367, 565th CA Bn (AA) (AW) is detailed as Personnel Adjutant this battalion.

16. 2nd Lieutenant CHARLES K. THIEBAUTH, 0-1052997, 565th CA Bn (AA) (AW) is designated as Motor Transport Officer this battalion.

17. 2nd Lieutenant MASON (NMI) TENAGLIA, 0-1052995, 565th CA Bn (AA) (AW) is designated as Munitions Officer this battalion.

18. 2nd Lieutenant ROBERT B. CARR, 0-1053081, 565th CA Bn (AA) AW) is designated as Communications Officer this battalion.

3. No enemy aircraft were engaged during this period.

4. During the month of Feb 45, approximately 10 F.E. shells fell in the area defended by this Battalion. No personnel injured or Material damaged.

5. By order of 207th AAA Gp., Battery B, 226th S/L Bn was attached for operational control as of 090600 Feb 45. All lights of Btry B were moved forward with exception of #4, 5, and 6, 13 February 1945. This Bn was relieved of Operational control of Battery B 226th S/L Bn as of 131700 Feb 45.

6. On 24 Feb 45 an EM of Btry C found a booby trap on a railroad track near the end of a tunnel, location P950262. The device was neutralized, removed, and the CO, 207th AAA Group was notified.

7. Relay of flash messages from Signal Corps OP's thru Battery C CP was discontinued 241200 Feb 45 due to the Signal Corps NCS having moved. OP#7 was set up in Battery C area, coordinates 951257.

8. The Battalion CP closed 843121, 260814 Feb 45 and opened 832137, 260814 Feb. 45.

Date	Unit	Mission	Coordinates
1-21 Mar 45	Btry "C"	RADIO LUXEMBOURG	P936247
22-26 Mar 45	Btry "C"	RR Bridge KONZ-KARTHAUS	L160230
27-28 Mar 45	Btry "C"	Cl V Supply Dump, APACH, FRANCE	Q012965
28-31 Mar 45	1st Platoon	AW protection 277th FA Bn	M230918
	2nd Platoon	AW protection 663rd FA Bn	M245890
1-28 Mar 45	Btry "D"	City of LUXEMBOURG	P852133
290330A-301200A	1st Platoon	AW protection 174th FA Bn	L984637
301800A-310840A	1st Platoon	AW protection 174th FA Bn vic HENOTHEL, GERMANY	M270810
290130-A-301140A	2nd Platoon	AW protection 578th FA Bn	L881726
301750A-311115A	2nd Platoon	AW protection 578th FA Bn vic LEMBACH, GERMANY	M320780
311900A Mar 45	Btry "D"	AW protection RHINE RIVER crossings, vic BOPPARD, GERMANY	L900815

Bn CP closed LUXEMBOURG CITY (P832137) 291130A Mar 45, and opened HAUSBAY (L873675) 291618A Mar 45. Bn CP closed at HAUSBAY (L873675) 311330A Mar 45 and opened at BOPPARD (L899916) 311430A Mar. 45.

6. On 31 Mar 45, Btry "B" assisted 578th FA Bn, vicinity of M320780, and Btry "C" assisted the 277th FA Bn, vicinity of M230918, in cleaning out pockets of German soldiers. Approximately 260 prisioners were taken.

K.L. YARNALL, Lt. Col., CAC Commanding

1st Ind.
Headquarters, 7th AAA Group, APO 403, U.S. Army, 7 April 1945.
TO: The Adjutant General, Washington, D.C.
THRU: Commanding General, 38th AAA Brigade, APO 403, U.S. Army

D.L. DUTTON, Colonel, CAC Commanding

**HEADQUARTERS
565th ANTIAIRCRAFT ARTILLERY
AUTOMATIC WEAPONS BATTALION (MOBILE)
APO 403
U.S. ARMY**

319.1   1 April 1945
SUBJECT: After Action Report
TO: The Adjutant General, Washington, D.C.

1. In compliance with letter, file 319.1, Hq 16th AAA GROUP, 26 Dec 44, subject as above, the following "After Action Report" for the 565th ANTIAIRCRAFT ARTILLERY AUTOMATIC WEAPONS BATTALION (MOBILE) is submitted for the period 1-31 March 1945.

2. This Bn is assigned to the THIRD UNITED STATES ARMY, and attached to the 7th AAA GROUP. All batteries are in IAZ Number 38, in defense of the crossings of the RHINE RIVER, vicinity of BOPPARD, GERMANY.

Coordinates of units of the Bn are as follows: Bn CP L899816, BOPPARD, GERMANY; Btry "A" M915813, KAMP, GERMANY; Btry "B" M897827, FILST, GERMANY; Btry "C" L904811, BOPPARD, GERMANY; Btry "D" L899811, BOPPARD, GERMANY.

3. No enemy aircraft were engaged during the period covered by this report.

4. During the month of March 1945, AW defenses of the following objectives were established:

Date	Unit	Mission	Coordinates
1-29 Mar 45	Btry "A"	City of LUXEMBOURG	P828134
30-31 Mar 45		Crossing of RHINE RIVER vie BOPPARD, GERMANY	L900815
1-28 Mar 45	Btry "B"	Air Strip A-97	P876148
29-31 Mar 45	1st Platoon	AW protection 578th FA Bn	M290775 Vic
	2nd Platoon	AW protection VIII CORPS Air strip, vic PANROD, GERMANY	M282840
311200A Mar 45	Btry "B"	AW defense of RHINE RIVER crossings, vic BOPPARD, GERMANY	L900815

**HEADQUARTERS
565 ANTIAIRCRAFT ARTILLERY AUTOMATIC
WEAPONS BATTALION (MOBILE)
APO 403
U.S. ARMY**

319.1   30 April 1945
SUBJECT: After Action Report
TO: The Adjutant General, Washington, D.C.

1. In compliance with AR 345-105, Change #4, dated 10 August, 1944, (par 10), subject as above, the following "After Action Report" for the 565th ANTIAIRCRAFT ARTILLERY AUTOMATIC WEAPONS BATTALION (MOBILE) is submitted for the period 1-30 April 1945.

2. Headquarters and Headquarters Battery, Batteries "B" and "C" were relieved from attachment to the 38th ANTIAIRCRAFT ARTILLERY BRIGADE and attached to the 112th ANTIAIRCRAFT ARTILLERY GROUP and the XX CORPS — effective 10 April 45, by Troop Assignment No. A-134, HEADQUARTERS THIRD UNITED STATES ARMY dated 17 April 45, and Batteries "A" and "D" were attached to the VIII CORPS 11 April 45 by Troop Assignment No. A-134 HEADQUARTERS THIRD UNITED STATES ARMY dated 17 April 1945. Batteries "A" and "D" were reattached to the 38th ANTIAIRCRAFT ARTILLERY BRIGADE 17 April 45 by Troop Assignment No. A-135 HEADQUARTERS THIRD UNITED STATES ARMY dated 20 April 1945.

3. The following is a narrative report of engagements with hostile aircraft for this period:

a. At 132000B Apr 45, from 20 to 25 E.A attacked a town occupied by 76th Infantry Division. One ME 109 was engaged by PFC J.E. VANN who manned a M32. The pilot attempted to evade the fire, but as plane turned, it burst into flames and disappeared below the skyline of the town. The crash was witnessed by Tec/Sgt. HITCHENS of Co. "F" 304th Infantry Regiment, 76th Infantry division. One Cat I was claimed.

b. At 232140 and 232325 Battery "C" engaged one JU 88 in each raid. Direction of flight was SW and NE, altitude approximately 400 feet. The raid of 232140 enemy aircraft was strafing. No damage to defended area or personnel injured. No claims.

c. At 252230 Battery "B" engaged on JU 88 which had been strafing Highway No. 4 and turned over ASP No. 56, coordinates O-385230, which was being defended by Battery "B". Altitude approximately 500 feet, direction of flight E. One 40mm burst observed on wing of plane but it did not crash. Cat III claimed.

d. At 262230 Battery "B" engaged a single JU 88 flying E over the Pontoon Bridge vic U-202675, altitude approximately 400 feet. No attacks were made on defended area. No claims.

4. During the month of April 1945, AW defense of the following objectives were established:

Date	Unit	Missions	Coordinates
1-5 Apr	Btry A	RHINE RIVER Crossings vic BOPPARD	L915813
5-13 Apr	Btry A	AIRFIELD Y74 vic SCHWALBACH	M595718
13 Apr	Btry A	Attached to 16th AA Group and assigned to 635th AAA AW Bn for operational control	
1-3 Apr	Btry B	RHINE RIVER Crossings vic BOPPARD	L897827
3-10 Apr	Btry B	RHINE RIVER Crossings vic LORCH	MO49605

10-13 Apr	Btry B	AIRFIELD R-2 vic LANCENSALZA	J0483
13-17 Apr	Btry B	AIRFIELD vic WEIMAR	J464689
19-26 Apr	Btry B	ASP No. 56 vic BAIERSDORF	O-380220
26-30 Apr	1st Plat	Pontoon Bridge 71st Inf Sector	U-286570
	2nd Plat	Pontoon Bridge 71st Inf Sector	U-290572
1-3 Apr	Btry C	RHINE RIVER Crossing vic BOPPARD	L-904811
3-10 Apr	Btry C	RHINE RIVER Crossing vic LORCH	M-038604
10-13 Apr	Btry C	AIRFIELD R-1 vic WENIGENLUPNITZ	H-8968
13-17 Apr	Btry C	AIRFIELD vic WEIMAR	J-464691
19-23 Apr	Btry C	Class III DP vic HOLLFELD	O-5555
23-24 Apr	Btry C	Class III DP vic LAUF	O-585082
24-26 Apr	Btry C	Decanning Area vic NURNBERG	O-457980
26-29 Apr	1st Plat	Pontoon Bridge 65th Inf Sector	U-124472
	2nd Plat	Pontoon Bridge 65th Inf Sector	U-125482
29-30 Apr	1st Plat	AIRFIELD vic REGENSBURG	U-159573
	2nd Plat	Pontoon Bridge vic REGENSBURG	U-161565
1-5 Apr	Btry D	RHINE RIVER Crossings vic BOPPARD	L-899811
5-8 Apr	Btry D	RHINE RIVER Crossings vic LORCH	M-039603
8-13 Apr	Btry D	AIRFIELD Y-74 vic SCHWALBACH	M-590698
13 Apr	Btry D	Attached to 16th Group and assigned to 635th AAA AW Bn for operational control.	

5. a. Bn CP closed vic HAUSBAY (L-873675) 311330B Apr 45, and opened at BOPPARD (L-899816) 311430B Apr 45.

b. Bn CP closed vic BOPPARD (L-899816) 051230B Apr 45, and opened at LORCH (M-048616) 051430B Apr 45.

c. Bn CP Closed vic LORCH (M-048606) 101812B Apr 45, and opened vic GROBEN-BEHRINGEN (H-9573) 111230B Apr 45.

d. Bn CP closed vic GROBEN-BEHRINGEN (H-9573) 131430B Apr 45, and opened vic WEIMAR (J-480696) 131800B Apr 45.

e. Bn CP closed vic Weimar (J-480696) 181015B Apr 45, and opened vic BREITENGUSSBACH (O-251587) 180130B Apr 45.

f. Bn CP closed vic BREITENGUSSBACH ()-251587) 220830B Apr 45, and opened vic NURNBERG (0-422030) 221145B Apr 45.

g. Bn CP closed vic NURNBERG (O-427030) 261410B Apr 45, and opened vic HEMAU (T-955582) 261730B Apr 45.

K.L. YARNALL, Lt. Col., CAC Commanding

HEADQUARTERS
565TH ANTIAIRCRAFT ARTILLERY AUTOMATIC
WEAPONS BATTALION (MOBILE)
APO 403
U.S. Army

319.1 1 June 1945

SUBJECT: After Action Report
TO: The Adjutant General, Washington, D.C.

1. In compliance with Change No. 4, AR 345-105, par 10, dated 10 August 1944, subject as above, the following final "After Action Report" for the 565TH ANTIAIRCRAFT ARTILLERY AUTOMATIC WEAPONS BATTALION (MOBILE) is submitted for the period 1-9 May 1945.

2. Headquarters and Headquarters Battery, Batteries "B" and "C" were relieved from attachment XX CORPS and attached to 38th AAA BRIGADE, and Batteries "A" and "D" were relieved from attachment III CORPS and attached to 38th AAA BRIGADE 8 May 1945, effective 5 May 1945, by Troop Assignment No. A-140, THIRD UNITED STATES ARMY, dated 8 May 1945. This battalion was relieved from attachment to the 38th AAA BRIGADE and attached to III CORPS 6 May 1945 by Troop Assignement No. A-142, THIRD UNITED STATES ARMY, dated 10 May 1945.

3. At 021947B May 1945, Battery "B" engaged one E/A flying Northwest at approximately 60 ft. altitude, over Airstrip R-68 (U-540365). No attack was made on the defended area. No claims.

4. a. Bn CP closed HEMAU (T-955582) 301830B April 45, and opened STRAUBING (U-542426) 302330B April 45.

b. Bn CP closed STRAUBING (U-542436) 040800B May 45, and opened SCHWARZENBERG (N-954230) 041600B May 45.

5. Objectives Defended:

Date	Unit	Location	Mission
1-4 May 45	Battery "A" CP	GAIMERSHEIM (wj 6729) Attached to III CORPS for operations	
4 May 45	Battery "A" CP	Closed CP GAIMERSHEIM and opened vic SCHEINFELD, vic Bn Assembly Area (N-954230)	
4-7 May 45	Battery "A" CP	CP at Bn Assembly Area (N-954230)	
7 May 45	Battery "A" CP	CP closed N-954230, opened	
	Battery "A" CP	O-291137	Security guard, traffic control, lines of communication, bridges
7-9 May 45	Battery "A" CP	O-291137	
1-4 May 45	Battery "B" CP	U-540365 AAA AW Defense Airstrip R-68, vic STRAUBING.	
4-7 May 45	Battery "B" CP	SCHWARZENBERG (N-954230) Bn Assembly Area	
7-9 May 45	Battery "B" CP	N-820253 Security Patrol, guarding of bridges, traffic control, lines of communication, etc.	
	Btry "B" 1st Plat CP	N-866233	
	Btry "B" 2st Plat CP	N-815250	
1-3 May 45	Btry "B" CP	U-498153 AAA AW Protection ISAR RIVER	
	BTRY "B" 1st Plat CP	U-498153	Crossing 80th Inf Div Sector
	Btry "B" 2nd Plat CP	U-513135	
3-7 May 45	Battery "C" CP	N-954230 SCHWARZENBERG Bn Assembly Area	
7-9 May 45	Battery "C" CP	O-75130 Security Guard, traffic control, guarding of bridges, lines of communication, etc.	
	Battery "C" 1st Plat	O-75130	
	Battery "C" 2nd Plat	O-16141	
1-3 May 45	Battery "D" CP	MAINBURG (wt 9813) Attached to III CORPS for operations	
3-4 May 45	Battery "D" CP	DORFEN (wZ 2874)	
4 May 45	Battery "D" CP	Closed DORFEN (wZ 2874)	
5 May 45	Battery "D" CP	SCHWARZENBERG (N-954230) Bn Assembly Area	
5-7 May 45	Battery "D" CP	SCHWARZENBERG (N-954230) Bn Assembly Area	
5-7 May 45	Battery "D" CP	SCHWARZENBERG (N-954230) Bn Assembly Area	
7-9 May 45	Battery "D" CP	N-940039 Security guard, traffic control, guarding of bridges, lines of communication	
	Battery "D" 1st Plat	T-059820	
	Battery "D" 2nd Plat	N-940039	

K.L. YARNALL, Lt. Col., CAC Commanding

WAR DEPARTMENT
THE ADJUTANT GENERAL'S OFFICE
WASHINGTON
WAR DEPARTMENT RECORDS BRANCH, A.G.O.
HISTORICAL RECORDS SECTION
ROOM MB-858 PENTAGON

HEADQUARTERS
565th Antiaircraft Artillery Automatic Weapons Battalion
APO 403
UNITED STATES ARMY

314.7 1 January 1945

SUBJECT: Unit History 1944.
TO: The Adjutant General, War Department, Washington, D.C.

1. Under the provisions of Par IIb AR 345-105, dated 18 November 1929 as amended, the history of the 565th Antiaircraft Artillery Automatic Weapons Battalion Mobile is submitted for the year 1944:

a. Original Unit.
(1) Designation: 565th Coast Artillery Battalion (Antiaircraft) (Automatic Weapons)
(2) Date of organization: 10 April 1943.
(3) Place of organization: Camp Stewart, Georgia.
(4) Authority for organization: Paragraph 7, Special Orders No. 17, Headquarters Antiaircraft Artillery Command, Richmond, Virginia, dated 22 January 1943 as amended by paragraph 2, Special Orders No. 38, Headquarters Antiaircraft Artillery Command, Richmond, Virginia, dated 26 February 1943.
(5) Sources from which personnel was obtained was by draft. Majority of personnel came from Fourth, Sixth, and Second Service Commands, with a minority coming from all other Service Commands.

b. Change in organization: This Battalion was reorganized under TO and E 44-25, 22 April 1944. Reorganized and redesignated as the 565th AAA AW Bn (Mbl) 27 May 1943 pursuant to authority contained in Paragraph 1, General Orders No. 45, Headquarters Antiaircraft Artillery Command, Richmond, Virginia, dated 20 May 1943.

c. Strength, commissioned, and enlisted of this organization by months was as follows:
(1) At beginning of period: Not available.
(2) Net increase each month:
(1) January 1944: Not available.

	Officers	Warrant Officers	EM
(b) 29 Feb. 1944:			60

(c) 31 March 1944	14		
(d) 30 April 1944			6
(2) 31 May 1944			5
(f) 30 June 1944			3
(g) 31 July 1944	18		3
(h) 31 August 1944			9
(i) 30 Nov. 1944			2

(3) Warrant Officer strength for the entire period remained at a total of 3.
(4) Net decrease each month:
 (a) January 1944: Not Available
 (b) 29 February 1944: 10
 (c) 31 March 1944 20
 (d) 30 April 1944 9
 (e) 31 May 1944 5
 (f) 30 June 1944 9
 (g) 31 August 1944 19
 (h) 30 Sept. 1944 13
 (i) 31 Oct. 1944 4
 (j) 31 Dec. 1944 1 26
(5) At end of period: 35 3 734

d. Stations, permanent and temporary of unit:
 (1) Unit participated in Tennessee Maneuvers under direction of Second Army from November 1943 to January 1944. On 17 January 1944 departed from vicinity of Murfreesboro, Tennessee at 0900, destination Camp Stewart, Georgia per Par 26 Special Orders No. 7, Maneuver Director Headquarters, Second Army, APO 402/ c/o Postmaster Nashville, Tennessee, dated 7 January 1944.
 (2) Unit arrived at Fort Oglethorpe, Georgia approximately 1700 17 January 1944 enroute to Camp Stewart, Georgia, and bivouaced for night.
 (3) Departed from Fort Oglethorpe, Georgia at 0600 18 January, destination Camp Stewart, Georgia, and arrived at Madison, Georgia approximately 2000 18 January 1944.
 (4) Departed Madison, Georgia 0700 19 January 1944 arriving at final destination, Camp Stewart, Georgia at 1700 19 January 1944.
 (5) Advance party for overseas movement departed from Camp Stewart, Georgia for NYPE, Fort Hamilton, New York, per Par 19, Special Orders No 201, Headquarters Antiaircraft Artillery Training Center, Camp Stewart, Georgia, dated 22 August 1944, on 26 August 1944. Also authority contained in Cryptographic Message, headquarters, Antiaircraft Artillery Command, Richmond, Virginia, GNSTO-1057, 14 August 1944.
 (6) Battalion departed from Camp Stewart, Georgia in two sections at 0700 and 0900 30 September 1944 with strength of 761 Enlisted men and 32 Officers, and 3 Warrant Officers for overseas movement. Destination NYPE, Camp Kilmer, New Brunswick, New Jersey, per Confidential Ltr Army Service Forces NYPE, Brookly, New York, file SPTAA 370.5 GM (CA))E7992) Subj: Movement Orders, Shipments 4516 AA and BB. Also Par 1 Special Orders No. 230, Headquarters, Antiaircraft Artillery Training Center, Camp Stewart, Georgia, 25 September 1944, and Immediate Action Ltr, WD file 370.5 (4 Aug 44) OB-S-E-M, dated 5 August 1944 Subj: Movement Orders 4516.
 (7) Battalion arrived at NYPE, Camp Kilmer, New Brunswick, New Jersey at 1300 1 October 1944.
 (8) Battalion departed Camp Kilmer, New Brunswick, New Jersey at 1900 5 October 1944 for movement to ship per authority Ltr, Headquarters Army Service Forces, Camp Kilmer, N.J. Subj: "Movement Orders", dated 3 October 1944.
 (9) Arrived at Staten Island NYPE at approximately 0030 6 October 1944 for embarkation.
 (10) Departed from Staten island Terminal at 1145 6 October 1944 aboard USAT Cristobal.
 (11) Arrived at Plymouth, England and anchored in harbor at 1900 16 October 1944.
 (12) Debarked at 1930 18 October 1944 departing by train for Leek, Staffordshire, England.
 (13) Arrived Camp Blackshaw Moor, Staffordshire, England at 1100 19 October 1944.
 (14) Five (5) officers, one hundred ninety seven (197) enlisted men from Batteries "B" and "C", and One (1) Medic proceeded on temporary duty from Camp Blackshaw Moor, England to Porthcawl, Glamorganshire on 26 October 1944 per Ltr Headquarters 111th AAA Group, file AG 300.4 Subj: "Orders" dated 25 October 1944.
 (15) One (1) officer and forty-eight (48) enlisted men from Battery "C" returned from temporary duty at Porthcawl, Glamorganshire on 6 November 1944.
 (16) Ninety-six enlisted men and two (2) officers from Battery "B", fifty-two (52) enlisted men and two (2) officers from Battery "C", and one (1) Medic returned from temporary duty at Porthcawl, Glamorganshire 13 November 1944. One (1) enlisted man remained absent sick in Porthcawl, Glamorganshire.
 (17) Organization departed from Camp Blackshawmoor, Staffordshire on 7 December 1944. Destination Southampton, England for embarkation for movement to Continent per authority OMI 1025 Part 25.
 (18) Arrived at Camp Hursley, Romsey, England at 2300.
 (19) Departed Camp Hursley for Southampton at 1200 8 December 1944. Headquarters Battery and Medics embarked on SS Charles M Hall at 1800. Lettered Batteries embarked on various other ships on 8 and 9 December 1944. Troops embarked on British transport Llangibby Castle. Vehicles and drivers from Btrys "A" and "B" embarked on the Joseph C Storey. Vehicles and drivers from Btrys "C" and "D" embarked on the Samuel Holt.
 (20) Departed for Continent at 2100 9 December 1944. Arrived at point about 5 miles off Le Harve, France, Sunday 10 December 1944 and anchored to await orders.
 (21) Debarked at 0900 15 December 1944 and proceeded to assembly point. Left by motor convoy at approximately 1200 for Red Horse Assembly Area, Camp Bertrimont, Pavilly, France arriving at destination at 1600.
 (22) Departed from Camp Bertrimont, Red Horse Assembly Area at 0500 20 December 1944 for Luxembourg per Auth TWX Headquarters First United States Army, District "D" DTO.
 (23) Arrived Luxembourg City, Luxembourg at 1600 21 December 1944 and moved into tactical position.
e. None
f. None
g. See attached summary
h. Lt. Col. Kenneth L. Yarnall, 021864
i. Unit Assignment and losses in action:
 (1) Antiaircraft defense of city of Luxembourg under command of Third United States Army.
 (2) Tec 5 Willie C Copeland, 34 731 104, Headquarters Battery (060) wounded by stray .50 caliber machine gun bullet on 30 December 1944 at 1420 at Battalion CP. Evacuated to 104th Evacuation Hospital condition SWA.
j. None
K. None

K L YARNALL
Lt. Col., CAC
Commanding

1 Incl.
Incl-1-Summary of Enemy Air Acitvity (in trip)
1st Ind.
HEADQUARTERS, 16th AAA GROUP, APO 230, US Army, 29 January 1945.
TO: The Adjutant General, Washington, D.C.
(Thru: Commanding General, Third U.S. Army, APO 403, Rear Echelon)
Approved.
For the Commanding Officer:

RALPH S. IRWIN, JR.,
1st Lt., A.G.D.,
Adjutant

AG314.7 - GNMCF
(1 Jan 45)
HQ THIRD US ARMY, APO 403, US Army, 31 January 1945.
To: Commanding General, European Theater of Operations, APO 887, US Army.

HEADQUARTERS
565th Artillery Antiaircraft Artillry Automatic Weapons Battalion
APO 403
UNITED STATES ARMY

1 January 1945
SUMMARY OF ENEMY AIR ACTIVITY AND ENGAGEMENTS
1. The 565th Antiaircraft Artillery Automatic Weapons Battalion became operational at 1200, 22 December 1944. Batteries "A" and "D" were assigned as part of the Antiaircraft Defense of the City of

Luxembourg. Battery "B" was given the mission of protecting Air Strip A-97 near the City of Luxembourg, and Battery "C" set up in tactical positions around Radio Luxembourg. The Battalion Command Post was established in the City of Luxembourg.

2. During the period of 22-31 December 1944 a total of 46 enemy air raids were engaged by batteries of this Battalion with an expenditure of 1467 rounds of 40mm HE, and 9444 rounds of cal. .50 ball, tracer, and AP ammunition. Thirty-nine raids were night raids with firing on 90mm bursts. Seven of the raids were seen targets. Type of fire control for machine gun fire was Mk9 sight, tracer control. Type of fire control for 40mm firing was Forward Area Sight, director Control, and Weissight. No ground targets were engaged during this period. One Category III claim was approved for Battery "B" during this period.

MEDICAL DETACHMENT
565th Antiaircraft Artillery Automatic Weapons Battalion
APO 403
UNITED STATES ARMY

319.1   10 Apr 43 - 30 Jun 45
SUB: Semi-annual Report of Medical Detachment Activities
TO: The Surgeon General, War Department, Washington, D.C.
(Thru Commanding Officer, 16th AAA Group)

In compliance with circular 58, Headquarters, European Theater of Operations, APO 887, 14 May 1945, Subject: "Period Reports, Medical Department Activities", the semi-annual report of the Medical Detachment, 565th Antiaircraft Artillery Automatic Weapons Battalion is submitted.

1. On 10 April 1943 the 565th Coast Artilley Battalion (Antiaircraft) (Automatic Weapons) with authorized Medical Detachment was activated with Harry D. Schell, O 411 233, 1st Lt., MC, as Battalion Surgeon, Murray M. Franklin, O 487 857, 1st Lt., DC, as Battalion Dentist, and with a cadre of three (3) enlisted men. Training as directed under provisions of MTP 8-1 was begun 20 May 1943 and was subsequently completed in twenty-two (22) weeks. This Detachment participated in Maneuvers on the Camp Stewart Reservation where the principles of treatment and evacuation of casualties were discussed, demonstrated, and practiced. This unit left Camp Stewart, Georgia, 13 November 1943 by motor convoy and preceeded to the Tennessee Maneuver Area. There the procedures of treatment and evacuation were practiced on simulated casualties. On 17 January 1944, this organization departed from the Tennessee Maneuver Area and arrived at Camp Stewart, Georgia, 19 January 1944. An eight (8) weeks course of refresher training as prescribed by Headquarters Antiaircraft Artillery Training Center, Camp Stewart, Georgia, was begun shortly after the return of this unit to this training center. On 30 September 1944 this unit entrained at Camp Stewart, Georgia, for the staging area Camp Kilmer, New Brunswick, New Jersey. On 5 October 1944 this unit entrained for the Port of Embarkation and debarked at Plymouth, England 18 October 1944. The organization left England 7 December 1944 and arrived at Le Havre, France 15 December 1944.

2. The 565th Antiaircraft Artillery Automatic Weapons Battalion was in active combat 140 days from 20 December 1944 to 8 May 1945. The mission of the Medical Detachment consisted of administering first aid, evacuating casualties, and supervision of field sanitation. The Detachment is composed of three (3) Officers and seventeen (17) enlisted men. Since 16 April 1945 we have operated with sixteen (16) enlisted men without lessening our efficiency or causing undue hardship.

3. The battalion aid station was included in the battalion command post which was usually set up in a building. When tents were used, the aid station was set up in the detachment command post tent. The following personnel comprised the aid station group: Battalion Surgeon, Battalion Dental Surgeon, Medical Administrative Officer, and nine (9) enlisted men. Two (2) medical aid men were attached to each of the four (4) line batteries. They were attached for rations, quarters, and supply.

4. The duties performed by each member of the Medical Detachment were as follows:

a. Battalion Surgeon: Held daily sick call at battalion and battery command posts, made frequent sanitary inspections, and served as a member of the Battalion Special Court Martial.

b. Battalion Dental Surgeon: Performed all dental work, including a complete dental survey of the battalion; accomplished all prosthetic work in nearby dental laboratories; served as Officer's Finance Agent, and later as Battalion Finance Agent.

c. Medical Administrative Officer: Served as assistant Battalion Surgeon by making sanitary inspections, acting as Detachment Supply Officer, supervising all clerical work of the detachment, and by compounding various pharmaceutical preparations in the aid station. He also served as Battalion Fire Marshall, Battalion Special Service Officer, and Assistant Defence Council on the Battalion Special Court Martial.

d. S/Sgt.: Worked in the battalion aid station as assistant to the Battalion Surgeon and actively supervised work of all enlisted personnel.

e. Tec 3: Served as detachment Supply Sergeant; served as assistant to the Battalion Surgeon; and taught classes in first aid to gun section aid men.

f. Tec. 3: Did all detachment clerical work; did all clerical work for the Battalion Special Service Officer; assisted the Battalion Surgeon in the aid station.

g. Tec 4 (2): Each served as a battery aid man.

h. Cpl.: Served as assistant to the Battalion Surgeon and acted as assistant truck driver.

i. Tec 5 Surgical (3): Two of these men served as battery aid men and one served as first aid man in the battalion aid station.

j. Tec 5 Dental Assistant: Served as assistant to the Battalion Dental surgeon and as first aid man in the battalion aid station.

k. Tec 5 Truck Driver: Drove 2½ ton truck and served as first aid man in the battalion aid station.

l. Tec 5 Medical: Served as a battery aid man.

m. PFC (3): Served as battery aid men.

n. PFC: Drove ¼ ton truck and served as first aid man in the battalion aid station.

o. PFC: Hospitalized for Combat Exhaustion on 16 April 1945.

5. The following equipment was routinely used in the battalion aid station:

a. MD Chest #2. (A useful expedient consisted in using the bottom shelf to carry used plasma bottles which were filled with various liquid medications.)

b. A dressed litter, set upon the upturned Chests #2 and 4.

c. The Dental Chest #60 with the chair set up. It was necessary to improvise adequate lighting. A satisfactory light was constructed by the battalion motor pool. The foot pedal of the foot engine has broken three (3) times through ordinary use and it was repaired each time by the battalion motor pool.

d. The folding table of MD Chest #4 was set up as the clerk's desk.

6. The battery aid men set up a battery aid station at the battery command post. They were equipped with their medical aid pouches, one (1) litter, one (1) Army leg splint, and a sufficient amount of expendable medical supplies. Their duties consisted of the following:

a. Evacuation of any seriously injured to the nearest medical installation.

b. Daily visits to each gun section to hold sick call. Any seriously ill patients were seen by the battalion surgeon in the battery or battalion aid stations.

c. Daily sanitary inspections were made of each section. Deficiencies were reported to the section chief and to the Battery Commander. If corrective action were not taken, the deficiency was then reported to the Battalion Surgeon. In the opinion of the undersigned, these daily inspections were of great importance in maintaining a low incidence of disease.

d. The chlorine content of the water was checked daily and recorded by the battery aid men. All water used for drinking and culinary purposes was obtained from engineer water points.

7. A useful portable shower, constructed by the Medical Administrative Officer, was improvised, using a ¼ ton trailer (as the water container), an immersion water heater, and a hand force-pump with hose and nozzle. Quartermaster shower units were usually available. Laundry was done both by Quartermaster laundries and by home laundry.

8. The supply of food was satisfactory. It was not thought necessary to supplement it with additional vitamins. There were few problems of insect control during the winter months. The problem of fly control during the warm summer months is difficult to solve because of the shortage of wire screening and other fly control supplies.

9. Venereal disease control is accomplished by making mechanical and chemical prophylaxis supplies available to men through the battery aid men. Men are informed of the location of prophylaxis stations in nearby towns.

10. The allotted transportation consisted of two trucks, one 2½ ton and one ¼ ton. A one ton trailer was borrowed from the ammunition section of Headquarters Battery to provide room in the 2½ ton truck to haul probable casualties while travelling as a motor convoy. The ¼ ton truck was very valuable. It permitted frequent visits of the Battalion Surgeon to the batteries and it was used on numerous occasions to evacuate casualties. Despite frequent cleanings, the instrument sterilizer continued to rust. A captured German sterilizer

proved to be superior.

11. The number of severe casualties was very low. The battery aid men administered first aid and in many instances evacuated the injured directly to an Evacuation Hospital.

HARRY D. SCHEEL,
Captain, M.C.
Battalion Surgeon

319.1   1st Indorsement
(30 Jun 45) HEADQUARTERS 565th AAA AW Bn., APO 403 U.S. Army 3 July 1945.

TO: Commanding Officer 16th AAA Group, APO 403 U.S. Army. Approved.

K.L. YARNALL
Lt. Col., 565th AAA AW Bn.
Commanding

2d Ind.
HEADQUARTERS, 16th AAA Group, APO 403, U.S. Army, 5 July 1945
TO: Commanding Officer, 35th AAA Brigade, APO 403. Approved.

J.H. MADISON
Colonel, CAC
Commanding

Basic: Semi-annual Report of Medical Detachment Activities.
AG 319.1   3rd Indorsement   JBF/dr
HEADQUARTERS, 35th AAA Brigade, APO 403, U.S. Army, 6 July 1945.
TO: Commanding General, XV Corps, APO 436, U.S. Army. Approved.

J.B. FRASER,
Colonel, CAC,
Commanding

4th Ind
HQ, XV CORPS, Office of the Surgeon, APO 436 U.S. Army, 9 July 1945.
TO: Surgeon, Third Army, APO 403 U.S. Army.

G.J.H.

AG 314.7 GNMCN-2   5th Indorsement
HEADQUARTERS THIRD U.S. ARMY, APO 403, U.S. Army, 12 July 1945.
TO: Commanding General, U.S. Forces, European Theater (Rear), APO 887, U.S. Army. (ATTN: Chief Surgeon)

Fighting Assignments of the 3rd Army

1) The Ardennes Counter Offensive
   3-28 January 1945

   Showing Third Army's efforts to chase the enemy eastward to the Aar River.

2) The Saar-Moselle Triangle
   13 January - 1 March 1945

   This piece of real estate was held by the Germans until the Bulge could be pushed back and the German Eifel to the north could be taken. Trier was about 25 miles from Luxembourg City. Some of our outpost could watch Germans in this area from the hills west of the Moselle.

3) The Drive To Pruem
   3-10 February 1945

   Once across the Aar River, the next obstacle was the western Wall, also known as the Sigfried Line. This map shows how the Wall was penetrated and the key city of Pruem was captured. This part of Germany is known as the Eifel because of its high hills and steep valleys, much as the Ardennes of Luxembourg and Belgium.

4) Clearing of the Viaden Bulge and the Capture of Bittburg
   6-8 February 1945

   Having captured Pruem, the Third Army swung to the south, Bittburg being the next most important crossroads. Viaden had proved to be an especially difficult part of the western wall to break through, thus it was accomplished from the back side. The Third Army could move south to aid in the Saar Moselle Triangle battle.

5) Operation Lumberjack
   1-7 March 1945

   This was the name given to the First and Third Armies sweeping east out of the Eifel to the Rhine River, basically from a northern attack eastward to Reniggen and the Moselle River to the south.

6) The Saar-Palatinate Triangle
   12-21 March 1945

   With great success in the lumberjack operation, the Third Army crossed the Moselle to the southeast of the Saar-Moselle Triangle. The area was to be taken by the U.S. Seventh Army, but it had met stiff resistance breaking through the Sigfried Line to the south. Thus, Patton's Third Army cut in behind the lines and shut off the Germans' supply to both the Saar-Moselle Triangle and enemy in the Harrdot Mountains.

7) The Rhine River Crossings in the South
   22-28 March 1945

   The first crossing of the Rhine was at Oppenheim, a relatively easy budgehead. The ones downstream, where the 565th took up defense in late March, were more difficult, not so much because of enemy action, but rather the swiftness of the Rhine at this point. No bridges existed between Manz and Koblenz. Thus, the Third Army engineer had to build floating bridges of one kind or another. Other assaults were made by Army and Naval landing craft. In late March, we took up position east and west of the Rhine with field artillery units. Later we were assigned to air defense of bridges at Boppard and Lorch.

8) Drive to the Elbe
   4-24 April 1945

   On March 10th, part of the 565th AAA was sent to Eisenach and the succeeding days to Erfurt and Weimar, the latter the site of the infamous Buchenwald concentration camp. Our S-3 had sent reconnaissance into Chemnitz only to find upon return we were to head south toward Hamburg. The Elbe River was the predesignated meeting spot of the American and Russian armies. While that was true to a degree, later arguments allowed them as far west as Gena, and postwar boundaries lay south of Weimar and Eisenach as well.

9) Into Austria and Czechoslovakia
   24 April - 8 May 1945

   This map traces the movements of the Third Army as well as the 565th AAA. Here the lettered batteries were often spread far and wide, ranging from Nurnburg to Munich to Passau. HQ and B Batteries ended command in Straubing. Later we all returned to Sheinfelt and Schwartzenburg Castle, also known as Julius Stricker Castle, and later to Forchheim. We began leaving Germany for Rowan, France on July 10th.

Commendations

HEADQUARTERS
THIRD UNITED STATES ARMY
APO 403

AG330.13 GNMCL   30 March 1945

SUBJECT: Commendation.

TO   : Commanding General, 38th Antiaircraft Artillery Brigade, APO 403, U.S. Army.

The following listed units are commended for their outstanding performance of duty during the period 16 March to 25 March 1945:

    38th Antiaircraft Artillery Brigade
     7th Antiaircraft Artillery Group
    24th Antiaircraft Artillery Group
    207th Antiaircraft Artillery Group
    119th Antiaircraft Artillery Gun Battalion
    120th Antiaircraft Artillery Gun Battalion
    129th Antiaircraft Artillery Gun Battalion
    217th Antiaircraft Artillery Gun Battalion
    411th Antiaircraft Artillery Gun Battalion
    456th Antiaircraft Artillery Automatic Weapons Battalion (M)
    <u>565th Antiaircraft Artillery Automatic Weapons Battalion (M)</u>
    567th Antiaircraft Artillery Automatic Weapons Battalion (M)
    599th Antiaircraft Artillery Automatic Weapons Battalion (M)

In addition to their primary, twenty-four-hour-per-day mission of furnishing antiaircraft protection for critical Third U.S. Army installations, these units hauled vitally needed gasoline and personnel reinforcements to forward armored and infantry elements during the critical period of operations when the Army swept to the Rhine River. On return trips many enemy prisoners of war were transported to rear areas. The skillful manner in which these missions were coordinated with frequent moves of antiaircraft units and the promptness with which they were accomplished, often under difficult conditions plus the enthusiasm and loyal, untiring devotion to duty of all officers and men, contributed materially to the success of Third U.S. Army operations and are in keeping with the highest traditions of the service.

                                                                        s/ G. S. Patton, Jr.
                                                                        t/ G. S. PATTON, JR.,
                                                                        Lieut. General, U.S. Army, Commanding

REPRODUCED, Hq 565th AAA AWBn.,
               6 April 1945
                       R.S.W.

<u>DISTRIBUTION:</u>
    20 Ea Btry
     5 Hq Btry
     1 File

Unit History

HEADQUARTERS
565th Antiaircraft Artillery Automatic Weapons Battalion
APO 562
UNITED STATES ARMY

317.7 6 October 1945
SUBJECT: Unit History, 1945.

TO : The Adjutant General, War Department, Washington, 25 D.C.

1. Under the provisions of Par 11b and AR. 345-105, dated 18 November 1929 as amended, the history of the 565th Antiaircraft Artillery Automatic Weapons Battalion (Mobile) is submitted for the period 1 January 1945 - 6 October 1945.
    a. Original Unit: No change.
    b. Change in Organization: No change.
    c. Strength, commissioned, and enlisted of this organization by month was as follows:

   (1) At beginning of period: 35 0; 3 WC; 732 EM
   (2) Net increase each month:

	Officers	Warrant Officers	EM
(a) January 1945	0	0	0
(b) 28 February 1945	0	0	14
(c) 31 March 1945	1	0	5
(d) 30 April 1945	1	0	0
(e) 31 May 1945	0	0	11
(f) 30 Jun 1945	0	0	11
(g) 31 Jul 1945	0	0	0
(h) 31 Aug 1945	0	0	0
(i) 30 Sep 1945	0	0	0

   (3) Net decrease each month:

(a) 31 January 1945	1	0	5
(b) 28 February 1945	1	0	0
(c) 31 March 1945	0	0	0
(d) 30 April 1945	0	0	15
(e) 31 May 1945	1	1	C
(f) 30 June 1945	3	0	0
(g) 31 July 1945	6	1	73
(h) 31 August 1945	3	0	17
(i) 30 September 1945	13	0	11

   (4) At end of period   9 0; 1 WO; 656 EM 4 Oct 45

    d. Stations, permanent and temporary of unit.

   (1) Battalion CP, with Batteries A and D located in and around Luxembourg City, Luxembourg providing AA protection for 19th Army Group and Third US Army Headquarters from 1 January 1945 to 26 February 1945. Battery B provided AA defense for Airstrip A-97, located N.E. of Luxembourg City, and Battery C provided AA defense for Radio Luxembourg during the same period. During the period the Battalion was attached to the 16th AAA Group and the 207th AAA Group.
   (2) During the period 28-30 March various units were attached to field artillery units on both sides of the Rhine River. The Battalion CP was located at Hausby, Germany.
   (3) On 31 March the Battalion under the 7th AAA Group set up AA defense of a pontoon bridge in the vicinity of Boppard, Germany on the Rhine River.
   (4) On 5 April the Battalion moved to the vicinity of Lerch, Germany to provide AA protection of river crossings.
   (5) Headquarters Battery, Batteries B and C were attached to the 112th AAA Group XX Corps on 10 April 1945. Battery B provided AA defense for airstrip at Lancensalya and Weimer, Germany during the period 10-17 April. Battery C furnished AA defense for airstrips near Weingenlupnitz and Weimer, Germany during the period 10-17 April 1945. Batteries A and D were attached to the 16th AAA Group and put under operational control of 635th AAA AW Bn providing AA defense of Airstrip 4-74 in the vicinity of Schwalbach during the period 13 April to 19 April 1945.
   (6) During the period 17-26 April when the XX Corps turned and headed to the south with Third Army, Batteries B and C provided AA defense for ASPs and Class III DP in and around Nurnberg. Batteries A and D continued under operation control of 635th AAA AW Bn in the III Corps Area until about 17 April when these batteries provided AA defense for the MSR in VIII Corps Area.

(7) Batteries B and C provided AA defense for pontoon bridges in the 71st and 65th Infantry Division sectors, respectively, on the Danube River from 26-30 April 1945. The battalion CP was located at Hemau during the operation. Batteries A and D remained attached to 16th AAA Group under VIII Corps.

(8) From 1-4 May 1945, Batteries B and C provided AA defense for river crossings on the Isar River, and AA defense for an airstrip at Straubing, Germany. The Battalion CP was located at Straubing during this period.

(9) On 4 May the Battalion was relieved of its tactical assignment and moved to Schwarzenberg, Germany to provide security guard on various bridges, roads, and lines of communications.

(10) On 24 May 1945 the Battalion moved to Forchheim, Germany and assumed control of the western part of Forchheir, Krois.

(11) The Battalion was relieved of assignment in Forchheim on 8 July 1945 and proceeded by motor convoy thru Aschaffensberg, Germany; Trier, Germany, Soissons, France; to Rouen, France, arriving there on 11 July 1945.

(12) Departed Rouen for duty at Antwerp, Belgium on 15 August 1945 to be assigned to 13th Port with station at Luchtbel Barracks, Antwerp, Belgium.

(13) Battalion CP moved to Camp Top Hat on 20 September 1945.

e. None.

f. No Change

g. Campaigns:

(1) Ardennes Campaign from 22 Dec 44 to 25 Jan 45.

(2) Rhineland Campaign from 22 Dec 44 to 21 Mar 45.

(3) Central European Campaign from 22 Mar 45 to 11 May 45.

h. No Change

i. Losses in action; officers and men.

(1) Ardennes Campaign. 2d Lt Dale E. Nelson 01057551, Battery D wounded in action on 4 January 1945 at Luxembourg City.

(2) Central European Campaign; Pfc Ernest C Tilton 31453975 Btry C died of injuries on 29 Apr 45 near Stadtamhof, Germany.

(3) CMO Guy F Boyle W2113935 slightly wounded in action on 3 May 45 and taken by the enemy. Later released to U.S. Forces.

(4) T Sgt Luther P Sheldon 33222760 Hq Btry, and Cpl Harris F Dake 32941117 Hq Btry reported missing in action on 3 May 45 and later found to have been captured by the enemy and released to U.S. Forces.

(5) Pfc Frank CR Orlandella 31424936 Btry A accidentally shot in Pilsen, Czechoslovakia on 26 Jun 45 and died of wounds.

j. Negative

k. Negative

l. The 565th AAA AWBn (M) is inactivating 6 October 1945 per Ltr Hq TGFET AC 322-GCT-ACO 21 Sep 45 Subj: Organization Order No 112 and War Department Cable 4096, 12 Sep 45.

                                              CALVIN M. PENTECOST
                                              Major CAC
                                              Commanding

Medical Reports

MEDICAL DETACHMENT

565th Antiaircraft Artillery Automatic Weapons Battalion
APO 403
UNITED STATES ARMY

319.1   10 Apr. 43 - 30 June 45   30 June 1945

To: The Surgeon General, War Department, Washington, D.C. (Thru Commanding Officer, 16th AAA Group)

      In compliance with circular 58, Headquarters, European Theater of Operations, APO 887, 14 May 1945, Subject: "Period Reports, Medical Department Activities," the semi-annual report of the Medical Detachment, 565th Antiaircraft Artillery Automatic Weapons Battalion is submitted.

      1. On 10 April 1943 the 565th Coast Artillery Battalion (Antiaircraft) (Automatic Weapons) with authorized Medical Detachment was activated with Harry D. Schell, 0 411 233, 1st Lt., MC, as Battalion Surgeon, Murray M. Franklin, 0 487 857, 1st Lt., DC, as Battalion Dentist, and with a cadre of three (3) enlisted men. Training as directed under provisions of MTP 8-1 was begun 20 May 1943 and was subsequently completed in twenty-two (22) weeks. This detachment participated in Maneuvers on the Camp Stewart Reservation where the principles of treatment and evacuation of casualties were discussed, demonstrated, and practiced. This unit left Camp Stewart, Georgia, 13 November 1943 by motor convoy and proceeded to the Tennessee Maneuver Area. There the procedures of treatment and evacuation were practiced on simulated casualties. On 17 January 1944, this organization departed from the Tennessee Maneuver Area and arrived at Camp Stewart, Georgia, 19 January 1944. An eight (8) weeks course of refresher training as prescribed by headquarters Antiaircraft Artillery Training Center, Camp Stewart, Georgia, was begun shortly after the return of this unit to this training center. On 30 September 1944 this unit entrained at Camp Stewart, Georgia, for the staging area Camp Kilmer, New Brunswick, New Jersey. On 5 October 1944 this unit entrained for the Port of Embarkation and debarked at Plymouth, England 18 October 1944. The organization left England 7 December 1944 and arrived at Le Havre, France 15 December 1944.

      2. The 565th Antiaircraft Artillery Automatic Weapons Battalion was in active combat 140 days from 20 December 1944 to 8 May 1945. The mission of the Medical Detachment consisted of administering first aid, evacuating casualties, and supervision of field sanitation. The Detachment is composed of three (3) officers and seventeen (17) enlisted men. Since 16 April 1945 we have operated with sixteen (16) enlisted men without lessening our efficiency or causing undue hardship.

      3. The battalion aid station was included in the battalion command post which was usually set up in a building. When tents were used, the aid station was set up in the detachment command post tent. The following personnel comprised the aid station group: Battalion Surgeon, Battalion Dental Surgeon, Medical Administrative Officer, and nine (9) enlisted men. Two (2) medical aid men were attached to each of the four (4) line batteries. They were attached for rations, quarters, and supplies.

      4. The duties performed by each member of the Medical Detachment were as follows:

          a. Battalion Surgeon: Held daily sick call at battalion and battery command posts, made frequent sanitary inspections, and served as a member of the Battalion Special Court Martial.

          b. Battalion Dental Surgeon: Performed all dental work, including a complete dental survey of the battalion; accomplished all prosthetic work in nearby dental laboratories; served as Officer's Finance Agent, and later as Battalion Finance Agent.

          c. Medical Administrative Officer: Served as assistant Battalion Surgeon by making sanitary inspections, acting as Detachment Supply Officer, supervising all clerical work of the detachment, and by compounding various pharmaceutical preparations in the aid station. He also served as Battalion Fire Marshall, Battalion Special Service Officer, and Assistant Defense Council on the Battalion Special Court Martial.

          d. S/Sgt.: Worked in the battalion aid station as assistant to the Battalion Surgeon and actively supervised work of all enlisted personnel.

          e. Tec 3: Served as detachment supply sergeant; served as assistant to the Battalion Surgeon; and taught classes in first aid to gun section aid men.

          f. Tec 3: Did all detachment clerical work; did all clerical work for the Battalion Special Service Officer; assisted the Battalion Surgeon in the aid station.

          g. Tec 4 (2): each served as a battery aid man.

          h. Cpl.: Served as assistant to the Battalion Surgeon and acted as assistant truck driver.

i. Tech 5 Surgical (3): Two of these men served as battery aid men and one served as first aid men in the battalion aid station.

j. Tec 5 Dental Assistant: Served as assistant to the Battalion Dental Surgeon and as first aid man in the battalion aid station.

k. Tec 5 Truck Driver: Drove 2-1/2 ton truck and served as first aid man in the battalion aid station.

l. Tech 5 Medical: Served as a battery aid man.

m. PFC (3): Served as battery aid man.

n. PFC: Drove 1/4 ton truck and served as first aid man in the battalion aid station.

o. PFC: Hospitalized for Combat Exhaustion on 16 April 1945.

History of the 565th AAA A/W BN

History of the 565th AAA A/W BN
By Colonel Edward D. Younis

1. Date of organization - 10 April, 1943 - As the 565th Coast Artillery Battalion (Antiaircraft), initial activation was the 123rd Provisional Automatic Weapons BN-per Special Orders 38, dated 26 February, 1943, Headquarters AAA Command, Richmond, Virginia. Reorganized and redesignated 565th AAA A/W BN (MBL) 27 May, 1943.

2. Place of organization - Camp Stewart, Georgia, under command of Lt. Col. Frank Courtenay, with Major Anthony R. Bayer as Executive Officer.

Headquarters Battery	Captain Griffin
Battery "A"	Captain Collier
Battery "B"	Captain Chapman
Battery "C"	Captain Bowron
Battery "D"	Captain Nesbitt

3. Training began in May, 1943 for a 16-week cycle.

4. November 1943, moved to the 2nd Army Maneuver Area (Tennessee), participated until 17 January, 1944, returned to Camp Stewart for further training and restructuring.

5. September 30, 1944, departed Camp Stewart for Camp Kilmer, New Jersey, boarded transport, USAT Cristobal for overseas duty, arrived Plymouth, England, 16 October, 1944, then to Midlands for training, departed 7 December, 1944 for Camp Hursley, then to Rouen, France.

6. 20 December, 1944, departed for combat assignment.

7. Participated in three major campaigns: Ardennes, Rhineland, and Central Europe.

8. Departed Germany, 8 July, 1945 for Rouen, France.

9. Departed France, 15 August, 1945 for Belgium and varied duties, assigned 13th Port, Luchtbal Barracks, Antwerp.

10. Deactivated 6 October, 1945.

BATTALION COMMANDERS

1. Courtenay	April 1943 to December 1943
2. Bayer	December 1943 to January 1944
3. Santilli	January 1944 to August 1944
4. Yarnall	August 1944 to July 1945
5. Pentecost	July 1945 to October 1945

Overseas- 6 October, 1944
Deactivated- 6 October, 1945

Ten Days in April, Twelve Days in May

Harris F. Dake's account of his capture and internment by the Germans in April and May of 1945

At the request of Secretary George Harber, I submit the following account of my capture and internment by the Germans in April and May of 1945.

It must be realized that at the age of 21, and in combat, we put little or no importance on keeping any record of our experiences. It is only later in our lives that unit histories and family records come to the limelight. It is only then that any fragment of note or memory is seized upon as the desert traveler searches for the water in the oasis. Fortunately, I was able to obtain a "Merkbuch" and pencil while prisoner and did make a few notes, not so much of historical value but of human interest.

My story begins with the southward movement of the 20th Corps, to which we were attached, the 19th of April, 1945. We moved to a position 25 miles east of Bamberg, Germany and were in the process of locating gun positions and OP's when the use of my jeep and myself were requested by Colonel Yarnall. We were to go to Chemnitz to attend an investigation of an incident in which we were to have shot down one of our own aircraft (a P-51 Mustang) resulting in the death of a U.S.A.F. colonel. I only know this because I was on the site minutes after the pilot crashed (after releasing his bombs) upside down into the side of a hill. He was beheaded in the crash. All other information pertaining to this Chemnitz meeting was contained in a brief carried by Warrant Officer Guy F. Boyle and his assistant T/Sgt. Luther Sheldon. This information was placed in the glove compartment of my jeep for the trip. I would love to read the official report of that incident!

We departed the CP area on the morning of the 21st of April with enough gas and rations for three days. Our barracks bags and personal belongings were left at the CP, except for the things on our own person. Warrant Officer Boyle occupied the seat next to me and Sgt. Sheldon rode in the back. We followed a route from Hollfeld to the German Autobahn and thence north to Chemnitz.

It sounded simple and, since Col. Yarnall assured us that Chemnitz was in U.S. hands, we looked forward to a quiet and relaxing journey - might even be fun! (How ignorant of danger are we when young!) Our trip up the German "Super Highway" was uneventful except for the detouring of many bridge locations. There were few bridges left standing so we had to drive around or through whatever they were spanning - drove through water above the floorboards several times - thanks for the durable jeep! Late in the afternoon we took the exit off the Autobahn and headed for Chemnitz. After a few miles we encountered a group of Army engineers working on a small bridge about four miles from Chemnitz. We asked them if we would have any trouble getting into Chemnitz. The sergeant assured us it was held by U.S. forces - "no problem." We continued on our way in the direction of the city. By now it was late afternoon, pouring rain, and getting dark. I was kept very busy dodging the shell holes in the road and burned-out vehicles. Suddenly about 50 yards ahead I spotted, through our rain-spattered windshield, a pile of trees across the road. I slammed on the brakes and stopped about five feet short of the trees.

Oh! Oh! Road Block! Ambush! In a frantic effort to shift to "reverse" and turn around, I only got as far as "neutral" when all hell broke loose. Small arms fire and one large caliber shot. The next thing I knew I was on my knees on the pavement and bullets were flying everywhere. Sheldon and I dove for the side of the road - no ditch for protection! Lying there I could see the grooves being made by the bullets hitting the pavement. I shouted to Sheldon, "We gotta get up or we'll lie here 'til they hit us." He said, "I ain't moving." I had two choices; get up and hope they stopped firing or lie there and possibly be killed. I chose the former, stood up, raised my hands and walked straight up to a group of about 15 young boys and old men with rifles leveled at me from the underbrush.

While we were being taken into custody, a German soldier rushed up to me with a first aid kit already opened. It was only then that I realized I was bleeding from the nose and left shin. He dressed the wounds and let me continue. I thanked him by saying "danka." I was next accosted by a young soldier, who turned out to be a young blond girl, who took my billfold. She gave me the billfold back after fleecing through it thoroughly and taking what she wanted. After a brief search we were loaded back into our jeep (Sgt. Sheldon and I - we were not to see W.O. Boyle again) and driven to the German headquarters deep inside the city. It was only then that I noticed the hole in the metal part of the center of the dashboard, clean and neat, about a 37mm. No wonder we were blown out of the jeep! The streets of Chemnitz were an absolute mess - wires, wreckage and rubble everywhere. Even the building where we were taken was half demolished. (I learned later that Warrant Officer Boyle had been hit in the left shoulder blade, the bullet exiting the left shoulder. He was taken to a German hospital. He later was sent to a hospital in Belgium and recovered.)

We were questioned thoroughly, and separately, by a German officer who spoke perfect English. The only thing that sticks in my memory from the interrogation are these two questions: "How many tanks are in your unit?" and "When will you fight the Russians?" The latter question I thought to be very humorous at the time. A very few years later, it became apparent that the seriousness of that question was much better analyzed by the Germans than ourselves.

Late that night we were put into a small black panel truck with no windows and driven to a POW facility at Gera where we were among a great many other prisoners being separated by nationality and rank. We were only there one or two days and then transported to Linda. We were told that the Russians were too close so the prisoners were being moved. The greatest dread of the Germans was to be captured by the Russians. The second was to be outnumbered in tanks.

The "prison" at Linda was an old rural schoolhouse. We were housed in one small room (18 of us) with double decker bunks and loose straw for bedding and a small wood-burning stove in one corner. There was a door to the rest of the building at which a guard was posted and another door to an outside barbed-wire enclosure of very small proportion. This was to be our "home" for the duration.

It is strange how humor can seep into the darkest hours - but somehow the American G.I. always managed to make that an important part of his survival kit. I remember an incident with T/Sgt. Lowery (Mulberry, Florida) who was an 8th Air Force crewman shot down over Germany. He had only a pocket full of wheat for food for several days before he was captured. There was a farmhouse about 50 yards from our enclosure and he got the idea to strew a line of wheat from outside the barbed-wire fence to the doorway in an attempt to lure one of the roaming chickens to our boiling pot. He proceeded to do so, and sure enough he grabbed it just inside the door, wrung its neck, skinned it and hid the entrails underneath the straw of one of the bunks - all in a matter of seconds. It was the only time we had any meat to go with our boiled potatoes or turnips or half slice of black bread - this to be washed down with some very bland weed they called "tea." It was a joyous occasion!

It did not last long! We were awakened very early the next morning with a shrill blast from the guard's whistle. He shouted for us to line up and, thrusting his Luger in each of our faces separately, he demanded, "Who took the chicken?" "Where is the chicken?" We did not need to know German to know what he said! It seems the farmer's wife had come running to the guards' quarters screaming we had stolen her chicken. Anyway, no one gave an answer. I felt sure someone was going to be shot as an example. Instead the guard searched for the chicken, didn't find it and ran out the door extremely upset. It was then that fright turned to laughter and my pulse returned to normal.

We entertained ourselves as best we could by playing cards, talking about our families, our outfits, and our capture. We even were able to have a long talk with our guard and learned that he was a pilot who had been shot down and as a result had lost the use of the fingers of his right hand. It was a terrible shame because he had been a concert pianist before the war! One day we were asked to go out into the woods and carry logs in for firewood, but we were told that we could not be forced to do this because we were non-commissioned officers. But we were very happy to get a chance for a change of scenery and much needed exercise. Can you imagine a German guard "asking" earlier in the war!

About two days after we were at Linda, we were told that President Roosevelt had died. Of course no one believed it, and I did not know the truth until after we were again with U.S. military forces. Being on an OP at the time and separated from the rest of the battalion, this information never reached me.

Somewhere around the end of April we began to hear faint artillery fire or bombs. We were not sure which. But as each day went by, it came nearer and nearer, and by the 2nd or 3rd of May we began to hear small arms fire. The nervousness and uneasiness of our guards was very obvious. The end was near. They knew it and we knew it. We cheered every time the nearby guns spoke.

On the 4th of May, part of our group decided that they wanted to attempt an escape that night. The following is a list of those men who chose to escape, and their home address at the time:

Pvt. Raymond Gutierrez - 308 8th St., Gilroy, California
Pvt. Owen S. Steele - 848 N.W. 76th St., Miami, Florida
Sgt. Lloyd Lowery - Box 2565, Mulberry, Florida
Pvt. Leland L. Davis - 5834 Cedros Ave., Van Nuys, California
Pfc. Roy Lance - Route #1, Erwin, Tennessee
Pvt. Frank Pedati - 68 Oakland Ave., Jersey City, New Jersey

The rest of their episode appears later in this account.

The 8th of May! The war was over - but not for us! This turned out to be a very dangerous interlude. Our guards had disappeared and we were still in a Russian combat zone. We were on our own - not yet in contact with the Russians and about 18 miles from the American lines. We decided to head for the village of Linda. I don't think it was much more than a mile or two. We followed the edge of a wooded area passing no more than 20 or 30 yards in the rear of the last German defenses which were a few machine guns and the rest riflemen. As their magazines were emptied they turned and fled the oncoming Russians. We kept going, paying no heed to the flying bullets until we got to the center of the village. Not one soul around - white flags in all the windows. We wondered. To whom were they surrendering? We went up the street, where the ground was higher, to try to get a better view. Russian tanks had completely encircled the town! A Russian convoy was almost to the town. What a mishmash of transport - lend-lease Studebaker trucks (most with no tires), hand-pulled carts, bicycles and horses and wagons. It looked like they just drove their vehicles until they quit - no maintenance, no repairs - leave them where they die.

Ed Gavlik (Elizabeth City, New Hampshire, 6th Armored Division) liberated a Luger from one of the German soldiers (now dressed in civilian clothes) and hid it inside his shirt. The Russians came storming into town, firing their machine guns at anything and everything. I remember that two of our men ran across the street from the cafe, where we had sought refuge, and into a shoe store. They were going to get some new shoes! We heard the sputtering of a machine gun and they came flying out the door. It seemed a Russian soldier had the same idea but first he did his usual thing by spraying the ceiling with bullets. Our poor guys were upstairs!

The Russians came into the cafe, sprayed the interior with bullets, and proceeded to drink anything and everything in sight. I wondered how many of their casualties were the result of this type of activity! Fortunately for us Ed Gavlik could understand and speak Russian so he hit it off with a Russian major, and from then on our wish was his command. A civilian pointed out a Nazi sympathizer. The Russian major pulled him outside, knelt him down by the side of the road and put a bullet through the man's head. We were taken to a farmhouse where the major demanded food. When the farmer pleaded that he had none, he was tied to a chair and ordered to produce some or be shot! It took a lot of talking by Ed Gavlik to prevent this from happening. From there we went to another home and we and the Russians were treated to the best meal we had had in a very long time. I still wonder where the farmer got the food. Whatever the source, it sure was a feast!

The next morning we were treated to very thick and very hot oatmeal from a huge Russian Army outdoor kettle. Now it was time to think about getting back to the American lines, but where were they and how far? The decision was made to take the first highway that looked like it might be a main highway and head west.

No way did we want to be the guests of the Russians for months! (Thousands of freed POWs were put in stockades by Russians. Many were not returned to the U.S. military until many months after the war, and many others were shot trying to escape.) Anyway, Gavlik with his pistol rounded up enough bicycles for everyone and off we went. The highway was clogged with refugees making their weary way east. It was difficult trying to make any headway against this massive human tide. (Russian planes strafed the refugee columns with P-38 Lightnings.) A few of us were separated from the rest at times but all managed to get back together. After approximately 18 miles of this we spotted a jeep in the distance, approaching from a side road. As it got nearer we were able to see a U.S. Army major standing up and waving his arms. He stopped a few yards from us and ran to us and shook our hands, saying loud and clear, "Welcome back!"

We finally felt safe! We finally felt free! He led us back to his infantry CP where we identified ourselves and were given our first G.I. meal in quite some time. Because our stomachs were considerably shrunken, we ate very little, but we sure enjoyed it. We were even offered "a spot of tea" by a British Army unit across the road. We respectfully declined! "Where ya bee, mate? Guests of the Jerries?"

After about an hour we were loaded into a truck and driven to Gera (May 10) to a POW debriefing center. We answered many, many questions and signed our statements. We were separated from the many nationalities May 11, packed 50 to a truck, standing room only, bound for Weimar airport. Our long convoy was passing through a wooded area when a whole series of tremendous explosions occurred! The truck in front of us was knocked out and the driver killed. Some of the trucks were turned over. Many were injured. We pulled around the wreckage and continued on our way. We soon encountered an MP who said that they had just blown up an ammunition dump! Great timing! Arrived at Weimar Airport with no further ado.

On May 12, 1945, 11:50 a.m., we boarded C-47s, which had been used as paratroop planes, with just an aluminum shell for a seat. We joined in formations of nine aircraft and flew very low all the way to Le Havre. We had a bird's-eye view of the destruction wrought through the years of the war - a terrible reminder of hundreds of battles and bombings and loss of human life. One sees the terrible price of liberty and freedom. Will we continue to take them for granted as we did before this struggle? Is there some other lunatic waiting in the wings to test our mettle?

We landed at Le Havre at 1:30 p.m., whereupon we were again loaded on trucks and transported to Camp Lucky Strike, about 40 miles from Le Havre. This was one of the five RAMP (Recovered American Military Personnel) camps in the area. They were all named after cigarette brands. Here we were deloused, had our first shower in months, questioned again, reoriented, given new uniforms (clean clothes at last!) and put up in tents. Much to our chagrin, we were not going home for a while. The almost constant rain and dampness in our tents further lowered our morale. As it turned out, I was to spend the next 25 days in this environment. I contracted an infection in both feet, which I was not able to get rid of until many months after the war.

We were put on an exclusive diet of stewed chicken and eggnog to gain back our weight and recondition our digestive systems. Remember, most of these men had spent years as POWs and their stomachs were down to the size of a baseball! Reconditioning had to be done very carefully or serious medical problems or even death could result.

I do not remember all that we did to occupy those days, but I had noted in my "Merkbuch" three movies: "Bowery to Broadway" with Jack Oakie, Maria Montez, Donald O'Connor and Peggy Ryan; "Two Down and One To Go"; and "Destination Tokyo." It was a distasteful reminder that we were still at war with Japan.

There were still men fighting and dying to complete the task that was before us in 1941.

One of the most moving moments for me was when General Eisenhower toured our camp and stopped every so often to stand up in his jeep and welcome us back. He was answered with rousing cheers each time.

It must also be noted here that we learned that the six fellow prisoners who escaped from Linda on May 4 (we had advised them it was too near the end of the war to take such a chance) were all recaptured. Two were recaptured by the S.S., one by the Russians and three by the Germans. Those captured by the fanatic S.S. were severely beaten and one had an extremely rough time before he was released from a Russian stockade. As it turned out, three more days was all that they would have had to wait!

On June 5, one day short of the first anniversary of D-Day, we boarded the Navy transport Admiral William S. Benson, together with 5,012 liberated prisoners and 194 members of the 97th Infantry Division headquarters staff. The voyage back across the Atlantic was much smoother and much faster than the North Atlantic was in October 1944! Finally, on June 12, we entered New York harbor - nine ships and 16,845 troops.* We were welcomed by that great lady, the Statue of Liberty. There were no words to express one's feelings at that instant! As promised in the last line of my poem "Troopship," we had indeed "Come back this way again."

---

*Some of the units represented were the 1st, 4th and 45th Divisions, the 3rd Ranger Division, the 4th, 7th and 9th Armored Divisions and 8th Air Force.

Addendum:

Arrived home June 15, 1945 on a 60-day convalescence furlough.

Lake Placid, New York - two weeks orientation and reassignment.

Reassigned to Infantry School, Fort Benning, Georgia.

Promoted to sergeant.

Requested discharge from the Army Dec. 5, 1945; discharged Dec. 6, 1945; Became Regular Army - Dec. 6, reenlisted in the Air Corps - assigned to Mitchell Field, Long Island, New York as Chief of Records, Adjutant General's Office, Squadron A, 116th Army Air Forces Base Unit, 1st AF. Final task - setting up files for the newly formed Air Defense Command.

Dec. 19, 1946 - discharged at Mitchell Field, Long Island, New York.

Three years, five months, 14 days, service, Army Antiaircraft, Infantry and Army Air Force.

Since I Left the United States

By Chester L. Krause
Member of Headquarters Battery 565th Antiaircraft Battalion
Written in summer 1945
Edited in February 1989

On Oct. 6, 1944, we left Pier No. 17 in Staten Island, New York, headed for Plymouth, England. There were about 2,300 combat-bound troops aboard the steamship Christobal, a converted freighter. We couldn't stay on deck as the ship pulled away from the pier. The war was at its height then, and all troop movements were top secret. When we got out into the harbor, we were allowed back on deck.

Many of the fellows aboard had been at sea before, mostly between the United States and Panama. They were more than willing to tell us what the voyage would be like and how to take care of ourselves if the sea got the best of us. I remember one fellow in particular who boasted of previous voyages. As perhaps could be expected, he was one of those who suffered the most. He really rode the tops of the waves almost the whole trip.

The voyage took 10 days, and we were thankful that only two of them were foggy. We must have been in the North Atlantic then; our course usually changed nightly.

Our destroyer escort brought us to our destination safely. Plymouth, from which the famous Mayflower sailed, is located on the southern coast of Britain. We passed by Land's End, the strip of Britain that stretches into the ocean on its southeastern corner.

Our ship had to wait a day in the harbor before it could dock. We were unexpected guests or another vessel was at the pier we were to dock at. We again had to go below deck as a tug pulled us to the pier.

While disembarking, we got our first look at what bombing can do. The docks had been hit heavily.

A few hundred yards from the pier, a British train waited to carry us inland. It traveled north and arrived at Leek, England, on the 19th. Leek is a large city near the pottery center of the world, Stoke on Trent, County of Staffs. Camp Blackshawmoor was about three miles from here, and when we arrived, hot meals and hot showers were waiting for us.

The fun began about two days later. The training schedule called for a hike every day except Sunday. They were rugged, too; the country was hilly and the distance anywhere from eight to 10 miles.

On the 26th we were given a detail to send a hundred men to Portcawl, Wales, to prepare camps like ours for more troops coming from the States. It seemed, though, that we were just marking time. Our advance party was in France, and all our equipment was there, too. The days were long and dreary - typical English weather.

Then in early November our equipment began to come in. We started drawing trucks and guns. We were getting ready to go to the continent and give the Jerry planes a little hell. On Dec. 6 we began our move. We left Blackshawmoor and went to South Hampton, nearly 200 miles away.

At the marshaling areas, individual batteries were placed on different ships, probably to prevent a total loss if one ship were lost in the crossing. I crossed on the Charles M. Hall, riding anchor and eating C rations. Six days later we docked at Le Havre; some of the other ships landed at Rouen.

Le Havre was a level wreckage; American engineers built the docks. Port battalions were already operating there. Under their supervision, we again assembled as a battalion in a town called Pavilly, a short distance from Rouen. It was now Dec. 15, the day before Rundstedt began his offensive.

We stayed in Pavilly only four days, but what a four days! It rained all the time, and we had to sleep in pup tents.

Rundstedt was really pushing forward and was reported to be giving more and more strength to his offensive. The Battle of the Ardennes was on, and we were ready to move up. The front line was about 300 miles from us.

On Dec. 20 we moved 280 miles, stopping in Neidercorn, Luxembourg. Our advance party had left a day earlier and was already there. Our original destination was nearly in enemy hands and would be before we could get enough rest to get there. Rundstedt was really pouring it on.

The next day we moved into Luxembourg City and set up defense for several high Third Army headquarters there (we had been transferred from the First Army). C battery went seven miles northeast to the towers of Radio Luxembourg; infantry was only a half-mile from there. B Battery set up around an airstrip (now Luxembourg Airport); A and D in the city.

Headquarters were set up in an old hotel on Highway 3 near the railroad station, which later proved to be a bad spot. The weather was cold that night, but the action was hot. The half-tracks we were relieving were still in position and were keeping their barrels warm. Our guns weren't officially in action until the next day, but there were some nervous trigger fingers that night.

This was the first fire I'd been near since we left training camp, and now they were playing for keeps. I think I slept about four hours that night.

Despite what was going on, our jobs at headquarters could not be neglected. In fact, it was more important now than ever that we serve our batteries. Communications had to be set up - first radio, then wire. Rations, ammunition and other supplies had to be drawn. My job - in this vast army now all around me - was maintenance. We worked in a large, open shed right across the street from the battalion command post. Everybody also had to take his turn at guard duty. At night the snow would be blowing and the wind would be howling, and just before you were to be relieved, a warning would come to watch for paratroopers.

Being assigned to Luxembourg City was tough and getting to be heartbreaking. Mail was slow because we had moved and because of the enemy's offensive. Morale was getting lower every day, but we were becoming better soldiers.

On the 23rd, roads, ammunition dumps and railheads were strafed behind us. The following day I went to Esch, France, with a couple of other fellows to get some parts off wrecked trucks. While we were there, two ME-109s strafed a locomotive there and killed its engineer. This was the closest I had been to the enemy, as far as I knew.

On the 29th, enemy planes appeared in daylight and got a very warm reception. So did a couple of American fighters that came in after them. To their misfortune and ours, one was the victim of a direct hit.

Nights now were never silent; rocket shells dropped close and thick. One came within a few yards of Third Army headquarters. The primary targets, however, seemed to be the antiaircraft gun positions. On the 28th, an A Battery gun was knocked out by one of them.

The Germans were reported to be massing at Merch for an attempt to break through and head for the city. We were warned to be ready for a quick march order, and each section chief was shown where his gun was to take up defense.

This would have been a bad time for a move, if one had developed. It was really cold and the guns were frozen down.

On the night of Dec. 31, it was very cold. Railroad artillery was coming in now. One could almost set his watch by them - exactly five minutes apart.

I was on guard duty that night, and I can't remember ever being more afraid. The following night was the same thing. Civilians had reported paratroopers in civilian clothes in the city.

The following day wire communications to D Battery were broken but readily restored by the efficient communications section. One of them narrowly escaped sniper fire one day while tying a wire on a post.

On Jan. 3 the Germans tried to break through again, but this time they got fooled. The Third Army had moved up from the south and was able to cut them off so they couldn't return.

The war was beginning to turn our way now. The Bulge was proving to be a major mistake and would probably hasten the war's end. But there was, of course, much hard fighting still going on and much more ahead.

By mid-January, the Germans were in full retreat. The First and Third armies had been successful in stamping out Rundstedt's Ardennes offensive. We had seen American bombers overhead almost every day, and their work was beginning to show.

Third Army headquarters remained in Luxembourg City, and we were glad. We weren't the best of troops yet and needed to rest for a while.

We were now rear-echelon troops. Passes to go downtown - some even to Paris - were issued. Our trucks were being used to haul gasoline to the front.

January passed, and February was well on its way. All we had done was move our CP to uptown quarters. We were expecting march orders any day, and finally in March, the word came.

On the 28th of that month we moved to the Rhine River and became part of the 20th Corps. We were no longer with headquarters now; the batteries were attached to field artillery and were going up with the fast-moving front. We were ready to establish headquarters further up when orders came to recall our batteries and establish protection for a bridge at Boppard.

We were in Germany now and couldn't fraternize with civilians, which was hard on many of the boys after being in Luxembourg for so long. After only four or five days at Boppard, we moved to Lorch, where a pontoon bridge was being built. A and D batteries spent only one night there before moving to Frankfurt to guard an airstrip.

At Lorch the Rhineland wine got the best of a few fellows. It was free; all one had to do was pick it up.

We were set up in a school equipped with two 35mm movie projectors. We watched movies two nights in a row - all German of course. One dealt with the German youth movement.

The bridge project had to be abandoned because of the river's swiftness at Lorch, so we were to move up. But our section had several trucks that couldn't move, so we had to stay behind. The front was way up now, and the move was about a hundred miles. Our mission was to guard two airstrips.

Our section moved the next day, April 11, and it proved to be disastrous. Nightfall overtook us, and while on a detour off the Autobahn near Hersfeld, our trucks were strafed. Fortunately, nobody was hurt, although bullets hit the highway between the first and second vehicles.

It was a very dark night, and driving was difficult. Another fellow and I had been riding in the back of a wrecker when we relieved the drivers of another truck. About 10 minutes later, the wrecker ran off the road and overturned. One fellow was unhurt; another suffered a broken collarbone and internal injuries.

We were near our destination and it was almost morning, so it was light enough to see. We had to spend the day getting the wrecker back on its wheels and in shape for duty. This was the longest I went without sleep since in Europe - 37 hours.

Our stay here was short and darkened by the news of President Roosevelt's death. We were on a spearhead, and the fields we were protecting were being used by C-47s to land food and gasoline. Another field near Wiemar had been taken, and we were ordered to go there for the same type of assignment.

The move was made without excitement. We were billeted near the airport in former homes of Luftwaffe officers. While here we went to see the Buchenwald concentration camp. Many also went to see Ohrduff, although I never made it there. I will never forget the smell of death and horrible living conditions I witnessed at Buchenwald.

The Third Army turned south, and we were soon far behind them again. On the 19th we moved southward on Highway N-4, a main supply route. Again, darkness overtook us, and we were afraid of being strafed. Planes were heard overhead several times, but they must not have seen our convoy because no shots were fired.

We stopped at a small town north of Bamburg. The next day, B Battery left to guard an ammunition dump, and C Battery went on another assignment that has slipped my mind.

One of the sections in B Battery killed a Jerry that night as he tried to sneak up on them. His grave still marks that section's position.

On April 24 we moved to the outskirts of Nuremberg to be closer to our batteries. The second night we were there one of the fellows had an attack of appendicitis and was rushed to the hospital. This left us short two mechanics, which were badly needed.

The 20th Corps was driving southeasterly along the border with Czechoslovakia. Regensburg was the next big city to take, but the Danube River had to be crossed first. Once a bridge head was established on both sides, we were called there to relieve another outfit that was there for the crossing and had taken a hard rub.

Because of heavy traffic during this drive, we stopped at Hemau, a small town on Route 8 north of Regensburg. Here we stayed until the 29th, when we moved to Straubing, the last stop before turning back to assume duties as MPs.

On May 4 we arrived at Scheinfelt, a small town near Route 8 between Nuremberg and Wurzburg. We were quartered in a large castle formerly owned by Julius Stricker, noted Jew hater and head of the German youth movement. The castle was named "Schwartzenberg" after its former owner, a Czech prince.

Our stay there was short, and we were assigned duties as MPs and POW guards at Forchheim, a city south of Bamberg. At Forchheim many of the fellows who had been with us ever since we arrived in Europe were transferred. Some went to other AA units; others went to outfits where high-point men were getting ready to go home. We stayed in Forchheim until July 8.

We then moved to Rouen, France, and thought for sure we would be going home. But instead, we were assigned guard duty on an oil line. More fellows were transferred from our section, leaving only six of the original 12.

Now we are in Antwerp, Belgium, pulling guard duty on the docks here. We're all happy that the war is over and there is peace once more.

One Year Furlough

    Left Camp Stewart, Georgia Sept. 30, 1944. Arrived at Camp Kilmer New Jersey, 12 O'clock Oct. 1, 1944. Had a super PX, good chow, officers received combat shoes, the first we ever saw, but no passes. Left Camp Kilmer 2130 hours for New York, New York, and took a ferry across Hudson Bay to Staten Island. Up the plank at 0259 Oct. 6 at pier 17 on Staten Island.

    Out to sea at Oct. 6 on the U.S. Cristobal. The trip was quiet, the sea choppy, and our destination England. Landed at Plymouth, England Oct. 16, in the middle of the night, debarked Oct. 17 at 1715 hours, and boarded the train for Leek, England. Arrived at 0600 hours Oct. 19, and motored to Blackshawmoor, two miles out of Leek. Nov. 3, 1944, thirty-two sergeants went to Whem to G16 to unload equipment and to assemble guns. Shrewsbury was 12 miles away. Came back to Leek Nov. 19, 1944.

    Our training finished, we left Leek Dec. 7, 1944, and arrived at Hamesey, England at 0300; left there Dec. 9, and went to South Hampton, to board ship and load equipment. Equipment was loaded Dec. 10, and we boarded ship at 2100, set sail Dec. 11. Crossed channel in the middle of the night; bad night for sleeping. Dropped anchor at mouth of Siene River Dec. 12, ship being the Samuel B. Colt. Sailed up the Siene River Dec. 14, and arrived at Rouen, France at 1730. Debarked at 2000 hours, and equipment was unloaded at 0500 Dec. 15.

    Went to bivouac area at Pavilly, France Dec. 16, the rest of the battery motored here from Le Havre. Our home was pup tents, and our pastime making mud pies. Left our bivouac area at 0530 on Dec. 20, arrived at Deffinines, Luxembourg at 2100, moving in blackout. The battle of the Bulge is on. Artillery flashes could be seen and heard and rumors were flying thick and fast, our bed being the main street of town. Moved to Luxembourg city on Dec 21, our mission being the city with the first Army; enemy planes were over the first night. First snow the 22 of December. Dec. 23 transferred to Third Army as Patton takes command of the right flanks. Enemy planes made their usual call on Christmas Eve and Christmas day. New overshoes were our Christmas present. New Year's Eve - The field artillery wished Hitler a Happy New Year at midnight.

    Jan. 1, 1945 - Last day we fired the 40mm but were beginning to have trouble with the V-1 and the V-2. "Schnapps was the favorite drink." Jan. 15, - Germans were on the run, gun sections were inspected by General Hines, General Theile, and very often by our young West Point colonel. Feb. 25, - Rockets were just about kaput; some came close and some didn't; ask sections 45 and 43. March 28, - March order; at last the front is gone. Assigned to the field artillery on the 29, crossed the Rhine at St. Goar on Good Friday, relieved of field artillery mission April 1, and crossed the Rhine again to guard a pontoon bridge at Boppard. Dug in Easter Sunday. April 6, up the river to a pontoon bridge at Bacharach. April 9 - Frankfurt on-Main, a P-47 base. Red-Yellow, and blue no e P-47 were working overtime. April 11 - Bridge at Vacha. Infantry was still there. General "Ike," Patton and Bradley rode by this morning and didn't even stop for coffee. April 13 - moved to Dienstadt to protect a bridge. Infantry was there, tanks were up the road, and dead men were found. Captain Nesbitt didn't like a few things we'd done (motorcycles and gun pits). Captured our first prisoners here; before that we were killing them. April 16 - Moved to Ilemeau to protect MSR No. 4. Was a main supply route and road to the front as four divisions moved by during our short stay. While we were there, the enemy planes kept their dates, usually at night. Auto-Bahn was strafed that night. April 20 - "One day rest" - protect Third Army headquarters at Arlangen. April 21 - bridge at Schwaback, also L-5 landed in gun sections area. Couple of sergeants ran into three star general. April 23 - C-47 airstrip at Schwaback, landing gasoline and rations, all sections got beaucoup rations. April 27 - "TWO YEARS IN THE ARMY." Moved to protect bridge at Beilngriens, could still smell the Hienes. Had trouble with about sixty SS troopers when they still thought they were supermen. April 29 - Moved to Mainburg, sections lost all night over Germany, but finally made it across the Danube River. April 50 - Last mission at Freising, a pontoon bridge across the Isar river. Had a lovely six-day stay, and on May 2 we had a blanket of snow. May 4 - Patton can't even catch the Germans, and for us the war is finished; moved to Dorfen to assemble as a battery. Battery moved to Neaustadt to become SG. May 8 - V-E day. Battery was now SG and MP Detachment at Neaustadt. May 15 - No more SG and MP return to the battery. Captain was in the hospital. May 19 - Battery moved to Forchheim, Germany. Set up MP detachment with the city, and battery lived in castle in Heroldsback. Things were more like home and every one began to gain weight. July 1 - "HOW MANY POINTS" was the main topic, rumors began to fly fast and thick, "C B I (China, Burma, India) HERE WE COME." July 6 - High point men partee (French, meaning departed), Captain and officers were transferred, and news is out we are Le Havre bound. July 8 - "MARCH ORDER" Le Havre to the States, "YES OR NO," you guessed it, no. Pulled in Rouen, France July 11 to guard the American gas pipeline. Was our first real look at France and the French mademoiselles, and they both stink.

    The outfit was credited with 134 continuous days of combat and were awarded three bronze stars.

    Aug. 11 Once again march orders, destination Charlroi, Belgium as security guards at the world's largest Signal Depot. Plenty chow and recreation facilities.

Combat Locations

565TH AAA Battalion CP Combat Locations

Dec. 20, 1944 - This unit closed its CP RED HORSE ASSEMBLY AREA, with an overnight stop at Niterborn, Luxembourg and moved by motor convoy to LUXEMBOURG CITY. Units are assigned to THIRD UNITED STATES ARMY, and attached to 16TH ANTIAIRCRAFT ARTILLERY GROUP. CP opened Dec. 21, near railroad station in LUXEMBOURG CITY.

Feb. 26, 1945 - The Battalion CP moved to a new location on the east side of the same city.

March 29, 1945 - The Battalion CP closed LUXEMBOURG CITY and opened HAUSBAY. Germans were southwest of BOPPARD.

March 31, 1945 - The Battalion CP closed at HAUSBAY and opened at BOPPARD.

April 5, 1945 - The Battalion CP closed vicinity BOPPARD and opened at LORCH.

April 10, 1945 - The Battalion CP closed vicinity LORCH and opened vicinity GROBEN-BEHRINGEN April 11, 1945.

April 13, 1945 - The Battalion CP closed vicinity GROBEN-BEHRINGEN and opened vicinity WEIMAR.

April 18, 1945 - The Battalion CP closed WEIMAR and opened vicinity BREITENGUSSBACH near BAMBURG.

April 22, 1945 - The Battalion CP closed vicinity BREITENGUSSBACH and opened vicinity NURNBERG.

April 26, 1945 - The Battalion CP closed vicinity NURNBERG and opened vicinity HEMAU.

April 30, 1945 - The Battalion CP closed HEMAU and opened STRAUBING.

May 4, 1945 - The Battalion CP closed STRAUBING and opened SCHWARZENBERG.

May 19, 1945 - The Battalion CP moved to FORCHHEIM to an assembly area.

July 8, 1945 - The Battalion CP leaves for ROUEN, FRANCE.

July 11, 1945 - The Battalion CP arrive ROUEN, FRANCE.

August 15, 1945 - Departed for ANTWERP, BELGIUM.

Sept. 19, 1945 - Moved to Camp Top Hat, ANTWERP, BELGIUM.

Oct. 6, 1945 - Battalion inactivated. (All troops transferred by Sept. 30, 1945.)

565TH AAA BATTERY "A" COMBAT ASSIGNMENTS AND LOCATIONS

Dec. 22, 1941 - Battery "A" became operational at 12:00 noon, Coordinates 828134, in the western half of the CITY OF LUXEMBOURG in the Inner Artillery (IAZ) Zone 16, from Dec. 22, 1941 to March 29, 1945.

March 30-31, 1945 - Crossed RHINE RIVER via BOPPARD, GERMANY.

April 1-5, 1945 - RHINE RIVER vicinity BOPPARD.

April 5-10, 1945 - AIRFIELD Y74 vicinity SCHWALBACH.

April 10, 1945 - Attached to 16th AA Group and assigned to 635th AAA AW Bn for operational control. Defense of 578 FA and 663 FA vicinity of REHESTAT.

April 12, 1945 - 1st platoon assigned to defense of R3 Supply Airfield vicinity ROHENSSE. 2nd platoon assigned to AA mission for Cl III supply dumps.

April 17, 1945 - (Attached to 113th Group of the VIII Corps as of April 11.)

April 23, 1945 - Attached to 16th AAA Group for assignment at NEUSTADT.

April 24, 1945 - Defense of Airstrip R28 and Budge.

April 27-29, 1945 - No records received by The Battalion CP.

May 1-4, 1945 - GAIMERSHEIM attached to III CORPS for operations.

May 4, 1945 - Closed CP GAIMERSHEIM and opened vicinity SCHEINFELD, vicinity Bn Assembly Area.

May 4-7, 1945 - CP at Bn Assembly Area, SCHWARTZENBERG.

May 7, 1945 - CP closed at SCHWARTZENBERG and moved out a few miles. Security guard, traffic control, lines of communication, bridges.

May 7-9, 1945 - Moved headquarters.

May 19, 1945 - Assembled with battalion at FORCHEIM.

July 9, 1945 - Bn leaves for ROUEN, FRANCE.

Aug. 15, 1945 - Battery moves to HOLLAND.

565TH AAA BATTERY "B" COMBAT ASSIGNMENTS AND LOCATIONS

Dec. 22, 1944 - AIRSTRIP A-97 (LUXEMBOURG AIRPORT).

March 1-28, 1945 - AIRSTRIP A-97, East of RHINE RIVER.

March 29-31, 1945 - 1st Platoon: AW protection 578th, FA Bn vicinity; 2nd Platoon: AW protection VIII, CORPS, Airstrip, vicinity PANROD, GERMANY.

March 31, 1945 - AW defense of RHINE RIVER Crossings, vicinity BOPPARD, GERMANY.

April 1-3, 1945 - RHINE RIVER Crossings vicinity BOPPARD.

April 3-10, 1945 - RHINE RIVER Crossings vicinity LORCH.

April 10-13, 1945 - AIRFIELD R-2 vicinity LANCENSALZA.

April 13-17, 1945 - AIRFIELD vicinity WIEMAR.

April 19-26, 1945 - ASP No. 56 vicinity BAIERSDORF.

April 26-30, 1945 - 1st Platoon: Pontoon Bridge 71st Inf Sector. 2nd Platoon: Pontoon Bridge 71st Inf Sector.

May 1-4, 1945 - AAA AW Defense Airstrip R-68, vicinity STRAUBING.

May 1-3, 1945 - AAA AW Protection ISAR RIVER. 1st Platoon CP, Crossing 80th Inf Div. 2nd Platoon CP.

May 4, 1945 - Moved to SCHWARZENBERG (Sheinfeld).

May 4-7, 1945 - SCHWARZENBERG Bn Assembly Area.

May 9, 1945 - Moved out to guard bridges.

May 7-9, 1945 - Security patrol, guarding of bridges, traffic control, lines of communication, etc.

May 19, 1945 - Assembled with battalion at FORCHEIM.

July 8, 1945 - Bn Leaves for ROUEN, FRANCE.

July 11, 1945 - Arrives in ROUEN, FRANCE.

Aug. 15, 1945 - Battery plus "B" & "C" move to ANTWERP.

565TH AAA BATTERY "C" COMBAT ASSIGNMENTS & LOCATIONS

Dec. 22, 1944 to March 21, 1945 - RADIO LUXEMBOURG. Battery "C" is in an unrestricted area.

March 22-26, 1945 - RR bridge KONZ-KARTHAUS.

March 27-28, 1945 - Cl V Supply Dump, APACH, FRANCE.

March 28-31, 1945 - 1st platoon AW protection 277th FA Bn, RHINE RIVER.

April 1-3, 1945 - RHINE RIVER Crossings vicinity BOPPARD.

April 3-10, 1945 - RHINE RIVER Crossings vicinity LORCH.

April 10-13, 1945 - AIRFIELD R-1 vicinity WENIGENLUPNITZ

April 13-17, 1945 - AIRFIELD vicinity WEIMAR.

April 19-23, 1945 - Class III DP vicinity HOLLFELD.

April 23-24, 1945 - Class III DP vicinity LAUF.

April 24-26, 1945 - Decanning Area vicinity NURNBERG.

April 26-29, 1945 - 1st Platoon: Pontoon Bridge 65th Inf Sector. 2nd Platoon: Pontoon bridge 65th Inf Sector.

April 29-30, 1945 - 1st Platoon: AIRFIELD vicinity REGENSBURG. 2nd Platoon: Pontoon Bridge vicinity REGENSBURG.

May 3-7, 1945 - SCHWARZENBERG Bn Assembly Area.

May 7-9, 1945 - Security Guard, traffic control, guarding of bridges, lines of communication, etc.

May 1-3, 1945 - MAINBURG attached to III CORPS for operations.

May 4, 1945 - Moved to SCHWARZENBERG.

May 9, 1945 - Moved out to guard bridges.

May 19, 1945 - Moved to FORCHEIM with battalion.

July 8, 1945 - Bn leaves for ROUEN, FRANCE.

July 11, 1945 - Bn arrives in ROUEN, FRANCE.

Aug. 15, 1945 - Hq, "B" Btry and "E" Btry to ANTWERP.

565TH AAA BATTERY "D" COMBAT ASSIGNMENTS & LOCATIONS

Dec. 22, 1944 to March 28, 1945 - CITY OF LUXEMBOURG, Eastern Sector.

March 29, 1945 - 1st Platoon: AW protection 174th FA Bn vicinity HENOTHEL, GERMANY. 2nd Platoon: AW protection 578th FA Bn.

March 30, 1945 - 2nd Platoon: AW protection 578 FA Bn vicinity LEMBACH, GERMANY.

March 31, 1945 - AW protection RHINE RIVER Crossings vicinity BOPPARD, GERMANY.

April 1-5, 1945 - RHINE RIVER Crossings vicinity BOPPARD.

April 5-8, 1945 - RHINE RIVER Crossings vicinity LORCH.

April 8-13, 1945 - AIRFIELD Y-74 vicinity SCHWALBACH.

April 13, 1945 - Attached to 16th AAA Group and assigned to 635th AAA AW Bn for operational control.

April 14, 1945 - At TANNRODE.

April 15, 1945 - Relieved, reassigned.

April 17, 1945 - Relieved from mission and 635th reported to 207th Group. Relieved of attachment to 38th Brigade attached to new mission. VIII CORPS effective April 11, 1945.

April 21, 1945 - Relieved of mission. Attached to 7th AAA Group, assigned mission protecting 3A Hq at ERLANGEN.

April 23, 1945 - Relieved of defense of 3A Hq. Attached to 16th AAA Group. 2nd Platoon assigned mission of defense of bridge at REICHELSDORF. 1st Platoon assigned defense of III CORPS Hq in SCHWABACH, also "D" Btry Hq.

April 25, 1945 - 2nd Platoon relieved and reassigned to AIRSTRIP R42-T.

April 26, 1945 - 1st Platoon moved with III CORPS CP.

April 27, 1945 - 2nd Platoon relieved from Airstrip R42, moved to bridge near BECHNRIES.

April 29, 1945 - D CP opens at MAINBURG. 1st Platoon and Btry CP Moved with III CORPS Hq from BECHNRIES to MAINBURG.

April 30, 1945 - 2nd Platoon relieved and moved to assemble area.

May 2, 1945 - Battalion reassigned to 38 AAA Brigade.

May 3-4, 1945 - Moved into assembly at DORFEN.

May 4, 1945 - Closed DORFEN.

May 5, 1945 - SCHWARZENBERG Bn Assembly Area.

May 7-9, 1945 - Security guard, traffic control, guarding of bridges, lines of communication.

May 19, 1945 - Moved to FORCHEIM with battalion.

July 8, 1945 - Battalion leaves for ROUEN, FRANCE.

July 11, 1945 - Arrive in ROUEN, FRANCE.

Aug. 8, 1945 - Advance party leaves for COURCELLES, BELGIUM.

Aug. 10, 1945 - "D" Battery departs.

Oct. 6, 1945 - 565th inactivated and transferred to 556th AAA Bn.

```
                        ORDER OF BATTLE
                       565TH AAA Bn (AW)
```

Date	Brigade	Group	Army/Corps	Batteries
12/22/44	—	16AAA	3rd Army (CO Gen Hines)	Hq ABCD
1/1/45	—	207AAA	3rd Army	Hq ABCD
2/5/45	—	38AAA	—	—
3/30/45	—	—	—	—
4/1/45	—	7AAA (CO Col Dutton)	XX Corps	Hq ABCD
4/11/45	38AAA	112AAA	XX Corps	Hq BC
4/17/45	—	—	VIII Corps	AD
5/2/45	38AAA	—	3rd Army	Hq ABCD
5/10/45	16AAA	XII Corps	Hq ABCD	—
7/11/45	—	Chanor Base	—	Hq ABCD

The 565th Served Under the Following AAA Commands:

38 Brigade - Departed New York 7 Apr 44 for England; landed France 18 July 44. Crossed Luxembourg 8 Feb 45, entered Germany 27 Mar 45 and was inactivated 30 June 46.

16 AAA Group - Assaulted Omaha Beach in France 6 June 44. Crossed into Belgium 7 Sep 44. Crossed into Luxembourg 22 Oct 44. Defended Luxembourg City until return to Belgium 4 Feb. 45. Entered Germany 14 Feb 45 and returned to ZI and inactivated 11 Oct. 45.

207 AAA Group - Departed New York 11 Feb 44 and landed on Omaha Beach in France 9 June 44. Crossed into Luxembourg 4 Feb 45. Entered Germany 30 Mar 45 and inactivated 22 Dec 45.

112 AAA Group - Departed New York 17 Nov 43 and landed in France 20 Jul 44. Entered Germany 18 Mar 45, Austria 5 May 45 and inactivated 18 Oct 45.

113 AAA Group - Departed Boston 18 Jan 44 and landed in France 30 June 44. Crossed into Belgium 29 Sept 44 and into Luxembourg City 1 Oct 44. Returned to Belgium 18 Dec 44 and entered Germany 6 Mar 45. Inactivated 15 Nov 45.

7 AAA Group - Departed USA 21 Oct 43 and landed in France 27 Jul 44. Attached to 38th AAA Brigade and defended Nancy until 25 Jan 45. Crossed into Luxembourg 19 Mar 45. Entered Germany 29 Mar 45. Inactivated 17 Feb 46.

Germany

- ⭐ National Capital
- Bonn • City
- — International Boundary
- — Administrative District Boundary
- *Bayern* Administrative District Name

0 — Miles — 100

178

Baltic Sea

North Sea

NETHERLANDS

BELGIUM

LUX.

FRANCE

SWITZERLAND

AUSTRIA

CZECHOSLOVAKIA

POLAND

Schleswig-Holstein
- Kiel
- Rostock

Mecklenburg
- Schwerin

- Emden
- Bremerhaven
- Hamburg
- Bremen

Niedersachsen
- Hanover

- ⭐ Berlin
- Potsdam

Brandenburg

- Magdeburg

Saxony-Anhalt
- Halle
- Leipzig
- Dresden
- Chemnitz

Nordrhein-Westfalen
- Dusseldorf
- Koln
- Bonn ⭐
- Koblenz
- Boppard
- Echternach
- Waldesh
- Laurenburg
- Panrod
- Hennethol

Hessen
- Behringen
- Eisenach
- Erfurt
- Weimar
- Bad Berka

Thuringia
- Tannroda
- Suhl

- Trier
- St. Goar
- St. Goarshausen
- Lorch
- Schwalbach
- Rohensee
- Breitengussbach
- Simmern
- Hausbay
- Frankfurt
- Rehestad
- Hollfeld
- Bingen
- Wiesbaden
- Mainz
- Herrnsdorf
- Forchheim

- Apaeh

Rhineland-Pfalz

- Schwartzenburg Castle
- Scheinfeld
- Neustadt
- Erlangen
- Lauf
- Keinburg
- Nurnberg

Saarland
- Saarbrucken

- Stuttgart

Baden-Wurttemberg
- Freiburg

Bayern
- Hemau
- Regensburg
- Deming
- Ilkofen
- Straubing
- Manching
- Mainburg
- Gaimersheim
- Sulzbach
- Augsburg
- Munich
- Dorfen

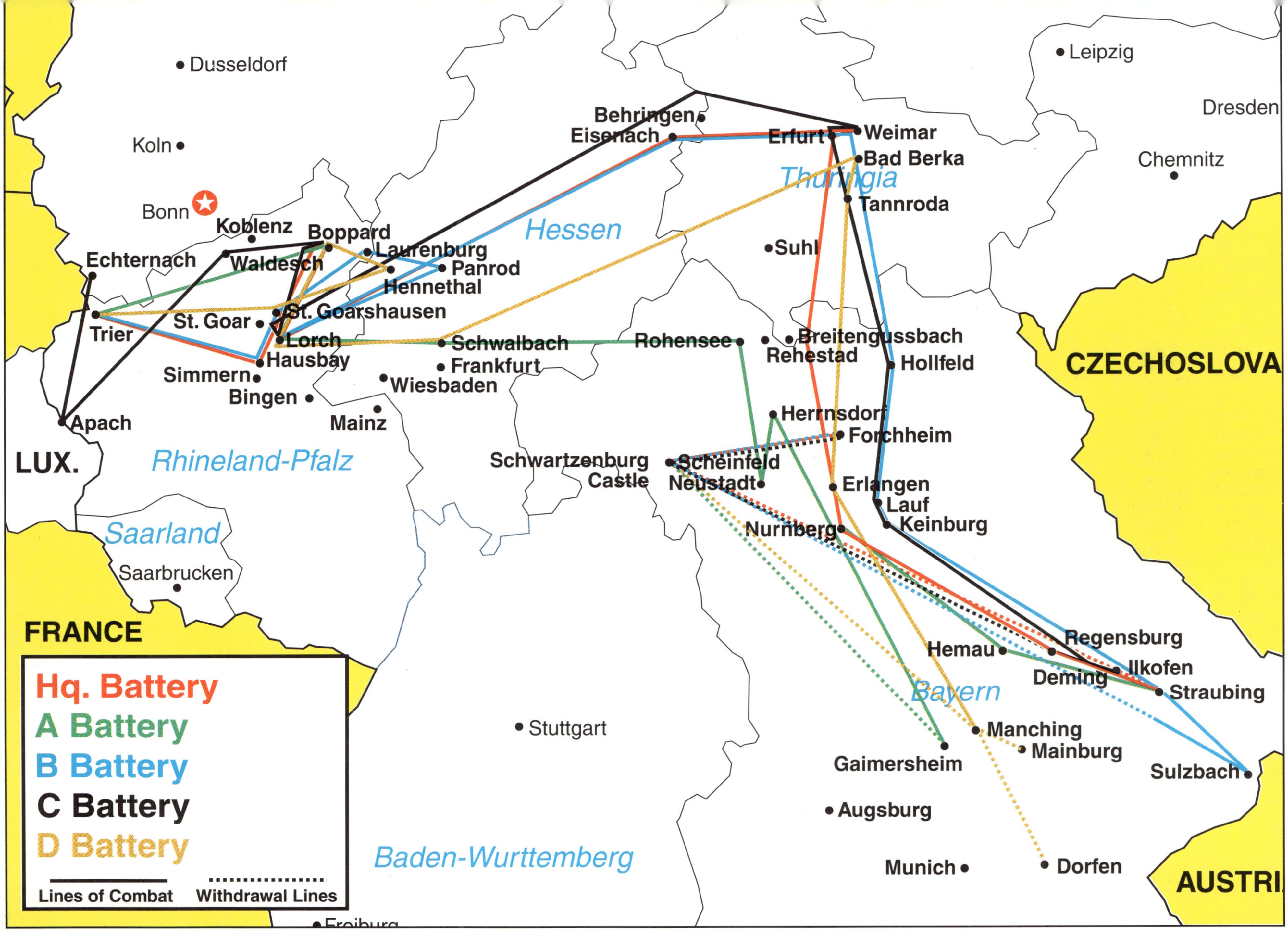
Dusseldorf
Koln
Bonn
Leipzig
Dresden
Chemnitz
Behringen
Eisenach
Erfurt
Weimar
Bad Berka
Thuringia
Tannroda
Suhl
Hessen
Koblenz
Boppard
Laurenburg
Panrod
Hennethal
Echternach
Waldesch
St. Goarshausen
St. Goar
Trier
Lorch
Schwalbach
Rohensee
Breitengussbach
Rehestad
Hollfeld
CZECHOSLOVA
Hausbay
Simmern
Frankfurt
Wiesbaden
Bingen
Mainz
Apach
Herrnsdorf
Forchheim
LUX.
Rhineland-Pfalz
Schwartzenburg Castle
Scheinfeld
Neustadt
Erlangen
Lauf
Keinburg
Nurnberg
Saarland
Saarbrucken
FRANCE
Regensburg
Hemau
Ilkofen
Deming
Straubing
Bayern
Stuttgart
Manching
Mainburg
Gaimersheim
Sulzbach
Augsburg
Munich
Dorfen
AUSTRI
Baden-Wurttemberg
Freiburg
Hq. Battery
A Battery
B Battery
C Battery
D Battery
Lines of Combat
Withdrawal Lines

Basic Military Map Symbols*

Symbols within a rectangle indicate a military unit, within a triangle an observation post, and within a circle a supply point.

Military Units - Identification

Antiaircraft Artillery	⟨triangle in rectangle⟩
Armored Command	⟨ellipse in rectangle⟩
Army Air Forces	⟨∞ in rectangle⟩
Artillery, except Antiaircraft and Coast Artillery	⟨dot in rectangle⟩
Cavalry, Horse	⟨diagonal line in rectangle⟩
Cavalry, Mechanized	⟨diagonal line with ellipse in rectangle⟩
Chemical Warfare Service	⟨G in rectangle⟩
Coast Artillery	⟨diamond in rectangle⟩
Engineers	⟨E in rectangle⟩
Infantry	⟨X in rectangle⟩
Medical Corps	⟨cross in rectangle⟩
Ordnance Department	⟨bomb in rectangle⟩
Quartermaster Corps	⟨Q in rectangle⟩
Signal Corps	⟨S in rectangle⟩
Tank Destroyer	⟨TD in rectangle⟩
Transportation Corps	⟨wheel in rectangle⟩
Veterinary Corps	⟨V-shape in rectangle⟩

Airborne units are designated by combining a gull wing symbol with the arm or service symbol:

Airborne Artillery	⟨dot with gull wing in rectangle⟩
Airborne Infantry	⟨X with gull wing in rectangle⟩

SIZE SYMBOLS

The following symbols placed either in boundary lines or above the rectangle, triangle, or circle enclosing the identifying arm or service symbol indicate the size of military organization:

Squad	•
Section	• •
Platoon	• • •
Company, troop, battery, Air Force flight	I
Battalion, cavalry squadron, or Air Force squadron	I I
Regiment or group; combat team (with abbreviation CT following identifying numeral)	I I I
Brigade, Combat Command of Armored Division, or Air Force Wing	X
Division or Command of an Air Force	XX
Corps or Air Force	XXX
Army	XXXX
Group of Armies	XXXXX

EXAMPLES

The letter or number to the left of the symbol indicates the unit designation; that to the right, the designation of the parent unit to which it belongs. Letters or numbers above or below boundary lines designate the units separated by the lines:

Company A, 137th Infantry	A ⊠ 137
8th Field Artillery Battalion	[•] 8
Combat Command A, 1st armored Division	A [⬭] 1
Observation Post, 23rd Infantry	△ 23
Command Post, 5th Infantry Division	⊠ 5
Boundary between 137th and 138th Infantry	137 —III— 138

WEAPONS

Machine gun	•→
Gun	●
Gun battery	⊔⊔⊔
Howitzer or Mortar	◆
Tank	◇
Self-propelled gun	●▷

Conclusion

It should be noted that I did not stay with the 565th until the very end; in fact, I am not familiar with anyone who did.

I left the 565th with a group of a dozen enlisted men from the 565th from Camp Top Hat and was transferred to the 563rd Antiaircraft Unit, which was in Camp Stewart, Georgia during our basic training period. I became the "B" Battery motor sergeant and stayed there for a period of two or three months before being transferred to Charleroi, Belgium, and I was in the motorpool with company "B" of the 769th MP Battalion as a mechanic. It was that unit with which I came home. As I recall, that wasn't an entire battalion, but rather a company and other mixed troops. We came back through Camp Top Hat, the same camp we had been members of for a short period of time. I came back on a liberty ship, the Frances A. Walker. The 769th left Antwerp in mid-January, arriving back in New York in late January. I got my discharge in early February.

The North Atlantic certainly was a rough piece of water, and those little liberty ships were certainly not the Queen Mary as far as comfort was concerned.

I do know that "D" Battery stayed on in Courcelles, Belgium. As a matter of fact, some had 565th AAA written on their discharges. Some of "B" Battery was also transferred with them. They became part of the 556th AAA Battalion. They operated there, doing the same thing as the 565th. They returned on the USS Wheaton.

Bibliography

Eisenhower At War 1943-1945, by David Eisenhower

A Soldier's Story, by Omar N. Bradley

Patton, A Study In Command, by H. Essame

The Memoirs Of Field Marshall Montgomery, An Autobiography

The Order Of Battle, US Army WWII, by Shelby L. Stanton

The War As I Knew It, by George S. Patton

1943 - The Victory That Never Was, by John Grigg

ETO - The Last Offensive, by Charles B. Andersen

Battle, The Story Of The Bulge, by John Toland

The Battle Of The Bulge - Then & Now, by Jean Paul Pollerd

Lucky Forward, by Col. Robert S. Allen

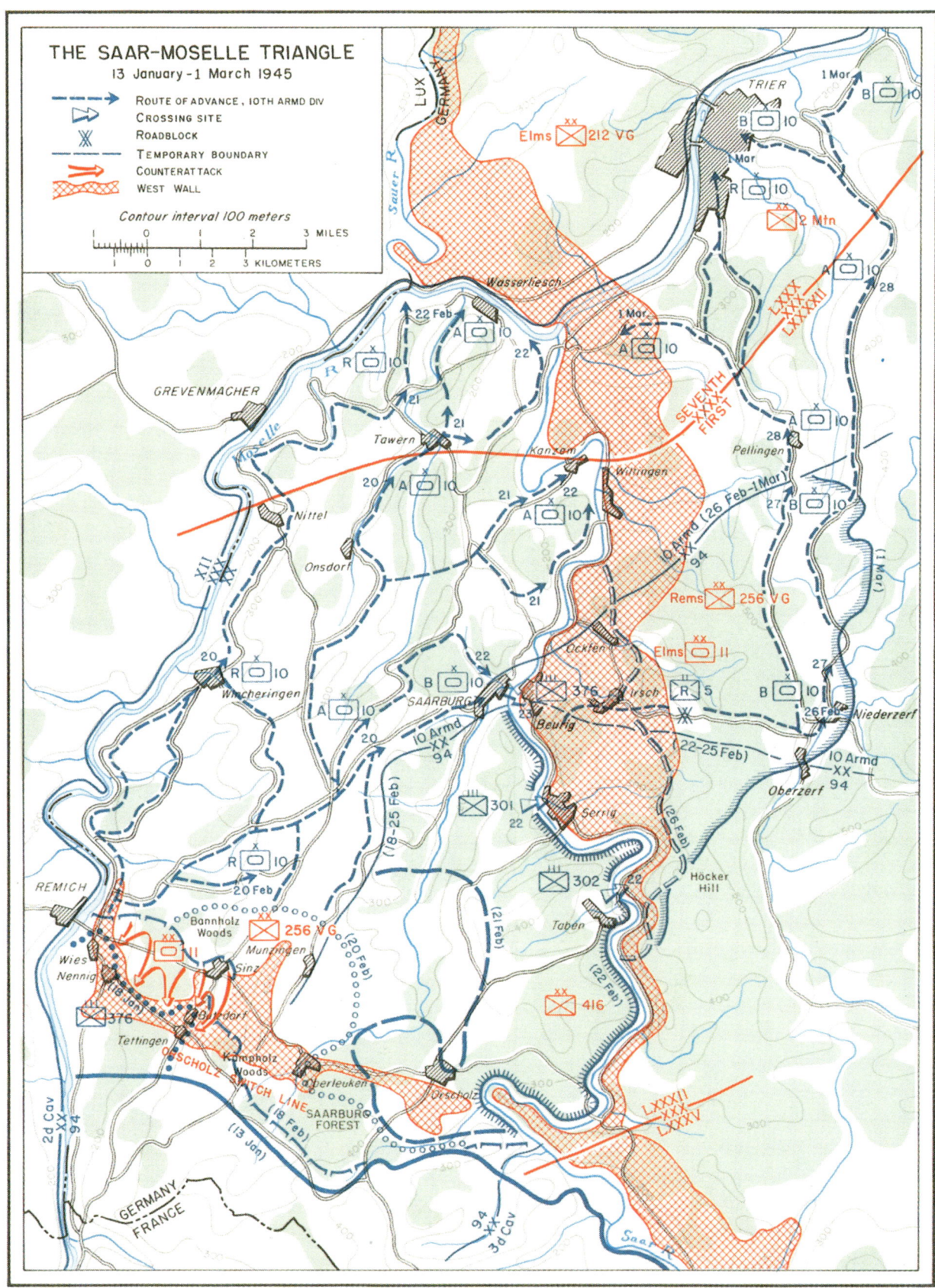

THE SAAR-MOSELLE TRIANGLE
13 January – 1 March 1945

MAP V